I0003652

AWS CodeCommit User Guide

A catalogue record for this book is available from the Hong Kong Public Libraries.

Published in Hong Kong by Samurai Media Limited.

Email: info@samuraimedia.org

ISBN 9789888407767

Copyright 2018 Amazon Web Services, Inc. and/or its affiliates.
Minor modifications for publication Copyright 2018 Samurai Media Limited.

This book is licensed under the Creative Commons Attribution-ShareAlike 4.0 International Public License.

Background Cover Image by https://www.flickr.com/people/webtreatsetc/

Contents

Copyright 2015 Amazon.com, Inc. or its affiliates. All Rights Reserved. Licensed under the Amazon Software License (the "License"). **208**

You may not use this file except in compliance with the License. A copy of the License is located at **208**

http://aws.amazon.com/asl/ **208**

This file is distributed on an "AS IS" BASIS, WITHOUT WARRANTIES OR CONDITIONS OF ANY KIND, express or implied. See the License for **208**

the specific language governing permissions and limitations under the License. **208**

helper = osxkeychain **220**

What Is AWS CodeCommit?

AWS CodeCommit is a version control service hosted by Amazon Web Services that you can use to privately store and manage assets (such as documents, source code, and binary files) in the cloud. For information about pricing for AWS CodeCommit, see Pricing.

Note
This is a HIPAA Eligible Service. For more information about AWS, U.S. Health Insurance Portability and Accountability Act of 1996 (HIPAA), and using AWS services to process, store, and transmit protected health information (PHI), see HIPAA Overview.
For information about this service and ISO 27001, a security management standard that specifies security management best practices, see ISO 27001 Overview.

Topics

- Introducing AWS CodeCommit
- How Does AWS CodeCommit Work?
- How Is AWS CodeCommit Different from File Versioning in Amazon S3?
- How Do I Get Started with AWS CodeCommit?
- Where Can I Learn More About Git?

Introducing AWS CodeCommit

AWS CodeCommit is a secure, highly scalable, managed source control service that hosts private Git repositories. AWS CodeCommit eliminates the need for you to manage your own source control system or worry about scaling its infrastructure. You can use AWS CodeCommit to store anything from code to binaries. It supports the standard functionality of Git, so it works seamlessly with your existing Git-based tools.

With AWS CodeCommit, you can:

- **Benefit from a fully managed service hosted by AWS**. AWS CodeCommit provides high service availability and durability and eliminates the administrative overhead of managing your own hardware and software. There is no hardware to provision and scale and no server software to install, configure, and update.
- **Store your code securely**. AWS CodeCommit repositories are encrypted at rest as well as in transit.
- **Work collaboratively on code**. AWS CodeCommit repositories support pull requests, where users can review and comment on each other's code changes before merging them to branches; notifications that automatically send emails to users about pull requests and comments; and more.
- **Easily scale your version control projects**. AWS CodeCommit repositories can scale up to meet your development needs. The service can handle repositories with large numbers of files or branches, large file sizes, and lengthy revision histories.
- **Store anything, anytime**. AWS CodeCommit has no limit on the size of your repositories or on the file types you can store.
- **Integrate with other AWS and third-party services**. AWS CodeCommit keeps your repositories close to your other production resources in the AWS Cloud, which helps increase the speed and frequency of your development lifecycle. It is integrated with IAM and can be used with other AWS services and in parallel with other repositories. For more information, see Product and Service Integrations with AWS CodeCommit.
- **Easily migrate files from other remote repositories**. You can migrate to AWS CodeCommit from any Git-based repository.
- **Use the Git tools you already know**. AWS CodeCommit supports Git commands as well as its own AWS CLI commands and APIs.

How Does AWS CodeCommit Work?

AWS CodeCommit will seem familiar to users of Git-based repositories, but even those unfamiliar should find the transition to AWS CodeCommit relatively simple. AWS CodeCommit provides a console for the easy creation of repositories and the listing of existing repositories and branches. In a few simple steps, users can find information about a repository and clone it to their computer, creating a local repo where they can make changes and then push them to the AWS CodeCommit repository. Users can work from the command line on their local machines or use a GUI-based editor.

The following figure shows how you use your development machine, the AWS CLI or AWS CodeCommit console, and the AWS CodeCommit service to create and manage repositories:

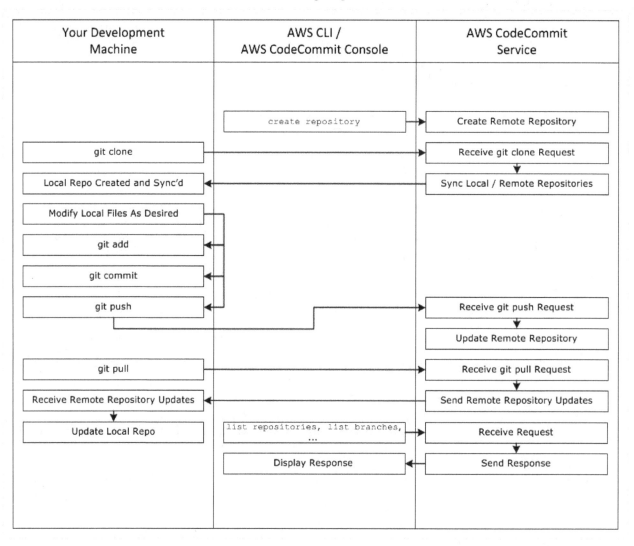

1. Use the AWS CLI or the AWS CodeCommit console to create an AWS CodeCommit repository.

2. From your development machine, use Git to run git clone, specifying the name of the AWS CodeCommit repository. This creates a local repo that connects to the AWS CodeCommit repository.

3. Use the local repo on your development machine to modify (add, edit, and delete) files, and then run git add to stage the modified files locally. Run git commit to commit the files locally, and then run git push to send the files to the AWS CodeCommit repository.

4. Download changes from other users. Run git pull to synchronize the files in the AWS CodeCommit repository with your local repo. This ensures you're working with the latest version of the files.

You can use the AWS CLI or the AWS CodeCommit console to track and manage your repositories.

How Is AWS CodeCommit Different from File Versioning in Amazon S3?

AWS CodeCommit is designed for team software development. It manages batches of changes across multiple files, which can occur in parallel with changes made by other developers. Amazon S3 versioning supports the recovery of past versions of files, but it's not focused on collaborative file tracking features that software development teams need.

How Do I Get Started with AWS CodeCommit?

To get started with AWS CodeCommit:

1. Follow the steps in Setting Up to prepare your development machines.
2. Follow the steps in one or more of the tutorials in Getting Started.
3. Create version control projects in AWS CodeCommit or migrate version control projects to AWS Code-Commit.

Where Can I Learn More About Git?

If you don't know it already, you should learn how to use Git. Here are some helpful resources:

- Pro Git, an online version of the *Pro Git* book. Written by Scott Chacon. Published by Apress.
- Git Immersion, a try-it-yourself guided tour that walks you through the fundamentals of using Git. Published by Neo Innovation, Inc.
- Git Reference, an online quick reference that can also be used as a more in-depth Git tutorial. Published by the GitHub team.
- Git Cheat Sheet with basic Git command syntax. Published by the GitHub team.
- Git Pocket Guide. Written by Richard E. Silverman. Published by O'Reilly Media, Inc.

Setting Up for AWS CodeCommit

You can sign in to the AWS Management Console and upload, add, or edit a file to a repository directly from the AWS CodeCommit console. This is a quick way to make a change. However, if you want to work with multiple files, files across branches, and so on, consider setting up your local computer to work with repositories. The easiest way to set up AWS CodeCommit is to configure HTTPS Git credentials for AWS CodeCommit. This HTTPS authentication method:

- Uses a static user name and password.
- Works with all operating systems supported by AWS CodeCommit.
- Is also compatible with integrated development environments (IDEs) and other development tools that support Git credentials.

You can use other methods if you do not want to or cannot use Git credentials for operational reasons. Read through these other options carefully, to decide which alternate method will work best for you.

- Setting Up Using Git Credentials
- Setting Up Using Other Methods
- Compatibility for AWS CodeCommit, Git, and Other Components

Setting Up Using Git Credentials

With HTTPS connections and Git credentials, you generate a static user name and password in IAM. You then use these credentials with Git and any third-party tool that supports Git user name and password authentication. This method is supported by most IDEs and development tools. It is the simplest and easiest connection method to use with AWS CodeCommit.

- For HTTPS Users Using Git Credentials: Follow these instructions to set up connections between your local computer and AWS CodeCommit repositories using Git credentials.
- For Connections from Development Tools: Follow these guidelines to set up connections between your IDE or other development tools and AWS CodeCommit repositories using Git credentials. IDEs that support Git credentials include (but are not limited to) Visual Studio, Eclipse, Xcode, and IntelliJ.

Setting Up Using Other Methods

You can use the SSH protocol instead of HTTPS to connect to your AWS CodeCommit repository. With SSH connections, you create public and private key files on your local machine that Git and AWS CodeCommit use for SSH authentication. You associate the public key with your IAM user. You store the private key on your local machine. Because SSH requires manual creation and management of public and private key files, you might find Git credentials simpler and easier to use with AWS CodeCommit.

Unlike Git credentials, SSH connection setup will vary, depending on the operating system on your local computer.

- For SSH Users Not Using the AWS CLI: Follow these abbreviated instructions if you already have a public-private key pair and are familiar with SSH connections on your local computer.
- For SSH Connections on Linux, macOS, or Unix: Follow these instructions for a step-by-step walkthrough of creating a public-private key pair and setting up connections on Linux, macOS, or Unix operating systems.
- For SSH Connections on Windows: Follow these instructions for a step-by-step walkthrough of creating public-private key pair and setting up connections on Windows operating systems.

If you are connecting to AWS CodeCommit and AWS using federated access or temporary credentials, or if you do not want to configure IAM users, you can set up connections to AWS CodeCommit repositories using the credential helper included in the AWS CLI. The credential helper allows Git to use HTTPS and a cryptographically signed version of your IAM user credentials or Amazon EC2 instance role whenever Git needs to authenticate with AWS to interact with AWS CodeCommit repositories. **This is the only connection** method for AWS CodeCommit repositories that does not require an IAM user, so it is the only method that supports federated access and temporary credentials. Some operating systems and Git versions have their own credential helpers, which conflict with the credential helper included in the AWS CLI. They can cause connectivity issues for AWS CodeCommit. For ease of use, consider creating IAM users and configuring Git credentials with HTTPS connections instead of using the credential helper.

- For HTTPS Connections on Linux, macOS, or Unix with the AWS CLI Credential Helper: Follow these instructions for a step-by-step walkthrough of installing and setting up the credential helper on Linux, macOS, or Unix systems.
- For HTTPS Connections on Windows with the AWS CLI Credential Helper: Follow these instructions for a step-by-step walkthrough of installing and setting up the credential helper on Windows systems.

If you are connecting to an AWS CodeCommit repository that is hosted in another AWS account, you can configure access and set up connections using roles, policies, and the credential helper included in the AWS CLI.

- Configure Cross-Account Access to an AWS CodeCommit Repository: Follow these instructions for a step-by-step walkthrough of configuring cross-account access in one AWS account to users in an IAM group in another AWS account.

Compatibility for AWS CodeCommit, Git, and Other Components

When working with AWS CodeCommit, you will use Git. You might use other programs, too. The following table provides the latest guidance for version compatibility.

Version Compatibility Information for AWS CodeCommit

Component	Version
Git	AWS CodeCommit supports Git versions 1.7.9 and later.
Curl	AWS CodeCommit requires curl 7.33 and later. However, there is a known issue with HTTPS and curl update 7.41.0. For more information, see Troubleshooting.

Setup for HTTPS Users Using Git Credentials

The simplest way to set up connections to AWS CodeCommit repositories is to configure Git credentials for AWS CodeCommit in the IAM console, and then use those credentials for HTTPS connections. You can also use these same credentials with any third-party tool or individual development environment (IDE) that supports HTTPS authentication using a static user name and password. For examples, see For Connections from Development Tools.

Note
If you have previously configured your local computer to use the credential helper for AWS CodeCommit, you must edit your .gitconfig file to remove the credential helper information from the file before you can use Git credentials. If your local computer is running macOS, you might need to clear cached credentials from Keychain Access.

Step 1: Initial Configuration for AWS CodeCommit

Follow these steps to set up an AWS account, create an IAM user, and configure access to AWS CodeCommit.

To create and configure an IAM user for accessing AWS CodeCommit

1. Create an AWS account by going to http://aws.amazon.com and choosing **Sign Up**.

2. Create an IAM user, or use an existing one, in your AWS account. Make sure you have an access key ID and a secret access key associated with that IAM user. For more information, see Creating an IAM User in Your AWS Account. **Note**
   AWS CodeCommit requires AWS Key Management Service. If you are using an existing IAM user, make sure there are no policies attached to the user that expressly deny the AWS KMS actions required by AWS CodeCommit. For more information, see AWS KMS and Encryption.

3. Sign in to the AWS Management Console and open the IAM console at https://console.aws.amazon.com/iam/.

4. In the IAM console, in the navigation pane, choose **Users**, and then choose the IAM user you want to configure for AWS CodeCommit access.

5. On the **Permissions** tab, choose **Add Permissions**.

6. In **Grant permissions**, choose **Attach existing policies directly**.

7. Select **AWSCodeCommitFullAccess** from the list of policies, or another managed policy for AWS CodeCommit access. For more information about managed policies for AWS CodeCommit, see AWS Managed (Predefined) Policies for AWS CodeCommit.

   After you have selected the policy you want to attach, choose** Next: Review** to review the list of policies that will be attached to the IAM user. If the list is correct, choose **Add permissions**.

   For more information about AWS CodeCommit managed policies and sharing access to repositories with other groups and users, see Share a Repository and Authentication and Access Control for AWS CodeCommit.

If you want to use AWS CLI commands with AWS CodeCommit, install the AWS CLI. For more information, see Command Line Reference.

Step 2: Install Git

To work with files, commits, and other information in AWS CodeCommit repositories, you must install Git on your local machine. AWS CodeCommit supports Git versions 1.7.9 and later.

To install Git, we recommend websites such as Git Downloads.

Note

Git is an evolving, regularly updated platform. Occasionally, a feature change might affect the way it works with AWS CodeCommit. If you encounter issues with a specific version of Git and AWS CodeCommit, review the information in Troubleshooting.

Step 3: Create Git Credentials for HTTPS Connections to AWS CodeCommit

After you have installed Git, create Git credentials for your IAM user in IAM. For more information, see Use Git Credentials and HTTPS with AWS CodeCommit in the *IAM User Guide*.

To set up HTTPS Git Credentials for AWS CodeCommit

1. Sign in to the AWS Management Console and open the IAM console at https://console.aws.amazon.com/iam/.

   Make sure to sign in as the IAM user who will create and use the Git credentials for connections to AWS CodeCommit.

2. In the IAM console, in the navigation pane, choose **Users**, and from the list of users, choose your IAM user.

3. On the user details page, choose the **Security Credentials** tab, and in **HTTPS Git credentials for AWS CodeCommit**, choose **Generate**.

Note

You cannot choose your own user name or password for Git credentials. For more information, see Use Git Credentials and HTTPS with AWS CodeCommit.

4. Copy the user name and password that IAM generated for you, either by showing, copying, and pasting this information into a secure file on your local computer, or by choosing **Download credentials** to download this information as a .CSV file. You will need this information to connect to AWS CodeCommit.

Git credentials generated   ✕

IAM has generated a user name and password for you to use when authenticating to AWS CodeCommit. You can use these credentials when connecting to AWS CodeCommit from your local computer and from tools that require a static user name and password. Learn more

User name   MyDemoUser-

Password   ✱✱✱✱✱✱✱✱ Show

This is the only time the password will be available to view, copy, or download. We recommend downloading these credentials and storing the file in a secure location. You can reset the password in IAM at any time.

[Download credentials]   [Close]

After you have saved your credentials, choose **Close**. **Important**
This is your only chance to save the user name and password. If you do not save them, you can copy the user name from the IAM console, but you cannot look up the password. You must reset the password and then save it.

Step 4: Connect to the AWS CodeCommit Console and Clone the Repository

If an administrator has already sent you the name and connection details for the AWS CodeCommit repository, you can skip this step and clone the repository directly.

To connect to an AWS CodeCommit repository

1. Open the AWS CodeCommit console at https://console.aws.amazon.com/codecommit.

2. In the region selector, choose the region where the repository was created. Repositories are specific to an AWS region. For more information, see Regions and Git Connection Endpoints.

3. Choose the repository you want to connect to from the list. This opens the **Code** page for that repository.

   If you see a **Welcome** page instead of a list of repositories, there are no repositories associated with your AWS account. To create a repository, see Create an AWS CodeCommit Repository or follow the steps in the Git with AWS CodeCommit Tutorial tutorial.

4. Choose **Connect**. Review the instructions and copy the URL to use when connecting to the repository.

5. Open a terminal, command line, or Git shell. Using the HTTPS URL you copied, run the git clone command to clone the repository. For example, to clone a repository named *MyDemoRepo* to a local repo named *my-demo-repo* in the US East (Ohio) region:

```
1 git clone https://git-codecommit.us-east-2.amazonaws.com/v1/repos/MyDemoRepo my-demo-repo
```

The first time you connect, you will be prompted to provide the user name and password for the repository. Depending on the configuration of your local computer, this prompt will either originate from a credential management system for the operating system (for example, Keychain Access for macOS), a credential manager utility for your version of Git (for example, the Git Credential Manager included in Git for Windows), your IDE, or Git itself. Provide the user name and password generated for Git credentials in IAM (the ones you created in Step 3: Create Git Credentials for HTTPS Connections to AWS CodeCommit). Depending on your operating system and other software, this information might be saved for you in a credential store or credential management utility. If so, you should not be prompted again unless you change the password, inactivate the Git credentials, or delete the Git credentials in IAM.

If you do not have a credential store or credential management utility configured on your local computer, you can install one. For more information about Git and how it manages credentials, see Credential Storage in the Git documentation.

For more information, see Connect to the AWS CodeCommit Repository by Cloning the Repository and Create a Commit.

Next Steps

You have completed the prerequisites. Follow the steps in AWS CodeCommit Tutorial to start using AWS CodeCommit.

Set Up Connections from Development Tools Using Git Credentials

After you have configured Git credentials for AWS CodeCommit in the IAM console, you can use those credentials with any development tool that supports Git credentials. For example, you can configure access to your AWS CodeCommit repository in AWS Cloud9, Visual Studio, Eclipse, Xcode, IntelliJ, or any integrated development environment (IDE) that integrates Git credentials. After configuring access, you can edit your code, commit your changes, and push directly from the IDE or other development tool.

Topics

- Integrate AWS Cloud9 with AWS CodeCommit
- Integrate Visual Studio with AWS CodeCommit
- Integrate Eclipse with AWS CodeCommit

When prompted by your IDE or development tool for the user name and password used to connect to the AWS CodeCommit repository, provide the Git credentials for **User name** and **Password** you created in IAM. For example, if you are prompted for a user name and password in Eclipse, you would provide your Git credentials as follows:

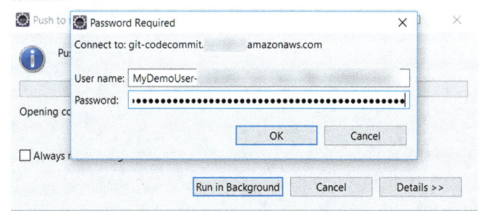

For more information about regions and endpoints for AWS CodeCommit, see Regions and Git Connection Endpoints.

You might also see a prompt from your operating system to store your user name and password. For example, in Windows, you would provide your Git credentials as follows:

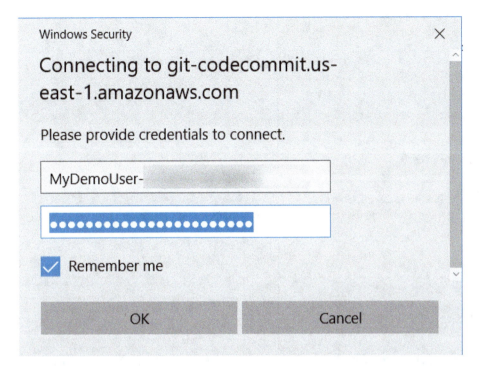

For more information about configuring Git credentials for a particular software program or development tool, consult the product documentation.

The following is not a comprehensive list of IDEs. AWS is not responsible for the content of any of these topics. The links are provided solely to help you learn more about these tools.

- AWS Cloud9

- Visual Studio

  Alternatively, install the AWS Toolkit for Visual Studio. For more information, see Integrate Visual Studio with AWS CodeCommit.

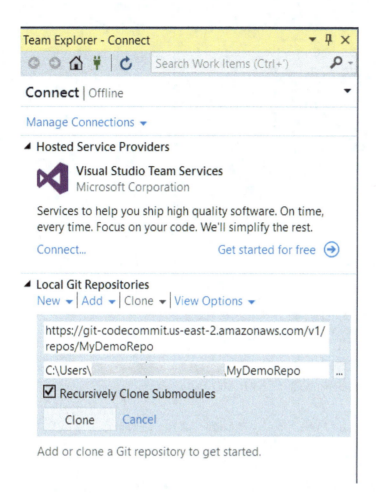

- EGit with Eclipse

  Alternatively, install the AWS Toolkit for Eclipse. For more information, see Integrate Eclipse with AWS CodeCommit.

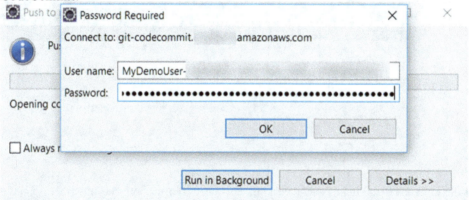

- IntelliJ

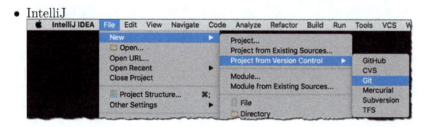

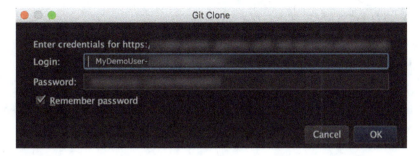

- XCode

Integrate AWS Cloud9 with AWS CodeCommit

You can use AWS Cloud9 to make code changes in an AWS CodeCommit repository. AWS Cloud9 contains a collection of tools that you can use to write code, as well as build, run, test, debug, and release software. You can clone existing repositories, create repositories, commit and push code changes to a repository, and more, all from your AWS Cloud9 EC2 development environment. The AWS Cloud9 EC2 development environment is generally preconfigured with the AWS CLI, an Amazon EC2 role, and Git, so in most cases, you can run a few simple commands and start interacting with your repository.

To use AWS Cloud9 with AWS CodeCommit, you need the following:

- An AWS Cloud9 EC2 development environment running on Amazon Linux.

- The AWS Cloud9 IDE open in a web browser.

- An IAM user with one of the AWS CodeCommit managed policies and one of the AWS Cloud9 managed policies applied to it.

  For more information, see AWS Managed (Predefined) Policies for AWS CodeCommit and Understanding and Getting Your Security Credentials.

Topics

- Step 1: Create an AWS Cloud9 Development Environment
- Step 2: Configure the AWS CLI Credential Helper On Your AWS Cloud9 EC2 Development Environment
- Step 3: Clone an AWS CodeCommit Repository Into Your AWS Cloud9 EC2 Development Environment
- Next Steps

Step 1: Create an AWS Cloud9 Development Environment

AWS Cloud9 will host your development environment on an Amazon EC2 instance. This is the easiest way to integrate, as you can use the AWS managed temporary credentials for the instance to connect to your AWS CodeCommit repository. If you want to use your own server instead, see the AWS Cloud9 User Guide.

To create an AWS Cloud9 environment

1. Sign in to AWS as the IAM user you've configured and open the AWS Cloud9 console.

2. In the AWS Cloud9 console, choose **Create environment**.

3. In **Step 1: Name environment**, type a name for your development environment in **Name**. Optionally add a description for the environment, and then choose **Next step**.

4. In **Step 2: Configure Settings**, configure your environment as follows:

   - In **Environment type**, choose **Create a new instance for environment (EC2)**.
   - In **Instance type**, choose the appropriate instance type for your development environment. For example, if you're just exploring the service, you might choose the default of t2.micro. If you intend to use this environment for development work, choose a larger instance type.
   - Accept the other default settings unless you have specific reasons to choose otherwise (for example, your organization uses a specific VPC, or your AWS account does not have any VPCs configured), and then choose **Next step**.

5. In **Step 3: Review**, review your settings. Choose **Previous step** if you want to make any changes. If not, choose **Create environment**.

   Creating an environment and connecting to it for the first time takes several minutes. If it seems to take an unusually long time, see Troubleshooting in the AWS Cloud9 User Guide.

6. Once you are connected to your environment, check to see if Git is already installed and is a supported version by running the git --version command in the terminal window.

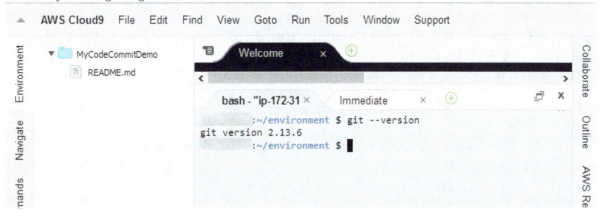

If Git is not installed, or if it is not a supported version, install a supported version. AWS CodeCommit supports Git versions 1.7.9 and later. To install Git, we recommend websites such as Git Downloads. **Tip** Depending on the operating system of your environment, you might be able to use the yum command with the sudo option to install updates, including Git. For example, an administrative command sequence might resemble the following three commands:

```
1 sudo yum -y update
2 sudo yum -y install git
3 git --version
```

7. Configure a user name and email to be associated with your Git commits by running the** git config** command. For example:

```
1     git config --global user.name "Mary Major"
2     git config --global user.email mary.major@example.com
```

Step 2: Configure the AWS CLI Credential Helper On Your AWS Cloud9 EC2 Development Environment

After you've created an AWS Cloud9 environment, you can configure the AWS CLI Credential Helper to manage the credentials for connections to your AWS CodeCommit repository. The AWS Cloud9 development environment comes with AWS managed temporary credentials that are associated with your IAM user. You will use these credentials with the AWS CLI credential helper.

1. Open the terminal window and type the following command to verify that the AWS CLI is installed:

```
1 aws --version
```

If successful, this command returns the currently-installed version of the AWS CLI. To upgrade an older version of the AWS CLI to the latest version, see Installing the AWS Command Line Interface.

2. At the terminal, type the following commands to configure the AWS CLI Credential Helper for HTTPS connections:

```
1 git config --global credential.helper '!aws codecommit credential-helper $@'
2 git config --global credential.UseHttpPath true
```

Tip
The credential helper will use the default Amazon EC2 instance role for your development environment. If you intend to use the development environment to connect to repositories that are not hosted in AWS CodeCommit, either configure SSH connections to those repositories, or configure a local .gitconfig file to use an alternative

credential management system when connecting to those other repositories. For more information, see Git Tools - Credential Storage on the Git website.

Step 3: Clone an AWS CodeCommit Repository Into Your AWS Cloud9 EC2 Development Environment

Once you've configured the AWS CLI credential helper, you can clone your AWS CodeCommit repository onto it. Then you can start working with the code.

1. In the terminal, run the git clone command, specifying the HTTPS clone URL of the repository you want to clone. For example, if you want to clone a repository named MyDemoRepo in the US East (Ohio) region, you would type:

```
1 git clone https://git-codecommit.us-east-2.amazonaws.com/v1/repos/MyDemoRepo
```

Tip
You can find the Clone URL for your repository in the AWS CodeCommit console, both on the **Dashboard**, and in the **Connect** information on the **Code** page of the repository itself.

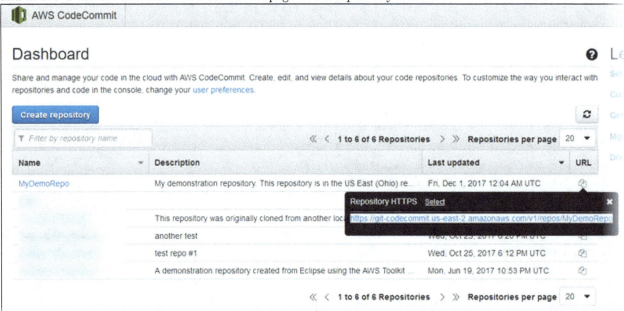

1. When the cloning is complete, expand the folder for your repository in the side navigation, and choose the file you want to open for editing. Alternatively, choose **File** and then choose **New File** to create a new file.

2. When you have finished editing or creating files, in the terminal window, change directories to your cloned repository and then commit and push your changes. For example, if you added a new file named *MyFile.py*:

```
1 cd MyDemoRepo
2 git commit -a MyFile.py
3 git commit -m "Added a new file with some code improvements"
4 git push
```

Next Steps

To learn more about using AWS Cloud9, see the AWS Cloud9 User Guide. To learn more about using Git with AWS CodeCommit, see Git with AWS CodeCommit Tutorial.

Integrate Visual Studio with AWS CodeCommit

You can use Visual Studio to make code changes in an AWS CodeCommit repository. The AWS Toolkit for Visual Studio now includes features that make working with AWS CodeCommit easier and more convenient when working from within Visual Studio Team Explorer. The Toolkit for Visual Studio integration is designed to work with Git credentials and an IAM user. You can clone existing repositories, create repositories, commit and push code changes to a repository, and more.

Important
The Toolkit for Visual Studio is available for installation on Windows operating systems only.

If you've used the Toolkit for Visual Studio before, you're probably already familiar with setting up AWS credential profiles that contain an access key and secret key. Credential profiles are used in the Toolkit for Visual Studio to enable calls to AWS service APIs (for example, to Amazon S3 to list buckets or to AWS CodeCommit to list repositories). To pull and push code to an AWS CodeCommit repository, you also need Git credentials. If you don't have Git credentials, the Toolkit for Visual Studio can generate and apply those credentials for you. This can save you a great deal of time.

To use Visual Studio with AWS CodeCommit, you need the following:

- An IAM user with a valid set of credentials (an access key and secret key) configured for it. This IAM user should also have:

  One of the AWS CodeCommit managed policies and the IAMSelfManageServiceSpecificCredentials managed policy applied to it.

  OR

  If the IAM user already has Git credentials configured, one of the AWS CodeCommit managed policies or equivalent permissions.

  For more information, see AWS Managed (Predefined) Policies for AWS CodeCommit and Understanding and Getting Your Security Credentials.

- The AWS Toolkit for Visual Studio installed on the computer where you've installed Visual Studio. For more information, see Setting Up the AWS Toolkit for Visual Studio.

Topics

- Step 1: Get an Access Key and Secret Key for Your IAM User
- Step 2: Install AWS Toolkit for Visual Studio and Connect to AWS CodeCommit
- Clone an AWS CodeCommit Repository from Visual Studio
- Create an AWS CodeCommit Repository from Visual Studio
- Working with AWS CodeCommit Repositories

Step 1: Get an Access Key and Secret Key for Your IAM User

If you do not already have a credential profile set up on the computer where Visual Studio is installed, you can configure one with the AWS CLI and the aws configure command. Alternatively, you can follow this procedure to create and download your credentials. Provide them to the Toolkit for Visual Studio when prompted.

To get the access key ID and secret access key for an IAM user

Access keys consist of an access key ID and secret access key, which are used to sign programmatic requests that you make to AWS. If you don't have access keys, you can create them from the AWS Management Console. We recommend that you use IAM access keys instead of AWS account root user access keys. IAM lets you securely control access to AWS services and resources in your AWS account.

The only time that you can view or download the secret access keys is when you create the keys. You cannot recover them later. However, you can create new access keys at any time. You must also have permissions to perform the required IAM actions. For more information, see Permissions Required to Access IAM Resources in the *IAM User Guide*.

1. Open the IAM console.

2. In the navigation pane of the console, choose **Users**.

3. Choose your IAM user name (not the check box).

4. Choose the **Security credentials** tab and then choose **Create access key**.

5. To see the new access key, choose **Show**. Your credentials will look something like this:

   - Access key ID: AKIAIOSFODNN7EXAMPLE
   - Secret access key: wJalrXUtnFEMI/K7MDENG/bPxRfiCYEXAMPLEKEY

6. To download the key pair, choose **Download .csv file**. Store the keys in a secure location.

   Keep the keys confidential in order to protect your AWS account, and never email them. Do not share them outside your organization, even if an inquiry appears to come from AWS or Amazon.com. No one who legitimately represents Amazon will ever ask you for your secret key.

Related topics

- What Is IAM? in the *IAM User Guide*
- AWS Security Credentials in *AWS General Reference*

Step 2: Install AWS Toolkit for Visual Studio and Connect to AWS CodeCommit

The Toolkit for Visual Studio is a software package you can add to Visual Studio. After you've installed it, you can connect to AWS CodeCommit from Team Explorer in Visual Studio.

To install the Toolkit for Visual Studio with the AWS CodeCommit module and configure access to your project repository

1. Install Visual Studio on your local computer if you don't have a supported version already installed.

2. Download and install the Toolkit for Visual Studio and save the file to a local folder or directory. Launch the installation wizard by opening the file. When prompted on the **Getting Started with the AWS Toolkit for Visual Studio** page, type or import your AWS credentials (your access key and secret key), and then choose** Save and Close**.

3. In Visual Studio, open **Team Explorer**. In **Hosted Service Providers**, find **AWS CodeCommit**, and choose **Connect**.

 AWS CodeCommit
Amazon, Inc.

AWS CodeCommit is a fully-managed source control service that makes it easy for companies to host secure and highly scalable private Git repositories.

Connect...   Sign up ➔

4. Do one of the following:

   - If you have a single credential profile already configured on your computer, the Toolkit for Visual Studio will apply it automatically. No action is required. The AWS CodeCommit connection panel appears in Team Explorer.
   - If you have more than one credential profile configured on your computer, you are prompted to choose the one you want to use. Choose the profile associated with the IAM user you'll use for connecting to AWS CodeCommit repositories, and then choose **OK**.
   - If you do not have a profile configured, a dialog box appears and asks for your AWS security credentials (your access key and secret key). Type or import them, and then choose **OK**.

After you are signed in with a profile, the AWS CodeCommit connection panel appears in Team Explorer with options to clone, create, or sign out. Choosing **Clone** clones an existing AWS CodeCommit repository to your local computer, so you can start working on code. This is the most frequently used option.

If you don't have repositories, or want to create a repository, choose **Create**. For more information, see Create an AWS CodeCommit Repository from Visual Studio.

Clone an AWS CodeCommit Repository from Visual Studio

After you're connected to AWS CodeCommit, you can clone a repository to a local repo on your computer. Then you can start working with the code.

1. In **Manage Connections**, choose **Clone**. In **Region**, choose the AWS region where the repository was created in AWS CodeCommit. Choose your project's repository and the folder on your local computer you want to clone the repository into, and then choose **OK**.

2. If you are prompted to create Git credentials, choose **Yes**. The toolkit attempts to create credentials on your behalf. You must have the IAMSelfManageServiceSpecificCredentials applied to your IAM user, or the equivalent permissions. When prompted, save the credentials file in a secure location. This is the only opportunity you will have to save these Git credentials.

   If the toolkit cannot create Git credentials on your behalf, or if you chose **No**, you must create and provide your own Git credentials. For more information, see For HTTPS Users Using Git Credentials, or follow the online directions.

3. When you have finished cloning the project, you're ready to start editing your code in Visual Studio and committing and pushing your changes to your project's repository in AWS CodeCommit.

Create an AWS CodeCommit Repository from Visual Studio

You can create AWS CodeCommit repositories from Visual Studio with the Toolkit for Visual Studio. As part of creating the repository, you also clone it to a local repo on your computer, so you can start working with it right away.

1. In **Manage Connections**, choose **Create**.

2. In **Region**, choose the AWS region where you want to create the repository. AWS CodeCommit repositories are organized by region.

3. In **Name**, type a name for this repository. Repository names must be unique within an AWS account. There are character and length limits. For more information, see Limits. Optionally, in **Description**, type a description for this repository. This helps others understand what the repository is for, and helps distinguish it from other repositories in the region.

4. In **Clone into**, type or browse to the folder or directory where you want to clone this repository on your local computer. Visual Studio automatically clones the repository after it's created and creates the local repo in the location you choose.

5. When you are satisfied with your choices, choose **OK**.

6. If prompted to create Git credentials, choose **Yes**. The toolkit attempts to create credentials on your behalf. You must have the IAMSelfManageServiceSpecificCredentials applied to your IAM user, or the equivalent permissions. When prompted, save the credentials file in a secure location. This is the only opportunity you will have to save these Git credentials.

   If the toolkit cannot create Git credentials on your behalf, or if you chose **No**, you must create and provide your own Git credentials. For more information, see For HTTPS Users Using Git Credentials, or follow the online directions.

Working with AWS CodeCommit Repositories

After you have connected to AWS CodeCommit, you can see a list of repositories associated with your AWS account. You can browse the contents of these repositories in Visual Studio. Open the context menu for the repository you're interested in, and choose **Browse in Console**.

Git operations in Visual Studio for AWS CodeCommit repositories work exactly as they do for any other Git-based repository. You can make changes to code, add files, and create local commits. When you are ready to share, you use the **Sync** option in Team Explorer to push your commits to the AWS CodeCommit repository. Because your Git credentials for your IAM user are already stored locally and associated with your connected AWS credential profile, you won't be prompted to supply them again when you push to AWS CodeCommit.

For more information about working with Toolkit for Visual Studio, see the AWS Toolkit for Visual Studio User Guide.

Integrate Eclipse with AWS CodeCommit

You can use Eclipse to make code changes in an AWS CodeCommit repository. The Toolkit for Eclipse integration is designed to work with Git credentials and an IAM user. You can clone existing repositories, create repositories, commit and push code changes to a repository, and more.

To use Toolkit for Eclipse with AWS CodeCommit, you need the following:

- Eclipse installed on your local computer.
- An IAM user with a valid set of credentials (an access key and secret key) configured for it. This IAM user should also have:

    One of the AWS CodeCommit managed policies and the IAMSelfManageServiceSpecificCredentials managed policy applied to it.

    OR

    If the IAM user already has Git credentials configured, one of the AWS CodeCommit managed policies or equivalent permissions .

    For more information, see AWS Managed (Predefined) Policies for AWS CodeCommit and Understanding and Getting Your Security Credentials.

- An active set of Git credentials configured for the user in IAM. For more information, see Step 3: Create Git Credentials for HTTPS Connections to AWS CodeCommit.

Topics

- Step 1: Get an Access Key and Secret Key for Your IAM User
- Step 2: Install AWS Toolkit for Eclipse and Connect to AWS CodeCommit
- Clone an AWS CodeCommit Repository from Eclipse
- Create an AWS CodeCommit Repository from Eclipse
- Working with AWS CodeCommit Repositories

Step 1: Get an Access Key and Secret Key for Your IAM User

If you do not already have a credential profile set up on the computer where Eclipse is installed, you can configure one with the AWS CLI and the aws configure command. Alternatively, you can follow this procedure to create and download your credentials. Provide them to the Toolkit for Eclipse when prompted.

To get the access key ID and secret access key for an IAM user

Access keys consist of an access key ID and secret access key, which are used to sign programmatic requests that you make to AWS. If you don't have access keys, you can create them from the AWS Management Console. We recommend that you use IAM access keys instead of AWS account root user access keys. IAM lets you securely control access to AWS services and resources in your AWS account.

The only time that you can view or download the secret access keys is when you create the keys. You cannot recover them later. However, you can create new access keys at any time. You must also have permissions to perform the required IAM actions. For more information, see Permissions Required to Access IAM Resources in the *IAM User Guide*.

1. Open the IAM console.

2. In the navigation pane of the console, choose **Users**.

3. Choose your IAM user name (not the check box).

4. Choose the **Security credentials** tab and then choose **Create access key**.

5. To see the new access key, choose **Show**. Your credentials will look something like this:

- Access key ID: AKIAIOSFODNN7EXAMPLE
- Secret access key: wJalrXUtnFEMI/K7MDENG/bPxRfiCYEXAMPLEKEY

6. To download the key pair, choose **Download .csv file**. Store the keys in a secure location.

   Keep the keys confidential in order to protect your AWS account, and never email them. Do not share them outside your organization, even if an inquiry appears to come from AWS or Amazon.com. No one who legitimately represents Amazon will ever ask you for your secret key.

Related topics

- What Is IAM? in the *IAM User Guide*
- AWS Security Credentials in *AWS General Reference*

Step 2: Install AWS Toolkit for Eclipse and Connect to AWS CodeCommit

The Toolkit for Eclipse is a software package you can add to Eclipse. After you've installed it and configured it with your AWS credential profile, you can connect to AWS CodeCommit from the AWS Explorer in Eclipse.

To install the Toolkit for Eclipse with the AWS CodeCommit module and configure access to your project repository

1. Install Toolkit for Eclipse on your local computer if you don't have a supported version already installed. If you need to update your version of Toolkit for Eclipse, follow the instructions in Set Up the Toolkit.

2. In Eclipse, either follow the firstrun experience, or open **Preferences** from the Eclipse menu system (the precise location will vary depending on your version and operating system) and choose **AWS Toolkit**.

3. Do one of the following:

   - If you are following the firstrun experience, provide your AWS security credentials when prompted to set up your credential profile.
   - If you are configuring in **Preferences** and have a credential profile already configured on your computer, choose it from the list in **Default Profile**.
   - If you are configuring in **Preferences** and you do not see the profile you want to use, or if the list is empty, choose **Add profile**. In **Profile Details**, provide a name for the proifle and the credentials for the IAM user (access key and secret key), or alternatively provide the location of the credentials file.
   - If you are configuring in **Preferences** and you do not have a profile configured, use the links for signing up for a new account or managing your existing AWS security credentials.

4. In Eclipse, expand the **AWS Toolkit** menu and choose **AWS CodeCommit**. Choose your credential profile, and then type the user name and password for your Git credentials or import them from the .csv file. Choose **Apply**, and then choose **OK**.

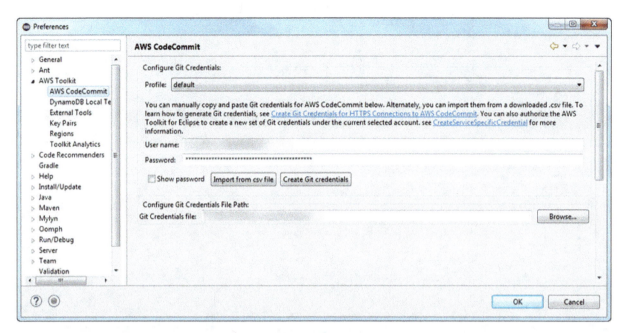

After you are signed in with a profile, the AWS CodeCommit connection panel appears in Team Explorer with options to clone, create, or sign out. Choosing **Clone** clones an existing AWS CodeCommit repository to your local computer, so you can start working on code. This is the most frequently used option.

If you don't have any repositories, or want to create a repository, choose **Create**.

Clone an AWS CodeCommit Repository from Eclipse

After you've configured your credentials, you can clone a repository to a local repo on your computer by checking it out in Eclipse. Then you can start working with the code.

1. In Eclipse, open **AWS Explorer**. For more information about where to find it, see How to Access AWS Explorer. Expand **AWS CodeCommit**, and choose the AWS CodeCommit repository you want to work in. You can view the commit history and other details of the repository, which can help you determine if this is the repository and branch you want to clone. **Note**
If you do not see your repository, choose the flag icon to open the AWS regions menu, and choose the region where the repository was created.

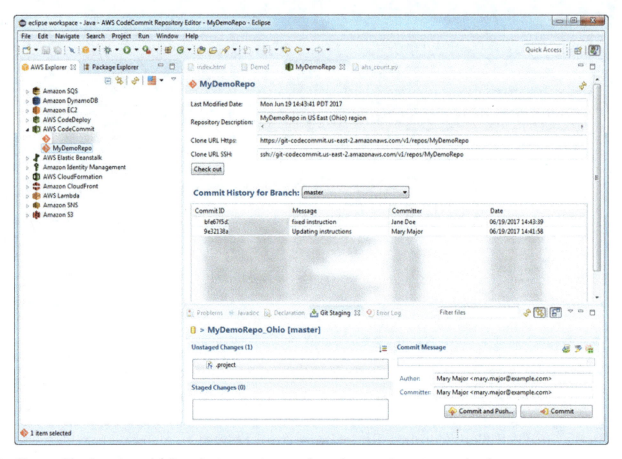

2. Choose **Check out**, and follow the instructions to clone the repository to your local computer.

3. When you have finished cloning the project, you're ready to start editing your code in Eclipse and staging, committing, and pushing your changes to your project's repository in AWS CodeCommit.

Create an AWS CodeCommit Repository from Eclipse

You can create AWS CodeCommit repositories from Eclipse with the Toolkit for Eclipse. As part of creating the repository, you'll also clone it to a local repo on your computer, so you can start working with it right away.

1. In AWS Explorer, right-click **AWS CodeCommit**, and then choose **Create repository**. **Note** Repositories are region-specific. Before you create the repository, make sure you have selected the correct AWS region. You cannot choose the region after you have started the repository creation process.

2. In **Repository Name**, type a name for this repository. Repository names must be unique within an AWS account. There are character and length limits. For more information, see Limits. Optionally, in **Repository Description**, type a description for this repository. This helps others understand what this repository is for, and helps distinguish it from other repositories in the region. Choose **OK**.

3. In AWS Explorer, expand **AWS CodeCommit**, and then choose the AWS CodeCommit repository you just created. You will see that this repository has no commit history. Choose **Check out**, and follow the instructions to clone the repository to your local computer.

Working with AWS CodeCommit Repositories

After you have connected to AWS CodeCommit, you can see a list of repositories associated with your AWS account, by region, in AWS Explorer. Choose the flag menu to change the region.

Note
AWS CodeCommit might not be available in all regions supported by Toolkit for Eclipse.

In Toolkit for Eclipse, you can browse the contents of these repositories from the **Navigation** and **Package Explorer** views. To open a file, choose it from the list.

Git operations in Toolkit for Eclipse for AWS CodeCommit repositories work exactly as they do for any other Git-based repository. You can make changes to code, add files, and create local commits. When you are ready to share, you use the **Git Staging** option to push your commits to the AWS CodeCommit repository. If you haven't configured your author and committer information in a Git profile, you can do this before you commit and push. Because your Git credentials for your IAM user are already stored locally and associated with your connected AWS credential profile, you won't be prompted to supply them again when you push to AWS CodeCommit.

For more information about working with Toolkit for Eclipse, see the AWS Toolkit for Eclipse Getting Started Guide.

Setup for SSH Users Not Using the AWS CLI

If you want to use SSH connections for your repository, you can connect to AWS CodeCommit without installing the AWS CLI. The AWS CLI includes commands that will be useful later when using and managing AWS CodeCommit repositories, but it is not required for initial setup.

This topic assumes:

- You have set up an IAM user with the policies or permissions required for AWS CodeCommit as well as the **IAMUserSSHKeys** managed policy or equivalent permissions required for uploading keys. For more information, see Using Identity-Based Policies (IAM Policies) for AWS CodeCommit.
- You already have, or know how to create, a public/private key pair. We strongly recommend you use a secure passphrase for your SSH key.
- You are familiar with SSH, your Git client, and its configuration files.
- If you are using Windows, you have installed a command-line utility, such as Git Bash, that emulates the bash shell.

If you need more guidance, follow the detailed instructions in For SSH Connections on Linux, macOS, or Unix or For SSH Connections on Windows.

Topics

- Step 1: Associate Your Public Key with Your IAM User
- Step 2: Add AWS CodeCommit to Your SSH Configuration
- Next Steps

Step 1: Associate Your Public Key with Your IAM User

1. Sign in to the AWS Management Console and open the IAM console at https://console.aws.amazon.com/iam/.

2. In the IAM console, in the navigation pane, choose **Users**, and from the list of users, choose your IAM user.

3. On the **Security Credentials** tab, choose **Upload SSH public key**.

4. Paste the contents of your SSH public key into the field, and then choose **Upload SSH Key**. **Tip** The public/private key pair must be SSH-2 RSA, in OpenSSH format, and contain 2048 bits. The key will look similar to this:

```
1  ssh-rsa EXAMPLE-AfICCQD6m7oRwOuXOjANBgkqhkiG9w0BAQUFADCBiDELMAkGA1UEBhMCVVMxCzAJB
2  gNVBAgTAldBMRAwDgYDVQQHEwdTZWF0dGxlMQ8wDQYDVQQKEwZBbWF6b24xFDASBgNVBAsTC01BTSBDb2
3  5zb2xlMRIwEAYDVQQDEwlUZXN0Q21sYWMxHzAdBgkqhkiG9w0BCQEWEG5vb251QGFtYXpvbi5jb20wHhc
4  NMTEwNDI1MjAONTIxWhcNMTIwNDIOMjAONTIxWjCBiDELMAkGA1UEBhMCVVMxCzAJBgNVBAgTAldBMRAw
5  DgYDVQQHEwdTZWF0dGxlMQ8wDQYDVQQKEwZBbWF6b24xFDAS=EXAMPLE user-name@ip-192-0-2-137
```

IAM accepts public keys in the OpenSSH format only. If you provide your public key in another format, you will see an error message stating the key format is not valid.

1. Copy the SSH key ID (for example, *APKAEIBAERJR2EXAMPLE*) and close the console.

SSH keys for AWS CodeCommit

Use SSH public keys to authenticate to AWS CodeCommit repositories. Learn more about SSH keys.

Upload SSH public key

SSH Key ID	Uploaded	Status	Actions
APKAEIBAERJR2EXAMPLE	2015-07-21 16:32 PDT	Active	Make Inactive | Show SSH Key | Delete

Step 2: Add AWS CodeCommit to Your SSH Configuration

1. At the terminal (Linux, macOS, or Unix) or bash emulator (Windows), edit your SSH configuration file by typing cat» ~/.ssh/config:

```
1 Host git-codecommit.*.amazonaws.com
2 User Your-SSH-Key-ID, such as APKAEIBAERJR2EXAMPLE
3 IdentityFile Your-Private-Key-File, such as ~/.ssh/codecommit_rsa or ~/.ssh/id_rsa
```

Tip

If you have more than one SSH configuration, make sure you include the blank lines before and after the content. Save the file by pressing the **Ctrl** and **d** keys simultaneously.

1. Run the following command to test your SSH configuration:

```
1 ssh git-codecommit.us-east-2.amazonaws.com
```

Type the passphrase for your SSH key file when prompted. If everything is configured correctly, you should see the following success message:

```
1 You have successfully authenticated over SSH. You can use Git to interact with AWS
    CodeCommit.
2 Interactive shells are not supported. Connection to git-codecommit.us-east-2.amazonaws.com
    closed by remote host.
```

Next Steps

You have completed the prerequisites. Follow the steps in AWS CodeCommit Tutorial to start using AWS CodeCommit.

To connect to an existing repository, follow the steps in Connect to a Repository. To create a repository, follow the steps in Create a Repository.

Setup Steps for SSH Connections to AWS CodeCommit Repositories on Linux, macOS, or Unix

Before you can connect to AWS CodeCommit for the first time, you must complete the initial configuration steps. This topic walks you through the steps for setting up your computer and AWS profile, connecting to an AWS CodeCommit repository, and cloning that repository to your computer (also known as creating a local repo). If you're new to Git, you might also want to review the information in Where Can I Learn More About Git?.

Topics

- Step 1: Initial Configuration for AWS CodeCommit
- Step 2: Install Git
- Step 3: Configure Credentials on Linux, macOS, or Unix
- Step 4: Connect to the AWS CodeCommit Console and Clone the Repository
- Next Steps

Step 1: Initial Configuration for AWS CodeCommit

Follow these steps to set up an AWS account, create an IAM user, and configure access to AWS CodeCommit.

To create and configure an IAM user for accessing AWS CodeCommit

1. Create an AWS account by going to http://aws.amazon.com and choosing **Sign Up**.

2. Create an IAM user, or use an existing one, in your AWS account. Make sure you have an access key ID and a secret access key associated with that IAM user. For more information, see Creating an IAM User in Your AWS Account. **Note**
AWS CodeCommit requires AWS Key Management Service. If you are using an existing IAM user, make sure there are no policies attached to the user that expressly deny the AWS KMS actions required by AWS CodeCommit. For more information, see AWS KMS and Encryption.

3. Sign in to the AWS Management Console and open the IAM console at https://console.aws.amazon.com/iam/.

4. In the IAM console, in the navigation pane, choose **Users**, and then choose the IAM user you want to configure for AWS CodeCommit access.

5. On the **Permissions** tab, choose **Add Permissions**.

6. In **Grant permissions**, choose **Attach existing policies directly**.

7. Select **AWSCodeCommitFullAccess** from the list of policies, or another managed policy for AWS CodeCommit access. For more information about managed policies for AWS CodeCommit, see AWS Managed (Predefined) Policies for AWS CodeCommit.

   After you have selected the policy you want to attach, choose** Next: Review** to review the list of policies that will be attached to the IAM user. If the list is correct, choose **Add permissions**.

   For more information about AWS CodeCommit managed policies and sharing access to repositories with other groups and users, see Share a Repository and Authentication and Access Control for AWS CodeCommit.

Note
If you want to use AWS CLI commands with AWS CodeCommit, install the AWS CLI. For more information, see Command Line Reference.

Step 2: Install Git

To work with files, commits, and other information in AWS CodeCommit repositories, you must install Git on your local machine. AWS CodeCommit supports Git versions 1.7.9 and later.

To install Git, we recommend websites such as Git Downloads.

Note
Git is an evolving, regularly updated platform. Occasionally, a feature change might affect the way it works with AWS CodeCommit. If you encounter issues with a specific version of Git and AWS CodeCommit, review the information in Troubleshooting.

Step 3: Configure Credentials on Linux, macOS, or Unix

SSH and Linux, macOS, or Unix: Set Up the Public and Private Keys for Git and AWS CodeCommit

1. From the terminal on your local machine, run the ssh-keygen command, and follow the directions to save the file to the .ssh directory for your profile. **Note**
   Be sure to check with your system administrator about where key files should be stored and which file naming pattern should be used.

   For example:

```
1 $ ssh-keygen
2
3 Generating public/private rsa key pair.
4 Enter file in which to save the key (/home/user-name/.ssh/id_rsa): Type /home/your-user-
      name/.ssh/ and a file name here, for example /home/your-user-name/.ssh/codecommit_rsa
5
6 Enter passphrase (empty for no passphrase): <Type a passphrase, and then press Enter>
7 Enter same passphrase again: <Type the passphrase again, and then press Enter>
8
9 Your identification has been saved in /home/user-name/.ssh/codecommit_rsa.
10 Your public key has been saved in /home/user-name/.ssh/codecommit_rsa.pub.
11 The key fingerprint is:
12 45:63:d5:99:0e:99:73:50:5e:d4:b3:2d:86:4a:2c:14 user-name@client-name
13 The key's randomart image is:
14 +--[ RSA 2048]----+
15 |        E.+.o*.++|
16 |        .o .=.=o.|
17 |        . .. *. +|
18 |        ..o . +..|
19 |        So . . . |
20 |        .        |
21 |                 |
22 |                 |
23 |                 |
24 +-----------------+
```

   This generates:

   - The *codecommit_rsa* file, which is the private key file.
   - The *codecommit_rsa*.pub file, which is the public key file.

2. Run the following command to display the value of the public key file (*codecommit_rsa*.pub):

```
1  cat ~/.ssh/codecommit_rsa.pub
```

Copy this value. It will look similar to the following:

```
1  ssh-rsa EXAMPLE-AfICCQD6m7oRwOuXOjANBgkqhkiG9wOBAQUFADCBiDELMAkGA1UEBhMCVVMxCzAJB
2  gNVBAgTAldBMRAwDgYDVQQHEwdTZWFOdGxlMQ8wDQYDVQQKEwZBbWF6b24xFDASBgNVBAsTCO1BTSBDb2
3  5zb2xlMRIwEAYDVQQDEwlUZXNOQ2lsYWMxHzAdBgkqhkiG9wOBCQEWEG5vb251QGFtYXpvbi5jb20wHhc
4  NMTEwNDI1MjAONTIxWhcNMTIwNDIOMjAONTIxWjCBiDELMAkGA1UEBhMCVVMxCzAJBgNVBAgTAldBMRAw
5  DgYDVQQHEwdTZWFOdGxlMQ8wDQYDVQQKEwZBbWF6b24xFDAS=EXAMPLE user-name@ip-192-0-2-137
```

3. Sign in to the AWS Management Console and open the IAM console at https://console.aws.amazon.com/iam/.

4. In the IAM console, in the navigation pane, choose **Users**, and from the list of users, choose your IAM user.

5. On the user details page, choose the **Security Credentials** tab, and then choose **Upload SSH public key**.

6. Paste the contents of your SSH public key into the field, and then choose **Upload SSH public key**.

7. Copy or save the information in **SSH Key ID** (for example, *APKAEIBAERJR2EXAMPLE*).

SSH keys for AWS CodeCommit

Use SSH public keys to authenticate to AWS CodeCommit repositories. Learn more about SSH keys.

Upload SSH public key

SSH Key ID	Uploaded	Status	Actions
APKAEIBAERJR2EXAMPLE	2015-07-21 16:32 PDT	Active	Make Inactive | Show SSH Key | Delete

8. On your local machine, use a text editor to create a config file in the ~/.ssh directory, and then add the following lines to the file, where the value for *User* is the SSH key ID you copied earlier:

```
1  Host git-codecommit.*.amazonaws.com
2    User APKAEIBAERJR2EXAMPLE
3    IdentityFile ~/.ssh/codecommit_rsa
```

Note
If you gave your private key file a name other than *codecommit_rsa*, be sure to use it here.

Save and name this file `config`.

1. From the terminal, run the following command to change the permissions for the config file:

```
1  chmod 600 config
```

2. Run the following command to test your SSH configuration:

```
1  ssh git-codecommit.us-east-2.amazonaws.com
```

You will be asked to confirm the connection because `git-codecommit.us-east-2.amazonaws.com` is not yet included in your known hosts file. The AWS CodeCommit server fingerprint is displayed as part of the verification (`a9:6d:03:ed:08:42:21:be:06:e1:e0:2a:d1:75:31:5e` for MD5 or `31B1W2g5xn /NA2Ck6dyeJIrQOWvn7n8UEs56fG6ZIzQ` for SHA256). **Note**
AWS CodeCommit server fingerprints are unique for every region. To view the server fingerprints for a specific region, see Server Fingerprints for AWS CodeCommit.

After you have confirmed the connection, you should see confirmation that you have added the server to your known hosts file and a successful connection message. If you do not see a success message, double-check that you saved the `config` file in the ~/.ssh directory of the IAM user you configured for access to AWS CodeCommit, and that you specified the correct private key file.

For information to help you troubleshoot problems, run the `ssh` command with the `-v` parameter:

```
1 ssh -v git-codecommit.us-east-2.amazonaws.com
```

You can find more information to help you troubleshoot connection problems in Troubleshooting.

Step 4: Connect to the AWS CodeCommit Console and Clone the Repository

If an administrator has already sent you the name and connection details for the AWS CodeCommit repository, you can skip this step and clone the repository directly.

To connect to an AWS CodeCommit repository

1. Open the AWS CodeCommit console at https://console.aws.amazon.com/codecommit.

2. In the region selector, choose the region where the repository was created. Repositories are specific to an AWS region. For more information, see Regions and Git Connection Endpoints.

3. Choose the repository you want to connect to from the list. This opens the **Code** page for that repository.

   If you see a **Welcome** page instead of a list of repositories, there are no repositories associated with your AWS account. To create a repository, see Create an AWS CodeCommit Repository or follow the steps in the Git with AWS CodeCommit Tutorial tutorial.

4. Copy the SSH URL to use when connecting to the repository.

5. Open a terminal. From the /tmp directory, using the SSH URL you copied, run the git clone command to clone the repository. For example, to clone a repository named *MyDemoRepo* to a local repo named *my-demo-repo* in the US East (Ohio) region:

   ```
   1 git clone ssh://git-codecommit.us-east-2.amazonaws.com/v1/repos/MyDemoRepo my-demo-repo
   ```

Note
If you successfully tested your connection, but the clone command fails, you might not have the necessary access to your config file, or another setting might be in conflict with your config file. Try connecting again, this time including the SSH key ID in the command. For example:

```
1 git clone ssh://Your-SSH-Key-ID@git-codecommit.us-east-2.amazonaws.com/v1/repos/MyDemoRepo my-
    demo-repo
```

For more information, see Access Error: Public Key Is Uploaded Successfully to IAM but Connection Fails on Linux, macOS, or Unix Systems.

For more information about how to connect to repositories, see Connect to the AWS CodeCommit Repository by Cloning the Repository.

Next Steps

You have completed the prerequisites. Follow the steps in AWS CodeCommit Tutorial to start using AWS CodeCommit.

Setup Steps for SSH Connections to AWS CodeCommit Repositories on Windows

Before you can connect to AWS CodeCommit for the first time, you must complete the initial configuration steps. This topic walks you through the steps for setting up your computer and AWS profile, connecting to an AWS CodeCommit repository, and cloning that repository to your computer (also known as creating a local repo). If you're new to Git, you might also want to review the information in Where Can I Learn More About Git?.

Topics

- Step 1: Initial Configuration for AWS CodeCommit
- Step 2: Install Git
- SSH and Windows: Set Up the Public and Private Keys for Git and AWS CodeCommit
- Step 4: Connect to the AWS CodeCommit Console and Clone the Repository
- Next Steps

Step 1: Initial Configuration for AWS CodeCommit

Follow these steps to set up an AWS account, create an IAM user, and configure access to AWS CodeCommit.

To create and configure an IAM user for accessing AWS CodeCommit

1. Create an AWS account by going to http://aws.amazon.com and choosing **Sign Up**.

2. Create an IAM user, or use an existing one, in your AWS account. Make sure you have an access key ID and a secret access key associated with that IAM user. For more information, see Creating an IAM User in Your AWS Account. **Note**
   AWS CodeCommit requires AWS Key Management Service. If you are using an existing IAM user, make sure there are no policies attached to the user that expressly deny the AWS KMS actions required by AWS CodeCommit. For more information, see AWS KMS and Encryption.

3. Sign in to the AWS Management Console and open the IAM console at https://console.aws.amazon.com/iam/.

4. In the IAM console, in the navigation pane, choose **Users**, and then choose the IAM user you want to configure for AWS CodeCommit access.

5. On the **Permissions** tab, choose **Add Permissions**.

6. In **Grant permissions**, choose **Attach existing policies directly**.

7. Select **AWSCodeCommitFullAccess** from the list of policies, or another managed policy for AWS CodeCommit access. For more information about managed policies for AWS CodeCommit, see AWS Managed (Predefined) Policies for AWS CodeCommit.

   After you have selected the policy you want to attach, choose** Next: Review** to review the list of policies that will be attached to the IAM user. If the list is correct, choose **Add permissions**.

   For more information about AWS CodeCommit managed policies and sharing access to repositories with other groups and users, see Share a Repository and Authentication and Access Control for AWS CodeCommit.

Note
If you want to use AWS CLI commands with AWS CodeCommit, install the AWS CLI. For more information, see Command Line Reference.

Step 2: Install Git

To work with files, commits, and other information in AWS CodeCommit repositories, you must install Git on your local machine. AWS CodeCommit supports Git versions 1.7.9 and later.

To install Git, we recommend websites such as Git Downloads.

Note
Git is an evolving, regularly updated platform. Occasionally, a feature change might affect the way it works with AWS CodeCommit. If you encounter issues with a specific version of Git and AWS CodeCommit, review the information in Troubleshooting.

If the version of Git you installed does not include a Bash emulator, such as Git Bash, install one. You will use this emulator instead of the Windows command line when you configure SSH connections.

SSH and Windows: Set Up the Public and Private Keys for Git and AWS Code-Commit

1. Open the Bash emulator. **Note**
   You might need to run the emulator with administrative permissions.

   From the emulator, run the ssh-keygen command, and follow the directions to save the file to the .ssh directory for your profile.

   For example:

```
1 $ ssh-keygen
2
3 Generating public/private rsa key pair.
4 Enter file in which to save the key (/drive/Users/user-name/.ssh/id_rsa): Type a file name
       here, for example /c/Users/user-name/.ssh/codecommit_rsa
5
6 Enter passphrase (empty for no passphrase): <Type a passphrase, and then press Enter>
7 Enter same passphrase again: <Type the passphrase again, and then press Enter>
8
9 Your identification has been saved in drive/Users/user-name/.ssh/codecommit_rsa.
10 Your public key has been saved in drive/Users/user-name/.ssh/codecommit_rsa.pub.
11 The key fingerprint is:
12 45:63:d5:99:0e:99:73:50:5e:d4:b3:2d:86:4a:2c:14 user-name@client-name
13 The key's randomart image is:
14 +--[ RSA 2048]----+
15 |        E.+.o*.++|
16 |       .o .=.=o. |
17 |       . .. *. +|
18 |        ..o . +..|
19 |        So . . . |
20 |          .      |
21 |                 |
22 |                 |
23 |                 |
24 +-----------------+
```

   This generates:

   - The *codecommit_rsa* file, which is the private key file.
   - The *codecommit_rsa*.pub file, which is the public key file.

2. Run the following commands to display the value of the public key file (*codecommit_rsa*.pub):

```
1 cd .ssh
2 notepad codecommit_rsa.pub
```

Copy the contents of the file, and then close Notepad without saving. The contents of the file will look similar to the following:

```
1 ssh-rsa EXAMPLE-AfICCQD6m7oRwOuXOjANBgkqhkiG9wOBAQUFADCBiDELMAkGA1UEBhMCVVMxCzAJB
2 gNVBAgTAldBMRAwDgYDVQQHEwdTZWF0dGxlMQ8wDQYDVQQKEwZBbWF6b24xFDASBgNVBAsTC01BTSBDb2
3 5zb2xlMRIwEAYDVQQDEwlUZXN0Q21ssYWMxHzAdBgkqhkiG9wOBCQEWEG5vb251QGFtYXpvbi5jb20wHhc
4 NMTEwNDI1MjAONTIxWhcNMTIwNDIOMjAONTIxWjCBiDELMAkGA1UEBhMCVVMxCzAJBgNVBAgTAldBMRAw
5 DgYDVQQHEwdTZWF0dGxlMQ8wDQYDVQQKEwZBbWF6b24xFDAS=EXAMPLE user-name@computer-name
```

3. Sign in to the AWS Management Console and open the IAM console at https://console.aws.amazon.com/iam/.

4. In the IAM console, in the navigation pane, choose **Users**, and from the list of users, choose your IAM user.

5. On the user details page, choose the **Security Credentials** tab, and then choose **Upload SSH public key**.

6. Paste the contents of your SSH public key into the field, and then choose **Upload SSH public key**.

7. Copy or save the information in **SSH Key ID** (for example, *APKAEIBAERJR2EXAMPLE*).

SSH keys for AWS CodeCommit

Use SSH public keys to authenticate to AWS CodeCommit repositories. Learn more about SSH keys.

Upload SSH public key

SSH Key ID	Uploaded	Status	Actions
APKAEIBAERJR2EXAMPLE	2015-07-21 16:32 PDT	Active	Make Inactive | Show SSH Key | Delete

8. In the Bash emulator, type the following commands to create a config file in the ~/.ssh directory, or edit it if one already exists:

```
1 notepad ~/.ssh/config
```

9. Add the following lines to the file, where the value for *User* is the SSH key ID you copied earlier, and the value for *IdentityFile* is the path to and name of the private key file:

```
1 Host git-codecommit.*.amazonaws.com
2   User APKAEIBAERJR2EXAMPLE
3   IdentityFile ~/.ssh/codecommit_rsa
```

Note
If you gave your private key file a name other than *codecommit_rsa*, be sure to use it here.

Save the file as config (not config.txt), and then close Notepad. **Important**
The name of the file must be **config** with no file extension, or the SSH connections will fail.

1. Run the following command to test your SSH configuration:

```
1 ssh git-codecommit.us-east-2.amazonaws.com
```

You will be asked to confirm the connection because `git-codecommit.us-east-2.amazonaws.com` is not yet included in your known hosts file. The AWS CodeCommit server fingerprint is displayed as part of the verification (`a9:6d:03:ed:08:42:21:be:06:e1:e0:2a:d1:75:31:5e` for MD5 or `31B1W2g5xn /NA2Ck6dyeJIrQOWvn7n8UEs56fG6ZIzQ` for SHA256). **Note**
AWS CodeCommit server fingerprints are unique for every region. To view the server fingerprints for a specific region, see Server Fingerprints for AWS CodeCommit.

After you have confirmed the connection, you should see confirmation that you have added the server to your known hosts file and a successful connection message. If you do not see a success message, double-check that you saved the `config` file in the ~/.ssh directory of the IAM user you configured for access to AWS CodeCommit, that the `config` file has no file extension (for example, it must not be named config.txt), and that you specified the correct private key file (*codecommit_rsa*, not *codecommit_rsa*.pub).

For information to help you troubleshoot problems, run the `ssh` command with the `-v` parameter:

```
1 ssh -v git-codecommit.us-east-2.amazonaws.com
```

You can find more information to help you troubleshoot connection problems in Troubleshooting.

Step 4: Connect to the AWS CodeCommit Console and Clone the Repository

If an administrator has already sent you the name and connection details for the AWS CodeCommit repository, you can skip this step and clone the repository directly.

To connect to an AWS CodeCommit repository

1. Open the AWS CodeCommit console at https://console.aws.amazon.com/codecommit.

2. In the region selector, choose the region where the repository was created. Repositories are specific to an AWS region. For more information, see Regions and Git Connection Endpoints.

3. Choose the repository you want to connect to from the list. This opens the **Code** page for that repository.

   If you see a **Welcome** page instead of a list of repositories, there are no repositories associated with your AWS account. To create a repository, see Create an AWS CodeCommit Repository or follow the steps in the Git with AWS CodeCommit Tutorial tutorial.

4. Choose **Clone URL**, and then copy the SSH URL.

5. In the Bash emulator, using the SSH URL you just copied, run the git clone command to clone the repository. This command will create the local repo in a subdirectory of the directory where you run the command. For example, to clone a repository named *MyDemoRepo* to a local repo named *my-demo-repo* in the US East (Ohio) region:

```
1 git clone ssh://git-codecommit.us-east-2.amazonaws.com/v1/repos/MyDemoRepo my-demo-repo
```

   Alternatively, open a command prompt, and using the URL and the SSH key ID for the public key you uploaded to IAM, run the git clone command. The local repo will be created in a subdirectory of the directory where you run the command. For example, to clone a repository named *MyDemoRepo* to a local repo named *my-demo-repo*:

```
1 git clone ssh://Your-SSH-Key-ID@git-codecommit.us-east-2.amazonaws.com/v1/repos/MyDemoRepo
    my-demo-repo
```

   For more information, see Connect to the AWS CodeCommit Repository by Cloning the Repository and Create a Commit.

Next Steps

You have completed the prerequisites. Follow the steps in AWS CodeCommit Tutorial to start using AWS CodeCommit.

Setup Steps for HTTPS Connections to AWS CodeCommit Repositories on Linux, macOS, or Unix with the AWS CLI Credential Helper

Before you can connect to AWS CodeCommit for the first time, you must complete the initial configuration steps. This topic walks you through the steps to set up your computer and AWS profile, connect to an AWS CodeCommit repository, and clone that repository to your computer, also known as creating a local repo. If you're new to Git, you might also want to review the information in Where Can I Learn More About Git?.

Topics

- Step 1: Initial Configuration for AWS CodeCommit
- Step 2: Install Git
- Step 3: Set Up the Credential Helper
- Step 4: Connect to the AWS CodeCommit Console and Clone the Repository
- Next Steps

Step 1: Initial Configuration for AWS CodeCommit

Follow these steps to set up an AWS account, create and configure an IAM user, and install the AWS CLI.

To create and configure an IAM user for accessing AWS CodeCommit

1. Create an AWS account by going to http://aws.amazon.com and choosing **Sign Up**.

2. Create an IAM user, or use an existing one, in your AWS account. Make sure you have an access key ID and a secret access key associated with that IAM user. For more information, see Creating an IAM User in Your AWS Account. **Note**
   AWS CodeCommit requires AWS Key Management Service. If you are using an existing IAM user, make sure there are no policies attached to the user that expressly deny the AWS KMS actions required by AWS CodeCommit. For more information, see AWS KMS and Encryption.

3. Sign in to the AWS Management Console and open the IAM console at https://console.aws.amazon.com/iam/.

4. In the IAM console, in the navigation pane, choose **Users**, and then choose the IAM user you want to configure for AWS CodeCommit access.

5. On the **Permissions** tab, choose **Add Permissions**.

6. In **Grant permissions**, choose **Attach existing policies directly**.

7. Select **AWSCodeCommitFullAccess** from the list of policies, or another managed policy for AWS CodeCommit access. For more information about managed policies for AWS CodeCommit, see AWS Managed (Predefined) Policies for AWS CodeCommit.

   After you have selected the policy you want to attach, choose** Next: Review** to review the list of policies that will be attached to the IAM user. If the list is correct, choose **Add permissions**.

   For more information about AWS CodeCommit managed policies and sharing access to repositories with other groups and users, see Share a Repository and Authentication and Access Control for AWS CodeCommit.

To install and configure the AWS CLI

1. On your local machine, download and install the AWS CLI. This is a prerequisite for interacting with AWS CodeCommit from the command line. For more information, see Getting Set Up with the AWS Command Line Interface. **Note**
   AWS CodeCommit works only with AWS CLI versions 1.7.38 and later. To determine which version of the AWS CLI you have installed, run the `aws --version` command.

To upgrade an older version of the AWS CLI to the latest version, see Installing the AWS Command Line Interface.

2. Run this command to verify the AWS CodeCommit commands for the AWS CLI are installed:

```
1 aws codecommit help
```

This command should return a list of AWS CodeCommit commands.

1. Configure the AWS CLI with the configure command, as follows:

```
1 aws configure
```

When prompted, specify the AWS access key and AWS secret access key of the IAM user you will use with AWS CodeCommit. Also, be sure to specify the region where the repository exists, such as us-east-2. When prompted for the default output format, specify json. For example:

```
1 AWS Access Key ID [None]: Type your target AWS access key ID here, and then press Enter
2 AWS Secret Access Key [None]: Type your target AWS secret access key here, and then press
      Enter
3 Default region name [None]: Type a supported region for AWS CodeCommit here, and then press
      Enter
4 Default output format [None]: Type json here, and then press Enter
```

To connect to a repository or a resource in another region, you must re-configure the AWS CLI with the default region name for that region. Supported default region names for AWS CodeCommit include:

- us-east-2
- us-east-1
- eu-west-1
- us-west-2
- ap-northeast-1
- ap-southeast-1
- ap-southeast-2
- eu-central-1
- ap-northeast-2
- sa-east-1
- us-west-1
- eu-west-2
- ap-south-1
- ca-central-1

For more information about AWS CodeCommit and regions, see Regions and Git Connection Endpoints. For more information about IAM, access keys, and secret keys, see How Do I Get Credentials? and Managing Access Keys for IAM Users.

Step 2: Install Git

To work with files, commits, and other information in AWS CodeCommit repositories, you must install Git on your local machine. AWS CodeCommit supports Git versions 1.7.9 and later.

To install Git, we recommend websites such as Git Downloads.

Note
Git is an evolving, regularly updated platform. Occasionally, a feature change might affect the way it works with AWS CodeCommit. If you encounter issues with a specific version of Git and AWS CodeCommit, review the information in Troubleshooting.

Step 3: Set Up the Credential Helper

1. From the terminal, use Git to run git config, specifying the use of the Git credential helper with the AWS credential profile, and enabling the Git credential helper to send the path to repositories:

```
1 git config --global credential.helper '!aws codecommit credential-helper $@'
2 git config --global credential.UseHttpPath true
```

Tip
The credential helper will use the default AWS credential profile or the Amazon EC2 instance role. You can specify a profile to use, such as `CodeCommitProfile`, if you have created a specific AWS credential profile to use with AWS CodeCommit:

```
1 git config --global credential.helper '!aws --profile CodeCommitProfile codecommit credential-
    helper $@'
```

If your profile name contains spaces, make sure you enclose the name in quotation marks (").
You can configure profiles per repository instead of globally by using `--local` instead of `--global`.

The Git credential helper writes the following value to `~/.gitconfig`:

```
1 [credential]
2     helper = !aws --profile CodeCommitProfile codecommit credential-helper $@
3     UseHttpPath = true
```

Important
If you want to use a different IAM user on the same local machine for AWS CodeCommit, you must run the git config command again and specify a different AWS credential profile.

1. Run git config --global --edit to verify the preceding value has been written to `~/.gitconfig`. If successful, you should see the preceding value (in addition to values that may already exist in the Git global configuration file). To exit, typically you would type **:q**, and then press Enter.

   If you experience problems after you configure your credential helper, see Troubleshooting. **Important**
   If you are using macOS, use the following steps to ensure the credential helper is configured correctly.

2. If you are using macOS, use HTTPS to connect to an AWS CodeCommit repository. After you connect to an AWS CodeCommit repository with HTTPS for the first time, subsequent access will fail after about fifteen minutes. The default Git version on macOS uses the Keychain Access utility to store credentials. For security measures, the password generated for access to your AWS CodeCommit repository is temporary, so the credentials stored in the keychain will stop working after about 15 minutes. To prevent these expired credentials from being used, you must either:

   - Install a version of Git that does not use the keychain by default.
   - Configure the Keychain Access utility to not provide credentials for AWS CodeCommit repositories.

   1. Open the Keychain Access utility. (You can use Finder to locate it.)

   2. Search for `git-codecommit.us-east-2.amazonaws.com`. Highlight the row, open the context menu or right-click it, and then choose **Get Info**.

   3. Choose the **Access Control** tab.

   4. In **Confirm before allowing access**, choose `git-credential-osxkeychain`, and then choose the minus sign to remove it from the list. **Note**
      After removing `git-credential-osxkeychain` from the list, you will see a pop-up dialog whenever you run a Git command. Choose **Deny** to continue. If you find the pop-ups too disruptive, here are some alternate options:
      Connect to AWS CodeCommit using SSH instead of HTTPS. For more information, see For SSH Connections on Linux, macOS, or Unix. In the Keychain Access utility, on the **Access Control** tab for `git-codecommit.us-east-2.amazonaws.com`, choose the **Allow all applications to access**

this item (access to this item is not restricted) option. This will prevent the pop-ups, but the credentials will eventually expire (on average, this takes about 15 minutes) and you will see a 403 error message. When this happens, you must delete the keychain item in order to restore functionality. Install a version of Git that does not use the keychain by default.

Step 4: Connect to the AWS CodeCommit Console and Clone the Repository

If an administrator has already sent you the name and connection details for the AWS CodeCommit repository, you can skip this step and clone the repository directly.

To connect to an AWS CodeCommit repository

1. Open the AWS CodeCommit console at https://console.aws.amazon.com/codecommit.

2. In the region selector, choose the region where the repository was created. Repositories are specific to an AWS region. For more information, see Regions and Git Connection Endpoints.

3. Choose the repository you want to connect to from the list. This opens the **Code** page for that repository.

   If you see a **Welcome** page instead of a list of repositories, there are no repositories associated with your AWS account. To create a repository, see Create an AWS CodeCommit Repository or follow the steps in the Git with AWS CodeCommit Tutorial tutorial.

4. Copy the HTTPS URL to use when connecting to the repository.

5. Open a terminal and from the /tmp directory, use the URL to clone the repository with the git clone command. For example, to clone a repository named *MyDemoRepo* to a local repo named *my-demo-repo* in the US East (Ohio) region:

```
1 git clone https://git-codecommit.us-east-2.amazonaws.com/v1/repos/MyDemoRepo my-demo-repo
```

   For more information, see Connect to the AWS CodeCommit Repository by Cloning the Repository and Create a Commit.

Next Steps

You have completed the prerequisites. Follow the steps in AWS CodeCommit Tutorial to start using AWS CodeCommit.

Setup Steps for HTTPS Connections to AWS CodeCommit Repositories on Windows with the AWS CLI Credential Helper

Before you can connect to AWS CodeCommit for the first time, you must complete the initial configuration steps. For most users, this can be done most easily by following the steps in For HTTPS Users Using Git Credentials. However, if you want to connect to AWS CodeCommit using a root account, federated access, or temporary credentials, you must use the credential helper that is included in the AWS CLI.

This topic walks you through the steps to install the AWS CLI, set up your computer and AWS profile, connect to an AWS CodeCommit repository, and clone that repository to your computer, also known as creating a local repo. If you're new to Git, you might also want to review the information in Where Can I Learn More About Git?.

Topics

- Step 1: Initial Configuration for AWS CodeCommit
- Step 2: Install Git
- Step 3: Set Up the Credential Helper
- Step 4: Connect to the AWS CodeCommit Console and Clone the Repository
- Next Steps

Step 1: Initial Configuration for AWS CodeCommit

Follow these steps to set up an AWS account, create and configure an IAM user, and install the AWS CLI. The AWS CLI includes a credential helper that you will configure for HTTPS connections to your AWS CodeCommit repositories.

To create and configure an IAM user for accessing AWS CodeCommit

1. Create an AWS account by going to http://aws.amazon.com and choosing **Sign Up**.

2. Create an IAM user, or use an existing one, in your AWS account. Make sure you have an access key ID and a secret access key associated with that IAM user. For more information, see Creating an IAM User in Your AWS Account. **Note**
AWS CodeCommit requires AWS Key Management Service. If you are using an existing IAM user, make sure there are no policies attached to the user that expressly deny the AWS KMS actions required by AWS CodeCommit. For more information, see AWS KMS and Encryption.

3. Sign in to the AWS Management Console and open the IAM console at https://console.aws.amazon.com/iam/.

4. In the IAM console, in the navigation pane, choose **Users**, and then choose the IAM user you want to configure for AWS CodeCommit access.

5. On the **Permissions** tab, choose **Add Permissions**.

6. In **Grant permissions**, choose **Attach existing policies directly**.

7. Select **AWSCodeCommitFullAccess** from the list of policies, or another managed policy for AWS CodeCommit access. For more information about managed policies for AWS CodeCommit, see AWS Managed (Predefined) Policies for AWS CodeCommit.

   After you have selected the policy you want to attach, choose** Next: Review** to review the list of policies that will be attached to the IAM user. If the list is correct, choose **Add permissions**.

   For more information about AWS CodeCommit managed policies and sharing access to repositories with other groups and users, see Share a Repository and Authentication and Access Control for AWS CodeCommit.

To install and configure the AWS CLI

1. On your local machine, download and install the AWS CLI. This is a prerequisite for interacting with AWS CodeCommit from the command line. For more information, see Getting Set Up with the AWS Command Line Interface. **Note**
   AWS CodeCommit works only with AWS CLI versions 1.7.38 and later. To determine which version of the AWS CLI you have installed, run the `aws --version` command.
   To upgrade an older version of the AWS CLI to the latest version, see Installing the AWS Command Line Interface.

2. Run this command to verify the AWS CodeCommit commands for the AWS CLI are installed:

```
1 aws codecommit help
```

This command should return a list of AWS CodeCommit commands.

1. Configure the AWS CLI with the configure command, as follows:

```
1 aws configure
```

When prompted, specify the AWS access key and AWS secret access key of the IAM user you will use with AWS CodeCommit. Also, be sure to specify the region where the repository exists, such as `us-east-2`. When prompted for the default output format, specify `json`. For example:

```
1 AWS Access Key ID [None]: Type your target AWS access key ID here, and then press Enter
2 AWS Secret Access Key [None]: Type your target AWS secret access key here, and then press
    Enter
3 Default region name [None]: Type a supported region for AWS CodeCommit here, and then press
    Enter
4 Default output format [None]: Type json here, and then press Enter
```

To connect to a repository or a resource in another region, you must re-configure the AWS CLI with the default region name for that region. Supported default region names for AWS CodeCommit include:

- us-east-2
- us-east-1
- eu-west-1
- us-west-2
- ap-northeast-1
- ap-southeast-1
- ap-southeast-2
- eu-central-1
- ap-northeast-2
- sa-east-1
- us-west-1
- eu-west-2
- ap-south-1
- ca-central-1

For more information about AWS CodeCommit and regions, see Regions and Git Connection Endpoints. For more information about IAM, access keys, and secret keys, see How Do I Get Credentials? and Managing Access Keys for IAM Users.

Step 2: Install Git

To work with files, commits, and other information in AWS CodeCommit repositories, you must install Git on your local machine. AWS CodeCommit supports Git versions 1.7.9 and later.

To install Git, we recommend websites such as Git for Windows. If you use this link to install Git, you can accept all of the installation default settings except for the following:

- When prompted during the **Adjusting your PATH environment** step, select the **Use Git from the Windows Command Prompt** option.
- (Optional) If you intend to use HTTPS with the credential helper that is included in the AWS CLI instead of configuring Git credentials for AWS CodeCommit, on the **Configuring extra options** page, make sure the **Enable Git Credential Manager** option is cleared. The Git Credential Manager is only compatible with AWS CodeCommit if IAM users configure Git credentials. For more information, see For HTTPS Users Using Git Credentials and Git for Windows: I Installed Git for Windows, but I Am Denied Access to My Repository (403).

Note

Git is an evolving, regularly updated platform. Occasionally, a feature change might affect the way it works with AWS CodeCommit. If you encounter issues with a specific version of Git and AWS CodeCommit, review the information in Troubleshooting.

Step 3: Set Up the Credential Helper

The AWS CLI includes a Git credential helper you can use with AWS CodeCommit. The Git credential helper requires an AWS credential profile, which stores a copy of an IAM user's AWS access key ID and AWS secret access key (along with a default region name and default output format). The Git credential helper uses this information to automatically authenticate with AWS CodeCommit so you don't need to type this information every time you use Git to interact with AWS CodeCommit.

1. Open a command prompt and use Git to run git config, specifying the use of the Git credential helper with the AWS credential profile, which enables the Git credential helper to send the path to repositories:

```
1 git config --global credential.helper "!aws codecommit credential-helper $@"
2 git config --global credential.UseHttpPath true
```

The Git credential helper writes the following to the .gitconfig file:

```
1 [credential]
2     helper = !aws codecommit credential-helper $@
3     UseHttpPath = true
```

Important

If you are using a Bash emulator instead of the Windows command line, you must use single quotes instead of double quotes. The credential helper will use the default AWS profile or the Amazon EC2 instance role. If you have created an AWS credential profile to use, such as *CodeCommitProfile*, you can modify the command as follows to use it instead:

```
1 ```
2 git config --global credential.helper "!aws codecommit credential-helper --profile
      CodeCommitProfile $@"
3 ```
```

This will write the following to the .gitconfig file:

```
1 ```
2 [credential]
3     helper = !aws codecommit credential-helper --profile=CodeCommitProfile $@
4     UseHttpPath = true
5 ```
```

If your profile name contains spaces, you must edit your .gitconfig file after you run this command to enclose it in single quotes ('); otherwise, the credential helper will not work. If your installation of Git for Windows

48

included the Git Credential Manager utility, you will see 403 errors or prompts to provide credentials into the Credential Manager utility after the first few connection attempts. The most reliable way to solve this problem is to uninstall and then reinstall Git for Windows without the option for the Git Credential Manager utility, as it is not compatible with AWS CodeCommit. If you want to keep the Git Credential Manager utility, you must perform additional configuration steps to also use AWS CodeCommit, including manually modifying the .gitconfig file to specify the use of the credential helper for AWS CodeCommit when connecting to AWS CodeCommit. Remove any stored credentials from the Credential Manager utility (you can find this utility in Control Panel). Once you have removed any stored credentials, add the following to your .gitconfig file, save it, and then try connecting again from a new command prompt window:

```
1  ```
2  [credential "https://git-codecommit.us-east-2.amazonaws.com"]
3      helper = !aws codecommit credential-helper $@
4      UseHttpPath = true
5
6  [credential "https://git-codecommit.us-east-1.amazonaws.com"]
7      helper = !aws codecommit credential-helper $@
8      UseHttpPath = true
9  ```
```

Additionally, you might have to re-configure your git config settings by specifying --system instead of --global or --local before all connections work as expected. If you want to use different IAM users on the same local machine for AWS CodeCommit, you should specify git config --local instead of git config --global, and run the configuration for each AWS credential profile.

1. Run git config --global --edit to verify the preceding values have been written to the .gitconfig file for your user profile (by default, `%HOME%\.gitconfig` or `drive:\Users\UserName\.gitconfig`). If successful, you should see the preceding values (in addition to values that may already exist in the Git global configuration file). To exit, typically you would type **:q** and then press Enter.

Step 4: Connect to the AWS CodeCommit Console and Clone the Repository

If an administrator has already sent you the name and connection details for the AWS CodeCommit repository, you can skip this step and clone the repository directly.

To connect to an AWS CodeCommit repository

1. Open the AWS CodeCommit console at https://console.aws.amazon.com/codecommit.

2. In the region selector, choose the region where the repository was created. Repositories are specific to an AWS region. For more information, see Regions and Git Connection Endpoints.

3. Choose the repository you want to connect to from the list. This opens the **Code** page for that repository.

   If you see a **Welcome** page instead of a list of repositories, there are no repositories associated with your AWS account. To create a repository, see Create an AWS CodeCommit Repository or follow the steps in the Git with AWS CodeCommit Tutorial tutorial.

4. Copy the HTTPS URL to use when connecting to the repository.

5. Open a command prompt and use the URL to clone the repository with the git clone command. The local repo will be created in a subdirectory of the directory where you run the command. For example, to clone a repository named *MyDemoRepo* to a local repo named *my-demo-repo* in the US East (Ohio) region:

```
1 git clone https://git-codecommit.us-east-2.amazonaws.com/v1/repos/MyDemoRepo my-demo-repo
```

   On some versions of Windows, you might see a pop-up dialog box asking for your user name and password. This is the built-in credential management system for Windows, but it is not compatible with the credential helper for AWS CodeCommit. Choose **Cancel**.

For more information about how to connect to repositories, see Connect to the AWS CodeCommit Repository by Cloning the Repository.

Next Steps

You have completed the prerequisites. Follow the steps in AWS CodeCommit Tutorial to start using AWS CodeCommit.

Getting Started with AWS CodeCommit

The easiest way to get started with AWS CodeCommit is to follow the steps in AWS CodeCommit Tutorial. If you are new to Git as well as AWS CodeCommit, you should also consider following the steps in Git with AWS CodeCommit Tutorial. This will help you familiarize yourself with AWS CodeCommit as well as the basics of using Git when interacting with your AWS CodeCommit repositories.

You can also follow the tutorial in Simple Pipeline Walkthrough with AWS CodePipeline and AWS CodeCommit to learn how to use your AWS CodeCommit repository as part of a continuous delivery pipeline.

The tutorials in this section assume you have completed the prerequisites and setup, including:

- Assigning permissions to the IAM user.
- Setting up credential management for HTTPS or SSH connections on the local machine you will use for this tutorial.
- Configuring the AWS CLI if you want to use the command line or terminal for all operations, including creating the repository.

Topics

- Getting Started with AWS CodeCommit Tutorial
- Git with AWS CodeCommit Tutorial

Getting Started with AWS CodeCommit Tutorial

If you're new to AWS CodeCommit, this tutorial helps you learn how to use its features. In this tutorial, you create a repository in AWS CodeCommit. After you create a local copy of that repository (a local repo) and push some changes to the AWS CodeCommit repository, you browse the files and view the changes. You can also create a pull request for others to review and comment on changes to your code.

If you are not familiar with Git, you might want to complete the Git with AWS CodeCommit Tutorial in addition to this tutorial. After you finish this tutorial, you should have enough practice to start using AWS CodeCommit for your own projects and in team environments.

Important
Before you begin, you must complete the prerequisites and setup, including:
Assigning permissions to the IAM user. Setting up credential management for HTTPS or SSH connections on the local machine you use for this tutorial. Configuring the AWS CLI if you want to use the command line or terminal for all operations, including creating the repository.

Topics

- Step 1: Create an AWS CodeCommit Repository
- Step 2: Add Files to Your Repository
- Step 3: Browse the Contents of Your Repository
- Step 4: Create and Collaborate on a Pull Request
- Step 5: Next Steps
- Step 6: Clean Up

Step 1: Create an AWS CodeCommit Repository

You can use the AWS CodeCommit console to create an AWS CodeCommit repository. If you already have a repository you want to use for this tutorial, you can skip this step.

Note
Depending on your usage, you might be charged for creating or accessing a repository. For more information, see Pricing on the AWS CodeCommit product information page.

To create the AWS CodeCommit repository (console)

1. Open the AWS CodeCommit console at https://console.aws.amazon.com/codecommit.

2. In the region selector, choose the region where you will create the repository. For more information, see Regions and Git Connection Endpoints.

3. On the **Welcome** page, choose **Get Started Now**. (If a **Dashboard** page appears instead, choose **Create repository**.)

4. On the **Create repository** page, in the **Repository name** box, type a name (for example, **MyDemoRepo**).

5. In **Description**, type a description (for example, **My demonstration repository**).

6. Choose **Create repository**.

7. In **Configure email notifications**, configure notifications so that repository users receive emails about important repository events. This step is optional, but recommended. You can choose the event types (for example, comments on code) and whether to use an existing Amazon SNS topic or create one specifically for this purpose. You can choose to skip this step and configure notifications at a later time. For more information, see Configuring Notifications for Events in an AWS CodeCommit Repository.

Create repository

Create a secure repository to store and share your code. Begin by typing a repository name and a description for your repository. Repository names are included in the URLs for that repository.

 Access to the repository
Users connecting to an AWS CodeCommit repository for the first time must complete setup steps before they can use it. Learn more

Repository name* | MyDemoRepo

Description | My demonstration repository

*Required

Cancel   **Create repository**

Note

If you use a name other than `MyDemoRepo` for your repository, be sure to use it in the remaining steps of this tutorial.

When the repository opens, you see information about connecting to it from your local computer and how to add files directly from the AWS CodeCommit console.

Step 2: Add Files to Your Repository

You can add files to your repository in the following ways:

- Creating a file directly from the AWS CodeCommit console.
- Uploading a file from your local computer using the AWS CodeCommit console.
- Using a Git client to clone the repository to your local computer, and then adding, committing, and pushing files to the AWS CodeCommit repository.

The simplest way to get started is to add a file from the AWS CodeCommit console.

1. In the navigation bar for the repository, choose **Code**.

2. Choose **Add file**, and then choose to create a file or upload a file from your computer.

3. In **Code: Create a file** or **Code: Upload a file**, in **Author name**, type the name you want displayed to other repository users. In **Commit message**, type a brief message. (Optional) Provide an email

address in **Email address**. If you're uploading a file, choose the file you want to upload. If you're creating a file, in the code editor, type a name for the file and the code you want to add .

Code: Upload a file

To upload a file from your computer to this repository, choose the branch where you want to add the file, and type a message about why you're adding the file to the repository

Branch: master ▼

MyDemoRepo

⬆
Choose a file to upload to the repository

Commit the file to the **master** branch

Author name	María García
Email address	maria_garcia@example.com
Commit message	Adding my first file to the repository

Cancel Commit file

4. Choose **Commit file**.

For more information, see Working with Files in AWS CodeCommit Repositories.

To use a Git client to clone the repository, install Git on your local computer, and then clone the AWS CodeCommit repository. Add some files to the local repo and push them to the AWS CodeCommit repository. For an in-depth introduction, try the Git with AWS CodeCommit Tutorial. If you are familiar with Git but are not sure how to do this with an AWS CodeCommit repository, you can view examples and instructions in Create a Commit, Step 2: Create a Local Repo, or Connect to a Repository.

After you have added some files to the AWS CodeCommit repository, you can view them from the console.

Step 3: Browse the Contents of Your Repository

You can use the AWS CodeCommit console to review the files in a repository or to quickly read the contents of a file. This helps you determine which branch to check out or whether to create a local copy of a repository.

1. From the AWS CodeCommit console, choose MyDemoRepo from the list of repositories.

2. The contents of the repository are displayed in the default branch for your repository. To change the view to another branch, choose the view selector button (here the view is set to **Branch: master**), and then choose the branch you want to view from the list.

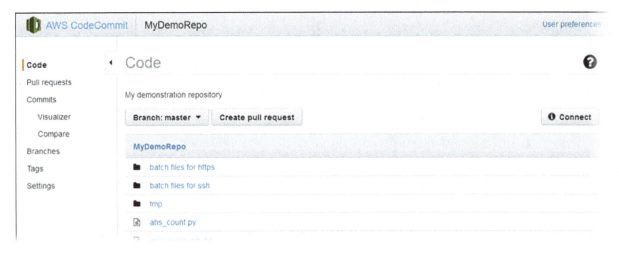

3. To view the contents of a file in your repository, choose the file from the list.

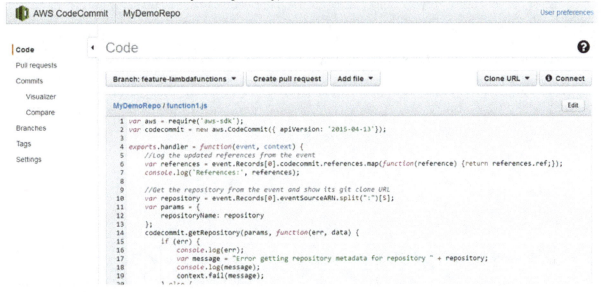

For more information, see Browse Files in a RepositoryCreate or Add a FileEdit the Contents of a File.

You can also browse the commit history of a repository. This helps you identify changes made in a repository, including when and by whom those changes were made.

1. In the navigation pane for a repository, choose **Commits**. In the commit history view, a history of commits for the repository in the default branch is displayed, in reverse chronological order.

2. Review the commit history by branch or by tag, and get details about commits by author, date, and more.

3. To view the differences between a commit and its parent, choose the abbreviated commit ID. You can choose how the changes are displayed, including showing or hiding white space changes, and whether to view changes inline (Unified view) or side by side (Split view). **Note**
If you are signed in as an IAM user, you can configure and save your preferences for viewing code and other console settings. For more information, see Working with User Preferences.

4. To view all comments on a commit, choose **Comments**, or scroll through the changes to view them inline. You can also add your own comments and reply to the comments made by others.

For more information, see Comment on a Commit.

5. To view the differences between any two commits specifiers, including tags, branches, and commit IDs, in the navigation pane, choose **Compare**.

For more information, see Browse the Commit History of a Repository and Compare Commits.

6. In the navigation pane, choose **Visualizer**.

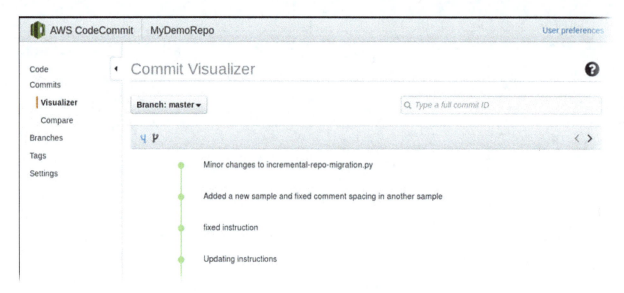

The commit graph is displayed, with the subject line for each commit shown next to its point in the graph. The subject line display is limited to 80 characters.

7. To see more details about a commit, choose its point in the graph.

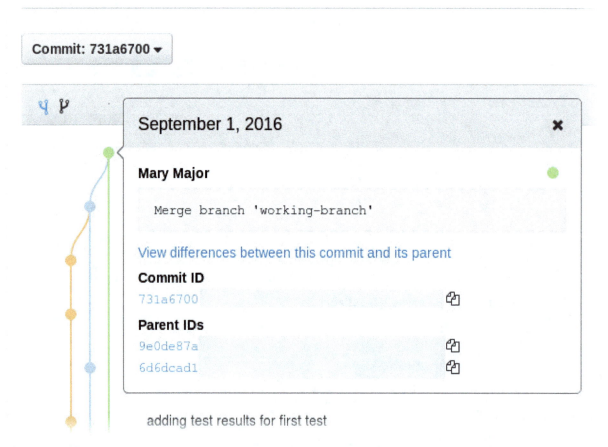

You can review the information in the detail pane, copy commit and parent commit IDs, render a graph from a different point, and more. For more information, see View a Graph of the Commit History of a

Repository .

Now that you have reviewed the content of your repository, consider whether you want to create a trigger. A trigger is an action that is taken in response to events in that repository, such as a push to a specific branch.

Step 4: Create and Collaborate on a Pull Request

When you work with other repository users, you might want to collaborate on code and review changes. You can create a pull request so that other users can review and comment on your code changes in a branch before you merge those changes into another branch.

Important
Before you can create a pull request, you must create a branch that contains the code changes you want to review. For more information, see Create a Branch.

1. In the navigation pane, choose **Branches**.

2. In **Branches**, find the branch that contains the changes you want reviewed, and then choose **Create pull request**.

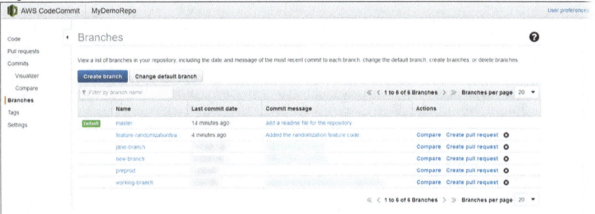

3. In **Create pull request**, in **Source**, choose the branch that contains the changes you want reviewed. By default, the destination branch is preconfigured for you with the default branch of the repository. (Optional) Choose a different branch if you want to merge code into a different branch when the pull request is complete, and then choose **Compare**.

4. Review the merge details and changes to confirm that the pull request contains the changes and commits you want reviewed. If so, in **Details**, provide a title for this review. This is the title that appears in the list of pull requests for the repository. In **Description**, provide details about what this review is about and any other useful information for reviewers. Choose **Create**.

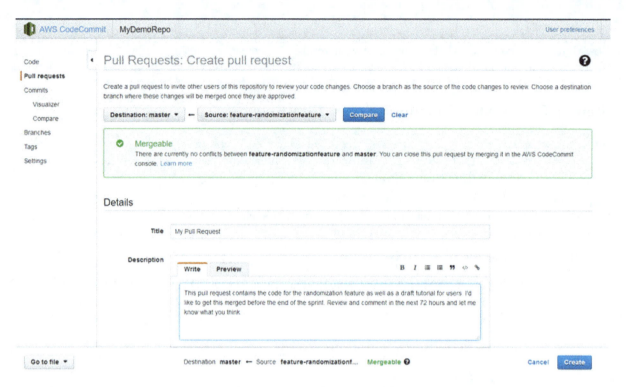

5. Your pull request appears in the list of pull requests for the repository. You can filter the view to show only open requests, closed requests, requests that you created, and more.

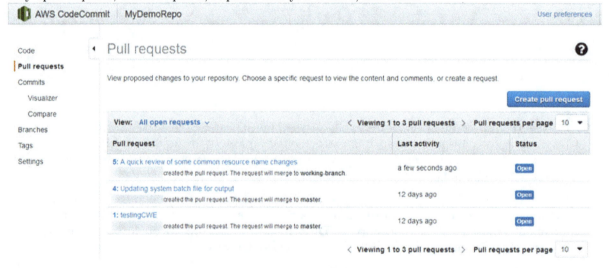

Tip

You can create pull requests directly from the **Pull requests** view.

6. If you configured notifications for your repository and chose to notify users of pull request events, users receive email about your new pull request. Users can view the changes and comment on specific lines of code, files, and the pull request itself. They can also reply to comments. If necessary, you can push changes to the pull request branch, which updates the pull request.

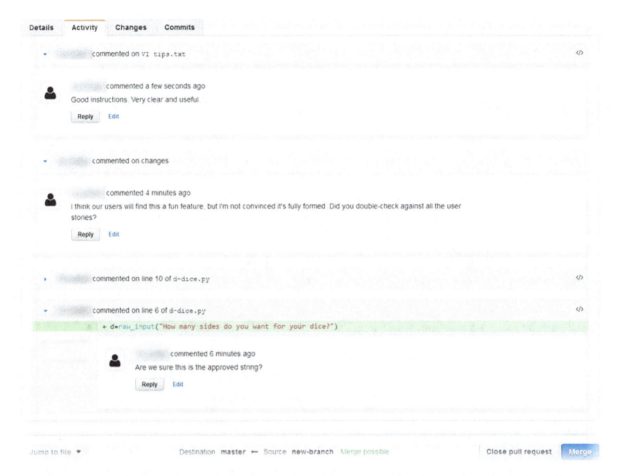

7. When you are satisfied that all the code changes have been reviewed and agreed to, from the pull request, do one of the following:

   - If you want to automatically merge the branches as part of closing the pull request using the fast-forward merge option, choose **Merge**.
   - If you want to close the pull request without using the automatic fast-forward merge option to merge branches, or if there are merge conflicts in the branches that cannot be automatically resolved, choose **Close pull request**. **Note**
     You can always manually merge branches, including pull request branches, by using the git merge command in your local repo and pushing your changes. AWS CodeCommit closes the pull request when you push the merged code.

For more information, see Working with Pull Requests.

Step 5: Next Steps

Now that you have familiarized yourself with AWS CodeCommit and some of its features, consider doing the following:

- If you are new to Git and AWS CodeCommit or want to review examples of using Git with AWS CodeCommit, continue to the Git with AWS CodeCommit Tutorial tutorial.
- If you want to work with others in an AWS CodeCommit repository, see Share a Repository. (If you want to share your repository with users in another AWS account, see Configure Cross-Account Access to an AWS CodeCommit Repository.)
- If you want to migrate a repository to AWS CodeCommit, follow the steps in Migrate to AWS CodeCommit.

- If you want to add your repository to a continuous delivery pipeline, follow the steps in Simple Pipeline Walkthrough.
- If you want to learn more about products and services that integrate with AWS CodeCommit, including examples from the community, see Product and Service Integrations.

Step 6: Clean Up

If you are done with exploring AWS CodeCommit and no longer need the repository, you should delete the AWS CodeCommit repository and other resources you used in this tutorial so you won't continue to be charged for the storage space.

Important
After you delete this repository, you can no longer clone it to any local repo or shared repo. You also can no longer pull data from it, push data to it, or perform any Git operations, from any local repo or shared repo. This action cannot be undone.
If you configured notifications for your repository, deleting the repository also deletes the Amazon CloudWatch Events rule created for the repository. It does not delete the Amazon SNS topic used as a target for that rule. If you configured triggers for your repository, deleting the repository does not delete the Amazon SNS topics or Lambda functions you configured as the targets of those triggers. Be sure to delete those resources if you don't need them. For more information, see Delete Triggers from a Repository.

To delete the AWS CodeCommit repository

1. Open the AWS CodeCommit console at https://console.aws.amazon.com/codecommit.

2. On the **Dashboard** page, in the list of repositories, choose **MyDemoRepo**.

3. In the navigation pane, choose **Settings**.

4. On the **Settings** page, in **General**, in **Delete repository**, choose **Delete repository**.

5. In the box next to **Type the name of the repository to confirm deletion**, type **MyDemoRepo**, and then choose **Delete**.

Git with AWS CodeCommit Tutorial

If you are new to Git and AWS CodeCommit, this tutorial helps you learn some simple commands to get you started. If you are already familiar with Git, you can skip this tutorial and go to AWS CodeCommit Tutorial.

In this tutorial, you create a repository that represents a local copy of the AWS CodeCommit repository, which we refer to here and in the rest of the documentation as a local repo.

After you create the local repo, you make some changes to it. Then you send (push) your changes to the AWS CodeCommit repository.

You also simulate a team environment where two users independently commit changes to their local repo and push those changes to the AWS CodeCommit repository. The users then pull the changes from the AWS CodeCommit repository to their own local repo to see the changes the other user made.

You also create branches and tags and manage some access permissions in the AWS CodeCommit repository.

After you complete this tutorial, you should have enough practice with the core Git and AWS CodeCommit concepts to use them for your own projects.

Complete the prerequisites and setup, including:

- Assign permissions to the IAM user.
- Set up credential management for HTTPS or SSH connections on the local machine you use for this tutorial.
- Configure the AWS CLI if you want to use the command line or terminal for all operations, including creating the repository.

Topics

- Step 1: Create an AWS CodeCommit Repository
- Step 2: Create a Local Repo
- Step 3: Create Your First Commit
- Step 4: Push Your First Commit
- Step 5: Share the AWS CodeCommit Repository and Push and Pull Another Commit
- Step 6: Create and Share a Branch
- Step 7: Create and Share a Tag
- Step 8: Set Up Access Permissions
- Step 9: Clean Up

Step 1: Create an AWS CodeCommit Repository

In this step, you use the AWS CodeCommit console to create the repository.

You can skip this step if you already have an AWS CodeCommit repository you want to use.

Note
Depending on your usage, you might be charged for creating or accessing a repository. For more information, see Pricing on the AWS CodeCommit product information page.

To create the AWS CodeCommit repository (console)

1. Open the AWS CodeCommit console at https://console.aws.amazon.com/codecommit.

2. In the region selector, choose the region where you will create the repository. For more information, see Regions and Git Connection Endpoints.

3. On the **Welcome** page, choose **Get Started Now**. (If a **Dashboard** page appears instead, choose **Create repository**.)

4. On the **Create repository** page, in the **Repository name** box, type a name (for example, **MyDemoRepo**).

5. In **Description**, type a description (for example, **My demonstration repository**).

6. Choose **Create repository**.

7. In **Configure email notifications**, configure notifications so that repository users receive emails about important repository events. This step is optional, but recommended. You can choose the event types (for example, comments on code) and whether to use an existing Amazon SNS topic or create one specifically for this purpose. You can choose to skip this step and configure notifications at a later time. For more information, see Configuring Notifications for Events in an AWS CodeCommit Repository.

Note

The remaining steps in this tutorial use `MyDemoRepo` for the name of your AWS CodeCommit repository. If you choose a different name, be sure to use it throughout this tutorial.

For more information about creating repositories, including how to create a repository from the terminal or command line, see Create a Repository.

Step 2: Create a Local Repo

In this step, you set up a local repo on your local machine to connect to your repository. To do this, you select a directory on your local machine that represents the local repo. You use Git to clone and initialize a copy of your empty AWS CodeCommit repository inside of that directory. Then you specify the user name and email address used to annotate your commits.

1. Open the AWS CodeCommit console at https://console.aws.amazon.com/codecommit.

2. In the region selector, choose the region where the repository was created. Repositories are specific to an AWS region. For more information, see Regions and Git Connection Endpoints.

3. On the **Dashboard** page, choose the name of the repository you want to share.

4. On the **Code** page, choose **Clone URL**, and then choose the protocol you want your users to use.

5. Copy the displayed URL for the connection protocol your users will use when connecting to your AWS CodeCommit repository.

6. Send your users the connection information along with any other instructions, such as installing the AWS CLI, configuring a profile, or installing Git. Make sure to include the configuration information for the connection protocol (for example, for HTTPS, configuring the credential helper for Git).

Step 3: Create Your First Commit

In this step, you create your first commit in your local repo. To do this, you create two example files in your local repo. You use Git to stage the change to, and then commit the change to, your local repo.

1. Use a text editor to create the following two example text files in your directory. Name the files `cat.txt` and `dog.txt`:

```
1 cat.txt
2 -------
3 The domestic cat (Felis catus or Felis silvestris catus) is a small, usually furry,
      domesticated, and carnivorous mammal.
```

```
1 dog.txt
2 -------
3 The domestic dog (Canis lupus familiaris) is a canid that is known as man's best friend.
```

2. Run git add to stage the change:

```
1 git add cat.txt dog.txt
```

3. Run git commit to commit the change:

```
1 git commit -m "Added cat.txt and dog.txt"
```

Tip
To see details about the commit you just made, run git log.

Step 4: Push Your First Commit

In this step, you push the commit from your local repo to your AWS CodeCommit repository.

Run git push to push your commit through the default remote name Git uses for your AWS CodeCommit repository (origin), from the default branch in your local repo (master):

```
1 git push -u origin master
```

Tip
After you have pushed files to your AWS CodeCommit repository, you can use the AWS CodeCommit console to view the contents. For more information, see Browse Files in a RepositoryCreate or Add a FileEdit the Contents of a File.

Step 5: Share the AWS CodeCommit Repository and Push and Pull Another Commit

In this step, you share information about the AWS CodeCommit repository with a fellow team member. The team member uses this information to get a local copy, make some changes to it, and then push the modified local copy to your AWS CodeCommit repository. You then pull the changes from the AWS CodeCommit repository to your local repo.

In this tutorial, you simulate the fellow user by having Git create a directory separate from the one you created in step 2. (Typically, this directory would be on a different machine.) This new directory is a copy of your AWS CodeCommit repository. Any changes you make to the existing directory or this new directory are made independently. The only way to identify changes to these directories is to pull from the AWS CodeCommit repository.

Even though they're on the same local machine, we call the existing directory your *local repo* and the new directory the *shared repo*.

From the new directory, you get a separate copy of the AWS CodeCommit repository. You then add a new example file, commit the changes to the shared repo, and then push the commit from the shared repo to your AWS CodeCommit repository.

Lastly, you pull the changes from your repository to your local repo and then browse it to see the changes committed by the other user.

1. Switch to the /tmp directory or the c:\temp directory.

2. Run git clone to pull down a copy of the repository into the shared repo:

   For HTTPS:

```
1 git clone https://git-codecommit.us-east-2.amazonaws.com/v1/repos/MyDemoRepo shared-demo-
     repo
```

   For SSH:

```
1 git clone ssh://git-codecommit.us-east-2.amazonaws.com/v1/repos/MyDemoRepo shared-demo-repo
```

Note

When you clone a repository using SSH on Windows operating systems, you must add the SSH key ID to the connection string as follows:

```
1 git clone ssh://Your-SSH-Key-ID@git-codecommit.us-east-2.amazonaws.com/v1/repos/MyDemoRepo my-
    demo-repo
```

For more information, see For SSH Connections on Windows.

In this command, `MyDemoRepo` is the name of your AWS CodeCommit repository. `shared-demo-repo` is the name of the directory Git creates in the `/tmp` directory or the `c:\temp` directory. After Git creates the directory, Git pulls down a copy of your repository into the `shared-demo-repo` directory.

1. Switch to the `shared-demo-repo` directory:

    ```
    1 (For Linux, macOS, or Unix) cd /tmp/shared-demo-repo
    2 (For Windows) cd c:\temp\shared-demo-repo
    ```

2. Run git config to add another user name and email address represented by placeholders *other-user-name* and *other-email-address* (for example, `John Doe` and `johndoe@example.com`). This makes it easier to identify the commits the other user made:

    ```
    1 git config --local user.name "other-user-name"
    2 git config --local user.email other-email-address
    ```

3. Use a text editor to create the following example text file in the `shared-demo-repo` directory. Name the file `horse.txt`:

    ```
    1 horse.txt
    2 --------
    3 The horse (Equus ferus caballus) is one of two extant subspecies of Equus ferus.
    ```

4. Run git add to stage the change to the shared repo:

    ```
    1 git add horse.txt
    ```

5. Run git commit to commit the change to the shared repo:

    ```
    1 git commit -m "Added horse.txt"
    ```

6. Run git push to push your initial commit through the default remote name Git uses for your AWS CodeCommit repository (`origin`), from the default branch in your local repo (`master`):

    ```
    1 git push -u origin master
    ```

7. Switch to your local repo and run git pull to pull into your local repo the commit the shared repo made to the AWS CodeCommit repository. Then run git log to see the commit that was initiated from the shared repo.

Step 6: Create and Share a Branch

In this step, you create a branch in your local repo, make a few changes, and then push the branch to your AWS CodeCommit repository. You then pull the branch to the shared repo from your AWS CodeCommit repository.

A branch allows you to independently develop a different version of the repository's contents (for example, to work on a new software feature without affecting the work of your team members). When that feature is stable, you merge the branch into a more stable branch of the software.

You use Git to create the branch and then point it to the first commit you made. You use Git to push the branch to the AWS CodeCommit repository. You then switch to your shared repo and use Git to pull the new branch into your shared local repo and explore the branch.

1. From your local repo, run git checkout, specifying the name of the branch (for example, `MyNewBranch`) and the ID of the first commit you made in the local repo.

   If you don't know the commit ID, run git log to get it. Make sure the commit has your user name and email address, not the user name and email address of the other user. This is to simulate that `master` is a stable version of the AWS CodeCommit repository and the `MyNewBranch` branch is for some new, relatively unstable feature:

   ```
   1 git checkout -b MyNewBranch commit-ID
   ```

2. Run git push to send the new branch from the local repo to the AWS CodeCommit repository:

   ```
   1 git push origin MyNewBranch
   ```

3. Now, pull the branch into the shared repo and check your results:

   1. Switch to the shared repo directory (shared-demo-repo).
   2. Pull in the new branch (git fetch origin).
   3. Confirm that the branch has been pulled in (git branch --all displays a list of all branches for the repository).
   4. Switch to the new branch (git checkout MyNewBranch).
   5. Confirm that you have switched to the `MyNewBranch` branch by running git status or git branch. The output shows which branch you are on. In this case, it should be `MyNewBranch`.
   6. View the list of commits in the branch (git log).

   Here's the list of Git commands to call:

   ```
   1 git fetch origin
   2 git branch --all
   3 git checkout MyNewBranch
   4 git branch or git status
   5 git log
   ```

4. Switch back to the `master` branch and view its list of commits. The Git commands should look like this:

   ```
   1 git checkout master
   2 git log
   ```

5. Switch to the `master` branch in your local repo. You can run git status or git branch. The output shows which branch you are on. In this case, it should be `master`. The Git commands should look like this:

   ```
   1 git checkout master
   2 git branch or git status
   ```

Step 7: Create and Share a Tag

In this step, you create two tags in your local repo, associate the tags with commits, and then push the tags to your AWS CodeCommit repository. You then pull the changes from the AWS CodeCommit repository to the shared repo.

A tag is used to give a human-readable name to a commit (or branch or even another tag). You would do this, for example, if you want to tag a commit as "v2.1." A commit, branch, or tag can have any number of tags associated with it, but an individual tag can be associated with only one commit, branch, or tag. In this tutorial, you tag one commit as release and one as beta.

You use Git to create the new tags, pointing the release tag to the first commit you made and the beta tag to the commit made by the other user. You then use Git to push the tags to the AWS CodeCommit repository. Then you switch to your shared repo and use Git to pull the tags into your shared local repo and explore the tags.

1. From your local repo, run git tag, specifying the name of the new tag (release) and the ID of the first commit you made in the local repo.

   If you don't know the commit ID, run git log to get it. Make sure the commit has your user name and email address, not the user name and email address of the other user. This is to simulate that your commit is a stable version of the AWS CodeCommit repository:

   ```
   1 git tag release commit-ID
   ```

   Run git tag again to tag the commit from the other user with the beta tag. This is to simulate that the commit is for some new, relatively unstable feature:

   ```
   1 git tag beta commit-ID
   ```

2. Run git push --tags to send the tags to the AWS CodeCommit repository.

3. Now pull the tags into the shared repo and check your results:

   1. Switch to the shared repo directory (shared-demo-repo).

   2. Pull in the new tags (git fetch origin).

   3. Confirm that the tags have been pulled in (git tag displays a list of tags for the repository).

   4. View information about each tag (git log release and git log beta).

   Here's the list of Git commands to call:

   ```
   1 git fetch origin
   2 git tag
   3 git log release
   4 git log beta
   ```

4. Try this out in the local repo, too:

   ```
   1 git log release
   2 git log beta
   ```

Step 8: Set Up Access Permissions

In this step, you give a user permission to synchronize the shared repo with the AWS CodeCommit repository. This is an optional step. It's recommended for users who are interested in learning about how to control access to AWS CodeCommit repositories.

To do this, you use the IAM console to create an IAM user, who, by default, does not have permissions to synchronize the shared repo with the AWS CodeCommit repository. You can run git pull to verify this. If the new user doesn't have permission to synchronize, the command doesn't work. Then you go back to the IAM console and apply a policy that allows the user to use git pull. Again, you can run git pull to verify this.

This step assumes you have permissions to create IAM users in your AWS account. If you don't have these permissions, then you can't perform the procedures in this step. Skip ahead to Step 9: Clean Up to clean up the resources you used for your tutorial.

1. Sign in to the AWS Management Console and open the IAM console at https://console.aws.amazon.com/iam/.

   Be sure to sign in with the same user name and password you used in Setting Up .

2. In the navigation pane, choose **Users**, and then choose **Create New Users**.

3. In the first **Enter User Names** box, type an example user name (for example, **JaneDoe-CodeCommit**). Select the **Generate an access key for each user** box, and choose **Create**.

4. Choose **Show User Security Credentials**. Make a note of the access key ID and secret access key or choose **Download Credentials**.

5. Follow the instructions in For HTTPS Users Using Git Credentials to generate and supply the credentials of the IAM user.

   If you want to use SSH, follow the instructions in SSH and Linux, macOS, or Unix: Set Up the Public and Private Keys for Git and AWS CodeCommit or SSH and Windows: Set Up the Public and Private Keys for Git and AWS CodeCommit to set up the user with public and private keys.

6. Run git pull. The following error should appear:

   For HTTPS:

   ```
   fatal: unable to access 'https://git-codecommit.us-east-2.amazonaws.com/v1/repos/
   repository-name/': The requested URL returned error: 403.
   ```

   For SSH:

   ```
   fatal: unable to access 'ssh://git-codecommit.us-east-2.amazonaws.com/v1/repos/
   repository-name/': The requested URL returned error: 403.
   ```

   The error appears because the new user doesn't have permission to synchronize the shared repo with the AWS CodeCommit repository.

7. Return to the IAM console. In the navigation pane, choose **Policies**, and then choose **Create Policy**. (If a **Get Started** button appears, choose it, and then choose **Create Policy**.)

8. Next to **Create Your Own Policy**, choose **Select**.

9. In the **Policy Name** box, type a name (for example, **CodeCommitAccess-GettingStarted**).

10. In the **Policy Document** box, type the following, which allows an IAM user to pull from any repository associated with the IAM user:

```
1  {
2    "Version": "2012-10-17",
3    "Statement": [
4      {
5        "Effect": "Allow",
6        "Action": [
7          "codecommit:GitPull"
8        ],
9        "Resource": "*"
10     }
11   ]
12 }
```

Tip

If you want the IAM user to be able to push commits to any repository associated with the IAM user, type this instead:

```
1  {
2    "Version": "2012-10-17",
3    "Statement": [
4      {
5        "Effect": "Allow",
6        "Action": [
7          "codecommit:GitPull",
8          "codecommit:GitPush"
9        ],
10       "Resource": "*"
11     }
12   ]
13 }
```

For information about other AWS CodeCommit action and resource permissions you can give to users, see Authentication and Access Control for AWS CodeCommit.

1. In the navigation pane, choose **Users**.

2. Choose the example user name (for example, **JaneDoe-CodeCommit**) to which you want to attach the policy.

3. Choose the **Permissions** tab.

4. In **Managed Policies**, choose **Attach Policy**.

5. Select the **CodeCommitAccess-GettingStarted** policy you just created, and then choose **Attach Policy**.

6. Run git pull. This time the command should work and an `Already up-to-date` message should appear.

7. If you are using HTTPS, switch to your original credentials. For more information, see the instructions in Step 3: Set Up the Credential Helper or Step 3: Set Up the Credential Helper.

   If you are using SSH, switch to your original keys. For more information, see SSH and Linux, macOS, or Unix: Set Up the Public and Private Keys for Git and AWS CodeCommit or SSH and Windows: Set Up the Public and Private Keys for Git and AWS CodeCommit.

You've reached the end of this tutorial.

Step 9: Clean Up

In this step, you delete the AWS CodeCommit repository you used in this tutorial, so you won't continue to be charged for the storage space.

You also remove the local repo and shared repo on your local machine because they won't be needed after you delete the AWS CodeCommit repository.

Important
After you delete this repository, you won't be able to clone it to any local repo or shared repo. You also won't be able to pull data from it, or push data to it, from any local repo or shared repo. This action cannot be undone.

To delete the AWS CodeCommit repository (console)

1. Open the AWS CodeCommit console at https://console.aws.amazon.com/codecommit.

2. On the **Dashboard** page, in the list of repositories, choose **MyDemoRepo**.

3. In the navigation pane, choose **Settings**.

4. On the **Settings** page, in **Delete repository**, choose **Delete repository**.

5. In the box next to **Type the name of the repository to confirm deletion**, type **MyDemoRepo**, and then choose **Delete**.

To delete the AWS CodeCommit repository (AWS CLI)

Run the delete-repository command:

```
1 aws codecommit delete-repository --repository-name MyDemoRepo
```

To delete the local repo and shared repo

For Linux, macOS, or Unix:

```
1 cd /tmp
2 rm -rf /tmp/my-demo-repo
3 rm -rf /tmp/shared-demo-repo
```

For Windows:

```
1 cd c:\temp
2 rd /s /q c:\temp\my-demo-repo
3 rd /s /q c:\temp\shared-demo-repo
```

Product and Service Integrations with AWS CodeCommit

By default, AWS CodeCommit is integrated with a number of AWS services. You can also use AWS CodeCommit with products and services outside of AWS. The following information can help you configure AWS CodeCommit to integrate with the products and services you use.

Note
You can automatically build and deploy commits to an AWS CodeCommit repository by integrating with AWS CodePipeline. To learn more, follow the steps in the AWS for DevOps Getting Started Guide.

Topics

- Integration with Other AWS Services
- Integration Examples from the Community

Integration with Other AWS Services

AWS CodeCommit is integrated with the following AWS services:

AWS Cloud9	AWS Cloud9 contains a collection of tools that you use to code, build, run, test, debug, and release software in the cloud. This collection of tools is referred to as the AWS Cloud9 integrated development environment, or IDE. You access the AWS Cloud9 IDE through a web browser. The IDE offers a rich code-editing experience with support for several programming languages and runtime debuggers, as well as a built-in terminal. Learn more: [See the AWS documentation website for more details]
Amazon CloudWatch Events	CloudWatch Events delivers a near real-time stream of system events that describe changes in Amazon Web Services (AWS) resources. Using simple rules that you can quickly set up, you can match events and route them to one or more target functions or streams. Cloud-Watch Events becomes aware of operational changes as they occur. CloudWatch Events responds to these operational changes and takes action as necessary, by sending messages to respond to the environment, activating functions, making changes, and capturing state information. You can configure CloudWatch Events to monitor AWS CodeCommit repositories and respond to repository events by targeting streams, functions, tasks, or other processes in other AWS services, such as Amazon Simple Queue Service, Amazon Kinesis, AWS Lambda, and many more. Learn more: [See the AWS documentation website for more details]

AWS CodeStar	AWS CodeStar is a cloud-based service for creating, managing, and working with software development projects on AWS. You can quickly develop, build, and deploy applications on AWS with an AWS CodeStar project. An AWS CodeStar project creates and integrates AWS services for your project development toolchain, including an AWS CodeCommit repository for the project. AWS CodeStar also assigns permissions to team members for that project. These permissions are applied automatically, including permissions for accessing AWS CodeCommit, creating and managing Git credentials, and more. You can configure repositories created for AWS CodeStar projects just as you would any other AWS CodeCommit repository by using the AWS CodeCommit console, AWS CodeCommit commands from the AWS CLI, the local Git client, and from the AWS CodeCommit API. Learn more: [See the AWS documentation website for more details]
AWS CloudTrail	CloudTrail captures AWS API calls and related events made by or on behalf of an AWS account and delivers log files to an Amazon S3 bucket that you specify. You can configure CloudTrail to capture API calls from the AWS CodeCommit console, AWS CodeCommit commands from the AWS CLI, the local Git client, and from the AWS CodeCommit API. Learn more: [See the AWS documentation website for more details]
AWS CodeBuild	AWS CodeBuild is a fully managed build service in the cloud that compiles your source code, runs unit tests, and produces artifacts that are ready to deploy. You can store the source code to be built and the build specification in an AWS CodeCommit repository. You can use AWS CodeBuild directly with AWS CodeCommit, or you can incorporate both AWS CodeBuild and AWS CodeCommit in a continuous delivery pipeline with AWS CodePipeline. Learn more: [See the AWS documentation website for more details]
AWS Elastic Beanstalk	Elastic Beanstalk is a managed service that makes it easy to deploy and manage applications in the AWS cloud without worrying about the infrastructure that runs those applications. You can use the Elastic Beanstalk command line interface (EB CLI) to deploy your application directly from a new or existing AWS CodeCommit repository. Learn more: [See the AWS documentation website for more details]

AWS CloudFormation	AWS CloudFormation is a service that helps you model and set up your AWS resources so that you can spend less time managing those resources and more time focusing on your applications. You create a template that describes resources, including an AWS Code-Commit repository, and AWS CloudForma-tion takes care of provisioning and configuring those resources for you. Learn more: [See the AWS documentation website for more details]
AWS CodePipeline	AWS CodePipeline is a continuous delivery service you can use to model, visualize, and automate the steps required to release your software. You can configure AWS Code-Pipeline to use an AWS CodeCommit repos-itory as a source action in a pipeline, and automate building, testing, and deploying your changes. Learn more: [See the AWS documentation website for more details]
AWS Key Management Service	AWS KMS is a managed service that makes it easy for you to create and control the en-cryption keys used to encrypt your data. By default, AWS CodeCommit uses AWS KMS to encrypt repositories. Learn more: [See the AWS documentation website for more details]
AWS Lambda	Lambda lets you run code without provision-ing or managing servers. You can configure triggers for AWS CodeCommit repositories that will invoke Lambda functions in response to repository events. Learn more: [See the AWS documentation website for more details]
Amazon Simple Notification Service	Amazon SNS is a web service that enables ap-plications, end users, and devices to instantly send and receive notifications from the cloud. You can configure triggers for AWS CodeCom-mit repositories that will send Amazon SNS notifications in response to repository events. You can also use Amazon SNS notifications to integrate with other AWS services. For example, you can use an Amazon SNS notifi-cation to send messages to an Amazon Simple Queue Service queue. Learn more: [See the AWS documentation website for more details]

Integration Examples from the Community

The following sections provide links to blog posts, articles, and community-provided examples.

Note
These links are provided for informational purposes only, and should not be considered either a comprehensive list or an endorsement of the content of the examples. AWS is not responsible for the content or accuracy of external content.

Topics

- Blog Posts
- Code Samples

Blog Posts

- **Refining Access to Branches in AWS CodeCommit**

  Learn how to restrict commits to repository branches by creating and applying an IAM policy that uses a context key.

  Published May 16, 2018

- **Replicate AWS CodeCommit Repositories Between Regions Using AWS Fargate**

  Learn how to set up continuous replication of an AWS CodeCommit repository from one AWS region to another using a serverless architecture.

  Published April 11, 2018

- **Distributing Your AWS OpsWorks for Chef Automate Infrastructure**

  Learn how to use AWS CodePipeline, AWS CodeCommit, AWS CodeBuild, and AWS Lambda to ensure that cookbooks and other configurations are consistently deployed across two or more Chef Servers residing in one or more AWS Regions.

  Published March 9, 2018

- **Peanut Butter and Chocolate: Azure Functions CI/CD Pipeline with AWS CodeCommit**

  Learn how to create a PowerShell-based Azure Functions CI/CD pipeline where the code is stored in an AWS CodeCommit repository.

  Published February 19, 2018

- **Continuous Deployment to Kubernetes using AWS CodePipeline, AWS CodeCommit, AWS CodeBuild, Amazon ECR, and AWS Lambda**

  Learn how to use Kubernetes and AWS together to create a fully managed, continuous deployment pipeline for container based applications.

  Published January 11, 2018

- **Use AWS CodeCommit Pull Requests to request code reviews and discuss code**

  Learn how to use pull requests to review, comment upon, and interactively iterate on code changes in an AWS CodeCommit repository.

  Published November 20, 2017

- **Build Serverless AWS CodeCommit Workflows using Amazon CloudWatch Events and JGit**

  Learn how to create CloudWatch Events rules that process changes in a repository using AWS CodeCommit repository events and target actions in other AWS services. Examples include AWS Lambda functions that enforce Git commit message policies on commits, replicate an AWS CodeCommit repository, and backing up an AWS CodeCommit repository to Amazon S3.

  Published August 3, 2017

- **Replicating and Automating Sync-Ups for a Repository with AWS CodeCommit**

  Learn how to back up or replicate an AWS CodeCommit repository to another AWS region, and how to back up repositories hosted on other services to AWS CodeCommit.

  Published March 17, 2017

- **Migrating to AWS CodeCommit**

  Learn how to push code to two repositories as part of migrating from using another Git repository to AWS CodeCommit when using SourceTree.

  Published September 6, 2016

- **Set Up Continuous Testing with Appium, AWS CodeCommit, Jenkins, and AWS Device Farm**

  Learn how to create a continuous testing process for mobile devices using Appium, AWS CodeCommit, Jenkins, and Device Farm.

  Published February 2, 2016

- **Using AWS CodeCommit with Git Repositories in Multiple AWS Accounts**

  Learn how to clone your AWS CodeCommit repository and, in one command, configure the credential helper to use a specific IAM role for connections to that repository.

  Published November 2015

- **Integrating AWS OpsWorks and AWS CodeCommit**

  Learn how AWS OpsWorks can automatically fetch Apps and Chef cookbooks from AWS CodeCommit.

  Published August 25 2015

- **Using AWS CodeCommit and GitHub Credential Helpers**

  Learn how to configure your gitconfig file to work with both AWS CodeCommit and GitHub credential helpers.

  Published September 2015

- **Using AWS CodeCommit from Eclipse**

  Learn how to use the EGit tools in Eclipse to work with AWS CodeCommit.

  Published August 2015

- **AWS CodeCommit with Amazon EC2 Role Credentials**

  Learn how to use an instance profile for Amazon EC2 when configuring automated agent access to an AWS CodeCommit repository.

  Published July 2015

- **Integrating AWS CodeCommit with Jenkins**

  Learn how to use AWS CodeCommit and Jenkins to support two simple continuous integration (CI) scenarios.

  Published July 2015

- **Integrating AWS CodeCommit with Review Board**

  Learn how to integrate AWS CodeCommit into a development workflow using the Review Board code review system.

  Published July 2015

Code Samples

The following are code samples that might be of interest to AWS CodeCommit users.

- **Mac OS X Script to Periodically Delete Cached Credentials in the OS X Certificate Store**

  If you use the credential helper for AWS CodeCommit on Mac OS X, you are likely familiar with the problem with cached credentials. This script demonstrate one solution.

  Author: Nico Coetzee

  Published February 2016

Working with Repositories in AWS CodeCommit

A repository is the fundamental version control object in AWS CodeCommit. It's where you securely store code and files for your project. It also stores your project history, from the first commit through the latest changes. You can share your repository with other users so you can work together on a project. You can set up notifications so that repository users receive email about events (for example, another user commenting on their code). You can also change the default settings for your repository, browse its contents, and more. You can create triggers for your repository so that code pushes or other events trigger actions, such as emails or code functions. You can even configure a repository on your local computer (a local repo) to push your changes to more than one repository.

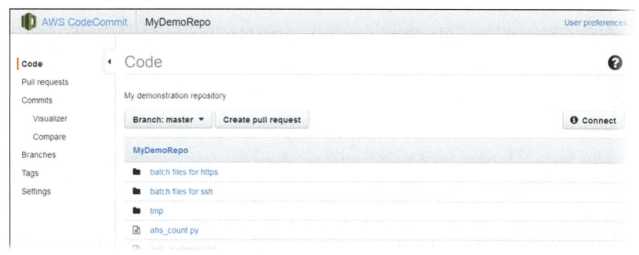

Before you can push changes to an AWS CodeCommit repository, you must configure your IAM user in your AWS account. For more information, see Step 1: Initial Configuration for AWS CodeCommit.

For information about working with other aspects of your repository in AWS CodeCommit, see Working with Files, Working with Pull Requests , Working with Commits, Working with Branches, and Working with User Preferences. To learn about migrating to AWS CodeCommit, see Migrate to AWS CodeCommit.

Topics

- Create an AWS CodeCommit Repository
- Connect to an AWS CodeCommit Repository
- Share an AWS CodeCommit Repository
- Configuring Notifications for Events in an AWS CodeCommit Repository
- Manage Triggers for an AWS CodeCommit Repository
- View AWS CodeCommit Repository Details
- Change AWS CodeCommit Repository Settings
- Synchronize Changes Between a Local Repo and an AWS CodeCommit Repository
- Push Commits to an Additional Git Repository
- Configure Cross-Account Access to an AWS CodeCommit Repository
- Delete an AWS CodeCommit Repository

Create an AWS CodeCommit Repository

Use AWS CLI or the AWS CodeCommit console to create a new, empty AWS CodeCommit repository.

These instructions assume you have already completed the steps in Setting Up .

Note
Depending on your usage, you might be charged for creating or accessing a repository. For more information, see Pricing on the AWS CodeCommit product information page.

Topics
- Use the AWS CodeCommit Console to Create a Repository
- Use the AWS CLI to Create an AWS CodeCommit Repository

Use the AWS CodeCommit Console to Create a Repository

To create a new AWS CodeCommit repository (console):

1. Open the AWS CodeCommit console at https://console.aws.amazon.com/codecommit.

2. In the region selector, choose the region where you will create the repository. For more information, see Regions and Git Connection Endpoints.

3. On the **Dashboard** page, choose **Create repository**. (If a welcome page appears instead of the **Dashboard** page, choose **Get Started Now**.)

4. On the **Create repository** page, in **Repository name**, type a name for the repository. **Note** This name must be unique in the region for your AWS account.

5. (Optional) In the **Description** box, type a description for the repository. This can help you and other users identify the purpose of the repository. **Note** The description field accepts all HTML characters and all valid Unicode characters. If you are an application developer using the `GetRepository` or `BatchGetRepositories` APIs and plan to display the repository description field in a web browser, see the AWS CodeCommit API Reference.

6. Choose **Create repository**.

7. In **Configure email notifications**, configure notifications so that repository users receive emails about important repository events. This step is optional, but recommended. You can choose the event types (for example, comments on code) and whether to use an existing Amazon SNS topic or create one specifically for this purpose. You can choose to skip this step and configure notifications at a later time. For more information, see Configuring Notifications for Events in an AWS CodeCommit Repository.

After you create a repository, you can connect to it and start adding code. To learn more, see Connect to a Repository. You can also add your repository to a continuous delivery pipeline. To learn more, see Simple Pipeline Walkthrough.

To get information about the new AWS CodeCommit repository, such as the URLs to use when cloning the repository, choose the repository's name from the list.

To share this repository with others, you will need to send them the HTTPS or SSH link to use to clone the repository. Make sure they have the permissions required to access the repository. For more information, see Share a Repository and Authentication and Access Control for AWS CodeCommit.

Use the AWS CLI to Create an AWS CodeCommit Repository

To create a new AWS CodeCommit repository (CLI):

1. Make sure that you have configured the AWS CLI with the region where the repository exists. To verify the region, type the following command at the command line or terminal and review the information for default region name:

```
1 aws configure
```

The default region name must match the region for the repository in AWS CodeCommit. For more information, see Regions and Git Connection Endpoints.

2. Run the create-repository command, specifying:

   - A name that uniquely identifies the AWS CodeCommit repository (with the `--repository-name` option). **Note**
     This name must be unique across an AWS account.
   - Optionally, a comment about the AWS CodeCommit repository (with the `--repository-description` option).

   For example, to create an AWS CodeCommit repository named `MyDemoRepo` with the description "My demonstration repository":

```
1 aws codecommit create-repository --repository-name MyDemoRepo --repository-description "My
    demonstration repository"
```

Note
The description field accepts all HTML characters and all valid Unicode characters. If you are an application developer using the `GetRepository` or `BatchGetRepositories` APIs and plan to display the repository description field in a web browser, see the AWS CodeCommit API Reference.

1. If successful, this command outputs a `repositoryMetadata` object with the following information:

   - The description (`repositoryDescription`).
   - The unique, system-generated ID (`repositoryId`).
   - The name (`repositoryName`).
   - The ID of the AWS account associated with the AWS CodeCommit repository (`accountId`).

   Here is some example output, based on the preceding example command:

```
1 {
2     "repositoryMetadata": {
3         "repositoryName": "MyDemoRepo",
4         "repositoryDescription": "My demonstration repository",
5         "repositoryId": "f7579e13-b83e-4027-aaef-650c0EXAMPLE",
6         "accountId": "creator-account-ID"
7     }
8 }
```

2. Note the AWS CodeCommit repository's name and ID. You will need them to monitor and change information about the AWS CodeCommit repository, especially if you use AWS CLI.

   If you forget the AWS CodeCommit repository's name or ID, follow the instructions in Use the AWS CLI to View AWS CodeCommit Repository Details.

After you create a repository, you can connect to it and start adding code. To learn more, see Connect to a Repository. You can also add your repository to a continuous delivery pipeline. To learn more, see Simple Pipeline Walkthrough.

Connect to an AWS CodeCommit Repository

When you connect to an AWS CodeCommit repository for the first time, you typically clone its contents to your local machine. Alternatively, if you already have a local repo, you can add an AWS CodeCommit repository as a remote. This topic provides instructions for connecting to an AWS CodeCommit repository. If you want to migrate an existing repository to AWS CodeCommit, see Migrate to AWS CodeCommit.

Note
Depending on your usage, you might be charged for creating or accessing a repository. For more information, see Pricing on the AWS CodeCommit product information page.

Topics

- Prerequisites for Connecting to an AWS CodeCommit Repository
- Connect to the AWS CodeCommit Repository by Cloning the Repository
- Connect a Local Repo to the AWS CodeCommit Repository

Prerequisites for Connecting to an AWS CodeCommit Repository

Before you can connect to an AWS CodeCommit repository:

- You must have configured your local computer with the software and settings required to connect to AWS CodeCommit. For more information, see Setting Up .

- You must have the clone URL of the AWS CodeCommit repository to which you want to connect. This URL includes the name of the repository as well as its AWS region. For more information, see View Repository Details.

  If you have not yet created an AWS CodeCommit repository, follow the instructions in Create a Repository, copy the clone URL of the new AWS CodeCommit repository, and return to this page.

  If you have an AWS CodeCommit repository but you do not know its name, follow the instructions in View Repository Details.

- You must have a location on your local machine to store a local copy of the AWS CodeCommit repository to which you will be connecting. (This local copy of the AWS CodeCommit repository is known as a *local repo*.) You then switch to and run Git commands from that location. For example, you could use /tmp (for Linux, macOS, or Unix) or c:\temp (for Windows). **Note**
  You can use any directory you want. If you use a different directory than /tmp or c:\temp, be sure to substitute it for ours when you follow these instructions.

Connect to the AWS CodeCommit Repository by Cloning the Repository

If you do not already have a local repo, follow the steps in this procedure to clone the AWS CodeCommit repository to your local machine.

1. Complete the prerequisites, including Setting Up . **Important**
   If you have not completed setup, you will not be able to connect to or clone the repository.

2. From the /tmp directory or the c:\temp directory, use Git to run the clone command, as shown in the following example for cloning a repository named *MyDemoRepo* in the US East (Ohio) region:

   For HTTPS:

   ```
   1 git clone https://git-codecommit.us-east-2.amazonaws.com/v1/repos/MyDemoRepo my-demo-repo
   ```

   For SSH:

   ```
   1 git clone ssh://git-codecommit.us-east-2.amazonaws.com/v1/repos/MyDemoRepo my-demo-repo
   ```

In this example, `git-codecommit.us-east-2.amazonaws.com` is the Git connection point for the US East (Ohio) region where the repository exists, `MyDemoRepo` represents the name of your AWS CodeCommit repository, and `my-demo-repo` represents the name of the directory Git will create in the `/tmp` directory or the `c:\temp` directory. For more information about the regions that support AWS CodeCommit and the Git connections for those regions, see Regions and Git Connection Endpoints. **Note** When you use SSH on Windows operating systems to clone a repository, you might need to add the SSH key ID to the connection string as follows:

```
1 git clone ssh://Your-SSH-Key-ID@git-codecommit.us-east-2.amazonaws.com/v1/repos/MyDemoRepo
    my-demo-repo
```

For more information, see For SSH Connections on Windows and Troubleshooting.

After Git creates the directory, it will pull down a copy of your AWS CodeCommit repository into the newly created directory.

If the AWS CodeCommit repository is new or otherwise empty, you will see a message that you are cloning an empty repository. This is expected. **Note** If you receive an error that Git can't find the AWS CodeCommit repository or that you don't have permission to connect to the AWS CodeCommit repository, make sure you completed the prerequisites, including assigning permissions to the IAM user and setting up your IAM user credentials for Git and AWS CodeCommit on the local machine. Also, make sure you specified the correct repository name.

After you successfully connect your local repo to your AWS CodeCommit repository, you are now ready to start running Git commands from the local repo to create commits, branches, and tags and push to and pull from the AWS CodeCommit repository.

Connect a Local Repo to the AWS CodeCommit Repository

Complete the following steps if you already have a local repo and want to add an AWS CodeCommit repository as the remote repository. If you already have a remote repository and want to push your commits to AWS CodeCommit as well as that other remote repository, follow the steps in Push Commits to Two Repositories instead.

1. Complete the prerequisites.

2. From the command prompt or terminal, switch to your local repo directory and run the git remote add command to add the AWS CodeCommit repository as a remote repository for your local repo.

   For example, the following command adds the remote nicknamed **origin** to https://git/-codecommit/.us/-east/-2/.amazonaws/.com/v1/repos/MyDemoRepo:

   For HTTPS:

```
1 git remote add origin https://git-codecommit.us-east-2.amazonaws.com/v1/repos/MyDemoRepo
```

   For SSH:

```
1 git remote add origin ssh://git-codecommit.us-east-2.amazonaws.com/v1/repos/MyDemoRepo
```

   This command returns nothing.

3. To verify you have added the AWS CodeCommit repository as a remote for your local repo, run the git remote -v command , which should create output similar to the following:

   For HTTPS:

```
1 origin  https://git-codecommit.us-east-2.amazonaws.com/v1/repos/MyDemoRepo (fetch)
2 origin  https://git-codecommit.us-east-2.amazonaws.com/v1/repos/MyDemoRepo (push)
```

   For SSH:

```
1 origin   ssh://git-codecommit.us-east-2.amazonaws.com/v1/repos/MyDemoRepo (fetch)
2 origin   ssh://git-codecommit.us-east-2.amazonaws.com/v1/repos/MyDemoRepo (push)
```

After you successfully connect your local repo to your AWS CodeCommit repository, you are ready to start running Git commands from the local repo to create commits, branches, and tags, and to push to and pull from the AWS CodeCommit repository.

Share an AWS CodeCommit Repository

After you have created an AWS CodeCommit repository, you can share it with other users. First, decide which protocol to recommend to users when connecting to your repository: HTTPS or SSH. Then send the URL and connection information to the users with whom you want to share the repository. Depending on your security requirements, sharing a repository may also require creating an IAM group, applying managed policies to that group, and editing IAM policies to refine access. This topic will walk you through these steps.

These instructions assume you have already completed the steps in Setting Up and Create a Repository.

Note
Depending on your usage, you might be charged for creating or accessing a repository. For more information, see Pricing on the AWS CodeCommit product information page.

Topics

- Choose the Connection Protocol to Share with Your Users
- Create IAM Policies for Your Repository
- Create an IAM Group for Repository Users
- Share the Connection Information with Your Users

Choose the Connection Protocol to Share with Your Users

When you create a repository in AWS CodeCommit, two endpoints are generated: one for HTTPS connections and one for SSH connections. Both provide secure connections over a network. Your users can use either protocol. Both endpoints remain active regardless of which protocol you recommend to your users.

HTTPS connections require either Git credentials, which IAM users can generate for themselves in IAM, or an AWS access key, which your repository users must configure in the credential helper included in the AWS CLI but is the only method available for root account or federated users. Git credentials are the easiest method for users of your repository to set up and use. SSH connections require your users to generate a public-private key pair, store the public key, associate the public key with their IAM user, configure their known hosts file on their local computer, and create and maintain a config file on their local computers. Because this is a more complex configuration process, we recommend you choose HTTPS and Git credentials for connections to AWS CodeCommit.

For more information about HTTPS, SSH, Git, and remote repositories, see Setting Up or consult your Git documentation. For a general overview of communication protocols and how each communicates with remote repositories, see Git on the Server - The Protocols.

Note
Although Git supports a variety of connection protocols, AWS CodeCommit does not support connections with unsecured protocols, such as the local protocol or generic HTTP.

Create IAM Policies for Your Repository

AWS provides three managed policies in IAM for AWS CodeCommit. These policies cannot be edited and apply to all repositories associated with your AWS account. However, you can use these policies as templates to create your own custom managed policies that apply only to the repository you want to share. Your customer managed policy can apply specifically to the repository you want to share. For more information about managed policies and IAM users, see Managed Policies and IAM Users and Groups.

Tip
For more fine-grained control over access to your repository, you can create more than one customer managed policy and apply the policies to different IAM users and groups.

To review the contents of the policy and the other managed policies for AWS CodeCommit and learn more about creating and applying permissions by using policies, see Authentication and Access Control for AWS CodeCommit.

Create a customer managed policy for your repository

1. Sign in to the AWS Management Console and open the IAM console at https://console.aws.amazon.com/iam/.

2. In the **Dashboard** navigation area, choose **Policies**, and then choose **Create Policy**.

3. On the **Create Policy** page, next to **Copy an AWS Managed Policy**, choose **Select**.

4. On the **Copy an AWS Managed Policy** page, type **AWSCodeCommitPowerUser** in the **Search Policies** search box. Choose **Select** next to that policy name.

5. On the **Review Policy** page, in **Policy Name**, type a new name for the policy (for example, *AWSCodeCommitPowerUser-MyDemoRepo*).

   In the **Policy Document** text box, replace the "*" portion of the `Resource` line with the Amazon Resource Name (ARN) of the AWS CodeCommit repository. For example:

```
1  "Resource": [
2    "arn:aws:codecommit:us-east-2:80398EXAMPLE:MyDemoRepo"
3  ]
```

Tip
To find the ARN for the AWS CodeCommit repository, go to the AWS CodeCommit console and choose the repository name from the list. For more information, see View Repository Details.

If you want this policy to apply to more than one repository, add each repository as a resource by specifying its ARN. Include a comma between each resource statement, as shown in the following example:

```
1  "Resource": [
2    "arn:aws:codecommit:us-east-2:80398EXAMPLE:MyDemoRepo",
3    "arn:aws:codecommit:us-east-2:80398EXAMPLE:MyOtherDemoRepo"
4  ]
```

1. Choose **Validate Policy**. After it is validated, choose **Create Policy. Tip**
   Creating a managed policy for a repository does not supply additional permissions required for individual users to set up Git credentials or SSH keys in IAM. You must apply these managed policies to individual IAM users.
   To allow users to use Git credentials to connect to AWS CodeCommit, select the **IAMSelfManage-ServiceSpecificCredentials** and **IAMReadOnlyAccess** managed policies and apply them to your users. To allow users to use SSH to connect to AWS CodeCommit, select the **IAMUserSSHKeys** and **IAMReadOnlyAccess** managed policies and apply them to your users.

Create an IAM Group for Repository Users

To manage access to your repository, create an IAM group for its users, add IAM users to that group, and then attach the customer managed policy you created in the previous step.

If you use SSH, you must attach another managed policy to the IAMUserSSHKeys group, the IAM managed policy that allows users to upload their SSH public key and associate it with the IAM user they use to connect to AWS CodeCommit.

1. Sign in to the AWS Management Console and open the IAM console at https://console.aws.amazon.com/iam/.

2. In the **Dashboard** navigation area, choose **Groups**, and then choose **Create New Group**.

3. On the **Set Group Name** page, in the **Group Name** box, type a name for the group (for example, *MyDemoRepoGroup*), and then choose **Next Step**. Consider including the repository name as part of the group name. **Note**
This name must be unique across an AWS account.

4. Select the check box next to the customer managed policy you created in the previous section (for example, **AWSCodeCommitPowerUser-MyDemoRepo**).

   - If your users will use HTTPS and Git credentials to connect to AWS CodeCommit, select the check boxes next to **IAMSelfManageServiceSpecificCredentials** and **IAMReadOnlyAccess**, and then choose **Next Step**.
   - If your users will use SSH to connect to your repository, select the check boxes next to **IAMUserSSHKeys** and **IAMReadOnlyAccess**, and then choose **Next Step**.

5. On the **Review** page, choose **Create Group**. The group will be created in IAM with the specified policies already attached. It will appear in the list of groups associated with your AWS account.

6. Choose your group from the list.

7. On the group summary page, choose the **Users** tab, and then choose **Add Users to Group**. On the list that shows all users associated with your AWS account, select the check boxes next to the users to whom you want to allow access to the AWS CodeCommit repository, and then choose **Add Users**. **Tip**
You can use the Search box to quickly find users by name.

8. When you have added your users, close the IAM console.

Share the Connection Information with Your Users

1. Open the AWS CodeCommit console at https://console.aws.amazon.com/codecommit.

2. In the region selector, choose the region where the repository was created. Repositories are specific to an AWS region. For more information, see Regions and Git Connection Endpoints.

3. On the **Dashboard** page, choose the name of the repository you want to share.

4. On the **Code** page, choose **Clone URL**, and then choose the protocol you want your users to use.

5. Copy the displayed URL for the connection protocol your users will use when connecting to your AWS CodeCommit repository.

6. Send your users the connection information along with any other instructions, such as installing the AWS CLI, configuring a profile, or installing Git. Make sure to include the configuration information for the connection protocol (for example, for HTTPS, configuring the credential helper for Git).

The following example email provides information for users connecting to the MyDemoRepo repository with the HTTPS connection protocol and Git credentials in the US East (Ohio) (us-east-2) region. This email assumes the user has already installed Git and is familiar with using it:

```
1 I've created an AWS CodeCommit repository for us to use while working on our project.
2 The name of the repository is MyDemoRepo, and
3 it is in the  US East (Ohio) (us-east-2) region.
4 Here's what you need to do in order to get started using it:
5
6 1. Make sure that your version of Git on your local computer is 1.7.9 or later.
7 2. Generate Git credentials for your IAM user by signing into the IAM console here: [https://
      console\.aws\.amazon\.com/iam/](https://console.aws.amazon.com/iam/).
8 Switch to the Security credentials tab for your IAM user and choose the Generate button in HTTPS
      Git credentials for AWS CodeCommit.
9 Make sure to save your credentials in a secure location!
```

10 3. Switch to a directory of your choice and clone the AWS CodeCommit repository to your local
   machine by running the following command:
11   git clone https://git-codecommit.us-east-2.amazonaws.com/v1/repos/MyDemoRepo my-demo-repo
12 4. When prompted for username and password, use the Git credentials you just saved.
13
14 That's it! If you'd like to learn more about using AWS CodeCommit, you can start with the
   tutorial [here](getting-started.md#getting-started-create-commit).

You can find complete setup instructions in Setting Up .

Configuring Notifications for Events in an AWS CodeCommit Repository

You can set up notifications for a repository so that repository users receive emails about the repository event types you specify. When you configure notifications, AWS CodeCommit creates an Amazon CloudWatch Events rule for your repository. This rule responds to the event types you select from the preconfigured options in the AWS CodeCommit console. Notifications are sent when events match the rule settings. You can create an Amazon SNS topic to use for notifications, or use an existing one in your AWS account.

You use the AWS CodeCommit console to configure notifications.

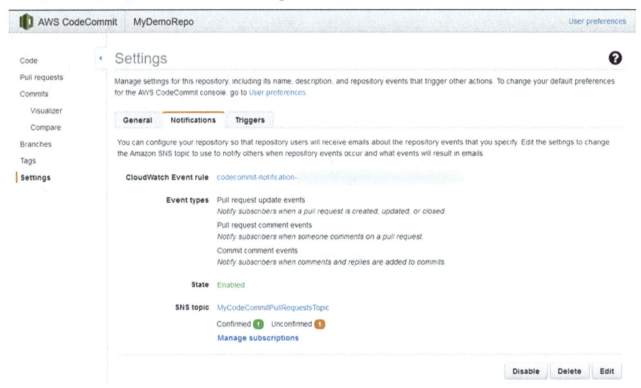

Topics

- Using Repository Notifications
- Configure Repository Notifications
- Change, Disable, or Enable Notifications
- Delete Notification Settings for a Repository

Using Repository Notifications

Configuring notifications helps your repository users by sending emails to users when someone takes an action that affects another user. For example, you can configure a repository to send notifications when comments are made on commits. In this configuration, when a repository user comments on a line of code in a commit, other repository users receive an email. They can sign in and view the comment. Responses to comments also generate emails, so repository users stay informed.

Notification event types are grouped into the following categories:

- **Pull request update events**: If you select this option, users receive emails when:
    - A pull request is created or closed.

- A pull request is updated with code changes.
- The title or description of the pull request changes.

- **Pull request comment events**: If you select this option, users receive emails when someone comments or replies to a comment in a pull request.

- **Commit comment events**: If you select this option, users receive emails when someone comments on a commit outside of a pull request. This includes comments on:

  - Lines of code in a commit.
  - Files in a commit.
  - The commit itself.

  For more information, see Comment on a Commit.

Repository notifications are different from repository triggers. Although you can configure a trigger to use Amazon SNS to send emails about some repository events, those events are limited to operational events such as creating branches and pushing code to a branch. Triggers do not use CloudWatch Events rules to evaluate repository events. They are more limited in scope. For more information about using triggers, see Manage Triggers for a Repository.

Configure Repository Notifications

You can keep repository users informed of repository events by configuring notifications. When you configure notifications, subscribed users receive emails about the events that you specify, such as when someone comments on a commit. For more information, see Using Repository Notifications.

To use the AWS CodeCommit console to configure notifications for a repository in AWS CodeCommit, you must have the following managed policy or the equivalent permissions attached to your IAM user:

- **CloudWatchEventsFullAccess**
- **AmazonSNSFullAccess**

Note

Equivalent permissions are included in the **AWSCodeCommitFullAccess** policy, which is required to configure repository notifications. If you have this policy applied, you do not need the other two policies. If you have a customized policy applied, you might need to modify it to include the required permissions for CloudWatch Events and Amazon SNS.

To configure notifications for a repository

1. Open the AWS CodeCommit console at https://console.aws.amazon.com/codecommit.

2. In the list of repositories, choose the name of the repository where you want to configure notifications.

3. In the navigation pane, choose **Settings**, and then choose **Notifications**.

4. In **Event types**, select the event types you want included in the CloudWatch Events rule for the repository.

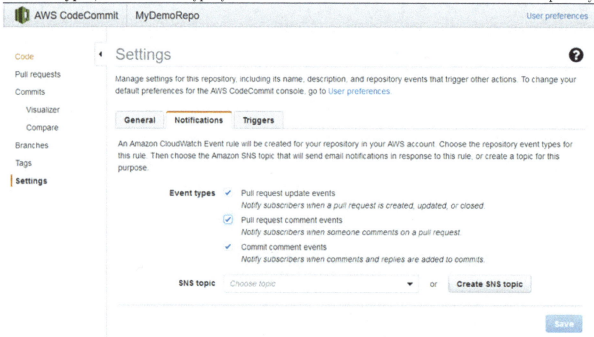

5. In **SNS topic**, either choose a topic from the list of Amazon SNS topics in your AWS account, or create a topic to use for this repository. **Note**
   If you create a topic, you can manage subscriptions for that policy from the AWS CodeCommit console. If you use an existing topic, you cannot manage subscriptions for that topic unless you have permissions to manage subscriptions for all topics in Amazon SNS. For more information, see Amazon Simple Notification Service Developer Guide.

   If you create a topic, in **Topic name**, type a name for the topic. Optionally, in **Display name**, type a short name . Choose **Create**.

6. To add the email addresses of the repository users, choose **Manage subscriptions**. In **Add email subscriber**, type the email address of a repository user, and then choose **Save**. You can add only one email address at a time. **Note**
A confirmation email is sent to the address as soon as you choose **Save**. However, the status of the subscription is not updated while you remain in **Manage subscriptions**.

After you have added all the email addresses to the list of subscribers, choose **Close**. **Tip**
Amazon SNS coordinates and manages the delivery and sending of messages to subscribing endpoints and email addresses. Endpoints include web servers, email addresses, Amazon Simple Queue Service queues, and AWS Lambda functions. For more information, see What Is Amazon Simple Notification Service? and Sending Amazon SNS Messages to HTTP/HTTPS Endpoints.

7. To finish configuring notifications, choose **Save**.

After you have configured notifications for a repository, you can view the CloudWatch Events rule automatically created for the repository.

Important
Do not edit or delete this rule. Changing or deleting the rule might cause operational issues. For example, emails might not be sent to subscribers or the inability to change notification settings for a repository in AWS CodeCommit.

To view the CloudWatch Events rule for a repository

1. Sign in to the AWS Management Console and open the CloudWatch console at https://console.aws.amazon.com/cloudwatch/.

2. In the navigation bar, under **Events**, choose **Rules**.

3. Choose the rule for your repository from the list. The rule name is displayed on the **Notifications** tab in your repository settings.

4. View the rule summary information. **Important**
Do not edit, delete, or disable this rule.

Change, Disable, or Enable Notifications

You can use the AWS CodeCommit console to change how notifications are configured, including the event types that send emails to users and the Amazon SNS topic used to send emails about the repository, or to manage the list of email addresses and endpoints subscribed to the topic. You can also use the console to temporarily disable notifications.

To change notification settings (console)

1. Open the AWS CodeCommit console at https://console.aws.amazon.com/codecommit.

2. In the list of repositories, choose the name of the repository where you want to configure notifications.

3. In the navigation pane, choose **Settings**, and then choose **Notifications**.

4. Choose **Edit**.

5. Make your changes, and then choose **Save**.

Disabling notifications is an easy way to temporarily prevent users from receiving emails about repository events. For example, you might want to disable notifications while you are performing repository maintenance. Because the configuration is preserved, you can quickly enable notifications when you are ready.

To permanently delete the notification settings, follow the steps in Delete Notification Settings for a Repository.

To disable notifications (console)

1. Open the AWS CodeCommit console at https://console.aws.amazon.com/codecommit.

2. In the list of repositories, choose the name of the repository where you want to disable notifications.

3. In the navigation pane, choose **Settings**, and then choose **Notifications**.

4. Choose **Disable**.

5. The notification state changes to **Disabled**. No emails about events are sent. When you disable notifications, the CloudWatch Events rule for the repository is disabled automatically. Do not manually change its status in the CloudWatch Events console.

To enable notifications (console)

1. Open the AWS CodeCommit console at https://console.aws.amazon.com/codecommit.

2. In the list of repositories, choose the name of the repository where notifications are disabled.

3. In the navigation pane, choose **Settings**, and then choose **Notifications**.

4. Choose **Enable**.

5. The notification state changes to **Enabled**. Emails about events are sent. The CloudWatch Events rule for the repository is enabled automatically.

Delete Notification Settings for a Repository

If you no longer want notifications for your repository, you can delete the settings. Deleting the settings also deletes the CloudWatch Events rule created for notifications for the repository. It does not delete any subscriptions or the Amazon SNS topic used for notifications.

Note
If you change the name of a repository from the console, notifications continue to work without modification. However, if you change the name of your repository from the command line or by using the API, notifications no longer work. The easiest way to restore notifications is to delete the notification settings and then configure them again.

To delete notification settings (console)

1. Open the AWS CodeCommit console at https://console.aws.amazon.com/codecommit.

2. In the list of repositories, choose the name of the repository where notifications are disabled.

3. In the navigation pane, choose **Settings**, and then choose **Notifications**.

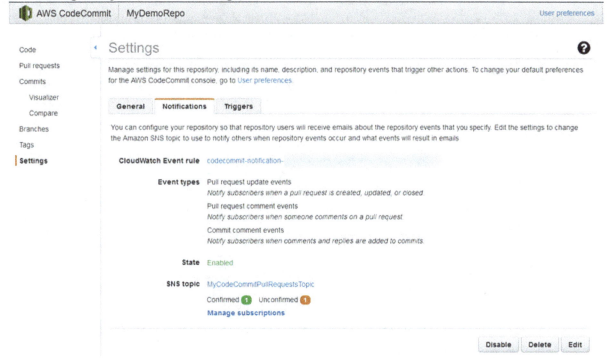

4. Choose **Delete**.

5. In **Delete notification settings**, choose **Delete notification settings**.

Delete notification settings   ✖

If you delete these settings, users of this repository will no longer receive emails about events in this repository. However, the SNS topic will not be deleted. Subscribers to that topic might still receive emails if other repositories or other AWS services are configured to use that topic. To delete the topic, go to the SNS Console.

Cancel   **Delete notification settings**

6. (Optional) To change or delete the Amazon SNS topic used for notifications after you delete notification settings, go to the Amazon SNS console at https://console.aws.amazon.com/sns/v2/home. For more information, see Clean Up in Amazon Simple Notification Service Developer Guide.

Manage Triggers for an AWS CodeCommit Repository

You can configure an AWS CodeCommit repository so that code pushes or other events trigger actions, such as sending a notification from Amazon Simple Notification Service (Amazon SNS) or invoking a function in AWS Lambda. You can create up to ten triggers for each AWS CodeCommit repository.

Triggers are commonly configured to:

- Send emails to subscribed users every time someone pushes to the repository.
- Notify an external build system to start a build after someone pushes to the main branch of the repository.

Scenarios like notifying an external build system require writing a Lambda function to interact with other applications. The email scenario simply requires creating an Amazon SNS topic.

In this topic, you will learn how to set permissions that allow AWS CodeCommit to trigger actions in Amazon SNS and Lambda. You will also find links to examples for creating, editing, testing, and deleting triggers.

Topics

- Create the Resource and Add Permissions for AWS CodeCommit
- Example: Create an AWS CodeCommit Trigger for an Amazon SNS Topic
- Example: Create an AWS CodeCommit Trigger for an AWS Lambda Function
- Example: Create a Trigger in AWS CodeCommit for an Existing AWS Lambda Function
- Edit Triggers for an AWS CodeCommit Repository
- Test Triggers for an AWS CodeCommit Repository
- Delete Triggers from an AWS CodeCommit Repository

Create the Resource and Add Permissions for AWS CodeCommit

You can integrate Amazon SNS topics and Lambda functions with triggers in AWS CodeCommit, but you must first create and then configure resources with a policy that allows AWS CodeCommit the permissions to interact with those resources. You must create the resource in the same region as the AWS CodeCommit repository. For example, if the repository is in US East (Ohio) (us-east-2), the Amazon SNS topic or Lambda function must be in US East (Ohio).

- For Amazon SNS topics, you do not need to configure additional IAM policies or permissions if the Amazon SNS topic is created using the same account as the AWS CodeCommit repository. You can create the AWS CodeCommit trigger as soon as you have created and subscribed to the Amazon SNS topic.
    - For more information about creating topics in Amazon SNS, see the Amazon SNS documentation.
    - For information about using Amazon SNS to send messages to Amazon SQS queues, see Sending Messages to Amazon SQS Queues.
    - For information about using Amazon SNS to invoke a Lambda function, see Invoking Lambda Functions.
- If you want to configure your trigger to use an Amazon SNS topic in another AWS account, you must first configure that topic with a policy that allows AWS CodeCommit to publish to that topic. For more information, see Example 1: Create a Policy That Enables Cross-Account Access to an Amazon SNS Topic.
- You can configure Lambda functions by creating the trigger in the Lambda console as part of the function. This is the simplest method, as triggers created in the Lambda console automatically include the permissions required for AWS CodeCommit to invoke the Lambda function. If you create the trigger in AWS CodeCommit, you must include a policy to allow AWS CodeCommit to invoke the function. For more information, see Create a Trigger for an Existing Lambda Function and Example 2: Create a Policy for AWS Lambda Integration.

Example: Create an AWS CodeCommit Trigger for an Amazon SNS Topic

You can create a trigger for an AWS CodeCommit repository so that events in that repository trigger notifications from an Amazon Simple Notification Service (Amazon SNS) topic. You might want to create a trigger to an Amazon SNS topic to enable users to subscribe to notifications about repository events, such as the deletion of branches. You can also take advantage of the integration of Amazon SNS topics with other services, such as Amazon Simple Queue Service (Amazon SQS) and AWS Lambda.

Note
You must point the trigger to an existing Amazon SNS topic that will be the action taken in response to repository events. For more information about creating and subscribing to Amazon SNS topics, see Getting Started with Amazon Simple Notification Service.

Topics

- Create a Trigger to an Amazon SNS Topic for an AWS CodeCommit Repository (Console)
- Create a Trigger to an Amazon SNS Topic for an AWS CodeCommit Repository (AWS CLI)

Create a Trigger to an Amazon SNS Topic for an AWS CodeCommit Repository (Console)

1. Open the AWS CodeCommit console at https://console.aws.amazon.com/codecommit.

2. From the list of repositories, choose the repository where you want to create triggers for repository events.

3. In the navigation pane for the repository, choose **Settings**. In **Settings**, choose **Triggers**.

4. Choose **Create trigger**.

5. In the **Create trigger** pane, do the following:

    - In **Trigger name**, type a name for the trigger, such as *MyFirstTrigger*.

    - In **Events**, select the repository events that will trigger the Amazon SNS topic to send notifications.

      If you choose **All repository events**, you cannot choose any other events. To choose a subset of events, remove **All repository events**, and then choose one or more events from the list. For example, if you want the trigger to run only when a user creates a branch or tag in the AWS CodeCommit repository, remove **All repository events**, and then choose **Create branch or tag**.

    - If you want the trigger to apply to all branches of the repository, in **Branches**, choose **All branches**. Otherwise, choose **Specific branches**. The default branch for the repository will be added by default. You can keep or delete this branch from the list. Choose up to ten branch names from the list of repository branches.

    - In **Send to**, choose **Amazon SNS**.

    - In **Amazon SNS Topic**, choose a topic name from the list, or choose **Add an Amazon SNS topic ARN** and then type the ARN for the function.

    - In **Custom data**, optionally provide any information you want included in the notification sent by the Amazon SNS topic (for example, an IRC channel name developers use when discussing development in this repository). This field is a string. It cannot be used to pass any dynamic parameters.

Create trigger

Triggers are actions taken in response to repository events. Triggers can be configured to send notifications to Amazon Simple Notification Service (SNS) or to an AWS Lambda function. Choose a trigger below to get started. Learn more

Trigger name* MyFirstTrigger

Events* All repository events ⊘ ▼

Branch names* All branches ⊘ ▼ ⓘ

Service

You can configure your trigger to use an existing SNS topic or Lambda function.

Send to* ● Amazon SNS ○ AWS Lambda

SNS topic* MyCodeCommitTopic ▼ ⓘ

Custom data For example, an IRC channel ID # ⓘ

AWS CodeCommit must have permission to publish to Amazon SNS topics from this trigger. Learn more

ⓘ Choose this option to test your trigger and confirm it functions as expected. ⚡ **Test trigger**

*Required Cancel **Create**

6. Optionally, choose **Test trigger**. This step will help you confirm have correctly configured access between AWS CodeCommit and the Amazon SNS topic. It will use the Amazon SNS topic to send a test notification using data from your repository, if available. If no real data is available, the test notification will contain sample data.

7. Choose **Create** to finish creating the trigger.

Create a Trigger to an Amazon SNS Topic for an AWS CodeCommit Repository (AWS CLI)

You can also use the command line to create a trigger for an Amazon SNS topic in response to AWS CodeCommit repository events, such as when someone pushes a commit to your repository.

To create a trigger for an Amazon SNS topic

1. Open a plain-text editor and create a JSON file that specifies:

   - The Amazon SNS topic name.
   - The repository and branches you want to monitor with this trigger. (If you do not specify any branches, the trigger will apply to all branches in the repository.)
   - The events that will activate this trigger.

Save the file.

For example, to create a trigger for a repository named *MyDemoRepo* that will publish all repository events to an Amazon SNS topic named *MySNSTopic* for two branches, *master* and *preprod*:

```
1  {
2      "repositoryName": "MyDemoRepo",
3      "triggers": [
4          {
5              "name": "MyFirstTrigger",
6              "destinationArn": "arn:aws:sns:us-east-2:80398EXAMPLE:MySNSTopic",
7              "customData": "",
8              "branches": [
9                  "master", "preprod"
10             ],
11             "events": [
12                 "all"
13             ]
14         }
15     ]
16 }
```

There must be a trigger block in the JSON for each trigger for a repository. To create more than one trigger for the repository, include more than one trigger block in the JSON. Remember that all triggers created in this file are for the specified repository. You cannot create triggers for multiple repositories in a single JSON file. For example, if you wanted to create two triggers for a repository, you could create a JSON file with two trigger blocks. In the following example, no branches are specified for the second trigger, so that trigger will apply to all branches:

```
1  {
2      "repositoryName": "MyDemoRepo",
3      "triggers": [
4          {
5              "name": "MyFirstTrigger",
6              "destinationArn": "arn:aws:sns:us-east-2:80398EXAMPLE:MySNSTopic",
7              "customData": "",
8              "branches": [
9                  "master", "preprod"
10             ],
11             "events": [
12                 "all"
13             ]
14         },
15         {
16             "name": "MySecondTrigger",
17             "destinationArn": "arn:aws:sns:us-east-2:80398EXAMPLE:MySNSTopic2",
18             "customData": "",
19             "branches": [],
20             "events": [
21                 "updateReference", "deleteReference"
22             ]
23         }
24     ]
25 }
```

You can create triggers for events you specify, such as when a commit is pushed to a repository. Event types include:

- **all** for all events in the specified repository and branches.
- **updateReference** for when commits are pushed to the specified repository and branches.
- **createReference** for when a new branch or tag is created in the specified repository.
- **deleteReference** for when a branch or tag is deleted in the specified repository. **Note**
  You can use more than one event type in a trigger. However, if you specify **all**, you cannot specify other events.

To see the full list of valid event types, at the terminal or command prompt, type aws codecommit put-repository-triggers help.

In addition, you can include a string in **customData** (for example, an IRC channel name developers use when discussing development in this repository). This field is a string. It cannot be used to pass any dynamic parameters. This string will be appended as an attribute to the AWS CodeCommit JSON returned in response to the trigger.

2. At a terminal or command prompt, optionally run the test-repository-triggers command. This test uses sample data from the repository (or generates sample data if no data is available) to send a notification to the subscribers of the Amazon SNS topic. For example, the following is used to test that the JSON in the trigger file named *trigger.json* is valid and that AWS CodeCommit can publish to the Amazon SNS topic:

```
1 aws codecommit test-repository-triggers --cli-input-json file://trigger.json
```

If successful, this command returns information similar to the following:

```
1 {
2     "successfulExecutions": [
3         "MyFirstTrigger"
4     ],
5     "failedExecutions": []
6 }
```

3. At a terminal or command prompt, run the put-repository-triggers command to create the trigger in AWS CodeCommit. For example, to use a JSON file named *trigger.json* to create the trigger:

aws codecommit put-repository-triggers --cli-input-json file://*trigger.json*

This command returns a configuration ID, similar to the following:

```
1 {
2     "configurationId": "0123456-I-AM-AN-EXAMPLE"
3 }
```

4. To view the configuration of the trigger, run the get-repository-triggers command, specifying the name of the repository:

aws codecommit get-repository-triggers --repository-name *MyDemoRepo*

This command returns the structure of all triggers configured for the repository, similar to the following:

```
1  {
2      "configurationId": "0123456-I-AM-AN-EXAMPLE",
3      "triggers": [
4          {
5              "events": [
6                  "all"
7              ],
8              "destinationArn": "arn:aws:sns:us-east-2:80398EXAMPLE:MySNSTopic",
9              "branches": [
10                 "master",
11                 "preprod"
```

```
12              ],
13              "name": "MyFirstTrigger",
14              "customData": "Project ID 12345"
15          }
16      ]
17 }
```

5. To test the functionality of the trigger itself, make and push a commit to the repository where you configured the trigger. You should see a response from the Amazon SNS topic. For example, if you configured the Amazon SNS topic to send an email, you should see an email from Amazon SNS in the email account subscribed to the topic.

The following is example output from an email sent from Amazon SNS in response to a push to an AWS CodeCommit repository:

```
1  {
2    "Records":[
3      {
4          "awsRegion":"us-east-2",
5          "codecommit":{
6              "references" : [
7                  {
8                      "commit":"317f8570EXAMPLE",
9                      "created":true,
10                     "ref":"refs/heads/NewBranch"
11                 },
12                 {
13                     "commit":"4c925148EXAMPLE",
14                     "ref":"refs/heads/preprod",
15                 }
16             ]
17         },
18         "eventId":"11111-EXAMPLE-ID",
19         "eventName":"ReferenceChange",
20         "eventPartNumber":1,
21         "eventSource":"aws:codecommit",
22         "eventSourceARN":"arn:aws:codecommit:us-east-2:80398EXAMPLE:MyDemoRepo",
23         "eventTime":"2016-02-09T00:08:11.743+0000",
24         "eventTotalParts":1,
25         "eventTriggerConfigId":"0123456-I-AM-AN-EXAMPLE",
26         "eventTriggerName":"MyFirstTrigger",
27         "eventVersion":"1.0",
28         "customData":"Project ID 12345",
29         "userIdentityARN":"arn:aws:iam::80398EXAMPLE:user/JaneDoe-CodeCommit",
30     }
31   ]
32 }
```

Example: Create an AWS CodeCommit Trigger for an AWS Lambda Function

You can create a trigger for an AWS CodeCommit repository so that events in the repository will invoke a Lambda function. In this example, you will create a Lambda function that returns the URL used to clone the repository to an Amazon CloudWatch log.

Topics

- Create the Lambda Function
- View the Trigger for the Lambda Function in the AWS CodeCommit Repository (Console)

Create the Lambda Function

You can create an AWS CodeCommit trigger for a Lambda function as part of creating the function itself in the Lambda console. The following steps include a sample Lambda function. The sample is available in two languages: JavaScript and Python. The function returns the URLs used for cloning a repository to a CloudWatch log.

To create a Lambda function using a Lambda blueprint

1. Sign in to the AWS Management Console and open the AWS Lambda console at https://console.aws. amazon.com/lambda/.

2. On the **Lambda Functions** page, choose **Create a Lambda function**. (If you have not used Lambda before, choose **Get Started Now**.)

3. On the **Select blueprint** page, choose **Blank function**.

4. On the **Configure triggers** page, choose AWS CodeCommit from the drop-down list of services to integrate with Lambda.

Configure triggers

Configure an optional trigger to automatically invoke your function.

CodeCommit ▶ Lambda   [Remove]

Repository name | MyDemoRepo ▼ | ❶

Trigger name | MyLambdaFunctionTrigger | ❶

Events | ❖ Push to existing branch ▼ | ❶

Branch names | ❖ All branches ▼ | ❶

Custom data | # | ❶

Lambda will add the necessary permissions for AWS CodeCommit to invoke your Lambda function. Learn more about the Lambda permissions model.

[Cancel] [Previous] [Next]

- In **Repository name**, choose the name of the repository where you want to configure a trigger that will use the Lambda function in response to repository events.
- In **Trigger name**, type a name for the trigger (for example, *MyLambdaFunctionTrigger*).
- In **Events**, choose the repository events that will trigger the Lambda function. If you choose **All repository events**, you cannot choose any other events. If you want to choose a subset of events, clear **All repository events**, and then choose the events you want from the list. For example, if you want the trigger to run only when a user creates a tag or a branch in the AWS CodeCommit repository, remove **All repository events**, and then choose **Create branch or tag**.
- If you want the trigger to apply to all branches of the repository, in **Branches**, choose **All branches**. Otherwise, choose **Specific branches**. The default branch for the repository will be added by default. You can keep or delete this branch from the list. Choose up to ten branch names from the list of repository branches.
- In **Custom data**, optionally provide information you want included in the Lambda function (for example, the name of the IRC channel used by developers to discuss development in the repository). This field is a string. It cannot be used to pass any dynamic parameters.

Choose **Next**.

5. On the **Configure function** page, in **Name**, type a name for the function (for example, *MyCodeCommit-Function*). Optionally, in **Description**, type a description for the function. If you want to create a sample JavaScript function, in **Runtime**, choose **Node.js**. If you want to create a sample Python function, choose **Python 2.7**.

6. In **Code entry type**, choose **Edit code inline**, and then replace the hello world code with one of the two following samples.

For Node.js:

```
1  var aws = require('aws-sdk');
2  var codecommit = new aws.CodeCommit({ apiVersion: '2015-04-13' });
```

```
3
4  exports.handler = function(event, context) {
5
6      //Log the updated references from the event
7      var references = event.Records[0].codecommit.references.map(function(reference) {return
         reference.ref;});
8      console.log('References:', references);
9
10     //Get the repository from the event and show its git clone URL
11     var repository = event.Records[0].eventSourceARN.split(":")[5];
12     var params = {
13         repositoryName: repository
14     };
15     codecommit.getRepository(params, function(err, data) {
16         if (err) {
17             console.log(err);
18             var message = "Error getting repository metadata for repository " + repository;
19             console.log(message);
20             context.fail(message);
21         } else {
22             console.log('Clone URL:', data.repositoryMetadata.cloneUrlHttp);
23             context.succeed(data.repositoryMetadata.cloneUrlHttp);
24         }
25     });
26 };
```

For Python:

```
1  import json
2  import boto3
3
4  codecommit = boto3.client('codecommit')
5
6  def lambda_handler(event, context):
7      #Log the updated references from the event
8      references = { reference['ref'] for reference in event['Records'][0]['codecommit']['
         references'] }
9      print("References: " + str(references))
10
11     #Get the repository from the event and show its git clone URL
12     repository = event['Records'][0]['eventSourceARN'].split(':')[5]
13     try:
14         response = codecommit.get_repository(repositoryName=repository)
15         print("Clone URL: " +response['repositoryMetadata']['cloneUrlHttp'])
16         return response['repositoryMetadata']['cloneUrlHttp']
17     except Exception as e:
18         print(e)
19         print('Error getting repository {}. Make sure it exists and that your repository is
             in the same region as this function.'.format(repository))
20         raise e
```

7. In **Lambda function handler and role**, do the following:

   - In **Handler**, leave the default value as derived from the function (`index.handler` for the Node.js sample or `lambda_function.lambda_handler` for the Python sample).
   - In **Role**, choose **Create a custom role** from the list. In the IAM console, do the following:

- In **IAM Role**, choose **lambda_basic_execution**.
- In **Policy Name**, choose **Create a new role policy**.
- Choose **Allow** to create the role and eturn to the Lambda console. A value of `lambda_basic_execution` should now be displayed for **Role**. **Note** If you choose a different role or a different name for the role, be sure to use it in the steps in this topic.

Choose **Next**.

8. On the **Review** page, review the settings for the function, and then choose **Create function**.

View the Trigger for the Lambda Function in the AWS CodeCommit Repository (Console)

After you have created the Lambda function, you can view and test the trigger in AWS CodeCommit. Testing the trigger will run the function in response to the repository events you specify.

To view and test the trigger for the Lambda function

1. Open the AWS CodeCommit console at https://console.aws.amazon.com/codecommit.

2. From the list of repositories, choose the repository where you want to view triggers.

3. In the navigation pane for the repository, choose **Settings**. In **Settings**, choose **Triggers**.

4. Review the list of triggers for the repository. You should see the trigger you created in the Lambda console. Choose it from the list.

5. In the **Edit trigger** pane, choose **Test trigger**. This option will attempt to invoke the function with sample data about your repository, including the most recent commit ID for the repository. (If no commit history exists, sample values consisting of zeroes will be generated instead.) This will help you confirm you have correctly configured access between AWS CodeCommit and the Lambda function.

6. Choose **Cancel** after you see a success message from the test.

7. To further verify the functionality of the trigger, make and push a commit to the repository where you configured the trigger. You should see a response from the Lambda function on the **Monitoring** tab for that function in the Lambda console. From the **Monitoring** tab, choose **View logs in CloudWatch**. The CloudWatch console will open in a new tab and display events for your function. Select the log stream from the list that corresponds to the time you pushed your commit. You should see event data similar to the following:

```
1 START RequestId: 70afdc9a-EXAMPLE Version: $LATEST
2 2015-11-10T18:18:28.689Z 70afdc9a-EXAMPLE    References: [ 'refs/heads/master' ]
3 2015-11-10T18:18:29.814Z 70afdc9a-EXAMPLE    Clone URL: https://git-codecommit.us-east-2.
    amazonaws.com/v1/repos/MyDemoRepo
4 END RequestId: 70afdc9a-EXAMPLE
5 REPORT RequestId: 70afdc9a-EXAMPLE Duration: 1126.87 ms Billed Duration: 1200 ms Memory
    Size: 128 MB Max Memory Used: 14 MB
```

Example: Create a Trigger in AWS CodeCommit for an Existing AWS Lambda Function

The easiest way to create a trigger that will invoke a Lambda function is to create that trigger in the Lambda console. This built-in integration ensures that AWS CodeCommit will have the permissions required to run the function. You can add a trigger for an existing Lambda function by going to the Lambda console, choosing the function, and on the **Triggers** tab for the function, and then following the steps in **Add trigger**. These are similar steps to the ones shown in Create the Lambda Function.

However, you can also create a trigger for a Lambda function in an AWS CodeCommit repository. Doing so requires that you choose an existing Lambda function to invoke, and also requires that you manually configure the permissions required for AWS CodeCommit to run the function.

Topics

- Manually Configure Permissions to Allow AWS CodeCommit to Run a Lambda Function
- Create a Trigger for the Lambda Function in an AWS CodeCommit Repository (Console)
- Create a Trigger to a Lambda Function for an AWS CodeCommit Repository (AWS CLI)

Manually Configure Permissions to Allow AWS CodeCommit to Run a Lambda Function

If you create a trigger in AWS CodeCommit that invokes a Lambda function, you must manually configure the permissions to allow AWS CodeCommit to run the Lambda function. To avoid this manual configuration, consider creating the trigger in the Lambda console for the function instead.

To allow AWS CodeCommit to run a Lambda function

1. Open a plain-text editor and create a JSON file that specifies the Lambda function name, the details of the AWS CodeCommit repository, and the actions you want to allow in Lambda, similar to the following:

```
1 {
2     "FunctionName": "MyCodeCommitFunction",
3     "StatementId": "1",
4     "Action": "lambda:InvokeFunction",
5     "Principal": "codecommit.amazonaws.com",
6     "SourceArn": "arn:aws:codecommit:us-east-1:80398EXAMPLE:MyDemoRepo",
7     "SourceAccount": "80398EXAMPLE"
8 }
```

2. Save the file as a JSON file with a name that is easy for you to remember (for example, *AllowAccessfrom-MyDemoRepo*.json).

3. At the terminal (Linux, macOS, or Unix) or command line (Windows), run the aws lambda add-permissions command to add a permission to the resource policy associated with your Lambda function, using the JSON file you just created:

```
1 aws lambda add-permission - -cli-input-json file://AllowAccessfromMyDemoRepo.json
```

This command returns the JSON of the policy statement you just added, similar to the following:

```
1 {
2     "Statement": "{\"Condition\":{\"StringEquals\":{\"AWS:SourceAccount\":\"80398EXAMPLE
       \"},\"ArnLike\":{\"AWS:SourceArn\":\"arn:aws:codecommit:us-east-1:80398EXAMPLE:
       MyDemoRepo\"}},\"Action\":[\"lambda:InvokeFunction\"],\"Resource\":\"arn:aws:lambda
       :us-east-1:80398EXAMPLE:function:MyCodeCommitFunction\",\"Effect\":\"Allow\",\"
       Principal\":{\"Service\":\"codecommit.amazonaws.com\"},\"Sid\":\"1\"}"
```

```
3 }
```

For more information about resource policies for Lambda functions, see AddPermission and The Pull/Push Event Models in the Lambda User Guide.

4. Sign in to the AWS Management Console and open the IAM console at https://console.aws.amazon.com/iam/.

5. In the **Dashboard** navigation pane, choose **Roles**, and in the list of roles, select *lambda_basic_execution*.

6. On the summary page for the role, choose the **Permissions** tab, and in the **Inline Policies** section, choose **Create Role Policy**.

7. On the **Set Permissions** page, choose **Policy Generator**, and then choose **Select**.

8. On the **Edit Permissions** page, do the following:

   - In **Effect**, choose **Allow**.
   - In **AWS Service**, choose **AWS CodeCommit**.
   - In **Actions**, select **GetRepository**.
   - In **Amazon Resource Name (ARN)**, type the ARN for the repository (for example, `arn:aws:codecommit:us-east-1:80398EXAMPLE:MyDemoRepo`).

   Choose **Add Statement**, and then choose **Next Step**.

9. On the **Review Policy** page, choose **Apply Policy**.

   Your policy statement should look similar to the following example:

```
1  {
2      "Version": "2012-10-17",
3      "Statement": [
4          {
5              "Sid": "Stmt11111111",
6              "Effect": "Allow",
7              "Action": [
8                  "codecommit:GetRepository"
9              ],
10             "Resource": [
11                 "arn:aws:codecommit:us-east-1:80398EXAMPLE:MyDemoRepo"
12             ]
13         }
14     ]
15 }
```

Create a Trigger for the Lambda Function in an AWS CodeCommit Repository (Console)

After you have created the Lambda function, you can create a trigger in AWS CodeCommit that will run the function in response to the repository events you specify.

Note
Before you can successfully test or run the trigger for the example, you must configure the policies that allow AWS CodeCommit to invoke the function and the Lambda function to get information about the repository. For more information, see To allow AWS CodeCommit to run a Lambda function.

To create a trigger for a Lambda function in the AWS CodeCommit console

1. Open the AWS CodeCommit console at https://console.aws.amazon.com/codecommit.

2. From the list of repositories, choose the repository where you want to create triggers for repository events.

3. In the navigation pane for the repository, choose **Settings**. In **Settings**, choose **Triggers**.

4. Choose **Create trigger**.

5. In the **Create trigger** pane, do the following:

   - In **Trigger name**, type a name for the trigger (for example, *MyLambdaFunctionTrigger*).

   - In **Events**, choose the repository events that will trigger the Lambda function.

     If you choose **All repository events**, you cannot choose any other events. If you want to choose a subset of events, clear **All repository events**, and then choose the events you want from the list. For example, if you want the trigger to run only when a user creates a tag or a branch in the AWS CodeCommit repository, remove **All repository events**, and then choose **Create branch or tag**.

   - If you want the trigger to apply to all branches of the repository, in **Branches**, choose **All branches**. Otherwise, choose **Specific branches**. The default branch for the repository will be added by default. You can keep or delete this branch from the list. Choose up to ten branch names from the list of repository branches.

   - In **Send to**, choose **AWS Lambda**.

   - In **Lambda function ARN**, choose the function name from the list, or choose **Add an AWS Lambda function ARN** and then type the ARN for the function.

   - In **Custom data**, optionally provide information you want included in the Lambda function (for example, the name of the IRC channel used by developers to discuss development in the repository). This field is a string. It cannot be used to pass any dynamic parameters.

6. Optionally, choose **Test trigger**. This option will attempt to invoke the function with sample data about your repository, including the most recent commit ID for the repository. (If no commit history exists, sample values consisting of zeroes will be generated instead.) This will help you confirm you have correctly configured access between AWS CodeCommit and the Lambda function.

7. Choose **Create** to finish creating the trigger.

8. To verify the functionality of the trigger, make and push a commit to the repository where you configured the trigger. You should see a response from the Lambda function on the **Monitoring** tab for that function in the Lambda console.

Create a Trigger to a Lambda Function for an AWS CodeCommit Repository (AWS CLI)

You can also use the command line to create a trigger for a Lambda function in response to AWS CodeCommit repository events, such as when someone pushes a commit to your repository.

To create a trigger for an Lambda function

1. Open a plain-text editor and create a JSON file that specifies:

   - The Lambda function name.
   - The repository and branches you want to monitor with this trigger. (If you do not specify any branches, the trigger will apply to all branches in the repository.)
   - The events that will activate this trigger.

   Save the file.

   For example, if you want to create a trigger for a repository named *MyDemoRepo* that will publish all repository events to a Lambda function named *MyCodeCommitFunction* for two branches, *master* and *preprod*:

```json
1  {
2      "repositoryName": "MyDemoRepo",
3      "triggers": [
4          {
5              "name": "MyLambdaFunctionTrigger",
6              "destinationArn": "arn:aws:lambda:us-east-1:80398EXAMPLE:function:
                  MyCodeCommitFunction",
7              "customData": "",
8              "branches": [
9                  "master", "preprod"
10             ],
11             "events": [
12                 "all"
13             ]
14         }
15     ]
16 }
```

There must be a trigger block in the JSON for each trigger for a repository. To create more than one trigger for a repository, include additional blocks in the JSON. Remember that all triggers created in this file are for the specified repository. You cannot create triggers for multiple repositories in a single JSON file. For example, if you wanted to create two triggers for a repository, you could create a JSON file with two trigger blocks. In the following example, no branches are specified in the second trigger block, so that trigger will apply to all branches:

```json
1  {
2      "repositoryName": "MyDemoRepo",
3      "triggers": [
4          {
5              "name": "MyLambdaFunctionTrigger",
6              "destinationArn": "arn:aws:lambda:us-east-1:80398EXAMPLE:function:
                  MyCodeCommitFunction",
7              "customData": "",
8              "branches": [
9                  "master", "preprod"
10             ],
11             "events": [
12                 "all"
13             ]
14         },
15         {
16             "name": "MyOtherLambdaFunctionTrigger",
17             "destinationArn": "arn:aws:lambda:us-east-1:80398EXAMPLE:function:
                  MyOtherCodeCommitFunction",
18             "customData": "",
19             "branches": [],
20             "events": [
21                 "updateReference", "deleteReference"
22             ]
23         }
24     ]
25 }
```

You can create triggers for events you specify, such as when a commit is pushed to a repository. Event types include:

- **all** for all events in the specified repository and branches.
- **updateReference** for when commits are pushed to the specified repository and branches.
- **createReference** for when a new branch or tag is created in the specified repository.
- **deleteReference** for when a branch or tag is deleted in the specified repository. **Note**
  You can use more than one event type in a trigger. However, if you specify **all**, you cannot specify other events.

To see the full list of valid event types, at the terminal or command prompt, type aws codecommit put-repository-triggers help.

In addition, you can include a string in **customData** (for example, an IRC channel name developers use when discussing development in this repository). This field is a string. It cannot be used to pass any dynamic parameters. This string will be appended as an attribute to the AWS CodeCommit JSON returned in response to the trigger.

2. At a terminal or command prompt, optionally run the test-repository-triggers command. For example, the following is used to test that the JSON file named *trigger.json* is valid and that AWS CodeCommit can trigger the Lambda function. This test uses sample data to trigger the function if no real data is available.

```
1 aws codecommit test-repository-triggers --cli-input-json file://trigger.json
```

If successful, this command returns information similar to the following:

```
1 {
2     "successfulExecutions": [
3         "MyLambdaFunctionTrigger"
4     ],
5     "failedExecutions": []
6 }
```

3. At a terminal or command prompt, run the put-repository-triggers command to create the trigger in AWS CodeCommit. For example, to use a JSON file named *trigger.json* to create the trigger:

aws codecommit put-repository-triggers - -cli-input-json file://*trigger.json*

This command returns a configuration ID, similar to the following:

```
1 {
2     "configurationId": "0123456-I-AM-AN-EXAMPLE"
3 }
```

4. To view the configuration of the trigger, run the get-repository-triggers command, specifying the name of the repository:

aws codecommit get-repository-triggers - -repository-name *MyDemoRepo*

This command returns the structure of all triggers configured for the repository, similar to the following:

```
 1 {
 2     "configurationId": "0123456-I-AM-AN-EXAMPLE",
 3     "triggers": [
 4         {
 5             "events": [
 6                 "all"
 7             ],
 8             "destinationArn": "arn:aws:lambda:us-east-1:80398EXAMPLE:MyCodeCommitFunction",
 9             "branches": [
10                 "master",
11                 "preprod"
12             ],
```

```
13              "name": "MyLambdaFunctionTrigger",
14              "customData": "Project ID 12345"
15          }
16      ]
17 }
```

5. To test the functionality of the trigger, make and push a commit to the repository where you configured the trigger. You should see a response from the Lambda function on the **Monitoring** tab for that function in the Lambda console.

Edit Triggers for an AWS CodeCommit Repository

You can edit the triggers that have been created for an AWS CodeCommit repository. You can change the events and branches for the trigger, the action taken in response to the event, and other settings.

Topics

- Edit a Trigger for a Repository (Console)
- Edit a Trigger for a Repository (AWS CLI)

Edit a Trigger for a Repository (Console)

1. Open the AWS CodeCommit console at https://console.aws.amazon.com/codecommit.

2. From the list of repositories, choose the repository where you want to edit a trigger for repository events.

3. In the navigation pane for the repository, choose **Settings**. In **Settings**, choose **Triggers**.

4. From the list of triggers for the repository, select the trigger you want to edit, and then choose **Edit**.

5. Make the changes you want to the trigger, and then choose **Update** to save your changes.

Edit a Trigger for a Repository (AWS CLI)

1. At a terminal (Linux, macOS, or Unix) or command prompt (Windows), run the get-repository-triggers command to create a JSON file with the structure of all of the triggers configured for your repository. For example, to create a JSON file named *MyTriggers.json* with the structure of all of the triggers configured for a repository named *MyDemoRepo*:

```
1 aws codecommit get-repository-triggers --repository-name MyDemoRepo >MyTriggers.json
```

This command returns nothing, but a file named *MyTriggers.json* is created in the directory where you ran the command.

2. Edit the JSON file in a plain-text editor and make changes to the trigger block of the trigger you want to edit. Replace the `configurationId` pair with a `repositoryName` pair. Save the file.

For example, if you want to edit a trigger named *MyFirstTrigger* in the repository named *MyDemoRepo* so that it applies to all branches, you would replace `configurationId` with `repositoryName`, and remove the specified `master` and `preprod` branches in *red italic text*. By default, if no branches are specified, the trigger will apply to all branches in the repository:

```
1  {
2      "repositoryName": "MyDemoRepo",
3      "triggers": [
4          {
5              "destinationArn": "arn:aws:sns:us-east-2:80398EXAMPLE:MyCodeCommitTopic",
6              "branches": [
7                  "master",
8                  "preprod"
9              ],
10             "name": "MyFirstTrigger",
11             "customData": "",
12             "events": [
13                 "all"
14             ]
15         }
```

```
16      ]
17  }
```

3. At the terminal or command line, run the put-repository-triggers command. This will update all triggers for the repository, including the changes you made to the *MyFirstTrigger* trigger:

```
1  aws codecommit put-repository-triggers --repository-name MyDemoRepo file://MyTriggers.json
```

This command returns a configuration ID, similar to the following:

```
1  {
2      "configurationId": "0123456-I-AM-AN-EXAMPLE"
3  }
```

Test Triggers for an AWS CodeCommit Repository

You can test the triggers that have been created for an AWS CodeCommit repository. Testing involves running the trigger with sample data from your repository, including the most recent commit ID. If no commit history exists for the repository, sample values consisting of zeroes will be generated instead. Testing triggers helps you confirm you have correctly configured access between AWS CodeCommit and the target of the trigger, whether that is an AWS Lambda function or an Amazon Simple Notification Service notification.

Topics

- Test a Trigger for a Repository (Console)
- Test a Trigger for a Repository (AWS CLI)

Test a Trigger for a Repository (Console)

1. Open the AWS CodeCommit console at https://console.aws.amazon.com/codecommit.

2. From the list of repositories, choose the repository where you want to test a trigger for repository events.

3. In the navigation pane for the repository, choose **Settings**. In **Settings**, choose **Triggers**.

4. Choose the trigger you want to edit from the list of triggers, and then choose **Edit**.

5. In the **Edit trigger** dialog box, choose **Test trigger**. You will see a success or failure message. If successful, you will also see a corresponding action response from the Lambda function or the Amazon SNS topic.

Test a Trigger for a Repository (AWS CLI)

1. At a terminal (Linux, macOS, or Unix) or command prompt (Windows), run the get-repository-triggers command to create a JSON file with the structure of all of the triggers configured for your repository. For example, to create a JSON file named *TestTrigger.json* with the structure of all of the triggers configured for a repository named MyDemoRepo:

```
1 aws codecommit get-repository-triggers --repository-name MyDemoRepo >TestTrigger.json
```

This command creates a file named *TestTriggers.json* in the directory where you ran the command.

2. Edit the JSON file in a plain-text editor and make the changes to the trigger statement. Replace the `configurationId` pair with a `repositoryName` pair. Save the file.

For example, if you want to test a trigger named *MyFirstTrigger* in the repository named *MyDemoRepo* so that it applies to all branches, you would replace the `configurationId` with `repositoryName` and then save a file that looks similar to the following as *TestTrigger.json*:

```
1  {
2      "repositoryName": "MyDemoRepo",
3      "triggers": [
4          {
5              "destinationArn": "arn:aws:sns:us-east-2:80398EXAMPLE:MyCodeCommitTopic",
6              "branches": [
7                  "master",
8                  "preprod"
9              ],
10             "name": "MyFirstTrigger",
11             "customData": "",
12             "events": [
```

```
13              "all"
14          ]
15      }
16  ]
17 }
```

3. At the terminal or command line, run the test-repository-triggers command. This will update all triggers for the repository, including the changes you made to the *MyFirstTrigger* trigger:

```
1 aws codecommit test-repository-triggers --cli-input-json file://TestTrigger.json
```

This command returns a response similar to the following:

```
1 {
2     "successfulExecutions": [
3         "MyFirstTrigger"
4     ],
5     "failedExecutions": []
6 }
```

Delete Triggers from an AWS CodeCommit Repository

You might want to delete triggers if they are no longer being used. You cannot undo the deletion of a trigger, but you can re-create one.

Note
If you configured one or more triggers for your repository, deleting the repository does not delete the Amazon SNS topics or Lambda functions you configured as the targets of those triggers. Be sure to delete those resources, too, if they are no longer needed.

Topics
- Delete a Trigger from a Repository (Console)
- Delete a Trigger from a Repository (AWS CLI)

Delete a Trigger from a Repository (Console)

1. Open the AWS CodeCommit console at https://console.aws.amazon.com/codecommit.

2. From the list of repositories, choose the repository where you want to delete triggers for repository events.

3. In the navigation pane for the repository, choose **Settings**. In **Settings**, choose **Triggers**.

4. Select the triggers you want to delete from the list of triggers, and then choose **Delete**.

5. In the dialog box, choose **Delete** to confirm.

Delete a Trigger from a Repository (AWS CLI)

1. At a terminal (Linux, macOS, or Unix) or command prompt (Windows), run the get-repository-triggers command to create a JSON file with the structure of all of the triggers configured for your repository. For example, to create a JSON file named *MyTriggers.json* with the structure of all of the triggers configured for a repository named MyDemoRepo:

```
1 aws codecommit get-repository-triggers --repository-name MyDemoRepo >MyTriggers.json
```

This command creates a file named *MyTriggers.json* in the directory where you ran the command.

2. Edit the JSON file in a plain-text editor and remove the trigger block for the trigger you want to delete. Replace the `configurationId` pair with a `repositoryName` pair. Save the file.

For example, if you want to remove a trigger named *MyFirstTrigger* from the repository named *MyDemoRepo*, you would replace `configurationId` with `repositoryName`, and remove the statement in *red italic text*:

```
1  {
2      "repositoryName": "MyDemoRepo",
3      "triggers": [
4          {
5              "destinationArn": "arn:aws:sns:us-east-2:80398EXAMPLE:MyCodeCommitTopic",
6              "branches": [
7                  "master",
8                  "preprod"
9              ],
10             "name": "MyFirstTrigger",
11             "customData": "",
12             "events": [
13                 "all"
```

```
14              ]
15          },
16          {
17              "destinationArn": "arn:aws:lambda:us-east-2:80398EXAMPLE:function:
                    MyCodeCommitJSFunction",
18              "branches": [],
19              "name": "MyLambdaTrigger",
20              "events": [
21                  "all"
22              ]
23          }
24      ]
25  }
```

3. At the terminal or command line, run the put-repository-triggers command. This will update the triggers for the repository and delete the *MyFirstTrigger* trigger:

```
1  aws codecommit put-repository-triggers --repository-name MyDemoRepo file://MyTriggers.json
```

This command returns a configuration ID, similar to the following:

```
1  {
2      "configurationId": "0123456-I-AM-AN-EXAMPLE"
3  }
```

Note

To delete all triggers for a repository named *MyDemoRepo*, your JSON file would look similar to this:

```
1  {
2      "repositoryName": "MyDemoRepo",
3      "triggers": []
4  }
```

View AWS CodeCommit Repository Details

To view information about available repositories, you can use:

- Git from a local repo connected to the AWS CodeCommit repository.
- The AWS CLI.
- The AWS CodeCommit console.

Before you follow these instructions, complete the steps in Setting Up .

Topics

- Use the AWS CodeCommit Console to View Repository Details
- Use Git to View AWS CodeCommit Repository Details
- Use the AWS CLI to View AWS CodeCommit Repository Details

Use the AWS CodeCommit Console to View Repository Details

Use the AWS CodeCommit console to quickly view all repositories created with your AWS account.

1. Open the AWS CodeCommit console at https://console.aws.amazon.com/codecommit.

2. Choose the name of the repository from the list.

3. Do one of the following:

   - To view the URL for cloning the repository, in the navigation pane, choose **Code**, choose **Clone URL**, and then choose the protocol you want to use when cloning the repository.
   - To view configurable details for the repository, in the navigation pane, choose **Settings**.

Note
If you are signed in as an IAM user, you can configure and save your preferences for viewing code and other console settings. For more information, see Working with User Preferences.

Use Git to View AWS CodeCommit Repository Details

To use Git from a local repo to view details about AWS CodeCommit repositories, run the git remote show command.

Before you perform these steps, connect the local repo to the AWS CodeCommit repository. For instructions, see Connect to a Repository.

1. Run the git remote show *remote-name* command, where *remote-name* is the alias of the AWS CodeCommit repository (by default, `origin`). **Tip**
   To get a list of AWS CodeCommit repository names along with their URLs, run the git remote -v command.

   For example, to view details about the AWS CodeCommit repository with the alias `origin`:

   ```
   1 git remote show origin
   ```

2. For HTTPS:

   ```
   1 * remote origin
   2   Fetch URL: https://git-codecommit.us-east-2.amazonaws.com/v1/repos/MyDemoRepo
   3   Push  URL: https://git-codecommit.us-east-2.amazonaws.com/v1/repos/MyDemoRepo
   4   HEAD branch: (unknown)
   5   Remote branches:
   6     MyNewBranch tracked
   7     master tracked
   ```

```
8    Local ref configured for 'git pull':
9      MyNewBranch merges with remote MyNewBranch (up to date)
10   Local refs configured for 'git push':
11     MyNewBranch pushes to MyNewBranch (up to date)
12     master pushes to master (up to date)
```

For SSH:

```
1  * remote origin
2    Fetch URL: ssh://git-codecommit.us-east-2.amazonaws.com/v1/repos/MyDemoRepo
3    Push  URL: ssh://git-codecommit.us-east-2.amazonaws.com/v1/repos/MyDemoRepo
4    HEAD branch: (unknown)
5    Remote branches:
6      MyNewBranch tracked
7      master tracked
8    Local ref configured for 'git pull':
9      MyNewBranch merges with remote MyNewBranch (up to date)
10   Local refs configured for 'git push':
11     MyNewBranch pushes to MyNewBranch (up to date)
12     master pushes to master (up to date)
```

Tip

To look up the SSH key ID for your IAM user, open the IAM console and expand **Security Credentials** on the IAM user details page. The SSH key ID can be found in **SSH Keys for AWS CodeCommit**.

For more options, see your Git documentation.

Use the AWS CLI to View AWS CodeCommit Repository Details

To use AWS CLI commands with AWS CodeCommit, install the AWS CLI. For more information, see Command Line Reference.

To use the AWS CLI to view repository details, run the following commands:

- list-repositories to view a list of AWS CodeCommit repository names and their corresponding IDs.
- get-repository to view information about a single AWS CodeCommit repository.
- batch-get-repositories to view information about multiple repositories in AWS CodeCommit.

To view a list of AWS CodeCommit repositories

1. Run the list-repositories command:

```
1  aws codecommit list-repositories
```

You can use the optional --sort-by or --order options to change the order of returned information.

2. If successful, this command outputs a repositories object that contains the names and IDs of all repositories in AWS CodeCommit associated with the AWS account.

Here is some example output based on the preceding command:

```
1  {
2      "repositories": [
3          {
4              "repositoryName": "MyDemoRepo"
5              "repositoryId": "f7579e13-b83e-4027-aaef-650c0EXAMPLE",
6          },
```

```
 7          {
 8              "repositoryName": "MyOtherDemoRepo"
 9              "repositoryId": "cfc29ac4-b0cb-44dc-9990-f6f51EXAMPLE"
10          }
11      ]
12  }
```

To view details about a single AWS CodeCommit repository

1. Run the get-repository command, specifying the name of the AWS CodeCommit repository with the
   --repository-name option. **Tip**
   To get the AWS CodeCommit repository's name, run the list-repositories command.

   For example, to view details about an AWS CodeCommit repository named MyDemoRepo:

```
1  aws codecommit get-repository --repository-name MyDemoRepo
```

2. If successful, this command outputs a repositoryMetadata object with the following information:

   - The repository's name (repositoryName).
   - The repository's description (repositoryDescription).
   - The repository's unique, system-generated ID (repositoryId).
   - The ID of the AWS account associated with the repository (accountId).

   Here is some example output, based on the preceding example command:

```
 1  {
 2          "repositoryMetadata": {
 3              "creationDate": 1429203623.625,
 4              "defaultBranch": "master",
 5              "repositoryName": "MyDemoRepo",
 6              "cloneUrlSsh": "ssh://git-codecommit.us-east-2.amazonaws.com/v1/repos/
                  MyDemoRepo",
 7              "lastModifiedDate": 1430783812.0869999,
 8              "repositoryDescription": "My demonstration repository",
 9              "cloneUrlHttp": "https://codecommit.us-east-2.amazonaws.com/v1/repos/MyDemoRepo
                  ",
10              "repositoryId": "f7579e13-b83e-4027-aaef-650c0EXAMPLE",
11              "Arn": "arn:aws:codecommit:us-east-2:80398EXAMPLE:MyDemoRepo
12              "accountId": "111111111111"
13          }
14  }
```

To view details about multiple AWS CodeCommit repositories

1. Run the batch-get-repositories command with the --repository-names option. Add a space between each
   AWS CodeCommit repository name. **Tip**
   To get the names of the repositories in AWS CodeCommit, run the list-repositories command.

   For example, to view details about two AWS CodeCommit repositories named MyDemoRepo and
   MyOtherDemoRepo:

```
1  aws codecommit batch-get-repositories --repository-names MyDemoRepo MyOtherDemoRepo
```

2. If successful, this command outputs an object with the following information:

- A list of any AWS CodeCommit repositories that could not be found (`repositoriesNotFound`).
- A list of AWS CodeCommit repositories (`repositories`). Each AWS CodeCommit repository's name is followed by:
  - The repository's description (`repositoryDescription`).
  - The repository's unique, system-generated ID (`repositoryId`).
  - The ID of the AWS account associated with the repository (`accountId`).

Here is some example output, based on the preceding example command:

```
 1  {
 2      "repositoriesNotFound": [],
 3      "repositories": [
 4          {
 5              "creationDate": 1429203623.625,
 6              "defaultBranch": "master",
 7              "repositoryName": "MyDemoRepo",
 8              "cloneUrlSsh": "ssh://git-codecommit.us-east-2.amazonaws.com/v1/repos/
                    MyDemoRepo",
 9              "lastModifiedDate": 1430783812.0869999,
10              "repositoryDescription": "My demonstration repository",
11              "cloneUrlHttp": "https://codecommit.us-east-2.amazonaws.com/v1/repos/
                    MyDemoRepo",
12              "repositoryId": "f7579e13-b83e-4027-aaef-650c0EXAMPLE",
13              "Arn": "arn:aws:codecommit:us-east-2:80398EXAMPLE:MyDemoRepo
14              "accountId": "111111111111"
15          },
16          {
17              "creationDate": 1429203623.627,
18              "defaultBranch": "master",
19              "repositoryName": "MyOtherDemoRepo",
20              "cloneUrlSsh": "ssh://git-codecommit.us-east-2.amazonaws.com/v1/repos/
                    MyOtherDemoRepo",
21              "lastModifiedDate": 1430783812.0889999,
22              "repositoryDescription": "My other demonstration repository",
23              "cloneUrlHttp": "https://codecommit.us-east-2.amazonaws.com/v1/repos/
                    MyOtherDemoRepo",
24              "repositoryId": "cfc29ac4-b0cb-44dc-9990-f6f51EXAMPLE",
25              "Arn": "arn:aws:codecommit:us-east-2:80398EXAMPLE:MyOtherDemoRepo
26              "accountId": "111111111111"
27          }
28      ],
29      "repositoriesNotFound": []
30  }
```

Change AWS CodeCommit Repository Settings

To change the settings of an AWS CodeCommit repository, such as its description or name, you can use the AWS CLI and the AWS CodeCommit console.

Important
Changing a repository's name may break any local repos that use the old name in their remote URL. Run the git remote set-url command to update the remote URL to use the new repository's name.

Topics

- Use the AWS CodeCommit Console to Change Repository Settings
- Use the AWS CLI to Change AWS CodeCommit Repository Settings

Use the AWS CodeCommit Console to Change Repository Settings

To use the AWS CodeCommit console to change an AWS CodeCommit repository's settings in AWS CodeCommit, follow these steps.

1. Open the AWS CodeCommit console at https://console.aws.amazon.com/codecommit.

2. In the list of repositories, choose the name of the repository where you want to change settings.

3. In the navigation pane, choose **Settings**.

4. To change the name of the repository, in the **General** tab, in **Repository name**, type a new name in the **Name** text box, choose **Change name**, and then choose **Change name** again. **Important**
   Changing the name of the AWS CodeCommit repository will change the SSH and HTTPS URLs that users need to connect to the repository. Users will not be able to connect to this repository until they update their connection settings. Also, because the repository's ARN will change, changing the repository name will invalidate any IAM user policies that rely on this repository's ARN.
   To connect to the repository after the name is changed, each user must use the git remote set-url command and specify the new URL to use. For example, if you changed the name of the repository from MyDemoRepo to MyRenamedDemoRepo, users who use HTTPS to connect to the repository would run the following Git command:

```
1 git remote set-url origin https://git-codecommit.us-east-2.amazonaws.com/v1/repos/
    MyRenamedDemoRepo
```

Users who use SSH to connect to the repository would run the following Git command:

```
1 git remote set-url origin ssh://git-codecommit.us-east-2.amazonaws.com/v1/repos/
    MyRenamedDemoRepo
```

For more options, see your Git documentation.

1. To change the repository's description, modify the text in the **Description** text box, and then choose **Save changes**. **Note**
   The description field accepts all HTML characters and all valid Unicode characters. If you are an application developer using the `GetRepository` or `BatchGetRepositories` APIs and plan to display the repository description field in a web browser, see the AWS CodeCommit API Reference.

2. To change the default branch, choose a different branch from the **Default branch** drop-down list, choose **Save changes**, and then choose **Change default**.

3. To delete the repository, choose **Delete repository**. In the box next to **Type the name of the repository to confirm deletion**, type the repository's name, and then choose **Delete**. **Important**
   After you delete this repository in AWS CodeCommit, you will no longer be able to clone it to any local repo or shared repo. You will also no longer be able to pull data from it, or push data to it, from any local repo or shared repo. This action cannot be undone.

Use the AWS CLI to Change AWS CodeCommit Repository Settings

To use AWS CLI commands with AWS CodeCommit, install the AWS CLI. For more information, see Command Line Reference.

To use AWS CLI to change an AWS CodeCommit repository's settings in AWS CodeCommit, run one or more of the following commands:

- update-repository-description to change an AWS CodeCommit repository's description.
- update-repository-name to change an AWS CodeCommit repository's name.

To change an AWS CodeCommit repository's description

1. Run the update-repository-description command, specifying:

    - The name of the AWS CodeCommit repository (with the `--repository-name` option). **Tip** To get the name of the AWS CodeCommit repository, run the list-repositories command.
    - The new repository description (with the `--repository-description` option). **Note** The description field accepts all HTML characters and all valid Unicode characters. If you are an application developer using the `GetRepository` or `BatchGetRepositories` APIs and plan to display the repository description field in a web browser, see the AWS CodeCommit API Reference.

    For example, to change the description for the AWS CodeCommit repository named `MyDemoRepo` to `This description was changed`:

    ```
    1 aws codecommit update-repository-description --repository-name MyDemoRepo --repository-
        description "This description was changed"
    ```

    This command produces output only if there are errors.

2. To verify the changed description, run the get-repository command, specifying the name of the AWS CodeCommit repository whose description you changed with the `--repository-name` option.

    The output of the command will show the changed text in `repositoryDescription`.

To change an AWS CodeCommit repository's name

1. Run the update-repository-name command, specifying:

    - The current name of the AWS CodeCommit repository (with the `--old-name` option). **Tip** To get the AWS CodeCommit repository's name, run the list-repositories command.
    - The new name of the AWS CodeCommit repository (with the `--new-name` option).

    For example, to change the repository named `MyDemoRepo` to `MyRenamedDemoRepo`:

    ```
    1 aws codecommit update-repository-name --old-name MyDemoRepo --new-name MyRenamedDemoRepo
    ```

    This command produces output only if there are errors. **Important** Changing the name of the AWS CodeCommit repository will change the SSH and HTTPS URLs that users need to connect to the repository. Users will not be able to connect to this repository until they update their connection settings. Also, because the repository's ARN will change, changing the repository name will invalidate any IAM user policies that rely on this repository's ARN.

2. To verify the changed name, run the list-repositories command and review the list of repository names.

Synchronize Changes Between a Local Repo and an AWS CodeCommit Repository

You use Git to synchronize changes between a local repo and the AWS CodeCommit repository connected to the local repo.

To push changes from the local repo to the AWS CodeCommit repository, run git push *remote-name branch-name*.

To pull changes to the local repo from the AWS CodeCommit repository, run git pull *remote-name branch-name*.

For both pushing and pulling, *remote-name* is the nickname the local repo uses for the AWS CodeCommit repository; *branch-name* is the name of the branch on the AWS CodeCommit repository to push to or pull from.

Tip
To get the nickname the local repo uses for the AWS CodeCommit repository, run git remote. To get a list of branch names, run git branch. An asterisk (*) appears next to the name of the current branch. (Alternatively, run git status to show the current branch name.)

Note
If you cloned the repository, from the local repo's perspective, *remote-name* is not the name of the AWS CodeCommit repository. When you clone a repository, *remote-name* is set automatically to origin.

For example, to push changes from the local repo to the master branch in the AWS CodeCommit repository with the nickname origin:

```
1 git push origin master
```

Similarly, to pull changes to the local repo from the master branch in the AWS CodeCommit repository with the nickname origin:

```
1 git pull origin master
```

Tip
If you add the -u option to git push, you will set upstream tracking information. For example, if you run git push -u origin master), in the future you can run git push and git pull without *remote-name branch-name*. To get upstream tracking information, run git remote show *remote-name* (for example, git remote show origin).

For more options, see your Git documentation.

Push Commits to an Additional Git Repository

You can configure your local repo to push changes to two remote repositories. For example, you might want to continue using your existing Git repository solution while you try out AWS CodeCommit. Follow these basic steps to push changes in your local repo to both AWS CodeCommit and a separate Git repository.

Tip
If you do not have a current Git repository, you can create an empty one on a service other than AWS CodeCommit and then migrate your AWS CodeCommit repository to it. You should follow steps similar to the ones in Migrate to AWS CodeCommit.

1. From the command prompt or terminal, switch to your local repo directory and run the git remote -v command. You should see output similar to the following:

   For HTTPS:

   ```
   1 origin  https://git-codecommit.us-east-2.amazonaws.com/v1/repos/MyDemoRepo (fetch)
   2 origin  https://git-codecommit.us-east-2.amazonaws.com/v1/repos/MyDemoRepo (push)
   ```

   For SSH:

   ```
   1 origin  ssh://git-codecommit.us-east-2.amazonaws.com/v1/repos/MyDemoRepo (fetch)
   2 origin  ssh://git-codecommit.us-east-2.amazonaws.com/v1/repos/MyDemoRepo (push)
   ```

2. Run the git remote set-url --add --push origin *git-repository-name* command where *git-repository-name* is the URL and name of the Git repository where you want to host your code. This changes the push destination of origin to that Git repository. **Note**
   git remote set-url --add --push overrides the default URL for pushes, so you will have to run this command twice, as demonstrated in later steps.

   For example, the following command changes the push of origin to *some-URL*/MyDestinationRepo:

   ```
   1 git remote set-url --add --push origin some-URL/MyDestinationRepo
   ```

   This command returns nothing. **Tip**
   If you are pushing to a Git repository that requires credentials, make sure you configure those credentials in a credential helper or in the configuration of the *some-URL* string; otherwise, your pushes to that repository will fail.

3. Run the git remote -v command again, which should create output similar to the following:

   For HTTPS:

   ```
   1 origin  https://git-codecommit.us-east-2.amazonaws.com/v1/repos/MyDemoRepo (fetch)
   2 origin  some-URL/MyDestinationRepo (push)
   ```

   For SSH:

   ```
   1 origin  ssh://git-codecommit.us-east-2.amazonaws.com/v1/repos/MyDemoRepo (fetch)
   2 origin  some-URL/MyDestinationRepo (push)
   ```

4. Now add the AWS CodeCommit repository. Run git remote set-url --add --push origin again, this time with the URL and repository name of your AWS CodeCommit repository.

   For example, the following command adds the push of **origin** to https://git/-codecommit/.us/-east/-2/.amazonaws/.com/v1/repos/MyDemoRepo:

   For HTTPS:

   ```
   1 git remote set-url --add --push origin https://git-codecommit.us-east-2.amazonaws.com/v1/
     repos/MyDemoRepo
   ```

For SSH:

```
1 git remote set-url --add --push origin ssh://git-codecommit.us-east-2.amazonaws.com/v1/
    repos/MyDemoRepo
```

This command returns nothing.

5. Run the git remote -v command again, which should create output similar to the following:

For HTTPS:

```
1 origin   https://git-codecommit.us-east-2.amazonaws.com/v1/repos/MyDemoRepo (fetch)
2 origin   some-URL/MyDestinationRepo (push)
3 origin   https://git-codecommit.us-east-2.amazonaws.com/v1/repos/MyDemoRepo (push)
```

For SSH:

```
1 origin   ssh://git-codecommit.us-east-2.amazonaws.com/v1/repos/MyDemoRepo (fetch)
2 origin   some-URL/MyDestinationRepo (push)
3 origin   ssh://git-codecommit.us-east-2.amazonaws.com/v1/repos/MyDemoRepo (push)
```

You now have two Git repositories as the destination for your pushes, but your pushes will go to *some-URL*/MyDestinationRepo first. If the push to that repository fails, your commits will not be pushed to either repository. **Tip**
If the other repository requires credentials you want to enter manually, consider changing the order of the pushes so that you push to AWS CodeCommit first. Run git remote set-url --delete to delete the repository that is pushed to first, and then run git remote set-url --add to add it again so that it becomes the second push destination in the list.
For more options, see your Git documentation.

6. To verify you are now pushing to both remote repositories, use a text editor to create the following text file in your local repo:

```
1 bees.txt
2 -------
3 Bees are flying insects closely related to wasps and ants, and are known for their role in
    pollination and for producing honey and beeswax.
```

7. Run git add to stage the change in your local repo:

```
1 git add bees.txt
```

8. Run git commit to commit the change in your local repo:

```
1 git commit -m "Added bees.txt"
```

9. To push the commit from the local repo to your remote repositories, run git push -u *remote-name branch-name* where *remote-name* is the nickname the local repo uses for the remote repositories and *branch-name* is the name of the branch to push to the repository. **Tip**
You only have to use the -u option the first time you push. The upstream tracking information will be set.

For example, running git push -u origin master would show the push went to both remote repositories in the expected branches, with output similar to the following:

For HTTPS:

```
1 Counting objects: 5, done.
2 Delta compression using up to 4 threads.
3 Compressing objects: 100% (3/3), done.
4 Writing objects: 100% (3/3), 5.61 KiB | 0 bytes/s, done.
5 Total 3 (delta 1), reused 0 (delta 0)
```

```
 6 To some-URL/MyDestinationRepo
 7    a5ba4ed..250f6c3  master -> master
 8 Counting objects: 5, done.
 9 Delta compression using up to 4 threads.
10 Compressing objects: 100% (3/3), done.
11 Writing objects: 100% (3/3), 5.61 KiB | 0 bytes/s, done.
12 Total 3 (delta 1), reused 0 (delta 0)
13 remote:
14 To https://git-codecommit.us-east-2.amazonaws.com/v1/repos/MyDemoRepo
15    a5ba4ed..250f6c3  master -> master
```

For SSH:

```
 1 Counting objects: 5, done.
 2 Delta compression using up to 4 threads.
 3 Compressing objects: 100% (3/3), done.
 4 Writing objects: 100% (3/3), 5.61 KiB | 0 bytes/s, done.
 5 Total 3 (delta 1), reused 0 (delta 0)
 6 To some-URL/MyDestinationRepo
 7    a5ba4ed..250f6c3  master -> master
 8 Counting objects: 5, done.
 9 Delta compression using up to 4 threads.
10 Compressing objects: 100% (3/3), done.
11 Writing objects: 100% (3/3), 5.61 KiB | 0 bytes/s, done.
12 Total 3 (delta 1), reused 0 (delta 0)
13 remote:
14 To ssh://git-codecommit.us-east-2.amazonaws.com/v1/repos/MyDemoRepo
15    a5ba4ed..250f6c3  master -> master
```

For more options, see your Git documentation.

Configure Cross-Account Access to an AWS CodeCommit Repository

You can configure access to AWS CodeCommit repositories for IAM users and groups in another AWS account. This is often referred to as *cross-account access*. This section provides examples and step-by-step instructions for configuring cross-account access for a repository named *MySharedDemoRepo* in the US East (Ohio) Region in an AWS account (referred to as AccountA) to IAM users who belong to an IAM group named *DevelopersWithCrossAccountRepositoryAccess* in another AWS account (referred to as AccountB).

This section is divided into three parts:

- Actions for the Administrator in AccountA.
- Actions for the Administrator in AccountB.
- Actions for the repository user in AccountB.

To configure cross-account access:

- The administrator in AccountA signs in as an IAM user with the permissions required to create and manage repositories in AWS CodeCommit and create roles in IAM. If you are using managed policies, apply IAMFullAccess and AWSCodeCommitFullAccess to this IAM user.

  The example account ID for AccountA is *111122223333*.

- The administrator in AccountB, signs in as an IAM user with the permissions required to create and manage IAM users and groups, and to configure policies for users and groups. If you are using managed policies, apply IAMFullAccess to this IAM user.

  The example account ID for AccountB is *888888888888*.

- The repository user in AccountB, to emulate the activities of a developer, signs in as an IAM user who is a member of the IAM group created to allow access to the AWS CodeCommit repository in AccountA. This account must be configured with:

  - AWS console access.
  - An access key and secret key to use when installing and configuring the AWS CLI credential helper on a local computer or Amazon EC2 instance, as described in For HTTPS Connections on Linux, macOS, or Unix with the AWS CLI Credential Helper or For HTTPS Connections on Windows with the AWS CLI Credential Helper.

  For more information, see IAM users.

Topics

Cross-Account Repository Access: Actions for the Administrator in AccountA

To allow users or groups in AccountB to access a repository in AccountA, an AccountA administrator must:

- Create a policy in AccountA that grants access to the repository.
- Create a role in AccountA that can be assumed by IAM users and groups in AccountB.
- Attach the policy to the role.

The following sections provide steps and examples.

Topics

- Step 1: Create a Policy for Repository Access in AccountA
- Step 2: Create a Role for Repository Access in AccountA

Step 1: Create a Policy for Repository Access in AccountA

You can create a policy in AccountA that grants access to the repository in AccountB. Depending on the level of access you want to allow, do one of the following:

- Configure the policy to allow AccountB users access to a specific repository, but do not allow them to view a list of all repositories in AccountA.
- Configure additional access to allow AccountB users to choose the repository from a list of all repositories in AccountA.

To create a role for repository access

1. Sign in to the AWS Management Console as an IAM user with permissions to create roles in AccountA.

2. Open the IAM console at https://console.aws.amazon.com/iam/.

3. In the navigation pane, choose **Policies**.

4. Choose **Create policy**.

5. Choose the **JSON** tab, and paste the following JSON policy document into the JSON text box. Replace *us-east-2* with the region for the repository, *111122223333* with the account ID for AccountA, and *MySharedDemoRepo* with the name for your AWS CodeCommit repository in AccountA:

```
{
"Version": "2012-10-17",
"Statement": [
    {
        "Effect": "Allow",
        "Action": [
            "codecommit:BatchGet*",
            "codecommit:Create*",
            "codecommit:DeleteBranch",
            "codecommit:Get*",
            "codecommit:List*",
            "codecommit:Describe*",
            "codecommit:Put*",
            "codecommit:Post*",
            "codecommit:Merge*",
            "codecommit:Test*",
            "codecommit:Update*",
            "codecommit:GitPull",
            "codecommit:GitPush"
```

```
20            ],
21            "Resource": [
22                "arn:aws:codecommit:us-east-2:111122223333:MySharedDemoRepo"
23            ]
24        }
25    ]
26 }
```

If you want users who assume this role to be able to view a list of repositories on the AWS CodeCommit console home page, add an additional statement to the policy, as follows:

```
1  {
2      "Version": "2012-10-17",
3      "Statement": [
4          {
5              "Effect": "Allow",
6              "Action": [
7                  "codecommit:BatchGet*",
8                  "codecommit:Create*",
9                  "codecommit:DeleteBranch",
10                 "codecommit:Get*",
11                 "codecommit:List*",
12                 "codecommit:Describe*",
13                 "codecommit:Put*",
14                 "codecommit:Post*",
15                 "codecommit:Merge*",
16                 "codecommit:Test*",
17                 "codecommit:Update*",
18                 "codecommit:GitPull",
19                 "codecommit:GitPush"
20             ],
21             "Resource": [
22                 "arn:aws:codecommit:us-east-2:111122223333:MySharedDemoRepo"
23             ]
24         },
25         {
26             "Effect": "Allow",
27             "Action": "codecommit:ListRepositories",
28             "Resource": "*"
29         }
30     ]
31 }
```

This access makes it easier for users who assume this role to find the repository to which they have access. They can choose the name of the repository from the list and be directed to the home page of the shared repository (Code). Users cannot access any of the other repositories they see in the list, but they can view the repositories in AccountA on the **Dashboard** page.

If you do not want to allow users who assume the role to be able to view a list of all repositories in AccountA, use the first policy example, but make sure that you send those users a direct link to the home page of the shared repository in the AWS CodeCommit console.

6. Choose **Review policy**. The policy validator reports syntax errors (for example, if you forget to replace the example AWS account ID and repository name with your AWS account ID and repository name).

7. On the **Review policy** page, type a name for the policy (for example, *CrossAccountAccessForMyShared-DemoRepo*). You can also provide an optional description for this policy. Choose **Create policy**.

Step 2: Create a Role for Repository Access in AccountA

After you have configured a policy, create a role that IAM users and groups in AccountB can assume, and attach the policy to that role.

To create a policy for repository access

1. In the IAM console, choose **Roles**.

2. Choose **Create role**.

3. Choose **Another AWS account**.

4. In **Account ID**, type the AWS account ID for AccountB (for example, *888888888888*). Choose **Next: Permissions**.

5. In **Attach permissions policies**, select the policy you created in the previous procedure (*CrossAccountAccessForMySharedDemoRepo*). Choose **Next: Review**.

6. In **Role name**, type a name for the role. For example, you could name this role *MyCrossAccountRepositoryContributorRole*. You can also type an optional description for the role to help others understand the purpose of the role.

7. Choose **Create role**.

8. Open the role you just created, and copy the role ARN (for example, `arn:aws:iam::111122223333:role/MyCrossAccountRepositoryContributorRole`). You need to provide this ARN to the AccountB administrator.

Cross Account Repository Access: Actions for the Administrator in AccountB

To allow users or groups in AccountB to access a repository in AccountA, the AccountB administrator must create a group in AccountB. This group must be configured with a policy that allows group members to assume the role created by the AccountA administrator.

The following sections provide steps and examples.

Topics

- Step 1: Create an IAM Group for Repository Access for AccountB Users
- Step 2: Create a Policy and Add Users to the IAM Group

Step 1: Create an IAM Group for Repository Access for AccountB Users

The simplest way to manage which IAM users in AccountB can access the AccountA repository is to create an IAM group in AccountB that has permission to assume the role in AccountA, and then add the IAM users to that group.

To create a group for cross-account repository access

1. Sign in to the AWS Management Console as an IAM user with the permissions required to create IAM groups and policies and manage IAM users in AccountB.

2. Open the IAM console at https://console.aws.amazon.com/iam/.

3. In the IAM console, choose **Groups**.

4. Choose **Create New Group**.

5. In **Group Name**, type a name for the group (for example, *DevelopersWithCrossAccountRepositoryAccess*). Choose **Next Step**.

6. In **Attach Policy**, choose **Next Step**. You create the cross-account policy in the next procedure. Finish creating the group.

Step 2: Create a Policy and Add Users to the IAM Group

Now that you have a group, create the policy that allows members of this group to assume the role that gives them access to the repository in AccountA. Then add to the group the IAM users in AccountB that you want to allow access in AccountA.

To create a policy for the group and add users to it

1. In the IAM console, choose **Groups**, and then choose the name of the group you just created (for example, *DevelopersWithCrossAccountRepositoryAccess*).

2. Choose the **Permissions** tab. Expand **Inline Policies**, and then choose the link to create an inline policy. (If you are configuring a group that already has an inline policy, choose **Create Group Policy**.)

3. Choose **Custom Policy**, and then choose **Select**.

4. In **Policy Name**, type a name for the policy (for example, *AccessPolicyForSharedRepository*).

5. In **Policy Document**, paste the following policy. In `Resource`, replace the ARN with the ARN of the policy created by the administrator in AccountA (for example, arn:aws:iam::*111122223333*:role/*MyCrossAccountRepositoryContributorRole*), and then choose **Apply Policy**. For more information about the policy created by the administrator in AccountA, see Step 1: Create a Policy for Repository Access in AccountA.

```
1 {
2   "Version": "2012-10-17",
3   "Statement": {
4     "Effect": "Allow",
5     "Action": "sts:AssumeRole",
6     "Resource": "arn:aws:iam::111122223333:role/MyCrossAccountRepositoryContributorRole"
7   }
8 }
```

6. Choose the **Users** tab. Choose **Add Users to Group**, and then add the AccountB IAM users. For example, you might add an IAM user with the user name *Saanvi_Sarkar* to the group. **Note**
Users in AccountB must have programmatic access, including an access key and secret key, to configure their local computers for access to the shared AWS CodeCommit repository. If you are creating IAM users, be sure to save the access key and secret key. To ensure the security of your AWS account, the secret access key is accessible only at the time you create it.

Cross-Account Repository Access: Actions for the Repository User in AccountB

To access the repository in AccountA, users in the AccountB group must configure their local computers for repository access. The following sections provide steps and examples.

Topics

- Step 1: Configure the AWS CLI and Git for an AccountB User to Access the Repository in AccountA
- Step 2: Clone and Access the AWS CodeCommit Repository in AccountA

Step 1: Configure the AWS CLI and Git for an AccountB User to Access the Repository in AccountA

You must use the credential helper, not SSH keys or Git credentials, to access repositories in another AWS account. AccountB users must configure their computers to use the credential helper to access the shared AWS CodeCommit repository in AccountA. You cannot use SSH keys or Git credentials to access repositories in another AWS account. However, you can continue to use SSH keys or Git credentials when accessing repositories in AccountB.

To configure the AWS CLI and Git for cross-account access

1. Install the AWS CLI on the local computer. For more information, see instructions for your operating system in Installing the AWS CLI.

2. Install Git on the local computer. To install Git, we recommend websites such as Git Downloads or Git for Windows.

   When you install Git, do not install the Git Credential Manager. The Git Credential Manager is not compatible with the credential helper included with the AWS CLI. **Note**
   AWS CodeCommit supports Git versions 1.7.9 and later. Git is an evolving, regularly updated platform. Occasionally, a feature change might affect the way it works with AWS CodeCommit. If you encounter issues with a specific version of Git and AWS CodeCommit, review the information in Troubleshooting.

3. From the terminal or command line, at the directory location where you want to clone the repository, run the git config --local user.name and git config --local user.email commands to set the user name and email for the commits you will make to the repository. For example:

```
1 git config --local user.name "Saanvi Sarkar"
2 git config --local user.email saanvi_sarkar@example.com
```

   These commands return nothing, but the email and user name you specify will be associated with the commits you make to the repository in AccountA.

4. Run the aws configure --profile command to configure a profile to use when connecting to the repository in AccountA. When prompted, provide the access key and secret key for your IAM user. For example, run the following command to create an AWS CLI profile named *MyCrossAccountAccessProfile* that you use to access a repository in AccountA in US East (Ohio) (us-east-2):

```
1 aws configure --profile MyCrossAccountAccessProfile
```

   When prompted, provide the following information:

```
1 AWS Access Key ID [None]: Your-IAM-User-Access-Key
2 AWS Secret Access Key ID [None]: Your-IAM-User-Secret-Access-Key
3 Default region name ID [None]: us-east-2
4 Default output format [None]: json
```

5. In a plain-text editor, open the `config` file, also known as the AWS CLI configuration file. Depending on your operating system, this file might be located at `~/.aws/config` on Linux, macOS, or Unix, or at *drive*:\Users*USERNAME*\\.aws\config on Windows.

6. In the file, find the entry that corresponds to the *MyCrossAccountAccessProfile* profile you just created. It should look similar to the following:

```
1 [profile MyCrossAccountAccessProfile]
2 region = US East (Ohio)
3 output = json
```

Add two lines to the profile configuration, `role_arn` and `source_profile`. Provide the ARN of the role in AccountA you will assume to access the repository in the other account, and the name of your IAM user in AccountB. For example:

```
1 [profile MyCrossAccountAccessProfile]
2 region = US East (Ohio)
3 role_arn = arn:aws:iam::111122223333:role/MyCrossAccountRepositoryContributorRole
4 source_profile = Saanvi_Sarkar
5 output = json
```

Save your changes, and close the plain-text editor.

7. Run the git config command twice: once to configure Git to use the AWS CLI credential helper with the AWS CLI profile you just created, and again to use HTTP. For example:

```
1 git config --global credential.helper "!aws codecommit credential-helper --profile
     MyCrossAccountAccessProfile $@"
```

```
1 git config --global credential.UseHttpPath true
```

8. Run the git config -l command to verify your configuration. A successful configuration contains lines similar to the following:

```
1 user.name=Saanvi Sarkar
2 user.email=saanvi_sarkar@example.com
3 credential.helper=!aws --profile MyCrossAccountAccessProfile codecommit credential-helper
     $@
4 credential.usehttppath=true
```

Note
If you see the following line in your configuration file, another credential manager is configured for your system, which can prevent the AWS CLI credential helper from working:

```
1 credential.helper=manager
```

To fix this problem, run the following command:

```
1 git config --system --unset credential.helper
```

Step 2: Clone and Access the AWS CodeCommit Repository in AccountA

Run git clone, git push, and git pull to clone, push to, and pull from, the cross-account AWS CodeCommit repository. You can also sign in to the AWS Management Console, switch roles, and use the AWS CodeCommit console to interact with the repository in the other account.

Note
Depending on how the IAM role was configured, you might be able to view repositories on the default page for AWS CodeCommit. If you cannot view the repositories, ask the repository administrator to email you a URL link to the **Code** page for that repository in the AWS CodeCommit console. The URL is similar to the following:

1 https://console.aws.amazon.com/codecommit/home?region=us-east-2#/repository/MySharedDemoRepo/
    browse/HEAD/--/
2 ```<a name="cross-account-clone-cross-account-repo"></a>
3
4 **To clone the cross\-account repository to your local computer**
5
6 1. At the command line or terminal, in the directory where you want to clone the repository, run
    the git clone command with the HTTPS clone URL\. For example:

git clone https://git-codecommit.us-east-2.amazonaws.com/v1/repos/MySharedDemoRepo

1
2 Unless you specify otherwise, the repository is cloned into a subdirectory with the same name as
    the repository\.
3
4 1. Change directories to the cloned repository, and either make a change to a file or add a file
    \. For example, you could add a file named *NewFile\.txt*\.
5
6 1. Add the file to the tracked changes for the local repo, commit the change, and push the file
    to the AWS CodeCommit repository\. For example:

git add NewFile.txt git commit -m "Added a file to test cross-account access to this repository" git push

1
2 For more information, see [Git with AWS CodeCommit Tutorial](getting-started.md)\.
3
4 Now that you've added a file, go to the AWS CodeCommit console to view your commit, review other
    users' changes to the repo, participate in pull requests, and more\.<a name="cross-account-
    console"></a>
5
6 **To access the cross\-account repository in the AWS CodeCommit console**
7
8 1. Sign in to the AWS Management Console in AccountB \(*888888888888*\) as the IAM user who has
    been granted cross\-account access to the repository in AccountA\.
9
10 1. Choose your user name on the navigation bar, and in the drop\-down list, choose **Switch Role
    **\.
11 **Note**
12 If this is the first time you have selected this option, review the information on the page, and
    then choose **Switch Role** again\.
13
14 1. On the **Switch Role** page, do the following:
15 + In **Account**, type the account ID for AccountA \(for example, *111122223333*\)\.
16 + In **Role**, type the name of the role you want to assume for access to the repository in
    AccountA \(for example, *MyCrossAccountRepositoryContributorRole*\)\.
17 + In **Display Name**, type a friendly name for this role\. This name appears in the console
    when you are assuming this role\. It also appears in the list of assumed roles the next time
    you want to switch roles in the console\.
18 + \(Optional\) In **Color**, choose a color label for the display name\.
19 + Choose **Switch Role**\.
20
21 For more information, see [Switching to a Role \(AWS Management Console\)](http://docs.aws.
    amazon.com/IAM/latest/UserGuide/id_roles_use_switch-role-console.html)\.
22
23 1. Open the AWS CodeCommit console at [https://console\.aws\.amazon\.com/codecommit](https://
    console.aws.amazon.com/codecommit)\.

If the assumed role has permission to view the names of repositories in AccountA, you see a list of repositories and an error message that informs you that you do not have permissions to view their status\. This is expected behavior\. Choose the name of the shared repository from the list\.

If the assumed role does not have permission to view the names of repositories in AccountA, you see an error message and a blank list with no repositories\. Paste the URL link to the repository or modify the console link and change `/list` to the name of the shared repository \(for example, `/MySharedDemoRepo`\)\.

1. In **Code**, find the name of the file you added from your local computer\. Choose it to browse the code in the file, and then browse the rest of the repository and start using its features\.

For more information, see [Getting Started with AWS CodeCommit Tutorial](getting-started-cc.md)\.

Delete an AWS CodeCommit Repository<a name="how-to-delete-repository"></a>

To delete an AWS CodeCommit repository, use the AWS CLI or the AWS CodeCommit console\.

Note
Deleting a repository does not delete any local copies of that repository \(local repos\)\. To delete a local repo, use your local machine's directory and file management tools\.

Topics
+ [Use the AWS CodeCommit Console to Delete a Repository](#how-to-delete-repository-console)
+ [Delete a Local Repo](#how-to-delete-repository-git)
+ [Use the AWS CLI to Delete an AWS CodeCommit Repository](#how-to-delete-repository-cli)

Use the AWS CodeCommit Console to Delete a Repository<a name="how-to-delete-repository-console"></a>

To use the AWS CodeCommit console to delete an AWS CodeCommit repository, follow these steps\.

Important
After you delete an AWS CodeCommit repository, you will no longer be able to clone it to any local repo or shared repo\. You will also no longer be able to pull data from it, or push data to it, from any local repo or shared repo\. This action cannot be undone\.

1. Open the AWS CodeCommit console at [https://console\.aws\.amazon\.com/codecommit](https://console.aws.amazon.com/codecommit)\.

1. In the list of repositories, choose the name of the repository you want to delete\.

1. In the navigation pane, choose **Settings**\.

1. In **General**, choose **Delete repository**\. In the box next to **Type the name of the repository to confirm deletion**, type the repository's name, and then choose **Delete**\. The repository is permanently deleted\.

62 **Note**
63 Deleting the repository in AWS CodeCommit does not delete any local repos\.

64

65 ## Delete a Local Repo<a name="how-to-delete-repository-git"></a>

66

67 Use your local machine's directory and file management tools to delete the directory that
contains the local repo\.

68

69 Deleting a local repo does not delete any AWS CodeCommit repository to which it might be
connected\.

70

71 ## Use the AWS CLI to Delete an AWS CodeCommit Repository<a name="how-to-delete-repository-cli
"></a>

72

73 To use AWS CLI commands with AWS CodeCommit, install the AWS CLI\. For more information, see [
Command Line Reference](cmd-ref.md)\.

74

75 To use the AWS CLI to delete an AWS CodeCommit repository, run the delete\-repository command,
specifying the name of the AWS CodeCommit repository to delete \(with the `--repository-name
` option\)\.

76

77 **Important**
78 After you delete an AWS CodeCommit repository, you will no longer be able to clone it to any
local repo or shared repo\. You will also no longer be able to pull data from it, or push
data to it, from any local repo or shared repo\. This action cannot be undone\.

79

80 **Tip**
81 To get the AWS CodeCommit repository's name, run the [list\-repositories](how-to-view-repository
-details.md#how-to-view-repository-details-no-name-cli) command\.

82

83 For example, to delete a repository named `MyDemoRepo`:

aws codecommit delete-repository --repository-name MyDemoRepo

1

2 If successful, the ID of the AWS CodeCommit repository that was permanently deleted will appear
in the output:

{ "repositoryId": "f7579e13-b83e-4027-aaef-650c0EXAMPLE" }

1

2 Deleting an AWS CodeCommit repository does not delete any local repos that may be connected to
it\.

3

4

5

6

7 # Working with Files in AWS CodeCommit Repositories<a name="files"></a>

8

9 In AWS CodeCommit, a file is a version\-controlled, self\-contained piece of information
available to you and other users of the repository and branch where the file is stored\. You
can organize your repository files with a directory structure, just as you would on a
computer\. Unlike your computer, AWS CodeCommit automatically tracks every change to a file
\. You can compare versions of a file, and store different versions of a file in different
repository branches\.

10

11 To add a file to a repository, or edit an existing file in a repository, you can use a Git client\. You can also use the AWS CodeCommit console, the AWS CLI, or the AWS CodeCommit API \.

12

13 ![\[A view of creating a file in the AWS CodeCommit console\]](http://docs.aws.amazon.com/codecommit/latest/userguide/images/codecommit-create-file.png)

14

15 For information about working with other aspects of your repository in AWS CodeCommit, see [Working with Repositories](repositories.md), [Working with Pull Requests](pull-requests.md), [Working with Branches](branches.md), [Working with Commits](commits.md), and [Working with User Preferences](user-preferences.md)\.

16

17 **Topics**

18 + [Browse Files in an AWS CodeCommit Repository](how-to-browse.md)

19 + [Create or Add a File to an AWS CodeCommit Repository](how-to-create-file.md)

20 + [Edit the Contents of a File in an AWS CodeCommit Repository](how-to-edit-file.md)

21

22

23

24

25 # Browse Files in an AWS CodeCommit Repository<a name="how-to-browse"></a>

26

27 After you connect to an AWS CodeCommit repository, you can clone it to a local repo or use the AWS CodeCommit console to browse its contents\. This topic provides instructions for browsing the content of an AWS CodeCommit repository by using the console\.

28

29 **Note**

30 For active AWS CodeCommit users, there is no charge for browsing code from the AWS CodeCommit console\. For information about when charges may apply, see [Pricing](http://aws.amazon.com/codecommit/pricing/)\.

31

32 ![\[A view of the contents of a file in the AWS CodeCommit console\]](http://docs.aws.amazon.com/codecommit/latest/userguide/images/codecommit-code-browse-file.png)

33

34 ## Browse an AWS CodeCommit Repository<a name="how-to-browse-console"></a>

35

36 You can use the AWS CodeCommit console to review the files contained in a repository or to quickly read the contents of a file\.

37

38 **To browse the content of a repository**

39

40 1. Open the AWS CodeCommit console at [https://console\.aws\.amazon\.com/codecommit](https://console.aws.amazon.com/codecommit)\.

41

42 1. On the **Dashboard** page, from the list of repositories, choose the repository you want to browse\.

43

44 1. In the **Code** view, browse the contents of the default branch for your repository\.

45

46   To change the view to a different branch or tag, choose the view selector button\. Either choose a branch or tag name from the drop\-down list, or in the filter box, type the name of the branch or tag, and then choose it from the list\.

47

48 1. Do one of the following:

49   + To view the contents of a directory, choose it from the list\. You can choose any of the
       directories in the navigation list to return to that directory view\. You can also use
       the up arrow at the top of the directory list\.
50   + To view the contents of a file, choose it from the list\. If the file is larger than the
       commit object limit, it cannot be displayed in the console and must be viewed in a local
       repo instead\. For more information, see [Limits](limits.md)\. To exit the file view,
       from the code navigation bar, choose the directory you want to view\.
51 **Note**
52 If you choose a binary file, a warning message appears, asking you to confirm that you want to
     display the contents\. To view the file, choose **Show file contents**\. If you do not want
     to view the file, from the code navigation bar, choose the directory you want to view\.
53 If you choose a markdown file \(\.md\), use the **Rendered Markdown** and **Markdown Source**
     buttons to toggle between the rendered and syntax views\.
54
55
56
57
58 # Create or Add a File to an AWS CodeCommit Repository<a name="how-to-create-file"></a>
59
60 You can use the AWS CodeCommit console, AWS CLI, or a Git client to add a file to a repository\.
     You can upload a file from your local computer to the repository, or you can use the code
     editor in the console to create the file\. The editor is a quick and easy way to add a
     simple file, such as a readme\.md file, to a branch in a repository\.
61
62 ![\[A view of uploading a file in the AWS CodeCommit console\]](http://docs.aws.amazon.com/
     codecommit/latest/userguide/images/codecommit-upload-file.png)
63
64 **Topics**
65 + [Create or Upload a File in the AWS CodeCommit Console](#how-to-create-file-console)
66 + [Add a File Using the AWS CLI](#how-to-create-file-cli)
67 + [Add a File Using Git](#how-to-edit-file-git)
68
69 ## Create or Upload a File in the AWS CodeCommit Console<a name="how-to-create-file-console"></a
     >
70
71 You can use the AWS CodeCommit console to create a file and add it to a branch in an AWS
     CodeCommit repository\. As part of creating the file, you can provide your user name and an
     email address\. You can also add a commit message so other users understand who added the
     file and why\. You can also upload a file directly from your local computer to a branch in a
     repository\.
72
73 **To add a file to a repository \(console\)**
74
75 1. Open the AWS CodeCommit console at [https://console\.aws\.amazon\.com/codecommit](https://
     console.aws.amazon.com/codecommit)\.
76
77 1. On the **Dashboard** page, from the list of repositories, choose the repository where you
     want to add a file\.
78
79 1. In the **Code** view, choose the branch where you want to add the file\. By default, the
     contents of the default branch are shown when you open the **Code** view\.
80
81   To change the view to a different branch, choose the view selector button\. Either choose a
       branch name from the drop\-down list, or in the filter box, type the name of the branch,

and then choose it from the list\.

82

83 1. Choose **Add file**, and then choose one of the following options:

84   + **Create file**, to use the code editor to create the contents of a file and add it to the repository\.

85   + **Upload file**, to upload a file from your local computer to the repository\.

86

87 1. Provide information to other users about who added this file to the repository and why\.

88   + In **Author name**, type your name\. This name is used as both the author name and the committer name in the commit information\. AWS CodeCommit defaults to using your IAM user name or a derivation of your console login as the author name\.

89   + In **Email address**, type an email address so that other repository users can contact you about this change\.

90   + In **Commit message**, type a brief description\.

91

92 1. Do one of the following:

93   + If you are uploading a file, choose the file from your local computer\.

94   + If you are creating a file, type the content you want to add in the code editor, and provide a name for the file\.

95

96 1. Choose **Commit file**\.

97

98 ## Add a File Using the AWS CLI<a name="how-to-create-file-cli"></a>

99

100 You can use the AWS CLI and the put\-file command to add a file in an AWS CodeCommit repository\. You can also use the put\-file command to add a directory or path structure for the file\.

101

102 **Note**

103 To use AWS CLI commands with AWS CodeCommit, install the AWS CLI\. For more information, see [Command Line Reference](cmd-ref.md)\.

104

105 **To add a file to a repository \(AWS CLI\)**

106

107 1. On your local computer, create the file you want to add to the AWS CodeCommit repository\.

108

109 1. At the terminal or command line, run the put\-file command, specifying:

110   + The repository where you want to add the file\.

111   + The branch where you want to add the file\.

112   + The full commit ID of the most recent commit made to that branch, also known as the tip or head commit\.

113   + The local location of the file\. The syntax used for this location varies depending on your local operating system\.

114   + The name of the file you want to add, including the path where the updated file is stored in the repository, if any\.

115   + The user name and email you want associated with this file\.

116   + A commit message that explains why you added this file\.

117

118 The user name, email address, and commit message are optional, but help other users know who made the change and why\. If you do not supply a user name, AWS CodeCommit defaults to using your IAM user name or a derivation of your console login as the author name\.

119

120 For example, to add a file named *ExampleSolution\.py* to a repository named *MyDemoRepo* to a branch named *feature\-randomizationfeature* whose most recent commit has an ID of *4

c925148EXAMPLE*:

aws codecommit put-file --repository-name MyDemoRepo --branch-name feature-randomizationfeature --file-content file://MyDirectory/ExampleSolution.py --file-path /solutions/ExampleSolution.py --parent-commit-id 4c925148EXAMPLE --name "María García" --email "maría_garcía@example.com" --commit-message "I added a third randomization routine."

1 **Note**
2 When you add binary files, make sure that you use `fileb://` to specify the local location of
    the file\.
3
4 If successful, this command returns output similar to the following:

  { "blobId": "2eb4af3bEXAMPLE", "commitId": "317f8570EXAMPLE", "treeId": "347a3408EXAMPLE" }

1
2 ## Add a File Using Git<a name="how-to-edit-file-git"></a>
3
4 You can add files in a local repo and push your changes to an AWS CodeCommit repository\. For
    more information, see [Git with AWS CodeCommit Tutorial](getting-started.md)\.
5
6
7
8
9 # Edit the Contents of a File in an AWS CodeCommit Repository<a name="how-to-edit-file"></a>
10
11 You can use the AWS CodeCommit console, AWS CLI, or a Git client to edit the contents of a file
    in an AWS CodeCommit repository\.
12
13 ![\[A view of editing a file in the AWS CodeCommit console\]](http://docs.aws.amazon.com/
    codecommit/latest/userguide/images/codecommit-edit-file.png)
14
15 **Topics**
16 + [Edit a File in the AWS CodeCommit Console](#how-to-edit-file-console)
17 + [Edit a File Using the AWS CLI](#how-to-edit-file-cli)
18 + [Edit a File Using Git](#how-to-edit-file-git)
19
20 ## Edit a File in the AWS CodeCommit Console<a name="how-to-edit-file-console"></a>
21
22 You can use the AWS CodeCommit console to edit a file that has been added to a branch in an AWS
    CodeCommit repository\. As part of editing the file, you can provide your user name and an
    email address\. You can also add a commit message so other users understand who made the
    change and why\.
23
24 **To edit a file in a repository \(console\)**
25
26 1. Open the AWS CodeCommit console at [https://console\.aws\.amazon\.com/codecommit](https://
    console.aws.amazon.com/codecommit)\.
27
28 1. On the **Dashboard** page, from the list of repositories, choose the repository you want to
    browse\.
29
30 1. In the **Code** view, choose the branch where you want to edit the file\. By default, the
    contents of the default branch are shown when you open the **Code** view\.
31

32 To change the view to a different branch, choose the view selector button\. Either choose a
   branch name from the drop\-down list, or in the filter box, type the name of the branch, and
   then choose it from the list\.

33

34 1. Navigate the contents of the branch and choose the file you want to edit\. In the file view,
   choose **Edit**\.

35 **Note**

36 If you choose a binary file, a warning message appears asking you to confirm that you want to
   display the contents\. You should not use the AWS CodeCommit console to edit binary files\.

37

38 1. Edit the file, and provide information to other users about who made this change and why\.

39 + In **Author name**, type your name\. This name is used as both the author name and the
   committer name in the commit information\. AWS CodeCommit defaults to using your IAM user
   name or a derivation of your console login as the author name\.

40 + In **Email address**, type an email address so that other repository users can contact you
   about this change\.

41 + In **Commit message**, type a brief description of your changes\.

42

43 1. Choose **Commit changes** to save your changes to the file and commit the changes to the
   repository\.

44

45 ## Edit a File Using the AWS CLI<a name="how-to-edit-file-cli"></a>

46

47 You can use the AWS CLI and the put\-file command to make changes to a file in an AWS CodeCommit
   repository\. You can also use the put\-file command to add a directory or path structure
   for the changed file, if you want to store the changed file in a location different from the
   original\.

48

49 **Note**

50 To use AWS CLI commands with AWS CodeCommit, install the AWS CLI\. For more information, see [
   Command Line Reference](cmd-ref.md)\.

51

52 **To edit a file in a repository \(AWS CLI\)**

53

54 1. Using a local copy of the file, make the changes you want to add to the AWS CodeCommit
   repository\.

55

56 1. At the terminal or command line, run the put\-file command, specifying:

57 + The repository where you want to add the edited file\.

58 + The branch where you want to add the edited file\.

59 + The full commit ID of the most recent commit made to that branch, also known as the tip or
   head commit\.

60 + The local location of the file\.

61 + The name of the updated file you want to add, including the path where the updated file is
   stored in the repository, if any\.

62 + The user name and email you want associated with this file change\.

63 + A commit message that explains the change you made\.

64

65 The user name, email address, and commit message are optional, but help other users know who
   made the change and why\. If you do not supply a user name, AWS CodeCommit defaults to using
   your IAM user name or a derivation of your console login as the author name\.

66

67 For example, to add edits made to a file named *ExampleSolution\.py* to a repository named *
   MyDemoRepo* to a branch named *feature\-randomizationfeature* whose most recent commit has

an ID of *4c925148EXAMPLE*:

aws codecommit put-file --repository-name MyDemoRepo --branch-name feature-randomizationfeature --file-content file://MyDirectory/ExampleSolution.py --file-path /solutions/ExampleSolution.py --parent-commit-id 4c925148EXAMPLE --name "María García" --email "maría_garcía@example.com" --commit-message "I fixed the bug Mary found."

1 **Note**
2 If you want to add a changed binary file, make sure to use `--file-content` with the notation `fileb://MyDirectory/MyFile.raw`\.
3
4 If successful, this command returns output similar to the following:

{ "blobId": "2eb4af3bEXAMPLE", "commitId": "317f8570EXAMPLE", "treeId": "347a3408EXAMPLE" }

1
2 ## Edit a File Using Git<a name="how-to-edit-file-git"></a>
3
4 You can edit files in a local repo and push your changes to an AWS CodeCommit repository\. For more information, see [Git with AWS CodeCommit Tutorial](getting-started.md)\.
5
6
7
8
9 # Working with Pull Requests in AWS CodeCommit Repositories<a name="pull-requests"></a>
10
11 A pull request is the primary way you and other repository users can review, comment on, and merge code changes from one branch to another\. You can use pull requests to collaboratively review code changes for minor changes or fixes, major feature additions, or new versions of your released software\. Here is one possible workflow for a pull request:
12
13 Li Juan, a developer working in a repo named MyDemoRepo, wants to work on a new feature for an upcoming version of a product\. To keep her work separate from production\-ready code, she creates a branch off of the default branch and names it *feature\-randomizationfeature*\. She writes code, makes commits, and pushes the new feature code into this branch\. She wants other repository users to review the code for quality before she merges her changes into the default branch\. To do this, she creates a pull request\. The pull request contains the comparison between her working branch and the branch of the code where she intends to merge her changes \(in this case, the default branch\)\. Other users review her code and changes, adding comments and suggestions\. She might update her working branch multiple times with code changes in response to comments\. Her changes are incorporated into the pull request every time she pushes them to that branch in AWS CodeCommit\. She might also incorporate changes that have been made in the intended destination branch while the pull request is open, so users can be sure they're reviewing all the proposed changes in context\. When she and her reviewers are satisfied, she merges her code and closes the pull request\.
14
15 ![\[Creating a pull request\]](http://docs.aws.amazon.com/codecommit/latest/userguide/images/codecommit-pull-request-create.png)
16
17 Pull requests require two branches: a source branch that contains the code you want reviewed, and a destination branch, where you merge the reviewed code\. The source branch contains the AFTER commit, which is the commit that contains the changes you want to merge into the destination branch\. The destination branch contains the BEFORE commit, which represents the "before" state of the code \(before the pull request branch is merged into the destination branch\)\.
18

19 ![\[The source and destination branches for a pull requests, showing the relationship between before and after commits\]](http://docs.aws.amazon.com/codecommit/latest/userguide/images/codecommit-pull-request-concepts.png)

20

21 The pull request displays the differences between these two branches, so users can view and comment on the changes\. You can update the pull request in response to comments by committing and pushing changes to the source branch\.

22

23 ![\[Adding a comment on a line in a pull request.\]](http://docs.aws.amazon.com/codecommit/latest/userguide/images/codecommit-pull-request-comment.png)

24

25 When your code has been reviewed, you can close the pull request in one of several ways:
26 + Merge the branches locally and push your changes\. This closes the request automatically\.
27 + Use the AWS CodeCommit console to either close the pull request without merging or, if there are no conflicts, to close and merge the branches\.
28 + Use the AWS CLI\.

29

30 Before you create a pull request:
31 + Create a branch that contains the code you want reviewed \(the source branch\)\.
32 + Commit and push the code you want reviewed to the source branch\.
33 + Set up notifications for your repository, so other users can be notified about the pull request and changes to it\. \(This step is optional, but recommended\.\)

34

35 Pull requests are more effective when you've set up IAM users for your repository users in your AWS account\. It's easier to distinguish which user made which comment\. IAM users also have the advantage of being able to use Git credentials for repository access\. For more information, see [Step 1: Initial Configuration for AWS CodeCommit](setting-up-gc.md#setting-up-gc-account)\. However, you can use pull requests with other kinds of users, including federated access users\.

36

37 For information about working with other aspects of your repository in AWS CodeCommit, see [Working with Repositories](repositories.md), [Working with Files](files.md), [Working with Commits](commits.md), [Working with Branches](branches.md), and [Working with User Preferences](user-preferences.md)\.

38

39 **Topics**
40 + [Create a Pull Request](how-to-create-pull-request.md)
41 + [View Pull Requests in an AWS CodeCommit Repository](how-to-view-pull-request.md)
42 + [Review a Pull Request](how-to-review-pull-request.md)
43 + [Update a Pull Request](how-to-update-pull-request.md)
44 + [Close a Pull Request in an AWS CodeCommit Repository](how-to-close-pull-request.md)

45

46

47

48

49 # Create a Pull Request<a name="how-to-create-pull-request"></a>

50

51 Creating pull requests helps other users see and review your code changes before you merge them into another branch\. First, you create a branch for your code changes\. This is referred to as the source branch for a pull request\. After you commit and push changes to the repository, you can create a pull request that compares the contents of that branch \(the source branch\) to the branch where you want to merge your changes after the pull request is closed \(the destination branch\)\.

52

53 You can use the AWS CodeCommit console or the AWS CLI to create pull requests for your
   repository\.

54

55 **Topics**
56 + [Use the AWS CodeCommit Console to Create a Pull Request](#how-to-create-pull-request-console)
57 + [Use the AWS CLI to Create a Pull Request](#how-to-create-pull-request-cli)

58

59 ## Use the AWS CodeCommit Console to Create a Pull Request<a name="how-to-create-pull-request-
   console"></a>

60

61 You can use the AWS CodeCommit console to create a pull request in an AWS CodeCommit repository
   \. If your repository is [configured with notifications](how-to-repository-email.md),
   subscribed users receive an email when you create a pull request\.

62

63 1. Open the AWS CodeCommit console at [https://console\.aws\.amazon\.com/codecommit](https://
   console.aws.amazon.com/codecommit)\.

64

65 1. In the list of repositories, choose the name of the repository\.

66

67 1. In the navigation pane, choose **Pull Requests**\.
68 **Tip**
69 You can also create pull requests from **Branches**, **Code**, or **Compare**\.

70

71 1. Choose **Create pull request**\.
72 ![\[Creating a pull request from the Pull Requests view in the AWS CodeCommit console.\]](http
   ://docs.aws.amazon.com/codecommit/latest/userguide/images/codecommit-pull-request-view.png)

73

74 1. In **Create pull request**, in **Source**, choose the branch that contains the changes you
   want reviewed\.

75

76 1. In **Destination**, review the branch where you intend to merge your code changes when the
   pull request is closed\. By default, the destination branch is preconfigured with the
   default branch of the repository, but you can choose a different branch\.

77

78 1. Choose **Compare**\. A comparison runs on the two branches, and the differences between them
   are displayed\. An analysis is also performed to determine whether the two branches can be
   merged automatically when the pull request is closed\.

79

80 1. Review the comparison details and the changes to be sure that the pull request contains the
   changes and commits you want reviewed\. If not, adjust your choices for source and
   destination branches, and choose **Compare** again\.

81

82 1. When you are satisfied with the comparison results for the pull request, in **Title**,
   provide a short but descriptive title for this review\. This is the title that appears in
   the list of pull requests for the repository\.

83

84 1. \(Optional\) In **Description**, provide details about this review and any other useful
   information for reviewers\.

85

86 1. Choose **Create**\.
87 ![\[Creating a pull request\]](http://docs.aws.amazon.com/codecommit/latest/userguide/images/
   codecommit-pull-request-create.png)

88

89 Your pull request appears in the list of pull requests for the repository\. If you [configured

notifications](how-to-repository-email.md), subscribers to the Amazon SNS topic receive an email to inform them of the newly created pull request\.

Use the AWS CLI to Create a Pull Request<a name="how-to-create-pull-request-cli"></a>

To use AWS CLI commands with AWS CodeCommit, install the AWS CLI\. For more information, see [Command Line Reference](cmd-ref.md)\.

To use the AWS CLI to create a pull request in an AWS CodeCommit repository:

1. Run the create\-pull\-request command, specifying:
+ The name of the pull request \(with the \-\-title option\)\.
+ The description of the pull request \(with the \-\-description option\)\.
+ A list of targets for the create\-pull\-request command, including:
   + The name of the AWS CodeCommit repository where the pull request is created \(with the repositoryName attribute\)\.
   + The name of the branch that contains the code changes you want reviewed, also known as the source branch \(with the sourceReference attribute\)\.
   + \(Optional\) The name of the branch where you intend to merge your code changes, also known as the destination branch, if you do not want to merge to the default branch \(with the destinationReference attribute\)\.
+ A unique, client\-generated idempotency token \(with the \-\-client\-request\-token option\)\.

For example, to create a pull request named *My Pull Request* with a description of *Please review these changes by Tuesday* that targets the *MyNewBranch* source branch and is to be merged to the default branch *master* in an AWS CodeCommit repository named `MyDemoRepo`:

aws codecommit create-pull-request --title "My Pull Request" --description "Please review these changes by Tuesday" --client-request-token 123Example --targets repositoryName=MyDemoRepo,sourceReference=MyNewBranch

1. If successful, this command produces output similar to the following:

{ "pullRequest": { "authorArn": "arn:aws:iam::111111111111:user/Jane_Doe", "clientRequestToken": "123Example", "creationDate": 1508962823.285, "description": "Please review these changes by Tuesday", "lastActivityDate": 1508962823.285, "pullRequestId": "42", "pullRequestStatus": "OPEN", "pullRequestTargets": [{ "destinationCommit": "5d036259EXAMPLE", "destinationReference": "refs/heads/master", "mergeMetadata": { "isMerged": false, }, "repositoryName": "MyDemoRepo", "sourceCommit": "317f8570EXAMPLE", "sourceReference": "refs/heads/MyNewBranch" }], "title": "My Pull Request" } }

View Pull Requests in an AWS CodeCommit Repository<a name="how-to-view-pull-request"></a>

You can use the AWS CodeCommit console or the the AWS CLI to view pull requests for your repository\. By default, you see only open pull requests, but you can change the filter to view all pull requests, only closed requests, only pull requests that you created, and more \.

Topics
+ [Use the AWS CodeCommit Console to View Pull Requests](#how-to-view-pull-request-console)
+ [Use the AWS CLI to View Pull Requests](#how-to-view-pull-request-cli)

Use the AWS CodeCommit Console to View Pull Requests<a name="how-to-view-pull-request-console"></a>

You can use the AWS CodeCommit console to view a list of pull requests in an AWS CodeCommit repository\. By changing the filter, you can change the list display to only show you a certain set of pull requests\. For example, you can view a list of pull requests you created with a status of **Open**, or you can choose a different filter and view pull requests you created with a status of **Closed**\.

1. Open the AWS CodeCommit console at [https://console\.aws\.amazon\.com/codecommit](https://console.aws.amazon.com/codecommit)\.

1. In the list of repositories, choose the name of the repository\.

1. In the navigation pane, choose **Pull Requests**\.

1. By default, a list of all open pull requests is displayed\. Pull requests are displayed in the order of most recent activity\.
![\[Open pull requests displayed in the AWS CodeCommit console.\]](http://docs.aws.amazon.com/codecommit/latest/userguide/images/codecommit-pull-request-view.png)

1. To display other pull requests, in **View**, choose the display filter that meets your needs:
+ **All open requests** \(default\): Displays all pull requests with a status of **Open**\.
+ **All requests**: Displays all pull requests\.
+ **All closed requests**: Displays all pull requests with a status of **Closed**\.
+ **All my requests**: Displays all pull requests that you created, regardless of the status\. It does not display reviews that you have commented on or otherwise participated in\.
+ **All my open requests**: Displays all pull requests that you created with a status of **Open**\.
+ **All my closed requests**: Displays all pull requests that you created with a status of **Closed**\.

1. When you find a pull request in the displayed list that you would like to view, choose it\.

Use the AWS CLI to View Pull Requests<a name="how-to-view-pull-request-cli"></a>

To use AWS CLI commands with AWS CodeCommit, install the AWS CLI\. For more information, see [Command Line Reference](cmd-ref.md)\.

To use the AWS CLI to view pull requests in an AWS CodeCommit repository, follow these steps\.

1. To view a list of pull requests in a repository, run the list\-pull\-requests command, specifying:
+ The name of the AWS CodeCommit repository where you want to view pull requests \(with the \-\-repository\-name option\)\.
+ \(Optional\) The status of the pull request \(with the \-\-pull\-request\-status option\)\.
+ \(Optional\) The Amazon Resource Name \(ARN\) of the IAM user who created the pull request \(with the \-\-author\-arn option\)\.
+ \(Optional\) An enumeration token that can be used to return batches of results \(with the \-\-next\-token option\)
+ \(Optional\) A limit on the number of returned results per request \(with the \-\-max\-results option\)\.

For example, to list pull requests created by an IAM user with the ARN *arn:aws:iam

::111111111111:user/Li_Juan* and the status of *CLOSED* in an AWS CodeCommit repository named `MyDemoRepo`:

aws codecommit list-pull-requests --author-arn arn:aws:iam::111111111111:user/Li_Juan --pull-request-status CLOSED --repository-name MyDemoRepo

1
2 If successful, this command produces output similar to the following:

{ "nextToken": "", "pullRequestIds": ["2","12","16","22","23","35","30","39","47"] }

1
2 Pull request IDs are displayed in the order of most recent activity\.
3
4 1. To view details of a pull request, run the get\-pull\-request command with the \-\-pull\-request\-id option, specifying the ID of the pull request\. For example, to view information about a pull request with the ID of *42*:

aws codecommit get-pull-request --pull-request-id 42

1
2 If successful, this command produces output similar to the following:

{ "pullRequest": { "authorArn": "arn:aws:iam::111111111111:user/Jane_Doe", "title": "Pronunciation difficulty analyzer" "pullRequestTargets": [{ "destinationReference": "refs/heads/master", "destinationCommit": "5d036259EXAMPLE", "sourceReference": "refs/heads/jane-branch" "sourceCommit": "317f8570EXAMPLE", "repositoryName": "MyDemoRepo", "mergeMetadata": { "isMerged": false, }, }], "lastActivityDate": 1508442444, "pullRequestId": "42", "clientRequestToken": "123Example", "pullRequestStatus": "OPEN", "creationDate": 1508962823, "description": "A code review of the new feature I just added to the service.", } }

1
2 1. To view events in a pull request, run the describe\-pull\-request\-events command with the \-\-pull\-request\-id option, specifying the ID of the pull request\. For example, to view the events for a pull request with the ID of *8*:

aws codecommit describe-pull-request-events --pull-request-id 8

1
2 If successful, this command produces output similar to the following:

{ "pullRequestEvents": [{ "pullRequestId": "8", "pullRequestEventType": "PULL_REQUEST_CREATED", "eventDate": 1510341779.53, "actor": "arn:aws:iam::111111111111:user/Zhang_Wei" }, { "pullRequestStatusChangedEventMetadata": { "pullRequestStatus": "CLOSED" }, "pullRequestId": "8", "pullRequestEventType": "PULL_REQUEST_STATUS_CHANGED", "eventDate": 1510341930.72, "actor": "arn:aws:iam::111111111111:user/Jane_Doe" }] }

1
2 1. To view whether there are any merge conflicts for a pull request, run the get\-merge\-conflicts command, specifying:
3 + The name of the AWS CodeCommit repository \(with the \-\-repository\-name option\)\.
4 + The branch, tag, HEAD, or other fully qualified reference for the source of the changes to use in the merge evaluation \(with the \-\-source\-commit\-specifier option\)\.
5 + The branch, tag, HEAD, or other fully qualified reference for the destination of the changes to use in the merge evaluation \(with the \-\-destination\-commit\-specifier option\)\.
6 + The merge option to use \(with the \-\-merge\-option option\)
7
8 For example, to view whether there are any merge conflicts between the tip of a source branch named *my\-feature\-branch* and a destination branch named *master* in a repository named `MyDemoRepo`:

```
aws codecommit get-merge-conflicts --repository-name MyDemoRepo --source-commit-specifier my-feature-branch
--destination-commit-specifier master --merge-option FAST_FORWARD_MERGE
```

If successful, this command returns output similar to the following:

```
{ "destinationCommitId": "fac04518EXAMPLE", "mergeable": false, "sourceCommitId": "16d097f03EXAMPLE"
}
```

Review a Pull Request<a name="how-to-review-pull-request"></a>

You can use the AWS CodeCommit console to review the changes included in a pull request\. You
    can add comments to the request, to the files, and to specific lines of code\. You can also
    reply to comments made by other users\. If your repository is [configured with notifications
    ](how-to-repository-email.md), you receive emails when users reply to your comments or when
    users comment on a pull request\.

You can use the AWS CLI to comment on a pull request and reply to comments\. To review the
    changes, you must use the git diff command or a diff tool\.

Topics
+ [Use the AWS CodeCommit Console to Review a Pull Request](#how-to-review-pull-request-console)
+ [Use the AWS CLI to Review Pull Requests](#how-to-review-pull-request-cli)

Use the AWS CodeCommit Console to Review a Pull Request<a name="how-to-review-pull-request-console"></a>

You can use the AWS CodeCommit console to review a pull request in an AWS CodeCommit repository
    \.

1. Open the AWS CodeCommit console at [https://console\.aws\.amazon\.com/codecommit](https://
    console.aws.amazon.com/codecommit)\.

1. In the list of repositories, choose the name of the repository\.

1. In the navigation pane, choose **Pull Requests**\.

1. By default, a list of all open pull requests is displayed\. Choose the open pull request you
    want to review\. You can also comment on a closed pull request\.
![\[Open pull requests displayed in the AWS CodeCommit console.\]](http://docs.aws.amazon.com/
    codecommit/latest/userguide/images/codecommit-pull-request-view.png)

1. In the pull request, choose **Changes**\.

1. Do one of the following:
+ To add a general comment, in **Comments on changes**, type a comment and then choose **Save
    **\. You can use [Markdown](https://docs.aws.amazon.com/general/latest/gr/aws-markdown.html)
    , or you can type your comment in plaintext\.
![\[A general comment on the changes in a pull request.\]](http://docs.aws.amazon.com/codecommit
    /latest/userguide/images/codecommit-commenting-changecomment.png)
+ To add a comment to a file in the commit, in **Changes**, find the name of the file\. Choose
    the comment bubble that appears next to the file name ![\[Image NOT FOUND\]](http://docs.aws
```

149
```

.amazon.com/codecommit/latest/userguide/images/codecommit-commentbubble.png), type a comment
, and then choose **Save**\.

34 ![\[Adding a comment on a file in a pull request.\]](http://docs.aws.amazon.com/codecommit/
latest/userguide/images/codecommit-commenting-addfilecomment.png)

35 + To add a comment to a changed line in the pull request, in **Changes**, go to the line you
want to comment on\. Choose the comment bubble ![\[Image NOT FOUND\]](http://docs.aws.amazon
.com/codecommit/latest/userguide/images/codecommit-commentbubble.png), type a comment, and
then choose **Save**\.

36 ![\[Adding a comment on a line in a pull request.\]](http://docs.aws.amazon.com/codecommit/
latest/userguide/images/codecommit-pull-request-comment.png)

37

38 1. To reply to comments on a commit, in **Changes** or **Activity**, choose **Reply**\.

39 ![\[Adding a reply to a comment in a pull request.\]](http://docs.aws.amazon.com/codecommit/
latest/userguide/images/codecommit-pull-request-reply-activity.png)

40

41 If [notifications](how-to-repository-email.md) are configured, the user who created the pull
request receives email about your comments\. You receive email if a user replies to your
comments or if the pull request is updated\.

42

43 ## Use the AWS CLI to Review Pull Requests<a name="how-to-review-pull-request-cli"></a>

44

45 To use AWS CLI commands with AWS CodeCommit, install the AWS CLI\. For more information, see [
Command Line Reference](cmd-ref.md)\.

46

47 To use the AWS CLI to review pull requests in an AWS CodeCommit repository:

48

49 1. To add a comment to a pull request in a repository, run the post\-comment\-for\-pull\-request
command, specifying:

50 + The ID of the pull request \(with the \-\-pull\-request\-id option\)\.

51 + The name of the repository that contains the pull request \(with the \-\-repository\-name
option\)\.

52 + The full commit ID of the commit in the destination branch where the pull request will be
merged \(with the \-\-before\-commit\-id option\)\.

53 + The full commit ID of the commit in the source branch that is the current tip of the branch
for the pull request when you post the comment \(with the \-\-after\-commit\-id option\)\.

54 + A unique, client\-generated idempotency token \(with the \-\-client\-request\-token option\)\.

55 + The content of your comment \(with the \-\-content option\)\.

56 + A list of location information about where to place the comment, including:

57 + The name of the file being compared, including its extension and subdirectory, if any \(with
the filePath attribute\)\.

58 + The line number of the change within a compared file \(with the filePosition attribute\)\.

59 + Whether the comment on the change is "before" or "after" in the comparison between the
source and destination branches \(with the relativeFileVersion attribute\)\.

60

61 For example, to add the comment *"These don't appear to be used anywhere\. Can we remove them?"*
on the change to the *ahs_count\.py* file in a pull request with the ID of *47* in a
repository named *MyDemoRepo*:

```
aws codecommit post-comment-for-pull-request --pull-request-id "47" --repository-name MyDemoRepo --before-commit-id 317f8570EXAMPLE --after-commit-id 5d036259EXAMPLE --client-request-token 123Example --content ""These don't appear to be used anywhere. Can we remove them?"" --location filePath=ahs_count.py,filePosition=367,relativeFileVersion=AFTER
```

1

2 If successful, this command produces output similar to the following:

{ "afterBlobId": "1f330709EXAMPLE", "afterCommitId": "5d036259EXAMPLE", "beforeBlobId": "80906a4cEXAMPLE", "beforeCommitId": "317f8570EXAMPLE", "comment": { "authorArn": "arn:aws:iam::111111111111:user/Saanvi_Sarkar", "clientRequestToken": "123Example", "commentId": "abcd1234EXAMPLEb5678efgh", "content": "These don't appear to be used anywhere. Can we remove them?", "creationDate": 1508369622.123, "deleted": false, "CommentId": "", "lastModifiedDate": 1508369622.123 } "location": { "filePath": "ahs_count.py", "filePosition": 367, "relativeFileVersion": "AFTER" }, "repositoryName": "MyDemoRepo", "pullRequestId": "47" }

```
1
2 1. To view comments for a pull request, run the get\-comments\-for\-pull\-request command,
     specifying:
3 + The AWS CodeCommit repository's name \(with the `--repository-name` option\)\.
4 + The full commit ID of the commit in the source branch that was the tip of the branch at the
     time the comment was made \(with the `--after-commit-id option`\)\.
5 + The full commit ID of the commit in the destination branch that was the tip of the branch at
     the time the pull request was created \(with the `--before-commit-id` option\)\.
6 + \(Optional\) An enumeration token to return the next batch of the results \(with the `--next-
     token` option\)\.
7 + \(Optional\) A non\-negative integer to limit the number of returned results \(with the `--max
     -results` option\)\.
8
9 For example, to view comments for a pull request in a repository named *MyDemoRepo*:
```

aws codecommit get-comments-for-pull-request --repository-name MyDemoRepo --before-commit-ID 317f8570EXAMPLE --after-commit-id 5d036259EXAMPLE

```
1
2 If successful, this command produces output similar to the following:
```

{ "commentsForPullRequestData": [{ "afterBlobId": "1f330709EXAMPLE", "afterCommitId": "5d036259EXAMPLE", "beforeBlobId": "80906a4cEXAMPLE", "beforeCommitId": "317f8570EXAMPLE", "comments": [{ "authorArn": "arn:aws:iam::111111111111:user/Saanvi_Sarkar", "clientRequestToken": "", "commentId": "abcd1234EXAMPLEb5678efgh", "content": "These don't appear to be used anywhere. Can we remove them?", "creationDate": 1508369622.123, "deleted": false, "lastModifiedDate": 1508369622.123 }, { "authorArn": "arn:aws:iam::111111111111:user/Li_Juan", "clientRequestToken": "", "commentId": "442b498bEXAMPLE5756813", "content": "Good catch. I'll remove them.", "creationDate": 1508369829.104, "deleted": false, "commentId": "abcd1234EXAMPLEb5678efgh", "lastModifiedDate": 150836912.273 }], "location": { "filePath": "ahs_count.py", "filePosition": 367, "relativeFileVersion": "AFTER" }, "repositoryName": "MyDemoRepo", "pullRequestId": "42" }], "nextToken": "exampleToken" }

```
1
2 1. To post a reply to a comment in a pull request, run the post\-comment\-reply command,
     specifying:
3 + The system\-generated ID of the comment to which you want to reply \(with the \-\-in\-reply\-
     to option\)\.
4 + A unique, client\-generated idempotency token \(with the \-\-client\-request\-token option\)\.
5 + The content of your reply \(with the \-\-content option\)\.
6
7  For example, to add the reply *"Good catch\. I'll remove them\."* to the comment with the
     system\-generated ID of *abcd1234EXAMPLEb5678efgh*:
```

aws codecommit post-comment-reply --in-reply-to abcd1234EXAMPLEb5678efgh --content "Good catch. I'll remove them." --client-request-token 123Example

```
1
2 If successful, this command produces output similar to the following:
```

{ "comment": { "authorArn": "arn:aws:iam::111111111111:user/Li_Juan", "clientRequestToken": "123Example", "commentId": "442b498bEXAMPLE5756813", "content": "Good catch. I'll remove them.", "creationDate": 1508369829.136, "deleted": false, "CommentId": "abcd1234EXAMPLEb5678efgh", "lastModifiedDate": 150836912.221 } }

1
2
3
4
5 # Update a Pull Request<a name="how-to-update-pull-request"></a>
6
7 You can use your local Git client to push commits to the source branch, which updates the pull request with code changes\. You might update the pull request with more commits because:
8 + You want users to review code changes you made to the source branch code in response to comments in the pull request\.
9 + One or more commits have been made to the destination branch since the pull request was created\. You want to incorporate those changes into the source branch as part of the review \(forward integration\)\. This changes the state of the pull request to **Mergeable** and enables the merging and closing of the pull request from the console\.
10
11 You can use the AWS CodeCommit console or the AWS CLI to update the title or description of a pull request\. You might want to update the pull request because:
12 + Other users don't understand the description, or the original title is misleading\.
13 + You want the title or description to reflect changes made to the source branch of an open pull request\.
14
15 **Topics**
16 + [Use Git to Update a Pull Request](#how-to-update-pull-request-git)
17 + [Use the AWS CodeCommit Console to Update a Pull Request](#how-to-update-pull-request-console)
18 + [Use the AWS CLI to Update Pull Requests](#how-to-update-pull-request-cli)
19
20 ## Use Git to Update a Pull Request<a name="how-to-update-pull-request-git"></a>
21
22 You can use Git to update the source branch of a pull request with changes to the code to:
23 + Add more code to the review\.
24 + Incorporate changes suggested in review comments\.
25 + Forward\-integrate changes to the destination branch in the source branch\.
26 + Make sure that all the changes to be merged into the destination branch have been reviewed in the pull request\.
27
28 You make the changes on your local computer, and then commit and push them to the source branch \. If [notifications are configured for the repository](how-to-repository-email.md), users subscribed to the topic receive emails when you push changes to the source branch of an open pull request\.
29
30 **To update the source branch with code changes**
31
32 1. From the local repo on your computer, at the terminal or command line, make sure you have pulled the latest changes to the repository, and then run the git checkout command, specifying the source branch of the pull request\. For example, to check out a source branch of a pull request named *pullrequestbranch*:

git checkout pullrequestbranch

1
2 1. Make any changes you want reviewed\. For example, if you want to change the code in the

source branch in responses to user comments, edit the files with those changes\. If you want to integrate changes that have been made to the destination branch into the source branch \(forward integration\), run the git merge command, specifying the destination branch, to merge those changes into the source branch\.

3 **Tip**

4 You might want to use diff tool or merge tool software to help view and choose the changes you want integrated into a source branch\.

5

6 1. After you have made your changes, run the git add and git commit commands to stage and commit them\.

7 **Tip**

8 You can run these commands separately, or you can use the `-a` option to add changed files to a commit automatically\. For example, you could run a command similar to the following:

git commit -am "This is an example commit message."

1

2 For more information, see [Basic Git Commands](how-to-basic-git.md) or consult your Git documentation\.

3

4 1. Run the **git push **command to push your changes to AWS CodeCommit\. Your pull request is updated with the changes you made to the source branch\.

5

6 ## Use the AWS CodeCommit Console to Update a Pull Request<a name="how-to-update-pull-request-console"></a>

7

8 You can use the AWS CodeCommit console to update the title and description of a pull request in an AWS CodeCommit repository\.

9

10 1. Open the AWS CodeCommit console at [https://console\.aws\.amazon\.com/codecommit](https://console.aws.amazon.com/codecommit)\.

11

12 1. In the list of repositories, choose the name of the repository\.

13

14 1. In the navigation pane, choose **Pull Requests**\.

15

16 1. By default, a list of all open pull requests is displayed\. Choose the open pull request you want to update\.

17 ![\[Open pull requests displayed in the AWS CodeCommit console.\]](http://docs.aws.amazon.com/codecommit/latest/userguide/images/codecommit-pull-request-view.png)

18

19 1. In the pull request, choose the option to edit the title or description\.

20

21 ## Use the AWS CLI to Update Pull Requests<a name="how-to-update-pull-request-cli"></a>

22

23 To use AWS CLI commands with AWS CodeCommit, install the AWS CLI\. For more information, see [Command Line Reference](cmd-ref.md)\.

24

25 To use the AWS CLI to update pull requests in an AWS CodeCommit repository:

26

27 1. To update the title of a pull request in a repository, run the update\-pull\-request\-title command, specifying:

28 + The ID of the pull request \(with the \-\-pull\-request\-id option\)\.

29 + The title of the pull request \(with the \-\-title option\)\.

30

31 For example, to update the title of a pull request with the ID of *47*:

aws codecommit update-pull-request-title --pull-request-id 47 --title "Consolidation of global variables - updated review"

1

2 If successful, this command produces output similar to the following:

{ "pullRequest": { "authorArn": "arn:aws:iam::111111111111:user/Li_Juan", "clientRequestToken": "", "creationDate": 1508530823.12, "description": "Review the latest changes and updates to the global variables. I have updated this request with some changes, including removing some unused variables.", "lastActivityDate": 1508372657.188, "pullRequestId": "47", "pullRequestStatus": "OPEN", "pullRequestTargets": [{ "destinationCommit": "9f31c968EXAMPLE", "destinationReference": "refs/heads/master", "mergeMetadata": { "isMerged": false, }, "repositoryName": "MyDemoRepo", "sourceCommit": "99132ab0EXAMPLE", "sourceReference": "refs/heads/variables-branch" }], "title": "Consolidation of global variables - updated review" } }

1

2 1. To update the description of a pull request, run the update\-pull\-request\-description command, specifying:
3 + The ID of the pull request \(with the \-\-pull\-request\-id option\)\.
4 + The description \(with the \-\-description option\)\.
5
6 For example, to update the description of a pull request with the ID of *47* :

aws codecommit update-pull-request-description --pull-request-id 47 --description "Updated the pull request to remove unused global variable."

1

2 If successful, this command produces output similar to the following:

{ "pullRequest": { "authorArn": "arn:aws:iam::111111111111:user/Li_Juan", "clientRequestToken": "", "creationDate": 1508530823.155, "description": "Updated the pull request to remove unused global variable.", "lastActivityDate": 1508372423.204, "pullRequestId": "47", "pullRequestStatus": "OPEN", "pullRequestTargets": [{ "destinationCommit": "9f31c968EXAMPLE", "destinationReference": "refs/heads/master", "mergeMetadata": { "isMerged": false, }, "repositoryName": "MyDemoRepo", "sourceCommit": "99132ab0EXAMPLE", "sourceReference": "refs/heads/variables-branch" }], "title": "Consolidation of global variables" } }

1
2
3
4
5 # Close a Pull Request in an AWS CodeCommit Repository<a name="how-to-close-pull-request"></a>
6
7 When you're satisfied that your code has been reviewed, you can close a pull request in one of several ways:
8 + <a name="why-git-merge"></a>On your local computer, you can use the git merge command to merge the source branch into the destination branch, and then push your merged code to the destination branch\. This closes the pull request automatically\. The git merge command also allows you to choose the merge option or strategy you use for the merge\. This is the only option available to merge the branches if the pull request status shows **Resolve conflicts **\. To learn more about git merge and merge options, see [git\-merge](https://git-scm.com/docs/git-merge) or your Git documentation\.
9 + In the console, you can close a pull request without merging the code\. You might want to do this if you want to use the git merge command to merge the branches manually, or if the code in the pull request source branch isn't code you want merged into the destination branch\. This is the only option available if the code cannot be merged automatically\. You see an

advisory message to resolve conflicts, which you must do on your local computer with the git merge command or a diff or merge tool\.

10 + <a name="is-mergable"></a>In the console, you might be able to merge your source branch to the destination branch automatically, which closes the pull request automatically\. You see an advisory message that the pull request is mergeable, and the **Merge** button in the pull request is active\. When you choose **Merge**, the merge is performed using the fast\-forward merge option\.

11 **Note**

12 The fast\-forward option does not create a commit or commit message for the merge\. If you want a merge commit to appear in the history of the destination branch, you can choose not to automatically merge the code as part of closing the pull request\. Instead, you can manually merge the branches using the git merge command with a different merge option\.

13 + AWS CodeCommit closes a pull request automatically if either the source or destination branch of the pull request is deleted\.

14 + In the AWS CLI, you can update the status of a pull request from `OPEN` to `CLOSED`\. This closes the pull request\. You can also use the AWS CLI to attempt to merge and close the pull request\.

15

16 **Topics**

17 + [Use the AWS CodeCommit Console to Close a Pull Request](#how-to-close-pull-request-console)

18 + [Use the AWS CLI to Close Pull Requests](#how-to-close-pull-request-cli)

19

20 ## Use the AWS CodeCommit Console to Close a Pull Request<a name="how-to-close-pull-request-console"></a>

21

22 You can use the AWS CodeCommit console to close a pull request in an AWS CodeCommit repository\. After the status of a pull request is changed to **Closed**, it cannot be changed back to **Open**, but users can still comment on the changes and reply to comments\.

23

24 1. Open the AWS CodeCommit console at [https://console\.aws\.amazon\.com/codecommit](https://console.aws.amazon.com/codecommit)\.

25

26 1. In the list of repositories, choose the name of the repository\.

27

28 1. In the navigation pane, choose **Pull Requests**\.

29

30 1. By default, a list of all open pull requests is displayed\. Choose the open pull request you would like to close\.

31 ![\[Open pull requests displayed in the AWS CodeCommit console.\]](http://docs.aws.amazon.com/codecommit/latest/userguide/images/codecommit-pull-request-view.png)

32

33 1. In the pull request, choose one of the following:

34 + **Merge**: This option, if available, closes the pull request and attempts to merge the code into the destination branch using the fast\-forward merge option\. You can also optionally select the option to automatically delete the pull request source branch after the merge is successful\. If the merge attempt is not successful, the source branch is not deleted\.

35 **Note**

36 The **Merge** option is available only if there are no merge conflicts detected between the source and destination branches\.

37 + **Close pull request**: This option closes the pull request without attempting to merge the source branch into the destination branch\. This option does not provide a way to delete the source branch as part of closing the pull request, but you can do it yourself after the request is closed\.

38

39 ## Use the AWS CLI to Close Pull Requests<a name="how-to-close-pull-request-cli"></a>

40

41 To use AWS CLI commands with AWS CodeCommit, install the AWS CLI\. For more information, see [
   Command Line Reference](cmd-ref.md)\.

42

43 To use the AWS CLI to close pull requests in an AWS CodeCommit repository:

44

45 1. To update the status of a pull request in a repository from `OPEN` to `CLOSED`, run the
   update\-pull\-request\-status command, specifying:

46 + The ID of the pull request \(with the \-\-pull\-request\-id option\)\.

47 + The status of the pull request \(with the \-\-pull\-request\-status option\)\.

48

49 For example, to update the status of a pull request with the ID of *42* to a status of *CLOSED*
   in an AWS CodeCommit repository named `MyDemoRepo`:

1

2 aws codecommit update-pull-request-status --pull-request-id 42 --pull-request-status CLOSED

1

2 If successful, this command produces output similar to the following:

{ "pullRequest": { "authorArn": "arn:aws:iam::111111111111:user/Jane_Doe", "clientRequestToken": "123Example", "creationDate": 1508962823.165, "description": "A code review of the new feature I just added to the service.", "lastActivityDate": 1508442444.12, "pullRequestId": "42", "pullRequestStatus": "CLOSED", "pullRequestTargets": [{ "destinationCommit": "5d036259EXAMPLE", "destinationReference": "refs/heads/master", "mergeMetadata": { "isMerged": false, }, "repositoryName": "MyDemoRepo", "sourceCommit": "317f8570EXAMPLE", "sourceReference": "refs/heads/jane-branch" }], "title": "Pronunciation difficulty analyzer" } }

1

2 1. To merge and close a pull request, run the merge\-pull\-request\-by\-fast\-forward command,
   specifying:

3 + The ID of the pull request \(with the \-\-pull\-request\-id option\)\.

4 + The full commit ID of the tip of the source branch \(with the \-\-source\-commit\-id option\)
   \.

5 + The name of the repository \(with the \-\-repository\-name option\)\.

6

7 For example, to merge and close a pull request with the ID of *47* and a source commit ID of
   99132ab0EXAMPLE in a repository named *MyDemoRepo*:

1

2 aws codecommit merge-pull-request-by-fast-forward --pull-request-id 47 --source-commit-id 99132ab0EXAMPLE
--repository-name MyDemoRepo

1

2 If successful, this command produces output similar to the following:

{ "pullRequest": { "authorArn": "arn:aws:iam::111111111111:user/Li_Juan", "clientRequestToken": "", "creationDate": 1508530823.142, "description": "Review the latest changes and updates to the global variables", "lastActivityDate": 1508887223.155, "pullRequestId": "47", "pullRequestStatus": "CLOSED", "pullRequestTargets": [{ "destinationCommit": "9f31c968EXAMPLE", "destinationReference": "refs/heads/master", "mergeMetadata": { "isMerged": true, "mergedBy": "arn:aws:iam::111111111111:user/Mary_Major" }, "repositoryName": "MyDemoRepo", "sourceCommit": "99132ab0EXAMPLE", "sourceReference": "refs/heads/variables-branch" }], "title": "Consolidation of global variables" } }

1

2

3

4

5 # Working with Commits in AWS CodeCommit Repositories<a name="commits"></a>

6

7 Commits to a repository are snapshots of the contents and changes to the contents of your repository\. Every time a user commits and pushes a change, that information is saved and stored\. So, too, is information that includes who committed the change, the date and time of the commit, and the changes made as part of the commit\. You can also add tags to commits, to easily identify specific commits\. In AWS CodeCommit, you can:

8 + Review commits\.

9 + View the history of commits in a graph\.

10 + Compare a commit to its parent or to another specifier\.

11 + Add comments to your commits and reply to comments made by others\.

12

13 ![\[Adding a comment to a changed line in a commit.\]](http://docs.aws.amazon.com/codecommit/latest/userguide/images/codecommit-commenting-savelinecomment.png)

14

15 Before you can push commits to an AWS CodeCommit repository, you must set up your local computer to connect to the repository\. For the simplest method, see [For HTTPS Users Using Git Credentials](setting-up-gc.md)\.

16

17 For information about working with other aspects of your repository in AWS CodeCommit, see [Working with Repositories](repositories.md), [Working with Files](files.md), [Working with Pull Requests](pull-requests.md) , [Working with Branches](branches.md), and [Working with User Preferences](user-preferences.md)\.

18

19 **Topics**

20 + [Create a Commit in AWS CodeCommit](how-to-create-commit.md)

21 + [View Commit Details in AWS CodeCommit](how-to-view-commit-details.md)

22 + [Compare Commits in AWS CodeCommit](how-to-compare-commits.md)

23 + [Comment on a Commit in AWS CodeCommit](how-to-commit-comment.md)

24 + [Create a Tag in AWS CodeCommit](how-to-create-tag.md)

25 + [View Tag Details in AWS CodeCommit](how-to-view-tag-details.md)

26 + [Delete a Tag in AWS CodeCommit](how-to-delete-tag.md)

27

28

29

30

31 # Create a Commit in AWS CodeCommit<a name="how-to-create-commit"></a>

32

33 Follow these steps to use Git to create a commit in a local repo\. If the local repo is connected to an AWS CodeCommit repository, you use Git to push the commit from the local repo to the AWS CodeCommit repository\.

34

35 1. Complete the prerequisites, including [Setting Up](setting-up.md)\.

36 **Important**

37 If you have not completed setup, you will not be able to connect or commit to the repository\.

38

39 1. Make sure you are creating a commit in the desired branch\. To see a list of available branches and find out which branch you are currently set to use, run git branch\. All branches will be displayed\. An asterisk \(`*`\) will appear next to your current branch\. To switch to a different branch, run git checkout *branch\-name*\.

40

41 1. Make a change to the branch \(such as adding, modifying, or deleting a file\)\.

42

43 For example, in the local repo, create a file named `bird.txt` with the following text:

bird.txt

Birds (class Aves or clade Avialae) are feathered, winged, two-legged, warm-blooded, egg-laying vertebrates.

1
2 1. Run git status, which should indicate that `bird.txt` has not yet been included in any
   pending commit:

...

Untracked files: (use "git add ..." to include in what will be committed)

1   bird.txt

1
2 1. Run git add bird\.txt to include the new file in the pending commit\.

3
4 1. If you run git status again, you should see output similar to the following\. It indicates
   that `bird.txt` is now part of the pending commit or staged for commit:

... Changes to be committed: (use "git reset HEAD ..." to unstage)

1   new file: bird.txt

1
2 1. To finalize the commit, run git commit with the `-m` option \(for example, git commit \-m "*
   Adding bird\.txt to the repository\.*"\) The `-m` option creates the commit message\.

3
4 1. If you run git status again, you should see output similar to the following\. It indicates
   that the commit is ready to be pushed from the local repo to the AWS CodeCommit repository:

...

nothing to commit, working directory clean

1
2 1. Before you push the finalized commit from the local repo to the AWS CodeCommit repository,
   you can see what will be pushed by running git diff \-\-stat *remote\-name*/*branch\-name*,
   where *remote\-name* is the nickname the local repo uses for the AWS CodeCommit repository
   and *branch\-name* is the name of the branch to compare\.
3 **Tip**
4 To get the nickname, run git remote\. To get a list of branch names, run git branch\. An
   asterisk \(`*`\) will appear next to the current branch\. You can also run git status to get
   the current branch name\.
5 **Note**
6 If you cloned the repository, from the local repo's perspective, *remote\-name* is not the name
   of the AWS CodeCommit repository\. When you clone a repository, *remote\-name* is set
   automatically to `origin`\.

7
8 For example, git diff \-\-stat origin/master would show output similar to the following:

bird.txt | 1 + 1 file changed, 1 insertion(+)

1
2 Of course, the output assumes you have already connected the local repo to the AWS CodeCommit
   repository\. \(For instructions, see [Connect to a Repository](how-to-connect.md)\.\)

3
4 1. When you're ready to push the commit from the local repo to the AWS CodeCommit repository,
   run git push *remote\-name* *branch\-name*, where *remote\-name* is the nickname the local
   repo uses for the AWS CodeCommit repository and *branch\-name* is the name of the branch to
   push to the AWS CodeCommit repository\.

For example, running git push origin master would show output similar to the following:

For HTTPS:

Counting objects: 7, done. Delta compression using up to 4 threads. Compressing objects: 100% (4/4), done. Writing objects: 100% (5/5), 516 bytes | 0 bytes/s, done. Total 5 (delta 2), reused 0 (delta 0) remote: To https://git-codecommit.us-east-2.amazonaws.com/v1/repos/MyDemoRepo b9e7aa6..3dbf4dd master -> master

For SSH:

Counting objects: 7, done. Delta compression using up to 4 threads. Compressing objects: 100% (4/4), done. Writing objects: 100% (5/5), 516 bytes | 0 bytes/s, done. Total 5 (delta 2), reused 0 (delta 0) remote: To ssh://git-codecommit.us-east-2.amazonaws.com/v1/repos/MyDemoRepo b9e7aa6..3dbf4dd master -> master

Tip

If you add the `-u` option to git push \(for example, git push \-u origin master\), then you only need to run git push in the future because upstream tracking information has been set\. To get upstream tracking information, run git remote show *remote\-name* \(for example, git remote show origin\)\.

For more options, see your Git documentation\.

View Commit Details in AWS CodeCommit<a name="how-to-view-commit-details"></a>

You can use the AWS CodeCommit console to browse the history of commits in a repository\. This can help you identify changes made in a repository, including:
+ When and by whom the changes were made\.
+ When specific commits were merged into a particular branch\.

Viewing the history of commits for a branch might also help you understand the difference between branches\. If you use tagging, you can also quickly view the commit that was labeled with a specific tag and the parents of that tagged commit\. At the command line, you can use Git to view details about the commits in a local repo or an AWS CodeCommit repository\.

Browse Commits in a Repository<a name="how-to-view-commit-details-console"></a>

You can use the AWS CodeCommit console to browse the history of commits to a repository\. You can also view a graph of the commits in the repository and its branches over time\. This can help you understand the history of the repository, including when changes were made\.

Note

Using the git rebase command to rebase a repository changes the history of a repository, which might cause commits to appear out of order\. For more information, see [Git Branching\-Rebasing](https://git-scm.com/book/en/v2/Git-Branching-Rebasing) or your Git documentation\.

Topics
+ [Browse the Commit History of a Repository](#how-to-view-commit-details-console-history)
+ [View a Graph of the Commit History of a Repository](#how-to-view-commit-details-console-visualizer)

28 ### Browse the Commit History of a Repository<a name="how-to-view-commit-details-console-history
   "></a>

29

30 You can browse the commit history for a specific branch or tag of the repository, including
   information about the committer and the commit message\. You can also view the code for a
   specific commit\.

31

32 **To browse the history of commits \(console\)**

33

34 1. Open the AWS CodeCommit console at [https://console\.aws\.amazon\.com/codecommit](https://
   console.aws.amazon.com/codecommit)\.

35

36 1. On the **Dashboard** page, from the list of repositories, choose the repository for which you
   want to review the commit history\.

37

38 1. In the navigation pane, choose **Commits**\. In the commit history view, a history of commits
   for the repository in the default branch is displayed, in reverse chronological order of
   the commit date\. Date and time are in coordinated universal time \(UTC\)\. You can view the
   commit history of a different branch by choosing the view selector button and then choosing
   a branch from the list\. If you are using tags in your repository, you can view a commit
   with a specific tag and its parents by choosing that tag in the view selector button\.

39 ![\[The commit history view in the console\]](http://docs.aws.amazon.com/codecommit/latest/
   userguide/images/codecommit-code-history.png)![\[The commit history view in the console\]](
   http://docs.aws.amazon.com/codecommit/latest/userguide/)

40

41 1. To view the difference between a commit and its parent, and to see any comments on the
   changes, choose the abbreviated commit ID\. For more information, see [Compare a Commit to
   Its Parent](how-to-compare-commits.md#how-to-compare-commits-parent) and [Comment on a
   Commit](how-to-commit-comment.md)\. To view the difference between a commit and any other
   commit specifier, including a branch, tag, or commit ID, see [Compare Any Two Commit
   Specifiers](how-to-compare-commits.md#how-to-compare-commits-compare)\.

42

43 1. Do one or more of the following:
44 + To view the date and time a change was made, hover over the days or months ago description\.
45 + To view the email associated with the author, hover over the user name\.
46 + To view the full commit ID, copy and then paste it into a text editor or other location\. To
   copy it, choose the copy icon\.
47 + To view the code as it was at the time of a commit, choose the code icon \(**< / >**\) for the
   commit\. The contents of the repository as they were at the time of that commit is
   displayed in the **Code** view\. The view selector button displays the abbreviated commit ID
   instead of a branch or tag\.
48 + If the full commit subject is too long to fit in the initial view, choose the arrow next to
   the message\. The commit message box expands to display up to 5,000 characters of the
   subject and message\.
49 + To collapse the list of commits for a particular date, choose the arrow next to that date\.
50
51 ### View a Graph of the Commit History of a Repository<a name="how-to-view-commit-details-
   console-visualizer"></a>

52

53 You can view a graph of the commits made to a repository\. The **Commit Visualizer** view is a
   directed acyclic graph \(DAG\) representation of all the commits made to a branch of the
   repository\. This graphical representation can help you understand when commits and
   associated features were added or merged\. It can also help you pinpoint when a change was
   made in relation to other changes\.

Note

Commits that are merged using the fast\-forward method do not appear as separate lines in the graph of commits\.

To view a graph of commits \(console\)

1. Open the AWS CodeCommit console at [https://console\.aws\.amazon\.com/codecommit](https://console.aws.amazon.com/codecommit)\.

1. On the **Dashboard** page, from the list of repositories, choose the repository for which you want to view a commit graph\.

1. In the navigation pane, choose **Visualizer**\.
![\[A graphical view of a repository in the console\]](http://docs.aws.amazon.com/codecommit/latest/userguide/images/codecommit-cv-simple1.png)![\[A graphical view of a repository in the console\]](http://docs.aws.amazon.com/codecommit/latest/userguide/)

In the commit graph, the subject for each commit message appears next to that point in the graph\. You can use the direction buttons to change which side of the graph shows branches\.
Note
The graph can display up to 35 branches on a page\. If there are more than 35 branches, the graph is too complex to display\. You can simplify the view in two ways:
By using the view selector button to show the graph for a specific branch\.
By pasting a full commit ID into the search box to render the graph from that commit\.

1. To see more details about a commit point, choose the point in the graph\.
![\[A detail view of a commit point\]](http://docs.aws.amazon.com/codecommit/latest/userguide/images/codecommit-cv-simple1-detail.png)![\[A detail view of a commit point\]](http://docs.aws.amazon.com/codecommit/latest/userguide/)

The detail view shows:
+ The date of the commit\.
+ The name of the author\.
+ The subject and contents of the commit message \(up to 200 characters\)\.
+ The full commit ID\.
+ The commit IDs of any parents of the commit\.

If the commit is a merge made by any method other than fast\-forward, multiple parent IDs are displayed\. To copy a commit ID, choose the copy icon next to that ID\.

1. To render a new graph from a commit, choose the commit ID in the detail view\. The view selector button changes to the abbreviated commit ID\.
![\[A new graph rendered from a specific commit\]](http://docs.aws.amazon.com/codecommit/latest/userguide/images/codecommit-cv-commit.png)![\[A new graph rendered from a specific commit\]](http://docs.aws.amazon.com/codecommit/latest/userguide/)

Use the AWS CLI to View Commit Details<a name="how-to-view-commit-details-cli"></a>

Git lets you view details about commits\. You can also use the AWS CLI to view details about the commits in a local repo or in an AWS CodeCommit repository, by running the following commands:
+ [aws codecommit get\-commit](#how-to-view-commit-details-cli-commit), to view information about a commit\.

92 + [aws codecommit get\-differences](#how-to-view-commit-details-cli-differences), to view
     information about changes for a commit specifier \(branch, tag, HEAD, or other fully
     qualified references, such as commit IDs\)\.
93 + [aws codecommit get\-blob](#how-to-view-commit-details-cli-blob), to view the base64\-encoded
     content of an individual Git blob object in a repository\.
94
95 ### To view information about a commit<a name="how-to-view-commit-details-cli-commit"></a>
96
97 1. Run the aws codecommit get\-commit command, specifying:
98 + The AWS CodeCommit repository's name \(with the `--repository-name` option\)\.
99 + The full commit ID\.
100
101 For example, to view information about a commit with the ID `317f8570EXAMPLE` in an AWS
     CodeCommit repository named `MyDemoRepo`:

aws codecommit get-commit --repository-name MyDemoRepo --commit-id 317f8570EXAMPLE

1
2 1. If successful, the output of this command includes the following:
3 + Information about the author of the commit \(as configured in Git\), including the date in
     time stamp format and the coordinated universal time \(UTC\) offset\.
4 + Information about the committer \(as configured in Git\) including the date in time stamp
     format and the UTC offset\.
5 + The ID of the Git tree where the commit exists\.
6 + The commit ID of the parent commit\.
7 + The commit message\.
8
9 Here is some example output, based on the preceding example command:

{ "commit": { "additionalData": "", "committer": { "date": "1484167798 -0800", "name": "Mary Major",
"email": "mary_major@example.com" }, "author": { "date": "1484167798 -0800", "name": "Mary Major",
"email": "mary_major@example.com" }, "treeId": "347a3408EXAMPLE", "parents": ["4c925148EXAMPLE"],
"message": "Fix incorrect variable name" } }

1
2 ### To view information about the changes for a commit specifier<a name="how-to-view-commit-
     details-cli-differences"></a>
3
4 1. Run the aws codecommit get\-differences command, specifying:
5 + The name of the AWS CodeCommit repository \(with the `--repository-name` option\)\.
6 + The commit specifiers you want to get information about\. Only `--after-commit-specifier` is
     required\. If you do not specify `--before-commit-specifier`, all files current as of the
     `--after-commit-specifier` will be shown\.
7
8 For example, to view information about the differences between commits with the IDs `317
     f8570EXAMPLE` and `4c925148EXAMPLE` in an AWS CodeCommit repository named `MyDemoRepo`:

aws codecommit get-differences --repository-name MyDemoRepo --before-commit-specifier 317f8570EXAMPLE
--after-commit-specifier 4c925148EXAMPLE

1
2 1. If successful, the output of this command includes the following:
3 + A list of differences, including the change type \(A for added, D for deleted, or M for
     modified\)\.
4 + The mode of the file change type\.
5 + The ID of the Git blob object that contains the change\.

6

7 Here is some example output, based on the preceding example command:

{ "differences": [{ "afterBlob": { "path": "blob.txt", "blobId": "2eb4af3bEXAMPLE", "mode": "100644" }, "changeType": "M", "beforeBlob": { "path": "blob.txt", "blobId": "bf7fcf28fEXAMPLE", "mode": "100644" } }] }

1

2 ### To view information about a Git blob object<a name="how-to-view-commit-details-cli-blob"></a
    >

3

4 1. Run the aws codecommit get\-blob command, specifying:
5 + The name of the AWS CodeCommit repository \(with the `--repository-name` option\)\.
6 + The ID of the Git blob \(with the `--blob-id `option\)\.

7

8 For example, to view information about a Git blob with the ID of `2eb4af3bEXAMPLE` in an AWS
    CodeCommit repository named `MyDemoRepo`:

aws codecommit get-blob --repository-name MyDemoRepo --blob-id 2eb4af3bEXAMPLE

1

2 1. If successful, the output of this command includes the following:
3 + The base64\-encoded content of the blob, usually a file\.

4

5 For example, the output of the previous command might be similar to the following:

{ "content": "QSBCaW5hcnkgTGFyToEXAMPLE=" }

1

2 ## Use Git to View Commit Details<a name="how-to-view-commit-details-git"></a>

3

4 Before you follow these steps, you should have already connected the local repo to the AWS
    CodeCommit repository and committed changes\. For instructions, see [Connect to a Repository
    ](how-to-connect.md)\.

5

6 To show the changes for the most recent commit to a repository, run the git show command\.

git show

1

2 The command produces output similar to the following:

commit 4f8c6f9d Author: Mary Major mary.major@example.com Date: Mon May 23 15:56:48 2016 -0700

1 Added bumblebee.txt

diff --git a/bumblebee.txt b/bumblebee.txt new file mode 100644 index 0000000..443b974 --- /dev/null +++
b/bumblebee.txt @@ -0,0 +1 @@ +A bumblebee, also written bumble bee, is a member of the bee genus Bombus,
in the family Apidae. \ No newline at end of file

1

2 **Note**
3 In this and the following examples, commit IDs have been abbreviated\. The full commit IDs are
    not shown\.

4

5 You can also use the git show command with the commit ID to view the changes that occurred:

git show 94ba1e60

commit 94ba1e60 Author: John Doe johndoe@example.com Date: Mon May 23 15:39:14 2016 -0700

1 `Added horse.txt`

diff --git a/horse.txt b/horse.txt new file mode 100644 index 0000000..080f68f --- /dev/null +++ b/horse.txt @@ -0,0 +1 @@ +The horse (Equus ferus caballus) is one of two extant subspecies of Equus ferus.

1

2 `To see the differences between two commits, run the git diff command and include the two commit`
`    IDs\.`

git diff ce22850d 4f8c6f9d

1

2 `In this example, the difference between the two commits is that two files were added\. The`
`    command produces output similar to the following:`

diff --git a/bees.txt b/bees.txt new file mode 100644 index 0000000..cf57550 --- /dev/null +++ b/bees.txt @@ -0,0 +1 @@ +Bees are flying insects closely related to wasps and ants, and are known for their role in pollination and for producing honey and beeswax. diff --git a/bumblebee.txt b/bumblebee.txt new file mode 100644 index 0000000..443b974 --- /dev/null +++ b/bumblebee.txt @@ -0,0 +1 @@ +A bumblebee, also written bumble bee, is a member of the bee genus Bombus, in the family Apidae. \ No newline at end of file

1

2 `To use Git to view details about the commits in a local repo, run the git log command:`

git log

1

2 `If successful, this command produces output similar to the following:`

commit 94ba1e60 Author: John Doe johndoe@example.com Date: Mon May 23 15:39:14 2016 -0700

1 `Added horse.txt`

commit 4c925148 Author: Jane Doe janedoe@example.com Date: Mon May 22 14:54:55 2014 -0700

1 `Added cat.txt and dog.txt`

1

2 `To show only commit IDs and messages, run the git log \-\-pretty=oneline command:`

git log --pretty=oneline

1

2 `If successful, this command produces output similar to the following:`

94ba1e60 Added horse.txt 4c925148 Added cat.txt and dog.txt

1

2 `For more options, see your Git documentation\.`

3

4

5

6

7 `# Compare Commits in AWS CodeCommit<a name="how-to-compare-commits"></a>`

8

9 You can use the AWS CodeCommit console to view the differences between commit specifiers in an
AWS CodeCommit repository\. You can quickly view the difference between a commit and its
parent\. You can also compare any two references, including commit IDs\.

10

11 **Topics**

12 + [Compare a Commit to Its Parent](#how-to-compare-commits-parent)

13 + [Compare Any Two Commit Specifiers](#how-to-compare-commits-compare)

14

15 ## Compare a Commit to Its Parent<a name="how-to-compare-commits-parent"></a>

16

17 You can quickly view the difference between a commit and its parent to review the commit message
, the committer, and exactly what changed\.

18

19 1. Open the AWS CodeCommit console at [https://console\.aws\.amazon\.com/codecommit](https://
console.aws.amazon.com/codecommit)\.

20

21 1. On the **Dashboard** page, from the list of repositories, choose the repository where you
want to view the difference between a commit and its parent\.

22

23 1. In the navigation pane, choose **Commits**\.

24

25 1. Choose the abbreviated commit ID of any commit in the list\. The view changes to show details
for this commit, including the differences between it and its parent commit\.

26 ![\[Choose the abbreviated commit ID to show differences between this commit and its parent\]](
http://docs.aws.amazon.com/codecommit/latest/userguide/images/codecommit-commit-changes1.png
)

27

28 You can show changes side by side \(**Split** view\) or inline \(**Unified** view\)\. You can
also hide or show white space changes\. You can also add comments\. For more information
, see [Comment on a Commit](how-to-commit-comment.md)\.

29 **Note**

30 If you are signed in as an IAM user, you can configure and save your preferences for viewing
code and other console settings\. For more information, see [Working with User Preferences](
user-preferences.md)\.

31 ![\[Changes shown in Split view, with white space changes visible\]](http://docs.aws.amazon.com/
codecommit/latest/userguide/images/codecommit-commit-changes2c.png)

32 ![\[Adding a comment to a changed line in a commit.\]](http://docs.aws.amazon.com/codecommit/
latest/userguide/images/codecommit-commenting-savelinecomment.png)

33 **Note**

34 Depending on line ending style, your code editor, and other factors, you might see entire lines
added or deleted instead of specific changes in a line\. The level of detail matches what'
s returned in the git show or git diff commands\.

35

36 ![\[Changes shown in Split view, with white space changes visible\]](http://docs.aws.amazon.com/
codecommit/latest/userguide/images/codecommit-commit-changes2b.png)

37

38 1. To compare a commit to its parent from the **Commit Visualizer page**, choose a reference
point on the graph, and then choose **View differences between this commit and its parent
**\.

39 ![\[The option to view differences between a commit and its parent in Commit Visualizer\]](http
://docs.aws.amazon.com/codecommit/latest/userguide/images/codecommit-commit-changes-
visualizer.png)

40

41 ## Compare Any Two Commit Specifiers<a name="how-to-compare-commits-compare"></a>

42

43 You can view the differences between any two commit specifiers in the AWS CodeCommit console\. Commit specifiers are references, such as branches, tags, and commit IDs\.

44

45 1. Open the AWS CodeCommit console at [https://console\.aws\.amazon\.com/codecommit](https://console.aws.amazon.com/codecommit)\.

46

47 1. On the **Dashboard** page, from the list of repositories, choose the repository where you want to compare commits, branches, or tagged commits\.

48

49 1. In the navigation pane, choose **Compare**\.
50 ![\[Compare any two commit specifiers\]](http://docs.aws.amazon.com/codecommit/latest/userguide/images/codecommit-compare-1.png)

51

52 1. Use the **Choose** buttons to compare two commit specifiers\.
53   + To compare the tip of a branch, choose the branch name\. This selects the most recent commit from that branch for the comparison\.
54   + To compare a commit with a specific tag associated with it, choose the tag name\. This selects the tagged commit for the comparison\.
55   + To compare a specific commit, paste the commit ID in the text box\. To get the full commit ID, choose **Commits** in the navigation bar, and copy the commit ID from the list\. On the **Compare** page, paste the full commit ID in the text box, and press **Enter**\. You can repeat this to copy and paste a second commit ID, if you want to compare two commit IDs\.
56 ![\[Compare branches, tags, or commit IDs\]](http://docs.aws.amazon.com/codecommit/latest/userguide/images/codecommit-compare-2.png)

57

58 1. After you have selected the specifiers, choose **Compare**\.
59 ![\[The comparison view between two commit specifiers\]](http://docs.aws.amazon.com/codecommit/latest/userguide/images/codecommit-compare-3.png)

60

61   You can show differences side by side \(**Split** view\) or inline \(**Unified** view\)\. You can also hide or show white space changes\.

62

63 1. To reverse the comparison, choose the Flip button \(![\[The flip button for changing the order of comparison.\]](http://docs.aws.amazon.com/codecommit/latest/userguide/images/codecommit-compare-flip.png)\), and then choose **Compare**\.

64

65 1. To clear your comparison choices, choose **Clear**\.

66

67

68

69

70 # Comment on a Commit in AWS CodeCommit<a name="how-to-commit-comment"></a>

71

72 You can use the AWS CodeCommit console to comment on commits in a repository, and view and reply to other users' comments on commits\. This can help you discuss changes made in a repository, including:
73 + Why specific changes were made\.
74 + Whether more changes or fixes are required\.
75 + Whether changes should be merged into another branch\.

76

77 You can comment on an overall commit, on a file within a commit, or on a specific line or change within a file\.

78

79 ![\[A commit with three comments.\]](http://docs.aws.amazon.com/codecommit/latest/userguide/images/codecommit-commenting-commitwithcomments.png)

80

81 **Note**

82 For best results, use commenting when you are signed in as an IAM user\. The commenting functionality is not optimized for users who sign in with root account credentials, federated access, or temporary credentials\.

83

84 **Topics**

85 + [View Comments on a Commit in a Repository](#how-to-commit-comment-view-console)

86 + [Add and Reply to Comments on a Commit in a Repository](#how-to-commit-comment-add-console)

87 + [Use the AWS CLI to View, Add, Update, and Reply to Commments](#how-to-commit-comment-cli)

88

89 ## View Comments on a Commit in a Repository<a name="how-to-commit-comment-view-console"></a>

90

91 You can use the AWS CodeCommit console to view comments on a commit\.

92

93 **To view comments on a commit \(console\)**

94

95 1. Open the AWS CodeCommit console at [https://console\.aws\.amazon\.com/codecommit](https://console.aws.amazon.com/codecommit)\.

96

97 1. On the **Dashboard** page, from the list of repositories, choose the repository for which you want to review comments on commits\.

98

99 1. In the navigation pane, choose **Commits**\. In the commit history view, a history of commits to the repository's default branch is displayed\. Choose the title of the commit where you want to view any comments\.

100

101 The page for that specific commit is displayed, along with any comments already present on that commit, in **Changes**\.

102 ![\[A commit showing a comment on a changed line of code.\]](http://docs.aws.amazon.com/codecommit/latest/userguide/images/codecommit-commenting-linecomment.png)

103

104 1. To only view the comments for a commit, choose **Comments**\. All file and line comments are shown, along with any comments on the changes in the commit itself, in reverse chronological order\.

105 ![\[The comments view for a commit, with three comments shown: one file comment, one line comment, and one change comment.\]](http://docs.aws.amazon.com/codecommit/latest/userguide/images/codecommit-commenting-commenttab.png)

106

107 To view the context of a comment, choose **Show context**\. The view changes to where the comment was made in the **Changes** view\.

108

109 ## Add and Reply to Comments on a Commit in a Repository<a name="how-to-commit-comment-add-console"></a>

110

111 You can use the AWS CodeCommit console to add comments to the comparison of a commit and a parent, or to the comparison between two specified commits\. You can also reply to existing comments\.

112

113 ### Add and Reply to Comments on a Commit<a name="how-to-commit-comment-add-cpage"></a>

114

115 You can add and reply to comments to a commit\. Your comments are marked as those belonging to the IAM user or role you used to sign in to the console\.

116

117 **To add and reply to comments on a commit \(console\)**

118

119 1. Open the AWS CodeCommit console at [https://console\.aws\.amazon\.com/codecommit](https://console.aws.amazon.com/codecommit)\.

120

121 1. On the **Dashboard** page, from the list of repositories, choose the repository where you want to comment on commits\.

122

123 1. In the navigation pane, choose **Commits**\. In the commit history view, choose the title of the commit where you want to add or reply to comments\.

124

125 The page for that commit is displayed, along with any comments\.

126

127 1. To add a comment, do one of the following:

128 + To add a general comment, in **Comments on changes**, type your comment, and then choose **Save**\. You can use [Markdown](https://en.wikipedia.org/wiki/Markdown), or you can type your comment in plaintext\.

129 ![\[A general comment on the changes in a commit.\]](http://docs.aws.amazon.com/codecommit/latest/userguide/images/codecommit-commenting-changecomment.png)

130 + To add a comment to a file in the commit, in **Changes**, find the name of the file\. Choose the comment bubble ![\[Image NOT FOUND\]](http://docs.aws.amazon.com/codecommit/latest/userguide/images/codecommit-commentbubble.png), type your comment, and then choose **Save**\.

131 ![\[Adding a comment on a file in a commit.\]](http://docs.aws.amazon.com/codecommit/latest/userguide/images/codecommit-commenting-addfilecomment.png)

132 + To add a comment to a changed line in the commit, in **Changes**, go to the line where the change appears\. Choose the comment bubble ![\[Image NOT FOUND\]](http://docs.aws.amazon.com/codecommit/latest/userguide/images/codecommit-commentbubble.png), type your comment, and then choose **Save**\.

133 ![\[Adding a comment on a line in a commit.\]](http://docs.aws.amazon.com/codecommit/latest/userguide/images/codecommit-commenting-addlinecomment.png)

134 **Note**

135 You can edit your comment after you have saved it, but you cannot delete it from the AWS CodeCommit console\. Consider using the **Preview** mode for your comment before you save your comment\.

136

137 1. To reply to comments on a commit, in either **Changes** or **Comments**, choose **Reply**\.

138 ![\[Choose Reply to add a comment to an existing comment on a commit.\]](http://docs.aws.amazon.com/codecommit/latest/userguide/images/codecommit-commenting-commenttab.png)

139

140 ### Add and Reply to Comments When Comparing Two Commit Specifiers<a name="how-to-commit-comment-console-compare"></a>

141

142 You can add comments to a comparison between branches, tags, or commits\.

143

144 **To add or reply to comments when comparing commit specifiers \(console\)**

145

146 1. Open the AWS CodeCommit console at [https://console\.aws\.amazon\.com/codecommit](https://console.aws.amazon.com/codecommit)\.

147

148 1. On the **Dashboard** page, from the list of repositories, choose the repository where you

want to compare commits, branches, or tagged commits\.

149

150 1. In the navigation pane, choose **Compare**\.

151 ![\[Compare any two commit specifiers\]](http://docs.aws.amazon.com/codecommit/latest/userguide/
      images/codecommit-compare-1.png)

152

153 1. Use the **Choose** buttons to compare two commit specifiers\. Use the drop\-down lists or
      paste in commit IDs\.

154

155 1. Do one or more of the following:

156   + To add comments to files or lines, choose the comment bubble ![\[Image NOT FOUND\]](http://
         docs.aws.amazon.com/codecommit/latest/userguide/images/codecommit-commentbubble.png)\.

157   + To add general comments on the compared changes, go to **Comments on changes**\.

158

159 ## Use the AWS CLI to View, Add, Update, and Reply to Commments<a name="how-to-commit-comment-
      cli"></a>

160

161 You can view, add, reply, update, and delete the contents of a comment by running the following
      commands:

162 + [get\-comments\-for\-compared\-commit](#how-to-commit-comment-cli-get-comments), to view the
      comments on the comparison between two commits\.

163 + [get\-comment](#how-to-commit-comment-cli-get-comment-info), to view details on a specific
      comment\.

164 + [delete\-comment\-content](#how-to-commit-comment-cli-commit-delete), to delete the contents
      of a comment that you created\.

165 + [post\-comment\-for\-compared\-commit](#how-to-commit-comment-cli-comment), to create a
      comment on the comparison between two commits\.

166 + [update\-comment](#how-to-commit-comment-cli-commit-update), to update a comment\.

167 + [post\-comment\-reply](#how-to-commit-comment-cli-commit-reply), to reply to a comment\.

168

169 ### To view comments on a commit<a name="how-to-commit-comment-cli-get-comments"></a>

170

171 1. Run the get\-comments\-for\-compared\-commit command, specifying:

172   + The AWS CodeCommit repository's name \(with the `--repository-name` option\)\.

173   + The full commit ID of the 'after' commit, to establish the directionality of the comparison
         \(with the `--after-commit-id option`\)\.

174   + The full commit ID of the 'before' commit, to establish the directionality of the
         comparison \(with the `--before-commit-id` option\)\.

175   + \(Optional\) An enumeration token to return the next batch of the results \(with the `--
         next-token` option\)\.

176   + \(Optional\) A non\-negative integer to limit the number of returned results \(with the `--
         max-results` option\)\.

177

178   For example, to view comments made on the comparison between two commits in a repository
         named *MyDemoRepo*:

aws codecommit get-comments-for-compared-commit --repository-name MyDemoRepo --before-commit-ID
6e147360EXAMPLE --after-commit-id 317f8570EXAMPLE

1

2 1. If successful, this command produces output similar to the following:

{ "commentsForComparedCommitData": [{ "afterBlobId": "1f330709EXAMPLE", "afterCommitId":
"317f8570EXAMPLE", "beforeBlobId": "80906a4cEXAMPLE", "beforeCommitId": "6e147360EXAMPLE",
"comments": [{ "authorArn": "arn:aws:iam::111111111111:user/Li__Juan", "clientRequestToken": "123Ex-

ample", "commentId": "ff30b348EXAMPLEb9aa670f", "content": "Whoops - I meant to add this comment to the line, not the file, but I don't see how to delete it.", "creationDate": 1508369768.142, "deleted": false, "CommentId": "123abc-EXAMPLE", "lastModifiedDate": 1508369842.278 }, { "authorArn": "arn:aws:iam::111111111111:user/Li_Juan", "clientRequestToken": "123Example", "commentId": "553b509bEXAMPLE56198325", "content": "Can you add a test case for this?", "creationDate": 1508369612.240, "deleted": false, "commentId": "456def-EXAMPLE", "lastModifiedDate": 1508369612.240 }], "location": { "filePath": "cl_sample.js", "filePosition": 1232, "relativeFileVersion": "after" }, "repositoryName": "MyDemoRepo" }], "nextToken": "exampleToken" }

To view details of a comment on a commit<a name="how-to-commit-comment-cli-get-comment-info"></a>

1. Run the get\-comment command, specifying the system\-generated comment ID\. For example:

aws codecommit get-comment --comment-id ff30b348EXAMPLEb9aa670f

1. If successful, this command returns output similar to the following:

{ "comment": { "authorArn": "arn:aws:iam::111111111111:user/Li_Juan", "clientRequestToken": "123Example", "commentId": "ff30b348EXAMPLEb9aa670f", "content": "Whoops - I meant to add this comment to the line, but I don't see how to delete it.", "creationDate": 1508369768.142, "deleted": false, "commentId": "", "lastModifiedDate": 1508369842.278 } }

To delete the contents of a comment on a commit<a name="how-to-commit-comment-cli-commit-delete"></a>

1. Run the delete\-comment\-content command, specifying the system\-generated comment ID\. For example:

aws codecommit delete-comment-content --comment-id ff30b348EXAMPLEb9aa670f

Note
You can only delete the content of a comment if you created the comment\.

1. If successful, this command produces output similar to the following:

{ "comment": { "creationDate": 1508369768.142, "deleted": true, "lastModifiedDate": 1508369842.278, "clientRequestToken": "123Example", "commentId": "ff30b348EXAMPLEb9aa670f", "authorArn": "arn:aws:iam::111111111111:user/Li_Juan" } }

To create a comment on a commit<a name="how-to-commit-comment-cli-comment"></a>

1. Run the `post-comment-for-compared-commit` command, specifying:
+ The AWS CodeCommit repository's name \(with the `--repository-name` option\)\.
+ The full commit ID of the 'after' commit, to establish the directionality of the comparison \(with the after\-commit\-id option\)\.
+ The full commit ID of the 'before' commit, to establish the directionality of the comparison \(with the before\-commit\-id option\)\.
+ A unique, client\-generated idempotency token \(with the \-\-client\-request\-token option\)\.
+ The content of your comment \(with the \-\-content option\)\.
+ A list of location information about where to place the comment, including:
  + The name of the file being compared, including its extension and subdirectory, if any \(with the filePath attribute\)\.

12   + The line number of the change within a compared file \(with the filePosition attribute\)\.
13   + Whether the comment on the change is "before" or "after" in the comparison between the
       source and destination branches \(with the relativeFileVersion attribute\)\.
14
15 For example, to add the comment *"Can you add a test case for this?"* on the change to the *cl\
     _sample\.js* file in the comparison between two commits in a repository named *MyDemoRepo*:

aws codecommit post-comment-for-compared-commit --repository-name MyDemoRepo --before-commit-id
317f8570EXAMPLE --after-commit-id 5d036259EXAMPLE --client-request-token 123Example --content "Can
you add a test case for this?" --location filePath=cl_sample.js,filePosition=1232,relativeFileVersion=AFTER

1
2 1. If successful, this command produces output similar to the following:

{ "afterBlobId": "1f330709EXAMPLE", "afterCommitId": "317f8570EXAMPLE", "beforeBlobId":
"80906a4cEXAMPLE", "beforeCommitId": "6e147360EXAMPLE", "comment": { "authorArn":
"arn:aws:iam::111111111111:user/Li_Juan", "clientRequestToken": "", "commentId": "553b509bEX-
AMPLE56198325", "content": "Can you add a test case for this?", "creationDate": 1508369612.203, "deleted":
false, "commentId": "abc123-EXAMPLE", "lastModifiedDate": 1508369612.203 }, "location": { "filePath":
"cl_sample.js", "filePosition": 1232, "relativeFileVersion": "AFTER" }, "repositoryName": "MyDemoRepo" }

1
2 ### To update a comment on a commit<a name="how-to-commit-comment-cli-commit-update"></a>
3
4 1. Run the `update-comment` command, specifying the system\-generated comment ID and the content
       with which you want to replace any existing content\.
5 **Note**
6 You can only update the content of a comment if you created the comment\.
7
8 For example, to add the content *"Fixed as requested\. I'll update the pull request\."* to a
       comment with an ID of *442b498bEXAMPLE5756813* :

aws codecommit update-comment --comment-id 442b498bEXAMPLE5756813 --content "Fixed as requested. I'll
update the pull request."

1
2 1. If successful, this command produces output similar to the following:

{ "comment": { "authorArn": "arn:aws:iam::111111111111:user/Li_Juan", "clientRequestToken": "", "commentId": "442b498bEXAMPLE5756813", "content": "Fixed as requested. I'll update the pull request.",
"creationDate": 1508369929.783, "deleted": false, "lastModifiedDate": 1508369929.287 } }

1
2 ### To reply to a comment on a commit<a name="how-to-commit-comment-cli-commit-reply"></a>
3
4 1. To post a reply to a comment in a pull request, run the post\-comment\-reply command,
       specifying:
5 + The system\-generated ID of the comment to which you want to reply \(with the \-\-in\-reply\-
       to option\)\.
6 + A unique, client\-generated idempotency token \(with the \-\-client\-request\-token option\)\.
7 + The content of your reply \(with the \-\-content option\)\.
8
9 For example, to add the reply *"Good catch\. I'll remove them\."* to the comment with the
       system\-generated ID of *abcd1234EXAMPLEb5678efgh*:

aws codecommit post-comment-reply --in-reply-to abcd1234EXAMPLEb5678efgh --content "Good catch. I'll
remove them." --client-request-token 123Example

1. If successful, this command produces output similar to the following:

```
{ "comment": { "authorArn": "arn:aws:iam::111111111111:user/Li_Juan", "clientRequestToken": "123Example", "commentId": "442b498bEXAMPLE5756813", "content": "Good catch. I'll remove them.", "creationDate": 1508369829.136, "deleted": false, "CommentId": "abcd1234EXAMPLEb5678efgh", "lastModifiedDate": 150836912.221 } }
```

Create a Tag in AWS CodeCommit<a name="how-to-create-tag"></a>

You can use a tag to mark a commit with a label that helps other repository users understand its importance\. To create a tag in an AWS CodeCommit repository, you can use Git from a local repo connected to the AWS CodeCommit repository\. After you have created a tag in the local repo, you can use git push \-\-tags to push it to the AWS CodeCommit repository\.

For more information about how to view tags in your repository, see [View Tag Details](how-to-view-tag-details.md)\.

Use Git to Create a Tag<a name="how-to-create-tag-git"></a>

To use Git from a local repo to create a tag in an AWS CodeCommit repository, follow these steps \.

In these steps, we assume that you have already connected the local repo to the AWS CodeCommit repository\. For instructions, see [Connect to a Repository](how-to-connect.md)\.

1. Run the git tag *new\-tag\-name* *commit\-id* command, where *new\-tag\-name* is the new tag's name and *commit\-id* is the ID of the commit to associate with the tag\.

For example, the following command creates a new tag named `beta` and associates it with the commit ID `dc082f9a...af873b88`:

```
git tag beta dc082f9a...af873b88
```

1. To push the new tag from the local repo to the AWS CodeCommit repository, run the git push *remote\-name* *new\-tag\-name* command, where *remote\-name* is the name of the AWS CodeCommit repository and *new\-tag\-name* is the name of the new tag\.

For example, to push a new tag named `beta` to an AWS CodeCommit repository named `origin`:

```
git push origin beta
```

Note
To push all new tags from your local repo to the AWS CodeCommit repository, run git push \-\-tags\.
To ensure your local repo is updated with all of the tags in the AWS CodeCommit repository, run git fetch followed by git fetch \-\-tags\.

For more options, see your Git documentation\.

View Tag Details in AWS CodeCommit<a name="how-to-view-tag-details"></a>

In Git, a tag is a label you can apply to a reference like a commit to mark it with information that might be important to other repository users\. For example, you might tag the commit that was the beta release point for a project with the tag **beta**\. For more information, see [Use Git to Create a Tag](how-to-create-tag.md#how-to-create-tag-git)\.

You can use the AWS CodeCommit console to view information about tags in your repository, including the date and commit message of the commit referenced by each tag\. From the console, you can compare the commit referenced by the tag with the head of the default branch of your repository\. Like any other commit, you can also view the code at the point of that tag\.

You can also use Git from your terminal or command line to view details about tags in a local repo\.

Topics
+ [Use the AWS CodeCommit Console to View Tag Details](#how-to-view-tag-details-console)
+ [Use Git to View Tag Details](#how-to-view-tag-details-git)

Use the AWS CodeCommit Console to View Tag Details<a name="how-to-view-tag-details-console"></a>

Use the AWS CodeCommit console to quickly view a list of tags for your repository and details about the commits referenced by the tags\.

1. Open the AWS CodeCommit console at [https://console\.aws\.amazon\.com/codecommit](https://console.aws.amazon.com/codecommit)\.

1. In the list of repositories, choose the name of the repository\.

1. In the navigation pane, choose **Tags**\.
![\[A view of tags in a repository.\]](http://docs.aws.amazon.com/codecommit/latest/userguide/images/codecommit-tags-view.png)
Note
You can adjust the number of tags displayed on the **Tags** page by changing the number of tags per page\.

1. Do one of the following:
+ To view the code as it was at that tagged commit, choose the tag name\.
+ To view a graph of the repository from that tagged commit, choose the abbreviated commit ID\.
+ To view details of the commit, including the full commit message, committer, and author, choose the commit message\.
+ To compare the tagged commit with the head of the default branch in your repository, choose **Compare**\.

Use Git to View Tag Details<a name="how-to-view-tag-details-git"></a>

To use Git to view details about tags in a local repo, run one of the following commands:
+ [git tag](#how-to-view-tag-details-git-tag) to view a list of tag names\.
+ [git show](#how-to-view-tag-details-git-show) to view information about a specific tag\.

47 + [git ls\-remote](#how-to-view-tag-details-git-remote) to view information about tags in an AWS
   CodeCommit repository\.

48

49 **Note**

50 To ensure that your local repo is updated with all of the tags in the AWS CodeCommit repository,
   run git fetch followed by git fetch \-\-tags\.

51

52 In the following steps, we assume that you have already connected the local repo to AWS
   CodeCommit repository\. For instructions, see [Connect to a Repository](how-to-connect.md)\.

53

54 ### To view a list of tags in a local repo<a name="how-to-view-tag-details-git-tag"></a>

55

56 1. Run the git tag command:

   git tag

1

2 1. If successful, this command produces output similar to the following:

   beta release

1 **Note**

2 If no tags have been defined, git tag returns nothing\.

3

4 For more options, see your Git documentation\.

5

6 ### To view information about a tag in a local repo<a name="how-to-view-tag-details-git-show"></
   a>

7

8 1. Run the git show *tag\-name* command\. For example, to view information about a tag named `
   beta`, run:

   git show beta

1

2 1. If successful, this command produces output similar to the following:

   commit 317f8570...ad9e3c09 Author: John Doe johndoe@example.com Date: Tue Sep 23 13:49:51 2014 -0700

1   Added horse.txt

   diff --git a/horse.txt b/horse.txt new file mode 100644 index 0000000..df42ff1 --- /dev/null +++ b/horse.txt @@
   -0,0 +1 @@ +The horse (Equus ferus caballus) is one of two extant subspecies of Equus ferus \ No newline at
   end of file

1 **Note**

2 To exit the output of the tag information, type :q\.

3

4 For more options, see your Git documentation\.

5

6 ### To view information about tags in an AWS CodeCommit repository<a name="how-to-view-tag-
   details-git-remote"></a>

7

8 1. Run the git ls\-remote \-\-tags command\.

   git ls-remote --tags

1. If successful, this command produces as output a list of the tags in the AWS CodeCommit repository:

    129ce87a...70fbffba refs/tags/beta 785de9bd...59b402d8 refs/tags/release

If no tags have been defined, git ls\-remote \-\-tags returns a blank line\.

For more options, see your Git documentation\.

Delete a Tag in AWS CodeCommit<a name="how-to-delete-tag"></a>

To delete a tag in an AWS CodeCommit repository, use Git from a local repo connected to the AWS CodeCommit repository\. \.

Use Git to Delete a Tag<a name="how-to-delete-tag-git"></a>

To use Git from a local repo to delete a tag in an AWS CodeCommit repository, follow these steps \.

These steps assume you have already connected the local repo to the AWS CodeCommit repository\. For instructions, see [Connect to a Repository](how-to-connect.md)\.

1. To delete the tag from the local repo, run the git tag \-d *tag\-name* command where *tag\-name* is the name of the tag you want to delete\.
Tip
To get a list of tag names, run git tag\.

For example, to delete a tag in the local repo named `beta`:

    git tag -d beta

1. To delete the tag from the AWS CodeCommit repository, run the git push *remote\-name* \-\-delete *tag\-name* command where *remote\-name* is the nickname the local repo uses for the AWS CodeCommit repository and *tag\-name* is the name of the tag you want to delete from the AWS CodeCommit repository\.
Tip
To get a list of AWS CodeCommit repository names along with their URLs, run the git remote \-v command\.

For example, to delete a tag named `beta` in the AWS CodeCommit repository named `origin`:

    git push origin --delete beta

Working with Branches in AWS CodeCommit Repositories<a name="branches"></a>

7 What is a branch? In Git, branches are simply pointers or references to a commit\. In
    development, they're a convenient way to organize your work\. You can use branches to
    separate work on a new or different version of files without impacting work in other
    branches\. You can use branches to develop new features, store a specific version of your
    project from a particular commit, and more\.

8

9 In AWS CodeCommit, you can change the default branch for your repository\. This default branch
    is the one used as the base or default branch in local repos when users clone the repository
    \. You can also create and delete branches and view details about a branch\. You can quickly
     compare differences between a branch and the default branch \(or any two branches\)\. To
    view the history of branches and merges in your repository, you can use the [Commit
    Visualizer](how-to-view-commit-details.md#how-to-view-commit-details-console-visualizer)\.

10

11 ![\[A view of branches in a repository\]](http://docs.aws.amazon.com/codecommit/latest/userguide
    /images/codecommit-branches.png)

12

13 For information about working with other aspects of your repository in AWS CodeCommit, see [
    Working with Repositories](repositories.md), [Working with Files](files.md), [Working with
    Pull Requests](pull-requests.md), [Working with Commits](commits.md), and [Working with User
    Preferences](user-preferences.md)\.

14

15 **Topics**
16 + [Create a Branch in AWS CodeCommit](how-to-create-branch.md)
17 + [Limit Pushes and Merges to Branches in AWS CodeCommit](how-to-conditional-branch.md)
18 + [View Branch Details in AWS CodeCommit](how-to-view-branch-details.md)
19 + [Compare Branches in AWS CodeCommit](how-to-compare-branches.md)
20 + [Change Branch Settings in AWS CodeCommit](how-to-change-branch.md)
21 + [Delete a Branch in AWS CodeCommit](how-to-delete-branch.md)

22

23

24

25

26 # Create a Branch in AWS CodeCommit<a name="how-to-create-branch"></a>

27

28 You can use the AWS CodeCommit console to create branches for your repository\. This is a quick
    way to separate work on a new or different version of files without impacting work in the
    default branch\. After creating a branch in the AWS CodeCommit console, you'll need to pull
    that change to your local repo\. Alternatively, you can create a branch locally and push
    that change to an AWS CodeCommit repository by using Git from a local repo connected to the
    AWS CodeCommit repository\. You can also use the AWS CLI\.

29

30 **Topics**
31 + [Use the AWS CodeCommit Console to Create a Branch](#how-to-create-branch-console)
32 + [Use Git to Create a Branch](#how-to-create-branch-git)
33 + [Use the AWS CLI to Create a Branch](#how-to-create-branch-cli)

34

35 ## Use the AWS CodeCommit Console to Create a Branch<a name="how-to-create-branch-console"></a>

36

37 You can use the AWS CodeCommit console to create a branch in an AWS CodeCommit repository\. When
    users next pull changes from the repository, they will see the new branch\.

38

39 1. Open the AWS CodeCommit console at [https://console\.aws\.amazon\.com/codecommit](https://
    console.aws.amazon.com/codecommit)\.

40

41 1. In the list of repositories, choose the name of the repository\.

42

43 1. In the navigation pane, choose **Branches**\.

44

45 1. Choose **Create branch**\.

46 !\[\[Creating a branch in the AWS CodeCommit console.\]\](http://docs.aws.amazon.com/codecommit/
   latest/userguide/images/codecommit-branches-create.png)

47

48 Type a name for the branch in **Branch name**\. In **Branch from**, the default branch is
   selected\. If you want to branch from a different branch or from a specific commit, expand
   the branch list, and either choose a branch from the list, or paste a specific commit ID\.
   Choose **Create**\.

49

50 ## Use Git to Create a Branch<a name="how-to-create-branch-git"></a>

51

52 To use Git from a local repo to create a branch in an local repo and then push that branch to
   the AWS CodeCommit repository, follow these steps\.

53

54 These steps assume you have already connected the local repo to the AWS CodeCommit repository\.
   For instructions, see [Connect to a Repository](how-to-connect.md)\.

55

56 1. Create a new branch in your local repo by running the git checkout \-b *new\-branch\-name*
   command, where *new\-branch\-name* is the name of the new branch\.

57

58 For example, the following command creates a new branch named `MyNewBranch` in the local repo:

git checkout -b MyNewBranch

1

2 1. To push the new branch from the local repo to the AWS CodeCommit repository, run the git push
   command, specifying both the *remote\-name* and the *new\-branch\-name*\.

3

4 For example, to push a new branch in the local repo named `MyNewBranch` to the AWS CodeCommit
   repository with the nickname `origin`:

git push origin MyNewBranch

1

2 **Note**

3 If you add the `-u` option to git push \(for example, git push \-u origin master\), then in the
   future you can run git push without *remote\-name* *branch\-name*\. Upstream tracking
   information will be set\. To get upstream tracking information, run git remote show *remote
   \-name* \(for example, git remote show origin\)\.

4 To see a list of all of your local and remote tracking branches, run git branch \-\-all\.

5 To set up a branch in the local repo that is connected to an existing branch in the AWS
   CodeCommit repository, run git checkout *remote\-branch\-name*\.

6

7 For more options, see your Git documentation\.

8

9 ## Use the AWS CLI to Create a Branch<a name="how-to-create-branch-cli"></a>

10

11 To use AWS CLI commands with AWS CodeCommit, install the AWS CLI\. For more information, see [
   Command Line Reference](cmd-ref.md)\.

12

13 To use the AWS CLI to create a branch in an AWS CodeCommit repository and then push that branch
   to the AWS CodeCommit repository, follow these steps\.

¹⁴

¹⁵ 1. Run the create\-branch command, specifying:

¹⁶ + The name of the AWS CodeCommit repository where the branch will be created \(with the \-\-repository\-name option\)\.

¹⁷ **Note**

¹⁸ To get the name of the AWS CodeCommit repository, run the [list\-repositories](how-to-view-repository-details.md#how-to-view-repository-details-no-name-cli) command\.

¹⁹ + The name of the new branch \(with the \-\-branch\-name option\)\.

²⁰ + The ID of the commit to which the new branch will point \(with the \-\-commit\-id option\)\.

²¹

²² For example, to create a new branch named `MyNewBranch` that points to commit ID `317f8570EXAMPLE` in an AWS CodeCommit repository named `MyDemoRepo`:

```
aws codecommit create-branch --repository-name MyDemoRepo --branch-name MyNewBranch --commit-id
317f8570EXAMPLE
```

¹

² This command produces output only if there are errors\.

³

⁴ 1. To update your local repo's list of available AWS CodeCommit repository branches with the new remote branch name, run git remote update *remote\-name*\.

⁵

⁶ For example, to update your local repo's list of available branches for the AWS CodeCommit repository with the nickname `origin`:

```
git remote update origin
```

¹ **Note**

² Alternatively, you can run the git fetch command\. You can also view all remote branches by running git branch \-\-all, but until you update your local repo's list, the remote branch you created will not appear in the list\.

³ For more options, see your Git documentation\.

⁴

⁵ 1. To set up a branch in the local repo that is connected to the new branch in the AWS CodeCommit repository, run git checkout *remote\-branch\-name*\.

⁶

⁷ **Note**

⁸ To get a list of AWS CodeCommit repository names, along with their URLs, run the git remote \-v command\.

⁹

¹⁰

¹¹

¹²

¹³ # Limit Pushes and Merges to Branches in AWS CodeCommit<a name="how-to-conditional-branch"></a>

¹⁴

¹⁵ By default, any AWS CodeCommit repository user who has sufficient permissions to push code to the repository can contribute to any branch in that repository\. This is true no matter how you add a branch to the repository: by using the console, the command line, or Git\. However, you might want to configure a branch so that only certain repository users can push or merge code to that branch\. For example, you might want to configure a branch used for production code so that only a subset of senior developers can push or merge changes to that branch\. Other developers can still pull from the branch, make their own branches, and create pull requests, but they cannot push or merge changes to that branch\. You can configure this access by creating a conditional policy that uses a context key for one or more branches in IAM\.

¹⁶

17 **Note**
18 To complete some of the procedures in this topic, you must sign in with an adminstrative user
that has sufficient permissions to configure and apply IAM policies\. For more information,
see [Creating an IAM Admin User and Group](http://docs.aws.amazon.com/IAM/latest/UserGuide/
getting-started_create-admin-group.html)\.

19

20 **Topics**
21 + [Configure an IAM Policy to Limit Pushes and Merges to a Branch](#how-to-conditional-branch-
create-policy)
22 + [Apply the IAM Policy to an IAM Group or Role](#how-to-conditional-branch-apply-policy)
23 + [Test the Policy](#how-to-conditional-branch-test)

24

25 ## Configure an IAM Policy to Limit Pushes and Merges to a Branch<a name="how-to-conditional-
branch-create-policy"></a>

26

27 You can create a policy in IAM that prevents users from updating a branch, including pushing
commits to a branch and merging pull requests to a branch\. To do this, your policy uses a
conditional statement, so that the effect of the `Deny` statement applies only if the
condition is met\. The APIs you include in the `Deny` statement determine which actions are
not allowed\. You can configure this policy to apply to only one branch in a repository, a
number of branches in a repository, or to all branches that match the criteria across all
repositories in an AWS account\. <a name="how-to-conditional-branch-create-policy-procedure
"></a>

28

29 **To create a conditional policy for branches**
30
31 1. Sign in to the AWS Management Console and open the IAM console at [https://console\.aws\.
amazon\.com/iam/](https://console.aws.amazon.com/iam/)\.

32

33 1. In the navigation pane, choose **Policies**\.

34

35 1. Choose **Create policy**\.

36

37 1. Choose **JSON**, and then paste the following example policy\. Replace the value of `Resource
` with the ARN of the repository that contains the branch for which you want to restrict
access\. Replace the value of `codecommit:References` with a reference to the branch or
branches to which you want to restrict access\. For example, this policy denies pushing
commits, merging pull requests, and adding files to a branch named *`master`* and a branch
named `prod` in a repository named `MyDemoRepo`:

{ ”Version”: ”2012-10-17”, ”Statement”: [{ ”Effect”: ”Deny”, ”Action”: [”codecommit:GitPush”, ”code-
commit:DeleteBranch”, ”codecommit:PutFile”, ”codecommit:MergePullRequestByFastForward”], ”Resource”:
”arn:aws:codecommit:us-east-2:80398EXAMPLE:MyDemoRepo”, ”Condition”: { ”StringEqualsIfExists”: {
”codecommit:References”: [”refs/heads/master”, ”refs/heads/prod”] }, ”Null”: { ”codecommit:References”:
false } } }] }

1
2 Branches in Git are simply pointers \(references\) to the SHA\-1 value of the head commit, which
is why the condition uses `References`\. The `Null` statement is required in any policy
whose effect is `Deny` and where `GitPush` is one of the actions\. This is required because
of the way Git and `git-receive-pack` work when pushing changes from a local repo to AWS
CodeCommit\.

3 **Tip**
4 To create a policy that applies to all branches named master in all repositories in an AWS
account, change the value of `Resource` from a repository ARN to an asterisk \(`*`\)\.

1. Choose **Review policy**\. Correct any errors in your policy statement, and then continue to **Create policy**\.

1. When the JSON is validated, the **Create policy** page is displayed\. A warning appears in the **Summary** section, advising you that this policy will not grant permissions\. This is expected\.
+ In **Name**, type a name for this policy, such as **DenyChangesToMaster**\.
+ In **Description**, type a description of the policy's purpose\. This is optional, but recommended\.
+ Choose **Create policy**\.

Apply the IAM Policy to an IAM Group or Role<a name="how-to-conditional-branch-apply-policy"></a>

You've created a policy that limits pushes and merges to a branch, but the policy has no effect until you apply it to an IAM user, group, or role\. As a best practice, consider applying the policy to an IAM group or role\. Applying policies to individual IAM users does not scale well\.<a name="how-to-conditional-branch-apply-policy-procedure"></a>

To apply the conditional policy to a group or role

1. Sign in to the AWS Management Console and open the IAM console at [https://console\.aws\.amazon\.com/iam/](https://console.aws.amazon.com/iam/)\.

1. In the navigation pane, choose **Groups**, if you want to apply the policy to an IAM group, or **Role**, if you want to apply the policy to a role that users assume\. Choose the name of the group or role\.

1. On the **Permissions** tab, choose **Attach Policy**\.

1. Select the conditional policy you created from the list of policies, and then choose **Attach policy**\.

For more information, see [Attaching and Detatching IAM Policies](http://docs.aws.amazon.com/IAM/latest/UserGuide/access_policies_manage-attach-detach.html)\.

Test the Policy<a name="how-to-conditional-branch-test"></a>

You should test the effects of the policy you've applied on the group or role to ensure that it acts as expected\. There are many ways you can do this\. For example, to test a policy similar to the one shown above, you can:
+ Sign in to the AWS CodeCommit console with an IAM user who is either a member of an IAM group that has the policy applied, or assumes a role that has the policy applied\. In the console, add a file on the branch where the restrictions apply\. You should see an error message when you attempt to save or upload a file to that branch\. Add a file to a different branch\. The operation should succeed\.
+ Sign in to the AWS CodeCommit console with an IAM user who is either a member of an IAM group that has the policy applied, or assumes a role that has the policy applied\. Create a pull request that will merge to the branch where the restrictions apply\. You should be able to create the pull request, but get an error if you try to merge it\.
+ From the terminal or command line, create a commit on the branch where the restrictions apply, and then push that commit to the AWS CodeCommit repository\. You should see an error message\. Commits and pushes made from other branches should work as usual\.

35

36

37

38

39 # View Branch Details in AWS CodeCommit<a name="how-to-view-branch-details"></a>

40

41 To view details about the branches in an AWS CodeCommit repository, you can use the AWS
CodeCommit console\. You can view the date of the last commit to a branch, the commit
message, and more\. You can also use Git from a local repo connected to the AWS CodeCommit
repository or the AWS CLI to view branch details\.

42

43 **Topics**

44 + [Use the AWS CodeCommit Console to View Branch Details](#how-to-view-branch-details-console)

45 + [Use Git to View Branch Details](#how-to-view-branch-details-git)

46 + [Use the AWS CLI to View Branch Details](#how-to-view-branch-details-cli)

47

48 ## Use the AWS CodeCommit Console to View Branch Details<a name="how-to-view-branch-details-console"></a>

49

50 Use the AWS CodeCommit console to quickly view a list of branches for your repository and
details about the branches\.

51

52 1. Open the AWS CodeCommit console at [https://console\.aws\.amazon\.com/codecommit](https://console.aws.amazon.com/codecommit)\.

53

54 1. In the list of repositories, choose the name of the repository\.

55

56 1. In the navigation pane, choose **Branches**\.

57 ![\[A view of branches in a repository.\]](http://docs.aws.amazon.com/codecommit/latest/userguide/images/codecommit-branches-list.png)

58

59 1. You can adjust the number of branches displayed on the **Branches** page by changing the
number of branches shown on a page\. The name of the branch used as the default for the
repository is displayed next to the **Default** label\. To view details about the most
recent commit to a branch, choose the commit message\. To view the files and code in a
branch, choose the branch name\.

60

61 ## Use Git to View Branch Details<a name="how-to-view-branch-details-git"></a>

62

63 To use Git from a local repo to view details about both the local and remote tracking branches
for an AWS CodeCommit repository, run the git branch command\.

64

65 The following steps assume you have already connected the local repo to the AWS CodeCommit
repository\. For instructions, see [Connect to a Repository](how-to-connect.md)\.

66

67 1. Run the git branch command, specifying the \-\-all option:

git branch --all

1

2 1. If successful, this command returns output similar to the following:

1 MyNewBranch

* master remotes/origin/MyNewBranch remotes/origin/master

2 The asterisk \(`*`\) appears next to the currently open branch\. The entries after that are remote tracking references\.
3 **Tip**
4 git branch shows local branches\.
5 git branch \-r shows remote branches\.
6 git checkout *existing\-branch\-name* switches to the specified branch name and, if git branch is run immediately afterward, displays it with an asterisk \(`*`\)\.
7 git remote update *remote\-name* updates your local repo with the list of available AWS CodeCommit repository branches\. \(To get a list of AWS CodeCommit repository names, along with their URLs, run the git remote \-v command\.\)
8
9 For more options, see your Git documentation\.
10
11 ## Use the AWS CLI to View Branch Details<a name="how-to-view-branch-details-cli"></a>
12
13 To use AWS CLI commands with AWS CodeCommit, install the AWS CLI\. For more information, see [Command Line Reference](cmd-ref.md)\.
14
15 To use the AWS CLI to view details about the branches in an AWS CodeCommit repository, run one or more of the following commands:
16 + [list\-branches](#how-to-view-branch-details-cli) to view a list of branch names\.
17 + [get\-branch](#how-to-view-branch-details-cli-details) to view information about a specific branch\.
18
19 ### To view a list of branch names<a name="how-to-view-branch-details-cli-list"></a>
20
21 1. Run the list\-branches command, specifying the name of the AWS CodeCommit repository \(with the `--repository-name` option\)\.
22 **Tip**
23 To get the name of the AWS CodeCommit repository, run the [list\-repositories](how-to-view-repository-details.md#how-to-view-repository-details-no-name-cli) command\.
24
25 For example, to view details about the branches in an AWS CodeCommit repository named ` MyDemoRepo`:

aws codecommit list-branches --repository-name MyDemoRepo

1
2 1. If successful, this command outputs a `branchNameList` object, with an entry for each branch \.
3
4 Here is some example output based on the preceding example command:

{ "branches": ["MyNewBranch", "master"] }

1
2 ### To view information about a branch<a name="how-to-view-branch-details-cli-details"></a>
3
4 1. Run the get\-branch command, specifying:
5 + The repository name \(with the \-\-repository\-name option\)\.
6 + The branch name \(with the \-\-branch\-name option\)\.
7
8 For example, to view information about a branch named `MyNewBranch` in an AWS CodeCommit repository named `MyDemoRepo`:

aws codecommit get-branch --repository-name MyDemoRepo --branch-name MyNewBranch

1. If successful, this command outputs the name of the branch and the ID of the last commit made to the branch\.

Here is some example output based on the preceding example command:

{ "branch": { "branchName": "MyNewBranch", "commitID": "317f8570EXAMPLE" } }

Compare Branches in AWS CodeCommit<a name="how-to-compare-branches"></a>

You can compare branches in an AWS CodeCommit repository by using the AWS CodeCommit console\. Comparing branches helps you quickly view the differences between a branch and the default branch, or view the differences between any two branches\.

Topics
+ [Compare a Branch to the Default Branch](#how-to-compare-branches-default)
+ [Compare Two Specific Branches](#how-to-compare-branches-two)

Compare a Branch to the Default Branch<a name="how-to-compare-branches-default"></a>

Use the AWS CodeCommit console to quickly view the differences between a branch and the default branch for your repository\.

1. Open the AWS CodeCommit console at [https://console\.aws\.amazon\.com/codecommit](https://console.aws.amazon.com/codecommit)\.

1. In the list of repositories, choose the name of the repository\.

1. In the navigation pane, choose **Branches**\.

1. In the list of branches, find the branch you want to compare to the default branch, and then choose **Compare**\.
![\[The list of branches in a repository, including information about the branches and the option to compare other branches to the default branch.\]](http://docs.aws.amazon.com/codecommit/latest/userguide/images/codecommit-branches.png)

The **Compare** view opens and displays the differences between the branch you chose and the default branch\.
![\[An abbreviated view of the differences between a branch and the default branch in a repository, including the number of changed files and the changes in those files.\]](http://docs.aws.amazon.com/codecommit/latest/userguide/images/codecommit-branches-compare1.png)

Compare Two Specific Branches<a name="how-to-compare-branches-two"></a>

Use the AWS CodeCommit console to view the differences between two branches that you want to compare\.

1. Open the AWS CodeCommit console at [https://console\.aws\.amazon\.com/codecommit](https://console.aws.amazon.com/codecommit)\.

35 1. In the list of repositories, choose the name of the repository\.

36

37 1. In the navigation pane, choose **Compare**\.

38

39 1. Choose the two branches to compare, and then choose **Compare**\. To view the list of changed
       files, expand the changed files list\. You can view changes in files side by side \(Split
       view\) or inline \(Unified view\)\.

40 **Note**

41 If you are signed in as an IAM user, you can configure and save your preferences for viewing
       code and other console settings\. For more information, see [Working with User Preferences](
       user-preferences.md)\.

42 ![\[An abbreviated view of the differences between two branches, including the number of changed
       files and the changes in those files.\]](http://docs.aws.amazon.com/codecommit/latest/
       userguide/images/codecommit-branches-compare1.png)

43

44

45

46

47 # Change Branch Settings in AWS CodeCommit<a name="how-to-change-branch"></a>

48

49 You can change the default branch to use in the AWS CodeCommit console\. You can also use the
       AWS CLI to change the default branch for a repository\. To change other branch settings, you
       can use Git from a local repo connected to the AWS CodeCommit repository\.

50

51 **Topics**

52 + [Use the AWS CodeCommit Console to Change the Default Branch](#how-to-change-branch-console)

53 + [Use the AWS CLI to Change Branch Settings](#how-to-change-branch-cli)

54

55 ## Use the AWS CodeCommit Console to Change the Default Branch<a name="how-to-change-branch-
       console"></a>

56

57 You can specify which branch is the default branch in an AWS CodeCommit repository in the AWS
       CodeCommit console\.

58

59 1. Open the AWS CodeCommit console at [https://console\.aws\.amazon\.com/codecommit](https://
       console.aws.amazon.com/codecommit)\.

60

61 1. In the list of repositories, choose the name of the repository where you want to change
       settings\.

62

63 1. In the navigation pane, choose **Branches**\.

64

65 1. Choose **Change default branch**\. In the **Default branch** drop\-down list, choose a
       different branch, and then choose **Change**\.

66 ![\[Changing the default branch used in an AWS CodeCommit repository.\]](http://docs.aws.amazon.
       com/codecommit/latest/userguide/images/codecommit-branches-change.png)

67

68 ## Use the AWS CLI to Change Branch Settings<a name="how-to-change-branch-cli"></a>

69

70 To use AWS CLI commands with AWS CodeCommit, install the AWS CLI\. For more information, see [
       Command Line Reference](cmd-ref.md)\.

71

72 To use the AWS CLI to change a repository's branch settings in an AWS CodeCommit repository, run
       the following command:

73 + [update\-default\-branch](#how-to-change-branch-cli-default) to change the default branch\.
74
75 ### To change the default branch<a name="how-to-change-branch-cli-default"></a>
76
77 1. Run the update\-default\-branch command, specifying:
78 + The name of the AWS CodeCommit repository where the default branch will be updated \(with the \-\-repository\-name option\)\.
79 **Tip**
80 To get the name of the AWS CodeCommit repository, run the [list\-repositories](how-to-view-repository-details.md#how-to-view-repository-details-no-name-cli) command\.
81 + The name of the new default branch \(with the \-\-default\-branch\-name option\)\.
82 **Tip**
83 To get the name of the branch, run the [list\-branches](how-to-view-branch-details.md#how-to-view-branch-details-cli) command\.
84
85 1. For example, to change the default branch to `MyNewBranch` in an AWS CodeCommit repository named `MyDemoRepo`:

aws codecommit update-default-branch --repository-name MyDemoRepo --default-branch-name MyNewBranch

1
2 This command produces output only if there are errors\.
3
4 For more options, see your Git documentation\.
5
6
7
8
9 # Delete a Branch in AWS CodeCommit<a name="how-to-delete-branch"></a>
10
11 You can use the AWS CodeCommit console to delete a branch in a repository\. Deleting a branch in AWS CodeCommit does not delete that branch in a local repo, so users might continue to have copies of that branch until the next time they pull changes\. To delete a branch locally and push that change to the AWS CodeCommit repository, use Git from a local repo connected to the AWS CodeCommit repository\.
12
13 Deleting a branch does not delete any commits, but it does delete all references to the commits in that branch\. If you delete a branch that contains commits that have not been merged into another branch in the repository, you cannot retrieve those commits unless you have their full commit IDs\.
14
15 **Note**
16 You cannot use the instructions in this topic to delete a repository's default branch\. If you want to delete the default branch, you must create a new branch, make the new branch the default branch, and then delete the old branch\. To learn how to create a new branch, see [Create a Branch](how-to-create-branch.md)\. To learn how to make a branch the default branch , see [Change Branch Settings](how-to-change-branch.md)\.
17
18 **Topics**
19 + [Use the AWS CodeCommit Console to Delete a Branch](#how-to-delete-branch-console)
20 + [Use the AWS CLI to Delete a Branch](#how-to-delete-branch-cli)
21 + [Use Git to Delete a Branch](#how-to-delete-branch-git)
22
23 ## Use the AWS CodeCommit Console to Delete a Branch<a name="how-to-delete-branch-console"></a>
24

25 You can use the AWS CodeCommit console to delete a branch in an AWS CodeCommit repository\.

26

27 1. Open the AWS CodeCommit console at [https://console\.aws\.amazon\.com/codecommit](https://console.aws.amazon.com/codecommit)\.

28

29 1. In the list of repositories, choose the name of the repository\.

30

31 1. In the navigation pane, choose **Branches**\.

32

33 1. Find the name of the branch that you want to delete, and choose the delete icon\. In the confirmation dialog, choose **Delete**\.

34 ![\[Deleting a branch from a repository.\]](http://docs.aws.amazon.com/codecommit/latest/userguide/images/codecommit-branches-delete-2step.png)

35

36 ## Use the AWS CLI to Delete a Branch<a name="how-to-delete-branch-cli"></a>

37

38 You can use the AWS CLI to delete a branch in an AWS CodeCommit repository, if that branch is not the default branch for the repository\. For more information about intalling and using the AWS CLI, see [Command Line Reference](cmd-ref.md)\.

39

40 1. At the terminal or command line, run the delete\-branch command, specifying:

41 + The name of the AWS CodeCommit repository where the branch will be deleted \(with the \-\-repository\-name option\)\.

42 **Tip**

43 To get the name of the AWS CodeCommit repository, run the [list\-repositories](how-to-view-repository-details.md#how-to-view-repository-details-no-name-cli) command\.

44 + The name of the branch to delete \(with the branch\-name option\)\.

45 **Tip**

46 To get the name of the branch, run the [list\-branches](how-to-view-branch-details.md#how-to-view-branch-details-cli) command\.

47

48 1. For example, to delete a branch named `MyNewBranch` in an AWS CodeCommit repository named `MyDemoRepo`:

aws codecommit delete-branch --repository-name MyDemoRepo --branch-name MyNewBranch

1

2 This command returns information about the deleted branch, including the name of the deleted branch and the full commit ID of the commit that was the head of the branch\. For example:

"deletedBranch": { "branchName": "MyNewBranch", "commitId": "317f8570EXAMPLE" }

1

2 ## Use Git to Delete a Branch<a name="how-to-delete-branch-git"></a>

3

4 To use Git from a local repo to delete a branch in an AWS CodeCommit repository, follow these steps\.

5

6 These steps assume you have already connected the local repo to the AWS CodeCommit repository\. For instructions, see [Connect to a Repository](how-to-connect.md)\.

7

8 1. To delete the branch from the local repo, run the git branch \-D *branch\-name* command where *branch\-name* is the name of the branch you want to delete\.

9 **Tip**

10 To get a list of branch names, run git branch \-\-all\.

11

12 For example, to delete a branch in the local repo named `MyNewBranch`:

git branch -D MyNewBranch

1
2 1. To delete the branch from the AWS CodeCommit repository, run the git push *remote\-name* \-\-delete *branch\-name* command where *remote\-name* is the nickname the local repo uses for the AWS CodeCommit repository and *branch\-name* is the name of the branch you want to delete from the AWS CodeCommit repository\.
3 **Tip**
4 To get a list of AWS CodeCommit repository names along with their URLs, run the git remote \-v command\.
5
6 For example, to delete a branch named `MyNewBranch` in the AWS CodeCommit repository named `origin`:

git push origin --delete MyNewBranch

1 **Tip**
2 This command will not delete a branch if it is the default branch\.
3
4 For more options, see your Git documentation\.
5
6
7
8
9 # Working with User Preferences<a name="user-preferences"></a>
10
11 Some default settings in the AWS CodeCommit console can be configured\. For example, you can change the number of repositories displayed on the dashboard\. If you are signed in to the console as an IAM user, you can store information about how you prefer to use the AWS CodeCommit console, also known as your user preferences\. This information is stored and applied every time you use the console\. These preferences are applied to all repositories in all regions for your IAM user any time you access the AWS CodeCommit console\. They are not repository\-specific or region\-specific\. They do not have any effect on your interactions with the AWS CLI, AWS CodeCommit API, or other services that interact with AWS CodeCommit\.
12
13 You can still change individual settings on console pages without having saved user preferences\. Those choices persist until you close the console window\. When you return to the console, any saved user preferences are applied\.
14
15 **Note**
16 User preferences are only available for IAM users\. You cannot set them if you use federated access, temporary access, or a root account to access the console\.
17
18 User preferences include:
19 + When viewing a list of repositories in your AWS account, the number of repositories displayed on the dashboard\.
20 + When viewing changes in code, whether to use **Unified** or **Split** view, and whether to show or hide whitespace changes\.
21 + When viewing a graph of commits, whether to display commits on branches to the left or to the right of the default branch\.
22
23 ## View and Save User Preferences<a name="user-preferences-how-to"></a>
24

25 You can view and change your user preferences for the AWS CodeCommit console\. These settings
    apply only to your IAM user in the AWS CodeCommit console\. They do not affect other IAM
    users in your AWS account\.

26

27 **To view and save preferences in the AWS CodeCommit console for your IAM user**

28

29 1. Open the AWS CodeCommit console at [https://console\.aws\.amazon\.com/codecommit](https://
    console.aws.amazon.com/codecommit)\.

30

31 You must sign in as an IAM user\. You cannot configure user preferences for other user types\.

32

33 1. In the title bar navigation, choose **User preferences**\.

34

35 1. In **User preferences**, make your changes to configure your preferences\.
36 ![\[A view of configurable user preferences in AWS CodeCommit.\]](http://docs.aws.amazon.com/
    codecommit/latest/userguide/images/codecommit-userprefs.png)

37

38 Do one of the following:
39 + To save and apply your changes, choose **Save**\.
40 + To view the AWS CodeCommit console defaults, choose **Restore**\. These defaults are applied
    if you choose **Save**\.
41 + To return to the console where you left off, choose **Back**\. Alternatively, choose **
    Dashboard** to go to the AWS CodeCommit console dashboard\.

42

43

44

45

46 # Migrate to AWS CodeCommit<a name="how-to-migrate-repository"></a>

47

48 You can migrate a Git repository to an AWS CodeCommit repository in a number of ways: by cloning
    it, mirroring it, migrating all or just some of the branches, and so on\. You can also
    migrate local, unversioned content on your computer to AWS CodeCommit\.

49

50 The following topics demonstrate some of the ways you can choose to migrate a repository\. Your
    steps may vary, depending on the type, style, or complexity of your repository and the
    decisions you make about what and how you want to migrate\. For very large repositories, you
    might want to consider [migrating incrementally](how-to-push-large-repositories.md)\.

51

52 **Note**
53 You can migrate to AWS CodeCommit from other version control systems, such as Perforce,
    Subversion, or TFS, but you will have to migrate to Git first\.
54 For more options, see your Git documentation\.
55 Alternatively, you can review the information about [migrating to Git](http://git-scm.com/book/
    en/v2/Git-and-Other-Systems-Migrating-to-Git) in the *Pro Git* book by Scott Chacon and Ben
    Straub\.

56

57 **Topics**
58 + [Migrate a Git Repository to AWS CodeCommit](how-to-migrate-repository-existing.md)
59 + [Migrate Content to AWS CodeCommit](how-to-migrate-repository-local.md)
60 + [Migrate a Repository in Increments](how-to-push-large-repositories.md)

61

62

63

64

Migrate a Git Repository to AWS CodeCommit<a name="how-to-migrate-repository-existing"></a>

You can migrate an existing Git repository to an AWS CodeCommit repository\. The procedures in this topic walk you through the process of migrating a project hosted on another Git repository to AWS CodeCommit\. As part of this process, you will:
+ Complete the initial setup required for AWS CodeCommit\.
+ Create an AWS CodeCommit repository\.
+ Clone the repository and push it to AWS CodeCommit\.
+ View files in the AWS CodeCommit repository\.
+ Share the AWS CodeCommit repository with your team\.

![\[Migrating a Git repository to AWS CodeCommit\]](http://docs.aws.amazon.com/codecommit/latest/userguide/images/codecommit-migrate-existing.png)![\[Migrating a Git repository to AWS CodeCommit\]](http://docs.aws.amazon.com/codecommit/latest/userguide/)

Topics
+ [Step 0: Setup Required for Access to AWS CodeCommit](#how-to-migrate-existing-setup)
+ [Step 1: Create an AWS CodeCommit Repository](#how-to-migrate-existing-create)
+ [Step 2: Clone the Repository and Push to the AWS CodeCommit Repository](#how-to-migrate-existing-clone)
+ [Step 3: View Files in AWS CodeCommit](#how-to-migrate-existing-view)
+ [Step 4: Share the AWS CodeCommit Repository](#how-to-migrate-existing-share)

Step 0: Setup Required for Access to AWS CodeCommit<a name="how-to-migrate-existing-setup"></a>

Before you can migrate a repository to AWS CodeCommit, you must create and configure an IAM user for AWS CodeCommit and configure your local computer for access\. You should also install the AWS CLI to manage AWS CodeCommit\. Although you can perform most AWS CodeCommit tasks without it, the AWS CLI offers flexibility when working with Git at the command line or terminal\.

If you are already set up for AWS CodeCommit, you can skip ahead to [Step 1: Create an AWS CodeCommit Repository](#how-to-migrate-existing-create)\.

To create and configure an IAM user for accessing AWS CodeCommit

1. Create an AWS account by going to [http://aws\.amazon\.com](http://aws.amazon.com) and choosing **Sign Up**\.

1. Create an IAM user, or use an existing one, in your AWS account\. Make sure you have an access key ID and a secret access key associated with that IAM user\. For more information, see [Creating an IAM User in Your AWS Account](http://docs.aws.amazon.com/IAM/latest/UserGuide/Using_SettingUpUser.html)\.
Note
AWS CodeCommit requires AWS Key Management Service\. If you are using an existing IAM user, make sure there are no policies attached to the user that expressly deny the AWS KMS actions required by AWS CodeCommit\. For more information, see [AWS KMS and Encryption](encryption.md)\.

1. Sign in to the AWS Management Console and open the IAM console at [https://console\.aws\.amazon\.com/iam/](https://console.aws.amazon.com/iam/)\.

1. In the IAM console, in the navigation pane, choose **Users**, and then choose the IAM user

you want to configure for AWS CodeCommit access\.

100

101 1. On the **Permissions** tab, choose **Add Permissions**\.

102

103 1. In **Grant permissions**, choose **Attach existing policies directly**\.

104

105 1. Select **AWSCodeCommitFullAccess** from the list of policies, or another managed policy for AWS CodeCommit access\. For more information about managed policies for AWS CodeCommit, see [AWS Managed \(Predefined\) Policies for AWS CodeCommit](auth-and-access-control-iam-identity-based-access-control.md#managed-policies)\.

106

107 After you have selected the policy you want to attach, choose** Next: Review** to review the list of policies that will be attached to the IAM user\. If the list is correct, choose ** Add permissions**\.

108

109 For more information about AWS CodeCommit managed policies and sharing access to repositories with other groups and users, see [Share a Repository](how-to-share-repository.md) and [Authentication and Access Control for AWS CodeCommit](auth-and-access-control.md)\.

110

111 **To install and configure the AWS CLI**

112

113 1. On your local machine, download and install the AWS CLI\. This is a prerequisite for interacting with AWS CodeCommit from the command line\. For more information, see [Getting Set Up with the AWS Command Line Interface](http://docs.aws.amazon.com/cli/latest/userguide/cli-chap-getting-set-up.html)\.

114 **Note**

115 AWS CodeCommit works only with AWS CLI versions 1\.7\.38 and later\. To determine which version of the AWS CLI you have installed, run the `aws --version` command\.

116 To upgrade an older version of the AWS CLI to the latest version, see [Installing the AWS Command Line Interface](http://docs.aws.amazon.com/cli/latest/userguide/installing.html)\.

117

118 1. Run this command to verify the AWS CodeCommit commands for the AWS CLI are installed:

aws codecommit help

1

2 This command should return a list of AWS CodeCommit commands\.

3

4 1. Configure the AWS CLI with the configure command, as follows:

aws configure

1

2 When prompted, specify the AWS access key and AWS secret access key of the IAM user you will use with AWS CodeCommit\. Also, be sure to specify the region where the repository exists, such as `us-east-2`\. When prompted for the default output format, specify `json`\. For example:

AWS Access Key ID [None]: Type your target AWS access key ID here, and then press Enter AWS Secret Access Key [None]: Type your target AWS secret access key here, and then press Enter Default region name [None]: Type a supported region for AWS CodeCommit here, and then press Enter Default output format [None]: Type json here, and then press Enter

1

2 To connect to a repository or a resource in another region, you must re\-configure the AWS CLI with the default region name for that region\. Supported default region names for AWS CodeCommit include:

```
 3 + us\-east\-2
 4 + us\-east\-1
 5 + eu\-west\-1
 6 + us\-west\-2
 7 + ap\-northeast\-1
 8 + ap\-southeast\-1
 9 + ap\-southeast\-2
10 + eu\-central\-1
11 + ap\-northeast\-2
12 + sa\-east\-1
13 + us\-west\-1
14 + eu\-west\-2
15 + ap\-south\-1
16 + ca\-central\-1
17
```

18 For more information about AWS CodeCommit and regions, see [Regions and Git Connection Endpoints](regions.md)\. For more information about IAM, access keys, and secret keys, see [How Do I Get Credentials?](http://docs.aws.amazon.com/IAM/latest/UserGuide/IAM_Introduction.html#IAM_SecurityCredentials) and [Managing Access Keys for IAM Users](http://docs.aws.amazon.com/IAM/latest/UserGuide/ManagingCredentials.html)\.

19

20 Next, you must install Git\.

21 + **For Linux, macOS, or Unix**:

22

23 To work with files, commits, and other information in AWS CodeCommit repositories, you must install Git on your local machine\. AWS CodeCommit supports Git versions 1\.7\.9 and later\.

24

25 To install Git, we recommend websites such as [Git Downloads](http://git-scm.com/downloads)\.

26 **Note**

27 Git is an evolving, regularly updated platform\. Occasionally, a feature change might affect the way it works with AWS CodeCommit\. If you encounter issues with a specific version of Git and AWS CodeCommit, review the information in [Troubleshooting](troubleshooting.md)\.

28 + **For Windows:**

29

30 To work with files, commits, and other information in AWS CodeCommit repositories, you must install Git on your local machine\. AWS CodeCommit supports Git versions 1\.7\.9 and later\.

31

32 To install Git, we recommend websites such as [Git for Windows](http://msysgit.github.io/)\. If you use this link to install Git, you can accept all of the installation default settings except for the following:

33 + When prompted during the **Adjusting your PATH environment** step, select the **Use Git from the Windows Command Prompt** option\.

34 + \(Optional\) If you intend to use HTTPS with the credential helper that is included in the AWS CLI instead of configuring Git credentials for AWS CodeCommit, on the **Configuring extra options** page, make sure the **Enable Git Credential Manager** option is cleared\. The Git Credential Manager is only compatible with AWS CodeCommit if IAM users configure Git credentials\. For more information, see [For HTTPS Users Using Git Credentials](setting-up-gc.md) and [Git for Windows: I Installed Git for Windows, but I Am Denied Access to My Repository \(403\)](troubleshooting-ch.md#troubleshooting-windowshttps)\.

35 **Note**

36 Git is an evolving, regularly updated platform\. Occasionally, a feature change might affect the way it works with AWS CodeCommit\. If you encounter issues with a specific version of Git and AWS CodeCommit, review the information in [Troubleshooting](troubleshooting.md)\.

37

38 AWS CodeCommit supports both HTTPS and SSH authentication\. To complete setup, you must
       configure either Git credentials for AWS CodeCommit \(HTTPS, recommended for most users\),
       an SSH key pair to use when accessing AWS CodeCommit \(SSH\), or the credential helper
       included in the AWS CLI \(HTTPS\)\.
39 + For Git credentials on all supported operating systems, see [Step 3: Create Git Credentials
       for HTTPS Connections to AWS CodeCommit](setting-up-gc.md#setting-up-gc-iam)\.
40 + For SSH on Linux, macOS, or Unix, see [SSH and Linux, macOS, or Unix: Set Up the Public and
       Private Keys for Git and AWS CodeCommit](setting-up-ssh-unixes.md#setting-up-ssh-unixes-keys
       -unixes)\.
41 + For SSH on Windows, see [SSH and Windows: Set Up the Public and Private Keys for Git and AWS
       CodeCommit](setting-up-ssh-windows.md#setting-up-ssh-windows-keys-windows)\.
42 + For the credential helper on Linux, macOS, or Unix, see [Set Up the Credential Helper \(Linux,
       macOS, or Unix\)](setting-up-https-unixes.md#setting-up-https-unixes-ch-config)\.
43 + For the credential helper on Windows, see [Set Up the Credential Helper \(Windows\)](setting-
       up-https-windows.md#setting-up-https-windows-ch-config)\.
44
45 ## Step 1: Create an AWS CodeCommit Repository<a name="how-to-migrate-existing-create"></a>
46
47 In this section, you will use the AWS CodeCommit console to create the AWS CodeCommit repository
       you will use for the rest of this tutorial\. To use the AWS CLI to create the repository,
       see [Use the AWS CLI to Create an AWS CodeCommit Repository](how-to-create-repository.md#how
       -to-create-repository-cli)\.
48
49 1. Open the AWS CodeCommit console at [https://console\.aws\.amazon\.com/codecommit](https://
       console.aws.amazon.com/codecommit)\.
50
51 1. In the region selector, choose the region where you will create the repository\. For more
       information, see [Regions and Git Connection Endpoints](regions.md)\.
52
53 1. On the **Dashboard** page, choose **Create repository**\. \(If a welcome page appears instead
       of the **Dashboard** page, choose **Get Started Now**\.\)
54
55 1. On the **Create repository** page, in **Repository name**, type a name for the repository\.
56 **Note**
57 This name must be unique in the region for your AWS account\.
58
59 1. \(Optional\) In the **Description** box, type a description for the repository\. This can
       help you and other users identify the purpose of the repository\.
60 **Note**
61 The description field accepts all HTML characters and all valid Unicode characters\. If you are
       an application developer using the `GetRepository` or `BatchGetRepositories` APIs and plan
       to display the repository description field in a web browser, see the [AWS CodeCommit API
       Reference](http://docs.aws.amazon.com/codecommit/latest/APIReference/)\.
62
63 1. Choose **Create repository**\.
64
65 1. In **Configure email notifications**, configure notifications so that repository users
       receive emails about important repository events\. This step is optional, but recommended\.
       You can choose the event types \(for example, comments on code\) and whether to use an
       existing Amazon SNS topic or create one specifically for this purpose\. You can choose to
       skip this step and configure notifications at a later time\. For more information, see [
       Configuring Notifications for Events in an AWS CodeCommit Repository](how-to-repository-
       email.md)\.
66

67 ![\[Creating a repository for migrating a Git repository to AWS CodeCommit\]](http://docs.aws.
amazon.com/codecommit/latest/userguide/images/codecommit-create-repo-migrate-existing.png)
![\[Creating a repository for migrating a Git repository to AWS CodeCommit\]](http://docs.
aws.amazon.com/codecommit/latest/userguide/)

68

69 After it is created, the repository will appear in the list of repositories in your dashboard\.
In the URL column, choose the copy icon, and then choose the protocol \(SSH or HTTPS\) you
will use to connect to AWS CodeCommit\. Copy the URL\.

70

71 For example, if you named your repository *MyClonedRepository* and you are using Git credentials
with HTTPS in the US West \(Oregon\) region, the URL would look like the following:

https://git-codecommit.us-east-2.amazonaws.com/v1/repos/MyClonedRepository

1

2 You will need this URL later in [Step 2: Clone the Repository and Push to the AWS CodeCommit
Repository](#how-to-migrate-existing-clone)\.

3

4 ## Step 2: Clone the Repository and Push to the AWS CodeCommit Repository<a name="how-to-migrate
-existing-clone"></a>

5

6 In this section, you will clone an existing Git repository to your local computer, creating what
is called a local repo\. You will then push the contents of the local repo to the AWS
CodeCommit repository you created earlier\.

7

8 1. From the terminal or command prompt on your local computer, run the git clone command with
the `--mirror` option to clone a bare copy of the remote repository into a new folder named
aws\-codecommit\-demo\. Note that this is a bare repo meant only for migration, and is not
the local repo for interacting with the migrated repository in AWS CodeCommit\. You'll want
to create that later, after the migration to AWS CodeCommit is complete\.

9

10 The following example clones a sample application created for AWS demonstration purposes and
hosted on GitHub \(*https://github\.com/awslabs/aws\-demo\-php\-simple\-app\.git*\) to a
local repo in a directory named *aws\-codecommit\-demo*\.

git clone --mirror https://github.com/awslabs/aws-demo-php-simple-app.git aws-codecommit-demo

1

2 1. Change directories to the directory where you made the clone\.

cd aws-codecommit-demo

1

2 1. Run the git push command, specifying the URL and name of the destination AWS CodeCommit
repository and the \-\-all option\. \(This is the URL you copied in [Step 1: Create an AWS
CodeCommit Repository](#how-to-migrate-existing-create)\)\.

3

4 For example, if you named your repository *MyClonedRepository* and you are set up to use HTTPS,
you would type the following command:

git push https://git-codecommit.us-east-2.amazonaws.com/v1/repos/MyClonedRepository --all

1 **Note**

2 The \-\-all option only pushes all branches for the repository\. It does not push other
references, such as tags\. If you want to push tags, wait until the initial push is complete
, and then push again, this time using the \-\-tags option, for example:

git push ssh://git-codecommit.us-east-2.amazonaws.com/v1/repos/MyClonedRepository --tags

1 For more information about git push and its options, see [Git push](https://git-scm.com/docs/git
   -push)\. For information about pushing large repositories, especially when pushing all
   references at once \(for example, with the \-\-mirror option\), see [Migrate a Repository in
   Increments](how-to-push-large-repositories.md)\.

2
3 You can delete the *aws\-codecommit\-demo* folder and its contents after you have migrated the
   repository to AWS CodeCommit\. To create a local repo with all the correct references for
   working with the repository in AWS CodeCommit, run the `git clone` command without the `--
   mirror` option\. For example:

git clone https://git-codecommit.us-east-2.amazonaws.com/v1/repos/MyClonedRepository

1
2 ## Step 3: View Files in AWS CodeCommit<a name="how-to-migrate-existing-view"></a>
3
4 After you have pushed the contents of your directory, you can use the AWS CodeCommit console to
   quickly view all of the files in that repository\.
5
6 1. Open the AWS CodeCommit console at [https://console\.aws\.amazon\.com/codecommit](https://
   console.aws.amazon.com/codecommit)\.
7
8 1. Choose the name of the repository from the list \(for example, *MyClonedRepository*\)\.
9
10 1. View the files in the repository for the branches, the clone URLs, the settings, and more\.
11 ![\[View of a cloned repository in AWS CodeCommit\]](http://docs.aws.amazon.com/codecommit/
   latest/userguide/images/codecommit-cloned-repo-url.png)![\[View of a cloned repository in
   AWS CodeCommit\]](http://docs.aws.amazon.com/codecommit/latest/userguide/)
12
13 ## Step 4: Share the AWS CodeCommit Repository<a name="how-to-migrate-existing-share"></a>
14
15 When you create a repository in AWS CodeCommit, two endpoints are generated: one for HTTPS
   connections and one for SSH connections\. Both provide secure connections over a network\.
   Your users can use either protocol\. Both endpoints remain active no matter which protocol
   you recommend to your users\. Before you can share your repository with others, you must
   create IAM policies that allow access to your repository to other users\. Provide those
   access instructions to your users\.
16
17 **Create a customer managed policy for your repository**
18
19 1. Sign in to the AWS Management Console and open the IAM console at [https://console\.aws\.
   amazon\.com/iam/](https://console.aws.amazon.com/iam/)\.
20
21 1. In the **Dashboard** navigation area, choose **Policies**, and then choose **Create Policy
   **\.
22
23 1. On the **Create Policy** page, next to **Copy an AWS Managed Policy**, choose **Select**\.
24
25 1. On the **Copy an AWS Managed Policy** page, type **AWSCodeCommitPowerUser** in the **Search
   Policies** search box\. Choose **Select** next to that policy name\.
26
27 1. On the **Review Policy** page, in **Policy Name**, type a new name for the policy \(for
   example, *AWSCodeCommitPowerUser\-MyDemoRepo*\)\.
28

29   In the **Policy Document** text box, replace the "*" portion of the `Resource` line with the
      Amazon Resource Name \(ARN\) of the AWS CodeCommit repository\. For example:

"Resource": ["arn:aws:codecommit:us-east-2:80398EXAMPLE:MyDemoRepo"]

1 **Tip**
2 To find the ARN for the AWS CodeCommit repository, go to the AWS CodeCommit console and choose
      the repository name from the list\. For more information, see [View Repository Details](how-
      to-view-repository-details.md)\.

3
4 If you want this policy to apply to more than one repository, add each repository as a resource
      by specifying its ARN\. Include a comma between each resource statement, as shown in the
      following example:

"Resource": ["arn:aws:codecommit:us-east-2:80398EXAMPLE:MyDemoRepo", "arn:aws:codecommit:us-east-
2:80398EXAMPLE:MyOtherDemoRepo"]

1
2 1. Choose **Validate Policy**\. After it is validated, choose **Create Policy**\.
3 **Tip**
4 Creating a managed policy for a repository does not supply additional permissions required for
      individual users to set up Git credentials or SSH keys in IAM\. You must apply these managed
      policies to individual IAM users\.
5 To allow users to use Git credentials to connect to AWS CodeCommit, select the **
      IAMSelfManageServiceSpecificCredentials** and **IAMReadOnlyAccess** managed policies and
      apply them to your users\.
6 To allow users to use SSH to connect to AWS CodeCommit, select the **IAMUserSSHKeys** and **
      IAMReadOnlyAccess** managed policies and apply them to your users\.

7
8 To manage access to your repository, create an IAM group for its users, add IAM users to that
      group, and then attach the customer managed policy you created in the previous step, as well
      as any additional policies required for access, such as IAMUserSSHKeys or
      IAMSelfManageServiceSpecificCredentials\.

9
10 1. Sign in to the AWS Management Console and open the IAM console at [https://console\.aws\.
      amazon\.com/iam/](https://console.aws.amazon.com/iam/)\.

11
12 1. In the **Dashboard** navigation area, choose **Groups**, and then choose **Create New Group
      **\.

13
14 1. On the **Set Group Name** page, in the **Group Name** box, type a name for the group \(for
      example, *MyDemoRepoGroup*\), and then choose **Next Step**\. Consider including the
      repository name as part of the group name\.
15 **Note**
16 This name must be unique across an AWS account\.

17
18 1. Select the check box next to the customer managed policy you created in the previous section
      \(for example, **AWSCodeCommitPowerUser\-MyDemoRepo**\)\.
19 + If your users will use HTTPS and Git credentials to connect to AWS CodeCommit, select the
      check boxes next to **IAMSelfManageServiceSpecificCredentials** and **IAMReadOnlyAccess**,
      and then choose **Next Step**\.
20 + If your users will use SSH to connect to your repository, select the check boxes next to **
      IAMUserSSHKeys** and **IAMReadOnlyAccess**, and then choose **Next Step**\.

21
22 1. On the **Review** page, choose **Create Group**\. The group will be created in IAM with the
      specified policies already attached\. It will appear in the list of groups associated with

your AWS account\.

23
24 1. Choose your group from the list\.

25
26 1. On the group summary page, choose the **Users** tab, and then choose **Add Users to Group**\.
On the list that shows all users associated with your AWS account, select the check boxes
next to the users to whom you want to allow access to the AWS CodeCommit repository, and
then choose **Add Users**\.
27 **Tip**
28 You can use the Search box to quickly find users by name\.

29
30 1. When you have added your users, close the IAM console\.

31
32 After you have created an IAM user that will access AWS CodeCommit using the policy group and
policies you configured, send that user the connection information they will use to connect
to the repository\.

33
34 1. Open the AWS CodeCommit console at [https://console\.aws\.amazon\.com/codecommit](https://
console.aws.amazon.com/codecommit)\.

35
36 1. In the region selector, choose the region where the repository was created\. Repositories are
specific to an AWS region\. For more information, see [Regions and Git Connection Endpoints
](regions.md)\.

37
38 1. On the **Dashboard** page, choose the name of the repository you want to share\.

39
40 1. On the **Code** page, choose **Clone URL**, and then choose the protocol you want your users
to use\.

41
42 1. Copy the displayed URL for the connection protocol your users will use when connecting to
your AWS CodeCommit repository\.

43
44 1. Send your users the connection information along with any other instructions, such as
installing the AWS CLI, configuring a profile, or installing Git\. Make sure to include the
configuration information for the connection protocol \(for example, for HTTPS, configuring
the credential helper for Git\)\.

45
46
47
48
49 # Migrate Local or Unversioned Content to AWS CodeCommit<a name="how-to-migrate-repository-local
"></a>

50
51 The procedures in this topic walk you through the process of migrating an existing project or
local content on your computer to an AWS CodeCommit repository\. As part of this process,
you will:
52 + Complete the initial setup required for AWS CodeCommit\.
53 + Create an AWS CodeCommit repository\.
54 + Place a local folder under Git version control and push the contents of that folder to the AWS
CodeCommit repository\.
55 + View files in the AWS CodeCommit repository\.
56 + Share the AWS CodeCommit repository with your team\.

57
58 ![\[Migrating a local project to AWS CodeCommit\]](http://docs.aws.amazon.com/codecommit/latest/

userguide/images/codecommit-migrate-local.png)![\[Migrating a local project to AWS
CodeCommit\]](http://docs.aws.amazon.com/codecommit/latest/userguide/)

Topics
+ [Step 0: Setup Required for Access to AWS CodeCommit](#how-to-migrate-local-setup)
+ [Step 1: Create an AWS CodeCommit Repository](#how-to-migrate-local-create)
+ [Step 2: Migrate Local Content to the AWS CodeCommit Repository](#how-to-migrate-local-version
)
+ [Step 3: View Files in AWS CodeCommit](#how-to-migrate-local-view)
+ [Step 4: Share the AWS CodeCommit Repository](#how-to-migrate-local-share)

Step 0: Setup Required for Access to AWS CodeCommit<a name="how-to-migrate-local-setup"></a>

Before you can migrate local content to AWS CodeCommit, you must create and configure an IAM
    user for AWS CodeCommit and configure your local computer for access\. You should also
    install the AWS CLI to manage AWS CodeCommit\. Although you can perform most AWS CodeCommit
    tasks without it, the AWS CLI offers flexibility when working with Git\.

If you are already set up for AWS CodeCommit, you can skip ahead to [Step 1: Create an AWS
    CodeCommit Repository](#how-to-migrate-local-create)\.

To create and configure an IAM user for accessing AWS CodeCommit

1. Create an AWS account by going to [http://aws\.amazon\.com](http://aws.amazon.com) and
    choosing **Sign Up**\.

1. Create an IAM user, or use an existing one, in your AWS account\. Make sure you have an
    access key ID and a secret access key associated with that IAM user\. For more information,
    see [Creating an IAM User in Your AWS Account](http://docs.aws.amazon.com/IAM/latest/
    UserGuide/Using_SettingUpUser.html)\.
Note
AWS CodeCommit requires AWS Key Management Service\. If you are using an existing IAM user, make
    sure there are no policies attached to the user that expressly deny the AWS KMS actions
    required by AWS CodeCommit\. For more information, see [AWS KMS and Encryption](encryption.
    md)\.

1. Sign in to the AWS Management Console and open the IAM console at [https://console\.aws\.
    amazon\.com/iam/](https://console.aws.amazon.com/iam/)\.

1. In the IAM console, in the navigation pane, choose **Users**, and then choose the IAM user
    you want to configure for AWS CodeCommit access\.

1. On the **Permissions** tab, choose **Add Permissions**\.

1. In **Grant permissions**, choose **Attach existing policies directly**\.

1. Select **AWSCodeCommitFullAccess** from the list of policies, or another managed policy for
    AWS CodeCommit access\. For more information about managed policies for AWS CodeCommit, see
    [AWS Managed \(Predefined\) Policies for AWS CodeCommit](auth-and-access-control-iam-
    identity-based-access-control.md#managed-policies)\.

After you have selected the policy you want to attach, choose** Next: Review** to review the
    list of policies that will be attached to the IAM user\. If the list is correct, choose **
    Add permissions**\.

92

93 For more information about AWS CodeCommit managed policies and sharing access to repositories with other groups and users, see [Share a Repository] (how-to-share-repository.md) and [Authentication and Access Control for AWS CodeCommit] (auth-and-access-control.md)\.

94

95 **To install and configure the AWS CLI**

96

97 1. On your local machine, download and install the AWS CLI\. This is a prerequisite for interacting with AWS CodeCommit from the command line\. For more information, see [Getting Set Up with the AWS Command Line Interface] (http://docs.aws.amazon.com/cli/latest/userguide/cli-chap-getting-set-up.html)\.

98 **Note**

99 AWS CodeCommit works only with AWS CLI versions 1\.7\.38 and later\. To determine which version of the AWS CLI you have installed, run the `aws --version` command\.

100 To upgrade an older version of the AWS CLI to the latest version, see [Installing the AWS Command Line Interface] (http://docs.aws.amazon.com/cli/latest/userguide/installing.html)\.

101

102 1. Run this command to verify the AWS CodeCommit commands for the AWS CLI are installed:

aws codecommit help

1

2 This command should return a list of AWS CodeCommit commands\.

3

4 1. Configure the AWS CLI with the configure command, as follows:

aws configure

1

2 When prompted, specify the AWS access key and AWS secret access key of the IAM user you will use with AWS CodeCommit\. Also, be sure to specify the region where the repository exists, such as `us-east-2`\. When prompted for the default output format, specify `json`\. For example:

AWS Access Key ID [None]: Type your target AWS access key ID here, and then press Enter AWS Secret Access Key [None]: Type your target AWS secret access key here, and then press Enter Default region name [None]: Type a supported region for AWS CodeCommit here, and then press Enter Default output format [None]: Type json here, and then press Enter

1

2 To connect to a repository or a resource in another region, you must re\-configure the AWS CLI with the default region name for that region\. Supported default region names for AWS CodeCommit include:

3 + us\-east\-2
4 + us\-east\-1
5 + eu\-west\-1
6 + us\-west\-2
7 + ap\-northeast\-1
8 + ap\-southeast\-1
9 + ap\-southeast\-2
10 + eu\-central\-1
11 + ap\-northeast\-2
12 + sa\-east\-1
13 + us\-west\-1
14 + eu\-west\-2
15 + ap\-south\-1
16 + ca\-central\-1

17

18 For more information about AWS CodeCommit and regions, see [Regions and Git Connection Endpoints](regions.md)\. For more information about IAM, access keys, and secret keys, see [How Do I Get Credentials?](http://docs.aws.amazon.com/IAM/latest/UserGuide/IAM_Introduction.html# IAM_SecurityCredentials) and [Managing Access Keys for IAM Users](http://docs.aws.amazon.com /IAM/latest/UserGuide/ManagingCredentials.html)\.

19

20 Next, you must install Git\.

21 + **For Linux, macOS, or Unix**:

22

23 To work with files, commits, and other information in AWS CodeCommit repositories, you must install Git on your local machine\. AWS CodeCommit supports Git versions 1\.7\.9 and later\.

24

25 To install Git, we recommend websites such as [Git Downloads](http://git-scm.com/downloads)\.

26 **Note**

27 Git is an evolving, regularly updated platform\. Occasionally, a feature change might affect the way it works with AWS CodeCommit\. If you encounter issues with a specific version of Git and AWS CodeCommit, review the information in [Troubleshooting](troubleshooting.md)\.

28 + **For Windows:**

29

30 To work with files, commits, and other information in AWS CodeCommit repositories, you must install Git on your local machine\. AWS CodeCommit supports Git versions 1\.7\.9 and later\.

31

32 To install Git, we recommend websites such as [Git for Windows](http://msysgit.github.io/)\. If you use this link to install Git, you can accept all of the installation default settings except for the following:

33 + When prompted during the **Adjusting your PATH environment** step, select the **Use Git from the Windows Command Prompt** option\.

34 + \(Optional\) If you intend to use HTTPS with the credential helper that is included in the AWS CLI instead of configuring Git credentials for AWS CodeCommit, on the **Configuring extra options** page, make sure the **Enable Git Credential Manager** option is cleared\. The Git Credential Manager is only compatible with AWS CodeCommit if IAM users configure Git credentials\. For more information, see [For HTTPS Users Using Git Credentials](setting-up-gc.md) and [Git for Windows: I Installed Git for Windows, but I Am Denied Access to My Repository \(403\)](troubleshooting-ch.md#troubleshooting-windowshttps)\.

35 **Note**

36 Git is an evolving, regularly updated platform\. Occasionally, a feature change might affect the way it works with AWS CodeCommit\. If you encounter issues with a specific version of Git and AWS CodeCommit, review the information in [Troubleshooting](troubleshooting.md)\.

37

38 AWS CodeCommit supports both HTTPS and SSH authentication\. To complete setup, you must configure either Git credentials for AWS CodeCommit \(HTTPS, recommended for most users\), an SSH key pair \(SSH\) to use when accessing AWS CodeCommit, or the credential helper included in the AWS CLI\.

39 + For Git credentials on all supported operating systems, see [Step 3: Create Git Credentials for HTTPS Connections to AWS CodeCommit](setting-up-gc.md#setting-up-gc-iam)\.

40 + For SSH on Linux, macOS, or Unix, see [SSH and Linux, macOS, or Unix: Set Up the Public and Private Keys for Git and AWS CodeCommit](setting-up-ssh-unixes.md#setting-up-ssh-unixes-keys -unixes)\.

41 + For SSH on Windows, see [SSH and Windows: Set Up the Public and Private Keys for Git and AWS CodeCommit](setting-up-ssh-windows.md#setting-up-ssh-windows-keys-windows)\.

42 + For the credential helper on Linux, macOS, or Unix, see [Set Up the Credential Helper \(Linux, macOS, or Unix\)](setting-up-https-unixes.md#setting-up-https-unixes-ch-config)\.

43 + For the credential helper on Windows, see [Set Up the Credential Helper \(Windows\)](setting-

up-https-windows.md#setting-up-https-windows-ch-config)\.

44

45 ## Step 1: Create an AWS CodeCommit Repository<a name="how-to-migrate-local-create"></a>

46

47 In this section, you will use the AWS CodeCommit console to create the AWS CodeCommit repository
   you will use for the rest of this tutorial\. To use the AWS CLI to create the repository,
   see [Use the AWS CLI to Create an AWS CodeCommit Repository](how-to-create-repository.md#how
   -to-create-repository-cli)\.

48

49 1. Open the AWS CodeCommit console at [https://console\.aws\.amazon\.com/codecommit](https://
   console.aws.amazon.com/codecommit)\.

50

51 1. In the region selector, choose the region where you will create the repository\. For more
   information, see [Regions and Git Connection Endpoints](regions.md)\.

52

53 1. On the **Dashboard** page, choose **Create repository**\. \(If a welcome page appears instead
   of the **Dashboard** page, choose **Get Started Now**\.\)

54

55 1. On the **Create repository** page, in **Repository name**, type a name for the repository\.
56 **Note**
57 This name must be unique in the region for your AWS account\.

58

59 1. \(Optional\) In the **Description** box, type a description for the repository\. This can
   help you and other users identify the purpose of the repository\.
60 **Note**
61 The description field accepts all HTML characters and all valid Unicode characters\. If you are
   an application developer using the `GetRepository` or `BatchGetRepositories` APIs and plan
   to display the repository description field in a web browser, see the [AWS CodeCommit API
   Reference](http://docs.aws.amazon.com/codecommit/latest/APIReference/)\.

62

63 1. Choose **Create repository**\.

64

65 1. In **Configure email notifications**, configure notifications so that repository users
   receive emails about important repository events\. This step is optional, but recommended\.
   You can choose the event types \(for example, comments on code\) and whether to use an
   existing Amazon SNS topic or create one specifically for this purpose\. You can choose to
   skip this step and configure notifications at a later time\. For more information, see [
   Configuring Notifications for Events in an AWS CodeCommit Repository](how-to-repository-
   email.md)\.

66

67 ![\[Creating a repository for migrating local content to AWS CodeCommit\]](http://docs.aws.
   amazon.com/codecommit/latest/userguide/images/codecommit-create-repo-migrate-local.png)![\[
   Creating a repository for migrating local content to AWS CodeCommit\]](http://docs.aws.
   amazon.com/codecommit/latest/userguide/)

68

69 After it is created, the repository will appear in the list of repositories in your dashboard\.
   In the URL column, choose the copy icon, and then choose the protocol \(HTTPS or SSH\) you
   will use to connect to AWS CodeCommit\. Copy the URL\.

70

71 For example, if you named your repository *MyFirstRepo* and you are using HTTPS, the URL would
   look like the following:

https://git-codecommit.us-east-2.amazonaws.com/v1/repos/MyFirstRepo

1

200

2 You will need this URL later in [Step 2: Migrate Local Content to the AWS CodeCommit Repository](#how-to-migrate-local-version)\.

3

4 ## Step 2: Migrate Local Content to the AWS CodeCommit Repository<a name="how-to-migrate-local-version"></a>

5

6 Now that you have an AWS CodeCommit repository, you can choose a directory on your local computer to convert into a local Git repository\. The git init command can be used to either convert existing, unversioned content to a Git repository or, if you do not yet have files or content, to initialize a new, empty repository\.

7

8 1. From the terminal or command line on your local computer, change directories to the directory you want to use as the source for your repository\.

9

10 1. Run the git init command to initialize Git version control in the directory\. This will create a \.git subdirectory in the root of the directory that enables version control tracking\. The \.git folder also contains all of the required metadata for the repository\.

git init

1

2 1. Add the files you want to add to version control\. In this tutorial, you will run the `git add` command with the `.` specifier to add all of the files in this directory\. For other options, consult your Git documentation\.

git add .

1

2 1. Create a commit for the added files with a commit message\.

git commit –m "Initial commit"

1

2 1. Run the git push command, specifying the URL and name of the destination AWS CodeCommit repository and the `--all` option\. \(This is the URL you copied in [Step 1: Create an AWS CodeCommit Repository](#how-to-migrate-local-create)\.\)

3

4 For example, if you named your repository *MyFirstRepo* and you are set up to use HTTPS, you would type the following command:

git push https://git-codecommit.us-east-2.amazonaws.com/v1/repos/MyFirstRepo --all

1

2 ## Step 3: View Files in AWS CodeCommit<a name="how-to-migrate-local-view"></a>

3

4 After you have pushed the contents of your directory, you can use the AWS CodeCommit console to quickly view all of the files in the repository\.

5

6 1. Open the AWS CodeCommit console at [https://console\.aws\.amazon\.com/codecommit](https://console.aws.amazon.com/codecommit)\.

7

8 1. Choose the name of the repository from the list \(for example, *MyFirstRepository*\)\.

9

10 1. View the files in the repository for the branches, the clone URLs, the settings, and more\.
11 ![\[View of the contents of a repository in AWS CodeCommit\]](http://docs.aws.amazon.com/codecommit/latest/userguide/images/codecommit-view-migrate-local.png)![\[View of the contents of a repository in AWS CodeCommit\]](http://docs.aws.amazon.com/codecommit/latest/userguide/)

12

13 ## Step 4: Share the AWS CodeCommit Repository<a name="how-to-migrate-local-share"></a>

14

15 When you create a repository in AWS CodeCommit, two endpoints are generated: one for HTTPS connections and one for SSH connections\. Both provide secure connections over a network\. Your users can use either protocol\. Both endpoints remain active no matter which protocol you recommend to your users\. Before you can share your repository with others, you must create IAM policies that allow access to your repository to other users\. Provide those access instructions to your users\.

16

17 **Create a customer managed policy for your repository**

18

19 1. Sign in to the AWS Management Console and open the IAM console at [https://console\.aws\.amazon\.com/iam/](https://console.aws.amazon.com/iam/)\.

20

21 1. In the **Dashboard** navigation area, choose **Policies**, and then choose **Create Policy**\.

22

23 1. On the **Create Policy** page, next to **Copy an AWS Managed Policy**, choose **Select**\.

24

25 1. On the **Copy an AWS Managed Policy** page, type **AWSCodeCommitPowerUser** in the **Search Policies** search box\. Choose **Select** next to that policy name\.

26

27 1. On the **Review Policy** page, in **Policy Name**, type a new name for the policy \(for example, *AWSCodeCommitPowerUser\-MyDemoRepo*\)\.

28

29 In the **Policy Document** text box, replace the "*" portion of the `Resource` line with the Amazon Resource Name \(ARN\) of the AWS CodeCommit repository\. For example:

"Resource": ["arn:aws:codecommit:us-east-2:80398EXAMPLE:MyDemoRepo"]

1 **Tip**
2 To find the ARN for the AWS CodeCommit repository, go to the AWS CodeCommit console and choose the repository name from the list\. For more information, see [View Repository Details](how-to-view-repository-details.md)\.

3

4 If you want this policy to apply to more than one repository, add each repository as a resource by specifying its ARN\. Include a comma between each resource statement, as shown in the following example:

"Resource": ["arn:aws:codecommit:us-east-2:80398EXAMPLE:MyDemoRepo", "arn:aws:codecommit:us-east-2:80398EXAMPLE:MyOtherDemoRepo"]

1

2 1. Choose **Validate Policy**\. After it is validated, choose **Create Policy**\.
3 **Tip**
4 Creating a managed policy for a repository does not supply additional permissions required for individual users to set up Git credentials or SSH keys in IAM\. You must apply these managed policies to individual IAM users\.
5 To allow users to use Git credentials to connect to AWS CodeCommit, select the **IAMSelfManageServiceSpecificCredentials** and **IAMReadOnlyAccess** managed policies and apply them to your users\.
6 To allow users to use SSH to connect to AWS CodeCommit, select the **IAMUserSSHKeys** and **IAMReadOnlyAccess** managed policies and apply them to your users\.

7

8 To manage access to your repository, create an IAM group for its users, add IAM users to that group, and then attach the customer managed policy you created in the previous step, as well as any additional policies required for access, such as IAMSelfManageServiceSpecificCredentials or IAMUserSSHKeys\.

9

10 1. Sign in to the AWS Management Console and open the IAM console at [https://console\.aws\.amazon\.com/iam/](https://console.aws.amazon.com/iam/)\.

11

12 1. In the **Dashboard** navigation area, choose **Groups**, and then choose **Create New Group **\.

13

14 1. On the **Set Group Name** page, in the **Group Name** box, type a name for the group \(for example, *MyDemoRepoGroup*\), and then choose **Next Step**\. Consider including the repository name as part of the group name\.

15 **Note**

16 This name must be unique across an AWS account\.

17

18 1. Select the check box next to the customer managed policy you created in the previous section \(for example, **AWSCodeCommitPowerUser\-MyDemoRepo**\)\.

19 + If your users will use HTTPS and Git credentials to connect to AWS CodeCommit, select the check boxes next to **IAMSelfManageServiceSpecificCredentials** and **IAMReadOnlyAccess**, and then choose **Next Step**\.

20 + If your users will use SSH to connect to your repository, select the check boxes next to **IAMUserSSHKeys** and **IAMReadOnlyAccess**, and then choose **Next Step**\.

21

22 1. On the **Review** page, choose **Create Group**\. The group will be created in IAM with the specified policies already attached\. It will appear in the list of groups associated with your AWS account\.

23

24 1. Choose your group from the list\.

25

26 1. On the group summary page, choose the **Users** tab, and then choose **Add Users to Group**\. On the list that shows all users associated with your AWS account, select the check boxes next to the users to whom you want to allow access to the AWS CodeCommit repository, and then choose **Add Users**\.

27 **Tip**

28 You can use the Search box to quickly find users by name\.

29

30 1. When you have added your users, close the IAM console\.

31

32 After you have created an IAM user that will access AWS CodeCommit using the policy group and policies you configured, send that user the connection information they will use to connect to the repository\.

33

34 1. Open the AWS CodeCommit console at [https://console\.aws\.amazon\.com/codecommit](https://console.aws.amazon.com/codecommit)\.

35

36 1. In the region selector, choose the region where the repository was created\. Repositories are specific to an AWS region\. For more information, see [Regions and Git Connection Endpoints](regions.md)\.

37

38 1. On the **Dashboard** page, choose the name of the repository you want to share\.

39

40 1. On the **Code** page, choose **Clone URL**, and then choose the protocol you want your users

```
40     to use\.

41

42  1. Copy the displayed URL for the connection protocol your users will use when connecting to
       your AWS CodeCommit repository\.

43

44  1. Send your users the connection information along with any other instructions, such as
       installing the AWS CLI, configuring a profile, or installing Git\. Make sure to include the
       configuration information for the connection protocol \(for example, for HTTPS, configuring
       the credential helper for Git\)\.

45

46

47

48
```

```
49  # Migrate a Repository Incrementally<a name="how-to-push-large-repositories"></a>

50

51  When migrating to AWS CodeCommit, consider pushing your repository in increments or chunks to
       reduce the chances an intermittent network issue or degraded network performance will cause
       the entire push to fail\. By using incremental pushes with a script like the following, you
       can restart the migration and push only those commits that did not succeed on the earlier
       attempt\.

52

53  The procedures in this topic show you how to create and run a script that will migrate your
       repository in increments and repush only those increments that did not succeed until the
       migration is complete\.

54

55  These instructions assume you have already completed the steps in [Setting Up ](setting-up.md)
       and [Create a Repository](how-to-create-repository.md)\.

56

57  **Topics**
58  + [Step 0: Determine Whether to Migrate Incrementally](#how-to-push-large-repositories-determine
       )
59  + [Step 1: Install Prerequisites and Add the AWS CodeCommit Repository as a Remote](#how-to-push
       -large-repositories-prereq)
60  + [Step 2: Create the Script to Use for Migrating Incrementally](#how-to-push-large-repositories
       -createscript)
61  + [Step 3: Run the Script and Migrate Incrementally to AWS CodeCommit](#how-to-push-large-
       repositories-runscript)
62  + [Appendix: Sample Script `incremental-repo-migration.py`](#how-to-push-large-repositories-
       sample)

63

64  ## Step 0: Determine Whether to Migrate Incrementally<a name="how-to-push-large-repositories-
       determine"></a>

65

66  There are several factors to consider to determine the overall size of your repository and
       whether to migrate incrementally\. The most obvious is the overall size of the artifacts in
       the repository\. Factors such as the accumulated history of the repository can also
       contribute to size\. A repository with years of history and branches can be very large, even
       though the individual assets are not\. There are a number of strategies you can pursue to
       make migrating these repositories simpler and more efficient, such as using a shallow clone
       strategy when cloning a repository with a long history of development, or turning off delta
       compression for large binary files\. You can research options by consulting your Git
       documentation, or you can choose to set up and configure incremental pushes for migrating
       your repository using the sample script included in this topic, `incremental-repo-migration.
       py`\.
```

₆₇

₆₈ You might want to configure incremental pushes if one or more of the following conditions is true:

₆₉ + The repository you want to migrate has more than five years of history\.

₇₀ + Your internet connection is subject to intermittent outages, dropped packets, slow response, or other interruptions in service\.

₇₁ + The overall size of the repository is larger than 2 GB and you intend to migrate the entire repository\.

₇₂ + The repository contains large artifacts or binaries that do not compress well, such as large image files with more than five tracked versions\.

₇₃ + You have previously attempted a migration to AWS CodeCommit and received an "Internal Service Error" message\.

₇₄

₇₅ Even if none of the above conditions are true, you can still choose to push incrementally\.

₇₆

₇₇ ## Step 1: Install Prerequisites and Add the AWS CodeCommit Repository as a Remote<a name="how-to-push-large-repositories-prereq"></a>

₇₈

₇₉ You can create your own custom script, which will have its own prerequisites\. If you choose to use the sample included in this topic, you must first install its prerequisites, as well as clone the repository to your local computer and add the AWS CodeCommit repository as a remote for the repository you want to migrate\.

₈₀

₈₁ **Set up to run incremental\-repo\-migration\.py**

₈₂

₈₃ 1. On your local computer, install Python 2\.6 or later, if it is not already installed\. For more information and the latest versions, see [the Python website](https://www.python.org/downloads/)\.

₈₄

₈₅ 1. On the same computer, install GitPython, which is a Python library used to interact with Git repositories, if it is not already installed\. For more information, see [the GitPython documentation](http://gitpython.readthedocs.org/en/stable/)\.

₈₆

₈₇ 1. Use the git clone \-\-mirror command to clone the repository you want to migrate to your local computer\. From the terminal \(Linux, macOS, or Unix\) or the command prompt \(Windows\), use the git clone \-\-mirror command to create a local repo for the repository, including the directory where you want to create the local repo\. For example, to clone a Git repository named *MyMigrationRepo* with a URL of *https://example\.com/my\-repo/* to a directory named *my\-repo*:

git clone --mirror https://example.com/my-repo/MyMigrationRepo.git my-repo

₁

₂ You should see output similar to the following, which indicates the repository has been cloned into a bare local repo named my\-repo:

Cloning into bare repository 'my-repo'... remote: Counting objects: 20, done. remote: Compressing objects: 100% (17/17), done. remote: Total 20 (delta 5), reused 15 (delta 3) Unpacking objects: 100% (20/20), done. Checking connectivity... done.

₁

₂ 1. Change directories to the local repo for the repository you just cloned \(for example, *my\-repo*\)\. From that directory, use the git remote add *DefaultRemoteName* *RemoteRepositoryURL* command to add the AWS CodeCommit repository as a remote repository for the local repo\.

₃ **Note**

4 When pushing large repositories, consider using SSH instead of HTTPS\. When pushing a large
change, a large number of changes, or a large repository, long\-running HTTPS connections
are often terminated prematurely due to networking issues or firewall settings\. For more
information about setting up AWS CodeCommit for SSH, see [For SSH Connections on Linux,
macOS, or Unix](setting-up-ssh-unixes.md) or [For SSH Connections on Windows](setting-up-ssh
-windows.md)\.

5

6 For example, to add the SSH endpoint for an AWS CodeCommit repository named MyDestinationRepo
as a remote repository for the remote named `codecommit`, use the following command:

git remote add codecommit ssh://git-codecommit.us-east-2.amazonaws.com/v1/repos/MyDestinationRepo

1 **Tip**
2 Because this is a clone, the default remote name \(`origin`\) will already be in use\. You must
use another remote name\. Although the example uses `codecommit`, you can use any name you
want\. Use the git remote show command to review the list of remotes set for your local repo
\.

3
4 1. Use the git remote \-v command to display the fetch and push settings for your local repo and
confirm they are set correctly\. For example:

codecommit ssh://git-codecommit.us-east-2.amazonaws.com/v1/repos/MyDestinationRepo (fetch) codecommit
ssh://git-codecommit.us-east-2.amazonaws.com/v1/repos/MyDestinationRepo (push)

1 **Tip**
2 If you still see fetch and push entries for a different remote repository \(for example, entries
for origin\), remove them using the git remote set\-url \-\-delete command\.

3
4 ## Step 2: Create the Script to Use for Migrating Incrementally<a name="how-to-push-large-
repositories-createscript"></a>

5
6 These steps assume you will use the `incremental-repo-migration.py` sample script\.
7
8 1. Open a text editor and paste the contents of [the sample script](#how-to-push-large-
repositories-sample) into an empty document\.

9
10 1. Save the document in a documents directory \(not the working directory of your local repo\)
and name it `incremental-repo-migration.py`\. Make sure the directory you choose is one
configured in your local environment or path variables, so you can run the Python script
from a command line or terminal\.

11
12 ## Step 3: Run the Script and Migrate Incrementally to AWS CodeCommit<a name="how-to-push-large-
repositories-runscript"></a>

13
14 Now that you have created your `incremental-repo-migration.py` script, you can use it to
incrementally migrate a local repo to an AWS CodeCommit repository\. By default, the script
pushes commits in batches of 1,000 commits and attempts to use the Git settings for the
directory from which it is run as the settings for the local repo and remote repository\.
You can use the options included in `incremental-repo-migration.py` to configure other
settings, if necessary\.

15
16 1. From the terminal or command prompt, change directories to the local repo you want to migrate
\.

17
18 1. From that directory, type the following command:

```
python incremental-repo-migration.py
```

1

2 1. The script runs and shows progress at the terminal or command prompt\. Some large
   repositories will be slow to show progress\. The script will stop if a single push fails
   three times\. You can then rerun the script, and it will start from the batch that failed\.
   You can rerun the script until all pushes succeed and the migration is complete\.

3

4 **Tip**

5 You can run `incremental-repo-migration.py` from any directory as long as you use the `-l` and
   `-r` options to specify the local and remote settings to use\. For example, to use the
   script from any directory to migrate a local repo located at /tmp/*my\-repo* to a remote
   nicknamed *codecommit*:

```
python incremental-repo-migration.py -l "/tmp/my-repo" -r "codecommit"
```

1 You might also want to use the `-b` option to change the default batch size used when pushing
   incrementally\. For example, if you are regularly pushing a repository with very large
   binary files that change often and are working from a location that has restricted network
   bandwidth, you might want to use the `-b` option to change the batch size to 500 instead of
   1,000\. For example:

```
python incremental-repo-migration.py -b 500
```

1 This will push the local repo incrementally in batches of 500 commits\. If you decide to change
   the batch size again when migrating the repository \(for example, if you decide to decrease
   the batch size after an unsuccessful attempt\), remember to use the `-c` option to remove
   the batch tags before resetting the batch size with `-b`:

```
python incremental-repo-migration.py -c python incremental-repo-migration.py -b 250
```

1

2 **Important**

3 Do not use the `-c` option if you want to rerun the script after a failure\. The `-c` option
   removes the tags used to batch the commits\. Use the `-c` option only if you want to change
   the batch size and start again, or if you decide you no longer want to use the script\.

4

5 ## Appendix: Sample Script `incremental-repo-migration.py`<a name="how-to-push-large-
   repositories-sample"></a>

6

7 For your convenience, we have developed a sample Python script, `incremental-repo-migration.py`,
   for pushing a repository incrementally\. This script is an open source code sample and
   provided as\-is\.

Copyright 2015 Amazon.com, Inc. or its affiliates. All Rights Reserved. Licensed under the Amazon Software License (the "License").

You may not use this file except in compliance with the License. A copy of the License is located at

http://aws.amazon.com/asl/

This file is distributed on an "AS IS" BASIS, WITHOUT WARRANTIES OR CONDITIONS OF ANY KIND, express or implied. See the License for

the specific language governing permissions and limitations under the License.

```
#!/usr/bin/env python
```

import os import sys from optparse import OptionParser from git import Repo, TagReference, RemoteProgress, GitCommandError

class PushProgressPrinter(RemoteProgress): def update(self, op_code, cur_count, max_count=None, message="): op_id = op_code & self.OP_MASK stage_id = op_code & self.STAGE_MASK if op_id == self.WRITING and stage_id == self.BEGIN: print("\tObjects: %d" % max_count)

class RepositoryMigration:

```
1  MAX_COMMITS_TOLERANCE_PERCENT = 0.05
2  PUSH_RETRY_LIMIT = 3
3  MIGRATION_TAG_PREFIX = "codecommit_migration_"
4
5  def migrate_repository_in_parts(self, repo_dir, remote_name, commit_batch_size, clean):
6      self.next_tag_number = 0
7      self.migration_tags = []
8      self.walked_commits = set()
9      self.local_repo = Repo(repo_dir)
10     self.remote_name = remote_name
11     self.max_commits_per_push = commit_batch_size
12     self.max_commits_tolerance = self.max_commits_per_push * self.MAX_COMMITS_TOLERANCE_PERCENT
13
14     try:
15         self.remote_repo = self.local_repo.remote(remote_name)
16         self.get_remote_migration_tags()
17     except (ValueError, GitCommandError):
18         print("Could not contact the remote repository. The most common reasons for this error
                 are that the name of the remote repository is incorrect, or that you do not have
                 permissions to interact with that remote repository.")
19         sys.exit(1)
20
21     if clean:
22         self.clean_up(clean_up_remote=True)
```

```
23            return
24
25        self.clean_up()
26
27        print("Analyzing repository")
28        head_commit = self.local_repo.head.commit
29        sys.setrecursionlimit(max(sys.getrecursionlimit(), head_commit.count()))
30
31        # tag commits on default branch
32        leftover_commits = self.migrate_commit(head_commit)
33        self.tag_commits([commit for (commit, commit_count) in leftover_commits])
34
35        # tag commits on each branch
36        for branch in self.local_repo.heads:
37            leftover_commits = self.migrate_commit(branch.commit)
38            self.tag_commits([commit for (commit, commit_count) in leftover_commits])
39
40        # push the tags
41        self.push_migration_tags()
42
43        # push all branch references
44        for branch in self.local_repo.heads:
45            print("Pushing branch %s" % branch.name)
46            self.do_push_with_retries(ref=branch.name)
47
48        # push all tags
49        print("Pushing tags")
50        self.do_push_with_retries(push_tags=True)
51
52        self.get_remote_migration_tags()
53        self.clean_up(clean_up_remote=True)
54
55        print("Migration to CodeCommit was successful")
56
57   def migrate_commit(self, commit):
58        if commit in self.walked_commits:
59            return []
60
61        pending_ancestor_pushes = []
62        commit_count = 1
63
64        if len(commit.parents) > 1:
65            # This is a merge commit
66            # Ensure that all parents are pushed first
67            for parent_commit in commit.parents:
68                pending_ancestor_pushes.extend(self.migrate_commit(parent_commit))
69        elif len(commit.parents) == 1:
70            # Split linear history into individual pushes
71            next_ancestor, commits_to_next_ancestor = self.find_next_ancestor_for_push(commit.
                parents[0])
72            commit_count += commits_to_next_ancestor
73            pending_ancestor_pushes.extend(self.migrate_commit(next_ancestor))
74
75        self.walked_commits.add(commit)
```

209

```
76
77        return self.stage_push(commit, commit_count, pending_ancestor_pushes)
78
79   def find_next_ancestor_for_push(self, commit):
80        commit_count = 0
81
82        # Traverse linear history until we reach our commit limit, a merge commit, or an initial
               commit
83        while len(commit.parents) == 1 and commit_count < self.max_commits_per_push and commit not
               in self.walked_commits:
84            commit_count += 1
85            self.walked_commits.add(commit)
86            commit = commit.parents[0]
87
88        return commit, commit_count
89
90   def stage_push(self, commit, commit_count, pending_ancestor_pushes):
91        # Determine whether we can roll up pending ancestor pushes into this push
92        combined_commit_count = commit_count + sum(ancestor_commit_count for (ancestor,
               ancestor_commit_count) in pending_ancestor_pushes)
93
94        if combined_commit_count < self.max_commits_per_push:
95            # don't push anything, roll up all pending ancestor pushes into this pending push
96            return [(commit, combined_commit_count)]
97
98        if combined_commit_count <= (self.max_commits_per_push + self.max_commits_tolerance):
99            # roll up everything into this commit and push
100           self.tag_commits([commit])
101           return []
102
103       if commit_count >= self.max_commits_per_push:
104           # need to push each pending ancestor and this commit
105           self.tag_commits([ancestor for (ancestor, ancestor_commit_count) in
                  pending_ancestor_pushes])
106           self.tag_commits([commit])
107           return []
108
109       # push each pending ancestor, but roll up this commit
110       self.tag_commits([ancestor for (ancestor, ancestor_commit_count) in pending_ancestor_pushes
               ])
111       return [(commit, commit_count)]
112
113  def tag_commits(self, commits):
114       for commit in commits:
115           self.next_tag_number += 1
116           tag_name = self.MIGRATION_TAG_PREFIX + str(self.next_tag_number)
117
118           if tag_name not in self.remote_migration_tags:
119               tag = self.local_repo.create_tag(tag_name, ref=commit)
120               self.migration_tags.append(tag)
121           elif self.remote_migration_tags[tag_name] != str(commit):
122               print("Migration tags on the remote do not match the local tags. Most likely your
                      batch size has changed since the last time you ran this script. Please run this
                      script with the --clean option, and try again.")
```

```python
123            sys.exit(1)
124
125    def push_migration_tags(self):
126        print("Will attempt to push %d tags" % len(self.migration_tags))
127        self.migration_tags.sort(key=lambda tag: int(tag.name.replace(self.MIGRATION_TAG_PREFIX, "")
               ))
128        for tag in self.migration_tags:
129            print("Pushing tag %s (out of %d tags), commit %s" % (tag.name, self.next_tag_number,
                   str(tag.commit)))
130            self.do_push_with_retries(ref=tag.name)
131
132    def do_push_with_retries(self, ref=None, push_tags=False):
133        for i in range(0, self.PUSH_RETRY_LIMIT):
134            if i == 0:
135                progress_printer = PushProgressPrinter()
136            else:
137                progress_printer = None
138
139            try:
140                if push_tags:
141                    infos = self.remote_repo.push(tags=True, progress=progress_printer)
142                elif ref is not None:
143                    infos = self.remote_repo.push(refspec=ref, progress=progress_printer)
144                else:
145                    infos = self.remote_repo.push(progress=progress_printer)
146
147                success = True
148                if len(infos) == 0:
149                    success = False
150                else:
151                    for info in infos:
152                        if info.flags & info.UP_TO_DATE or info.flags & info.NEW_TAG or info.flags &
                           info.NEW_HEAD:
153                            continue
154                        success = False
155                        print(info.summary)
156
157                if success:
158                    return
159            except GitCommandError as err:
160                print(err)
161
162        if push_tags:
163            print("Pushing all tags failed after %d attempts" % (self.PUSH_RETRY_LIMIT))
164        elif ref is not None:
165            print("Pushing %s failed after %d attempts" % (ref, self.PUSH_RETRY_LIMIT))
166            print("For more information about the cause of this error, run the following command
                   from the local repo: 'git push %s %s'" % (self.remote_name, ref))
167        else:
168            print("Pushing all branches failed after %d attempts" % (self.PUSH_RETRY_LIMIT))
169        sys.exit(1)
170
171    def get_remote_migration_tags(self):
172        remote_tags_output = self.local_repo.git.ls_remote(self.remote_name, tags=True).split('\n')
```

```
173    self.remote_migration_tags = dict((tag.split()[1].replace("refs/tags/",""), tag.split()[0])
           for tag in remote_tags_output if self.MIGRATION_TAG_PREFIX in tag)
174
175 def clean_up(self, clean_up_remote=False):
176     tags = [tag for tag in self.local_repo.tags if tag.name.startswith(self.MIGRATION_TAG_PREFIX
           )]
177
178     # delete the local tags
179     TagReference.delete(self.local_repo, *tags)
180
181     # delete the remote tags
182     if clean_up_remote:
183         tags_to_delete = [":" + tag_name for tag_name in self.remote_migration_tags]
184         self.remote_repo.push(refspec=tags_to_delete)
```

parser = OptionParser() parser.add_option("-l", "--local", action="store", dest="localrepo", default=os.getcwd(), help="The path to the local repo. If this option is not specified, the script will attempt to use current directory by default. If it is not a local git repo, the script will fail.") parser.add_option("-r", "--remote", action="store", dest="remoterepo", default="codecommit", help="The name of the remote repository to be used as the push or migration destination. The remote must already be set in the local repo ('git remote add ...'). If this option is not specified, the script will use 'codecommit' by default.") parser.add_option("-b", "--batch", action="store", dest="batchsize", default="1000", help="Specifies the commit batch size for pushes. If not explicitly set, the default is 1,000 commits.") parser.add_option("-c", "--clean", action="store_true", dest="clean", default=False, help="Remove the temporary tags created by migration from both the local repo and the remote repository. This option will not do any migration work, just cleanup. Cleanup is done automatically at the end of a successful migration, but not after a failure so that when you re-run the script, the tags from the prior run can be used to identify commit batches that were not pushed successfully.")

(options, args) = parser.parse_args()

migration = RepositoryMigration() migration.migrate_repository_in_parts(options.localrepo, options.remoterepo, int(options.batchsize), options.clean)

```
1
2
3
4
5 # Troubleshooting AWS CodeCommit<a name="troubleshooting"></a>
6
7 The following information might help you troubleshoot common issues in AWS CodeCommit\.
8
9 **Topics**
10 + [Troubleshooting Git Credentials and HTTPS Connections to AWS CodeCommit](troubleshooting-gc.
      md)
11 + [Troubleshooting SSH Connections to AWS CodeCommit](troubleshooting-ssh.md)
12 + [Troubleshooting the Credential Helper and HTTPS Connections to AWS CodeCommit](
      troubleshooting-ch.md)
13 + [Troubleshooting Git Clients and AWS CodeCommit](troubleshooting-git.md)
14 + [Troubleshooting Access Errors and AWS CodeCommit](troubleshooting-ae.md)
15 + [Troubleshooting Configuration Errors and AWS CodeCommit](troubleshooting-cf.md)
16 + [Troubleshooting Console Errors and AWS CodeCommit](troubleshooting-cs.md)
17 + [Troubleshooting Triggers and AWS CodeCommit](troubleshooting-ti.md)
18 + [Turn on Debugging](#troubleshooting-debug)
19
20 ## Turn on Debugging<a name="troubleshooting-debug"></a>
21
```

Problem: I want to turn on debugging to get more information about my repository and how Git is executing commands\.

Possible fixes: Try the following:

1. At the terminal or command prompt, run the following commands on your local machine before running Git commands:

   On Linux, macOS, or Unix:

export GIT_TRACE_PACKET=1 export GIT_TRACE=1 export GIT_CURL_VERBOSE=1

On Windows:

set GIT_TRACE_PACKET=1 set GIT_TRACE=1 set GIT_CURL_VERBOSE=1

Note

Setting `GIT_CURL_VERBOSE` is useful for HTTPS connections only\. SSH does not use the `libcurl` library\.

1. To get more information about your Git repository, create a shell script similar to the following, and then run the script:

```sh
#!/bin/sh

gc_output=script -q -c 'git gc' | grep Total object_count=$(echo $gc_output | awk -F ' |(|)' '{print $2}') delta_count=$(echo $gc_output | awk -F ' |(|)' '{print $5}')

verify_pack_output=git verify-pack -v objects/pack/pack-*.pack .git/objects/pack/pack-*.pack 2>/dev/null largest_object=$(echo "$verify_pack_output" | grep blob | sort -k3nr | head -n 1 | awk '{print $3/1024" KiB"}') largest_commit=$(echo "$verify_pack_output" | grep 'tree|commit|tag' | sort -k3nr | head -n 1 | awk '{print $3/1024" KiB"}') longest_delta_chain=$(echo "$verify_pack_output" | grep chain | tail -n 1 | awk -F ' |:' '{print $4}')

branch_count=git branch -a | grep remotes/origin | grep -v HEAD | wc -l if [ $branch_count -eq 0 ]; then branch_count=git branch -l | wc -l fi

echo "Size:  git count-objects -v | grep size-pack | awk '{print $2}' KiB" echo "Branches: $branch_count" echo "Tags: git show-ref --tags | wc -l" echo "Commits: git rev-list --all | wc -l" echo "Objects: $object_count" echo "Delta objects: $delta_count" echo "Largest blob: $largest_object" echo "Largest commit/tag/tree: $largest_commit" echo "Longest delta chain: $longest_delta_chain"
```

1. If these steps do not provide enough information for you to resolve the issue on your own, ask for help on [the AWS CodeCommit forum](https://forums.aws.amazon.com///forum.jspa?forumID=189)\. Be sure to include relevant output from these steps in your post\.

Troubleshooting Git Credentials and HTTPS Connections to AWS CodeCommit<a name="troubleshooting-gc"></a>

The following information might help you troubleshoot common issues when using Git credentials and HTTPS to connect to AWS CodeCommit repositories\.

Topics

12 + [Git Credentials for AWS CodeCommit: I Keep Seeing a Prompt for Credentials When Connecting to My AWS CodeCommit Repository at the Terminal or Command Line](#troubleshooting-gc1)

13 + [Git Credentials for AWS CodeCommit: I Set Up Git Credentials, But My System Is Not Using Them As I Expected](#troubleshooting-gc2)

14

15 ## Git Credentials for AWS CodeCommit: I Keep Seeing a Prompt for Credentials When Connecting to My AWS CodeCommit Repository at the Terminal or Command Line<a name="troubleshooting-gc1"></a>

16

17 **Problem:** When you try to push, pull, or otherwise interact with an AWS CodeCommit repository from the terminal or command line, you are prompted to provide a user name and password, and you must supply the Git credentials for your IAM user\.

18

19 **Possible fixes:** The most common causes for this error are that your local computer is running an operating system that does not support credential management, or it does not have a credential management utility installed, or the Git credentials for your IAM user have not been saved to one of these credential management systems\. Depending on your operating system and local environment, you might need to install a credential manager, configure the credential manager that is included in your operating system, or customize your local environment to use credential storage\. For example, if your computer is running macOS, you can use the Keychain Access utility to store your credentials\. If your computer is running Windows, you can use the Git Credential Manager that is installed with Git for Windows\. For more information, see [For HTTPS Users Using Git Credentials](setting-up-gc.md) and [Credential Storage](https://git-scm.com/book/en/v2/Git-Tools-Credential-Storage) in the Git documentation\.

20

21 ## Git Credentials for AWS CodeCommit: I Set Up Git Credentials, But My System Is Not Using Them As I Expected<a name="troubleshooting-gc2"></a>

22

23 **Problem:** When you try to use AWS CodeCommit with a Git client, the client does not appear to use the Git credentials for your IAM user\.

24

25 **Possible fixes:** The most common cause for this error is that you previously set up your computer to use the credential helper that is included with the AWS CLI\. Check your \.gitconfig file for configuration sections similar to the following, and remove them:

[credential ”https://git-codecommit.*.amazonaws.com”] helper = !aws codecommit credential-helper $@ Use-HttpPath = true

1

2 Save the file, and then open a new command line or terminal session before you attempt to connect again\.

3

4 You may also have multiple credential helpers or managers set up on your computer, and your system might be defaulting to another configuration\. To reset which credential helper is used as the default, you can use the \-\-system option instead of \-\-global or \-\-local when running the git config command\.

5

6 For more information, see [For HTTPS Users Using Git Credentials](setting-up-gc.md) and [Credential Storage](https://git-scm.com/book/en/v2/Git-Tools-Credential-Storage) in the Git documentation\.

7

8

9

10

Troubleshooting SSH Connections to AWS CodeCommit<a name="troubleshooting-ssh"></a>

The following information might help you troubleshoot common issues when using SSH to connect to AWS CodeCommit repositories\.

Topics
+ [Access Error: Public Key Is Uploaded Successfully to IAM but Connection Fails on Linux, macOS, or Unix Systems](#troubleshooting-ae4)
+ [Access Error: Public Key Is Uploaded Successfully to IAM and SSH Tested Successfully but Connection Fails on Windows Systems](#troubleshooting-ae5)
+ [Authentication Challenge: Authenticity of Host Can't Be Established When Connecting to an AWS CodeCommit Repository](#troubleshooting-ac1)
+ [IAM Error: 'Invalid format' when attempting to add a public key to IAM](#troubleshooting-iam1)
+ [Git on Windows: Bash Emulator or Command Line Freezes When Attempting to Connect Using SSH](#troubleshooting-gw2)

Access Error: Public Key Is Uploaded Successfully to IAM but Connection Fails on Linux, macOS, or Unix Systems<a name="troubleshooting-ae4"></a>

Problem: When you try to connect to an SSH endpoint to communicate with an AWS CodeCommit repository, either when testing the connection or cloning a repository, the connection fails or is refused\.

Possible fixes: The SSH Key ID assigned to your public key in IAM might not be associated with your connection attempt\. [You might not have configured a config file](setting-up-ssh-unixes.md#cc-configure-config), you might not have access to the configuration file, another setting might be preventing a successful read of the config file, or you might have provided the ID of the IAM user instead of the key ID\.

The SSH Key ID can be found in the IAM console in the profile for your IAM user:

![\[The SSH Key ID in the IAM console\]](http://docs.aws.amazon.com/codecommit/latest/userguide/images/codecommit-ssh-key-id-iam.png)![\[The SSH Key ID in the IAM console\]](http://docs.aws.amazon.com/codecommit/latest/userguide/)

Try testing the connection with the following command:

ssh Your-SSH-Key-ID@git-codecommit.us-east-2.amazonaws.com

If you see a success message after confirming the connection, your SSH Key ID is valid\. Edit your config file to associate your connection attempts with your public key in IAM\. If you do not want to edit your config file for some reason, you can preface all connection attempts to your repository with your SSH Key ID\. For example, if you wanted to clone a repository named *MyDemoRepo* without modifying your config file to associate your connection attempts, you would type the following command:

git clone ssh://Your-SSH-Key-ID@git-codecommit.us-east-2.amazonaws.com/v1/repos/MyDemoRepo my-demo-repo

For more information, see [For SSH Connections on Linux, macOS, or Unix](setting-up-ssh-unixes.md)\.

4 ## Access Error: Public Key Is Uploaded Successfully to IAM and SSH Tested Successfully but Connection Fails on Windows Systems<a name="troubleshooting-ae5"></a>

5

6 **Problem:** When you try to use an SSH endpoint to clone or communicate with an AWS CodeCommit repository, an error message appears containing the phrase `No supported authentication methods available`\.

7

8 **Possible fixes:** The most common reason for this error is that you have a Windows system environment variable set that directs Windows to use another program when you attempt to use SSH\. For example, you might have set a GIT_SSH variable to point to one of the PuTTY set of tools \(plink\.exe\)\. This might be a legacy configuration, or it might be necessary for one or more other programs installed on your computer\. If you are sure that this environment variable is not needed, you can remove it by opening your system properties and deleting the environment variable\.

9

10 To work around this issue, open a Bash emulator and then try your SSH connection again, but include `GIT_SSH_COMMAND="SSH"` as a prefix\. For example, to clone a repository using SSH:

GIT_SSH_COMMAND="ssh" git clone ssh://git-codecommit.us-east-2.amazonaws.com/v1/repos/MyDemoRepo my-demo-repo

1

2 A similar problem might occur if your version of Windows requires that you include the SSH Key ID as part of the connection string when connecting using SSH at the Windows command line\. Try your connection again, this time including the SSH Key ID copied from IAM as part of the command\. For example:

git clone ssh://Your-SSH-Key-ID@git-codecommit.us-east-2.amazonaws.com/v1/repos/MyDemoRepo my-demo-repo

1

2 ## Authentication Challenge: Authenticity of Host Can't Be Established When Connecting to an AWS CodeCommit Repository<a name="troubleshooting-ac1"></a>

3

4 **Problem:** When you try to use an SSH endpoint to communicate with an AWS CodeCommit repository, a warning message appears containing the phrase `The authenticity of host 'hostname' can't be established.`

5

6 **Possible fixes:** Your credentials might not be set up correctly\. Follow the instructions in [For SSH Connections on Linux, macOS, or Unix](setting-up-ssh-unixes.md) or [For SSH Connections on Windows](setting-up-ssh-windows.md)\.

7

8 If you have followed those steps and the problem persists, someone might be attempting a man\-in\-the\-middle attack\. When you see the following message, type `no`, and press Enter\.

Are you sure you want to continue connecting (yes/no)?

1

2 Make sure the fingerprint and public key for AWS CodeCommit connections match those documented in the SSH setup topics before you continue with the connection\.

3

4

5 **Public fingerprints for AWS CodeCommit**

6

7 | Server | Cryptographic hash type | Fingerprint |
8 | --- | --- | --- |

```
 9 | git\-codecommit\.us\-east\-2\.amazonaws\.com | MD5 | a9:6d:03:ed:08:42:21:be:06:e1:e0:2a:d1
     :75:31:5e |
10 | git\-codecommit\.us\-east\-2\.amazonaws\.com | SHA256 | 31B1W2g5xn/
     NA2Ck6dyeJIrQOWvn7n8UEs56fG6ZIzQ |
11 | git\-codecommit\.us\-east\-1\.amazonaws\.com | MD5 | a6:9c:7d:bc:35:f5:d4:5f:8b:ba:6f:c8:bc:d4
     :83:84 |
12 | git\-codecommit\.us\-east\-1\.amazonaws\.com | SHA256 | eLMY1jODKA4uvDZcl/KgtIayZANwX6t8\+8
     isPtotBoY |
13 | git\-codecommit\.us\-west\-2\.amazonaws\.com | MD5 | a8:68:53:e3:99:ac:6e:d7:04:7e:f7
     :92:95:77:a9:77 |
14 | git\-codecommit\.us\-west\-2\.amazonaws\.com | SHA256 | 0
     pJx9SQpkbPUAHwy58UVIq0IHcyo1fwCpOOuVgcAWPo |
15 | git\-codecommit\.eu\-west\-1\.amazonaws\.com | MD5 | 93:42:36:ea:22:1f:f1:0f:20:02:4a:79:ff:ea
     :12:1d |
16 | git\-codecommit\.eu\-west\-1\.amazonaws\.com | SHA256 | tKjRkOL8dmJyTmSbeSdN1S8F/
     f0iql3RlvqgTOP1UyQ |
17 | git\-codecommit\.ap\-northeast\-1\.amazonaws\.com | MD5 | 8e:a3:f0:80:98:48:1c:5c:6f:59:db:a7
     :8f:6e:c6:cb |
18 | git\-codecommit\.ap\-northeast\-1\.amazonaws\.com | SHA256 | Xk/WeYD/K/
     bnBybzhiuu4dWpBJtXPf7E30jHU7se4Ow |
19 | git\-codecommit\.ap\-southeast\-1\.amazonaws\.com | MD5 | 65:e5:27:c3:09:68:0d:8e:b7:6d
     :94:25:80:3e:93:cf |
20 | git\-codecommit\.ap\-southeast\-1\.amazonaws\.com | SHA256 | ZIsVa7OVzxrTIf\+
     Rk4UbhPv6Es22mSB3uTBojfPXIno |
21 | git\-codecommit\.ap\-southeast\-2\.amazonaws\.com | MD5 | 7b:d2:c1:24:e6:91:a5:7b:fa:c1:0c
     :35:95:87:da:a0 |
22 | git\-codecommit\.ap\-southeast\-2\.amazonaws\.com | SHA256 | nYp\+
     gHas80HY3DqbP4yanCDFhqDVjseefVbHEXqH2Ec |
23 | git\-codecommit\.eu\-central\-1\.amazonaws\.com | MD5 | 74:5a:e8:02:fc:b2:9c:06:10:b4
     :78:84:65:94:22:2d |
24 | git\-codecommit\.eu\-central\-1\.amazonaws\.com | SHA256 |
     MwGrkiEki8QkkBtlAgXbYt0hoZYBnZF62VY5RzGJEUY |
25 | git\-codecommit\.ap\-northeast\-2\.amazonaws\.com | MD5 | 9f:68:48:9b:5f:fc
     :96:69:39:45:58:87:95:b3:69:ed |
26 | git\-codecommit\.ap\-northeast\-2\.amazonaws\.com | SHA256 |
     eegAPQrWY9YsYo9ZHIKOmxetfXBHzAZd8Eya53Qcwko |
27 | git\-codecommit\.sa\-east\-1\.amazonaws\.com | MD5 | 74:99:9d:ff:2b:ef:63:c6:4b:b4:6a:7f:62:c5
     :4b:51 |
28 | git\-codecommit\.sa\-east\-1\.amazonaws\.com | SHA256 | kW\+VKBOjpRaG/
     ZbXkgbtMQbKgEDK7JnISV3SVoyCmzU |
29 | git\-codecommit\.us\-west\-1\.amazonaws\.com | MD5 | 3b:76:18:83:13:2c:f8:eb:e9:a3:d0
     :51:10:32:e7:d1 |
30 | git\-codecommit\.us\-west\-1\.amazonaws\.com | SHA256 |
     gzauWTWXDK2u5KuMMi5vbKTmfyerdIwgSbzYBODLpzg |
31 | git\-codecommit\.eu\-west\-2\.amazonaws\.com | MD5 | a5:65:a6:b1:84:02:b1:95:43:f9:0e:de:dd:ed
     :61:d3 |
32 | git\-codecommit\.eu\-west\-2\.amazonaws\.com | SHA256 | rORwz5k/IHp/
     QyrRnfiM9jO2D5UEqMbtFNTuDG2hNbs |
33 | git\-codecommit\.ap\-south\-1\.amazonaws\.com | MD5 | da:41:1e:07:3b:9e:76:a0:c5:1e
     :64:88:03:69:86:21 |
34 | git\-codecommit\.ap\-south\-1\.amazonaws\.com | SHA256 | hUKwnTj7\+
     Xpx4Kddb6p45j4RazIJ4IhAMD8k29itOfE |
35 | git\-codecommit\.ca\-central\-1\.amazonaws\.com | MD5 | 9f:7c:a2:2f:8c:b5:74:fd:ab:b7:e1:fd:af
     :46:ed:23 |
```

36 | git\-codecommit\.ca\-central\-1\.amazonaws\.com | SHA256 |
   Qz5puafQdANVprLlj6r0Qyh4lCNsF6ob61dGcPtFS7w |
37 | git\-codecommit\.eu\-west\-3\.amazonaws\.com | MD5 | 1b:7f:97:dd:d7:76:8a:32:2c:bd:2c:7b
   :33:74:6a:76 |
38 | git\-codecommit\.eu\-west\-3\.amazonaws\.com | SHA256 | uw7c2FL564jVoFgtc\+ikzILnKBsZz7t9\+
   CFdSJjKbLI |
39
40 ## IAM Error: 'Invalid format' when attempting to add a public key to IAM<a name="
   troubleshooting-iam1"></a>
41
42 **Problem:** In IAM, when attempting to set up to use SSH with AWS CodeCommit, an error message
   appears containing the phrase `Invalid format` when you attempt to add your public key\.
43
44 **Possible fixes:** IAM accepts public keys in the OpenSSH format only\. If you provide your
   public key in another format, or if the key does not contain the required number of bits,
   you will see this error\. This problem most commonly occurs when the public/private key
   pairs are generated on Windows computers\. To generate a key pair and copy the OpenSSH
   format required by IAM, see [SSH and Windows: Set Up the Public and Private Keys for Git and
   AWS CodeCommit](setting-up-ssh-windows.md#setting-up-ssh-windows-keys-windows)\.
45
46 ## Git on Windows: Bash Emulator or Command Line Freezes When Attempting to Connect Using SSH<a
   name="troubleshooting-gw2"></a>
47
48 **Problem:** After you configure SSH access for Windows and confirm connectivity at the command
   line or terminal, you see a message that the server's host key is not cached in the registry
   , and the prompt to store the key in the cache is frozen \(does not accept y/n/return input
   \) when you attempt to use commands such as git pull, git push, or git clone at the command
   prompt or Bash emulator\.
49
50 **Possible fixes:** The most common cause for this error is that your Git environment is
   configured to use something other than OpenSSH for authentication \(probably PuTTY\)\. This
   is known to cause problems with the caching of keys in some configurations\. To fix this
   problem, try one of the following:
51 + Open a Bash emulator and add the `GIT_SSH_COMMAND="ssh"` parameter before the Git command\.
   For example, if you are attempting to push to a repository, instead of typing git push, type
   :

   GIT_SSH_COMMAND="ssh" git push

1 + If you have PuTTY installed, open PuTTY, and in **Host Name \(or IP address\)**, type the AWS
   CodeCommit endpoint you want to reach \(for example, git\-codecommit\.us\-east\-2\.amazonaws
   \.com\)\. Choose **Open**\. When prompted by the PuTTY Security Alert, choose **Yes** to
   permanently cache the key\.
2 + Rename or delete the `GIT_SSH` environment variable if you are no longer using it\. Then open
   a new command prompt or Bash emulator session, and try your command again\.
3
4 For other solutions, see [Git clone/pull continually freezing at Store key in cache](http://
   stackoverflow.com/questions/33240137/git-clone-pull-continually-freezing-at-store-key-in-
   cache) on Stack Overflow\.
5
6
7
8
9 # Troubleshooting the Credential Helper and HTTPS Connections to AWS CodeCommit<a name="
   troubleshooting-ch"></a>

The following information might help you troubleshoot common issues when using the credential helper included with the AWS CLI and HTTPS to connect to AWS CodeCommit repositories\.

Topics
+ [Git for macOS: I Configured the Credential Helper Successfully, but Now I Am Denied Access to My Repository \(403\)](#troubleshooting-macoshttps)
+ [Git for Windows: I Installed Git for Windows, but I Am Denied Access to My Repository \(403\)](#troubleshooting-windowshttps)

Git for macOS: I Configured the Credential Helper Successfully, but Now I Am Denied Access to My Repository \(403\)<a name="troubleshooting-macoshttps"></a>

Problem: On macOS, the credential helper does not seem to access or use your credentials as expected\. This can be caused by two different problems:
+ The AWS CLI is configured for a different AWS region than the one where the repository exists \.
+ The Keychain Access utility has saved credentials which have since expired\.

Possible fixes: To verify whether the AWS CLI is configured for the correct region, run the aws configure command, and review the displayed information\. If the AWS CodeCommit repository is in a different region than the one shown for the AWS CLI, you must run the aws configure command and change the values to the appropriate ones for that region\. For more information, see [Step 1: Initial Configuration for AWS CodeCommit](setting-up-https-unixes.md#setting-up-https-unixes-account)\.

The default version of Git released on OS X and macOS uses the Keychain Access utility to save generated credentials\. For security reasons, the password generated for access to your AWS CodeCommit repository is temporary, so the credentials stored in the keychain will stop working after about 15 minutes\. If you are only accessing Git with AWS CodeCommit, try the following:

1. In Terminal, run the git config command to find the Git configuration file \(gitconfig\) where the Keychain Access utility is defined\. Depending on your local system and preferences, you might have more than one gitconfig file\.

   $ git config -l --show-origin

In the output from this command, find a line that contains the following option:

   helper = osxkeychain

The file listed at the beginning of this line is the Git configuration file you must edit\.

1. To edit the Git configuration file, use a plain\-text editor or run the following command:

   $ nano /usr/local/git/etc/gitconfig

1. Comment out the following line of text:

219

helper = osxkeychain

Alternatively, if you want to continue to use the Keychain Access utility to cache credentials for other Git repositories, modify the header instead of commenting out the line\. For example, to allow cached credentials for GitHub, you could modify the header as follows:

[credential "https://github.com"] helper = osxkeychain

If you are accessing other repositories with Git, you can configure the Keychain Access utility so that it does not supply credentials for your AWS CodeCommit repositories\. To configure the Keychain Access utility:

1. Open the Keychain Access utility\. \(You can use Finder to locate it\.\)

1. Search for `git-codecommit.us-east-2.amazonaws.com`\. Highlight the row, open the context \(right\-click\) menu, and then choose **Get Info**\.

1. Choose the **Access Control** tab\.

1. In **Confirm before allowing access**, choose `git-credential-osxkeychain`, and then choose the minus sign to remove it from the list\.

Note

After removing `git-credential-osxkeychain` from the list, you will see a pop\-up dialog box whenever you run a Git command\. Choose **Deny** to continue\. If you find the pop\-ups too disruptive, here are some alternatives:

Connect to AWS CodeCommit using SSH instead of HTTPS\. For more information, see [For SSH Connections on Linux, macOS, or Unix](setting-up-ssh-unixes.md)\.

In the Keychain Access utility, on the **Access Control** tab for `git-codecommit.us-east-2.amazonaws.com`, choose the **Allow all applications to access this item \(access to this item is not restricted\)** option\. This will prevent the pop\-ups, but the credentials will eventually expire \(on average, this takes about 15 minutes\) and you will see a 403 error message\. When this happens, you must delete the keychain item in order to restore functionality\.

Install a version of Git that does not use the keychain by default\.

Consider a scripting solution for deleting the keychain item\. To view a community\-generated sample of a scripted solution, see [Mac OS X Script to Periodically Delete Cached Credentials in the OS X Certificate Store](integrations.md#integrations-community-code) in [Product and Service Integrations](integrations.md)\.

Git for Windows: I Installed Git for Windows, but I Am Denied Access to My Repository \(403\) <a name="troubleshooting-windowshttps"></a>

Problem: On Windows, the credential helper does not seem to access or use your credentials as expected\. This can be caused by different problems:

+ The AWS CLI is configured for a different AWS region than the one where the repository exists \.

+ By default, Git for Windows installs a Git Credential Manager utility that is not compatible with AWS CodeCommit connections that use the AWS credential helper\. When installed, it will cause connections to repository to fail even thought the credential helper has been installed with the AWS CLI and configured for connections to AWS CodeCommit\.

+ Some versions of Git for Windows might not be in full compliance with [RFC 2617](https://tools.ietf.org/html/rfc2617#page-5) and [RFC 4559](https://tools.ietf.org/html/rfc4559#page-2), which could potentially cause issues with both Git credentials and the credential helper included with the AWS CLI\. For more information, see [Version 2\.11\.0\(3\) does not ask for username/password](https://github.com/git-for-windows/git/issues/1034)\.

24

25 **Possible fixes:**

26 + If you are attempting to use the credential helper included with the AWS CLI, consider connecting with Git credentials over HTTPS instead of using the credential helper\. Git credentials configured for your IAM user are compatible with the Git Credential Manager for Windows, unlike the credential helper for AWS CodeCommit\. For more information, see [For HTTPS Users Using Git Credentials](setting-up-gc.md)\.

27

28 If you want to use the credential helper, to verify whether the AWS CLI is configured for the correct region, run the aws configure command, and review the displayed information\. If the AWS CodeCommit repository is in a different region than the one shown for the AWS CLI, you must run the aws configure command and change the values to the appropriate ones for that region\. For more information, see [Step 1: Initial Configuration for AWS CodeCommit](setting-up-https-windows.md#setting-up-https-windows-account)\.

29 + If possible, uninstall and reinstall Git for Windows\. When installing Git for Windows, clear the check box for the option for installing the Git Credential Manager utility\. This credential manager is not compatible with the credential helper for AWS CodeCommit\. If you installed the Git Credential Manager or another credential management utility and you do not want to uninstall it, you can modify your \.gitconfig file and add specific credential management for AWS CodeCommit:

30

31 1. Open **Control Panel**, choose **Credential Manager**, and remove any stored credentials for AWS CodeCommit\.

32

33 1. Open your \.gitconfig file in any plain\-text editor, such as Notepad\.

34 **Note**

35 If you work with multiple Git profiles, you might have both local and global \.gitconfig files\. Be sure to edit the appropriate file\.

36

37 1. Add the following section to your \.gitconfig file:

38

39 ```

40 [credential "https://git-codecommit.*.amazonaws.com"]

41   helper = !aws codecommit credential-helper $@

42   UseHttpPath = true

43 ```

44

45 1. Save the file, and then open a new command line session before you attempt to connect again\.

46

47 You can also use this approach if you want to use the credential helper for AWS CodeCommit when connecting to AWS CodeCommit repositories and another credential management system when connecting to other hosted repositories, such as GitHub repositories\.

48

49 To reset which credential helper is used as the default, you can use the \-\-system option instead of \-\-global or \-\-local when running the git config command\.

50 + If you are using Git credentials on a Windows computer, you can try to work around any RFC noncompliance issues by including your Git credential user name as part of the connection string\. For example, to work around the issue and clone a repository named *MyDemoRepo* in the US East \(Ohio\) region:

git clone https://Your-Git-Credential-Username@git-codecommit.us-east-2.amazonaws.com/v1/repos/MyDemoRepo my-demo-repo

Note

This approach will not work if you have an `@` character in your Git credentials username\. You
must URL encode \(also known as URL escaping or [percent\-encoding](https://en.wikipedia.org
/wiki/Percent-encoding)\) the character before it will work\.

Troubleshooting Git Clients and AWS CodeCommit<a name="troubleshooting-git"></a>

The following information might help you troubleshoot common issues when using Git with AWS
CodeCommit repositories\. For troubleshooting problems specific to Git clients when using
HTTPS or SSH, also see [Troubleshooting Git Credentials \(HTTPS\)](troubleshooting-gc.md), [
Troubleshooting SSH Connections](troubleshooting-ssh.md), and [Troubleshooting the
Credential Helper \(HTTPS\)](troubleshooting-ch.md)\.

Topics
+ [Git Error: error: RPC failed; result=56, HTTP code = 200 fatal: The remote end hung up
unexpectedly](#troubleshooting-ge1)
+ [Git Error: Too many reference update commands](#troubleshooting-ge2)
+ [Git Error: push via HTTPS is broken in some versions of Git](#troubleshooting-ge3)
+ [Git Error: 'gnutls_handshake\(\) failed'](#troubleshooting-ge4)
+ [Git Error: Git cannot find the AWS CodeCommit repository or does not have permission to
access the repository](#troubleshooting-ge5)
+ [Git on Windows: No Supported Authentication Methods Available \(publickey\)](#troubleshooting
-gw1)

Git Error: error: RPC failed; result=56, HTTP code = 200 fatal: The remote end hung up
unexpectedly<a name="troubleshooting-ge1"></a>

Problem: When pushing a large change, a large number of changes, or a large repository, long
\-running HTTPS connections are often terminated prematurely due to networking issues or
firewall settings\.

Possible fixes: Push with SSH instead, or when migrating a large repository, follow the
steps in [Migrate a Repository in Increments](how-to-push-large-repositories.md)\. Also,
make sure you are not exceeding the size limits for individual files\. For more information,
see [Limits](limits.md)\.

Git Error: Too many reference update commands<a name="troubleshooting-ge2"></a>

Problem: The maximum number of reference updates per push is 4,000\. This error appears when
the push contains more than 4,000 reference updates\.

Possible fixes: Try pushing branches and tags individually with `git push --all` and `git
push --tags`\. If you have too many tags, split the tags into multiple pushes\. For more
information, see [Limits](limits.md)\.

Git Error: push via HTTPS is broken in some versions of Git<a name="troubleshooting-ge3"></a>

Problem: An issue with the curl update to 7\.41\.0 causes SSPI\-based digest authentication
to fail\. Known affected versions of Git include 1\.9\.5\.msysgit\.1\. Additionally, some
versions of Git for Windows might not be in full compliance with [RFC 2617](https://tools.
ietf.org/html/rfc2617#page-5) and [RFC 4559](https://tools.ietf.org/html/rfc4559#page-2),

which could potentially cause issues with HTTPS connections using either Git credentials or the credential helper included with the AWS CLI\.

Possible fixes: Check your version of Git for known issues or use an earlier or later version\. For more information about mysysgit, see [Push to HTTPS Is Broken](https://github .com/msysgit/git/issues/332) in the GitHub forums\. For more information about Git for Windows version issues, see [Version 2\.11\.0\(3\) does not ask for username/password](https ://github.com/git-for-windows/git/issues/1034)\.

Git Error: 'gnutls_handshake\(\) failed'<a name="troubleshooting-ge4"></a>

Problem: In Linux, when you try to use Git to communicate with an AWS CodeCommit repository, an error message appears containing the phrase `error: gnutls_handshake() failed`\.

Possible fixes: Compile Git against OpenSSL\. For one approach, see ["Error: gnutls_handshake\(\) failed" When Connecting to HTTPS Servers](http://askubuntu.com/questions /186847/error-gnutls-handshake-falied-when-connecting-to-https-servers) in the Ask Ubuntu forums\.

Alternatively, use SSH instead of HTTPS to communicate with AWS CodeCommit repositories\.

Git Error: Git cannot find the AWS CodeCommit repository or does not have permission to access the repository<a name="troubleshooting-ge5"></a>

Problem: A trailing slash in the connection string can cause connection attempts to fail\.

Possible fixes: Make sure that you have provided the correct name and connection string for the repository, and that there are no trailing slashes\. For more information, see [Connect to a Repository](how-to-connect.md)\.

Git on Windows: No Supported Authentication Methods Available \(publickey\)<a name="troubleshooting-gw1"></a>

Problem: After you configure SSH access for Windows, you see an access denied error when you attempt to use commands such as git pull, git push, or git clone\.

Possible fixes: The most common cause for this error is that a GIT_SSH environment variable exists on your computer and is configured to support another connection utility, such as PuTTY\. To fix this problem, try one of the following:
+ Open a Bash emulator and add the `GIT_SSH_COMMAND="ssh"` parameter before the Git command\. For example, if you are attempting to clone a repository, instead of typing git clone ssh:// git\-codecommit\.us\-east\-2\.amazonaws\.com/v1/repos/MyDemoRepo my\-demo\-repo, type:

GIT_SSH_COMMAND="ssh" git clone ssh://git-codecommit.us-east-2.amazonaws.com/v1/repos/MyDemoRepo my-demo-repo

+ Rename or delete the `GIT_SSH` environment variable if you are no longer using it\. Then open a new command prompt or Bash emulator session, and try your command again\.

For more information about troubleshooting Git issues on Windows when using SSH, see [Troubleshooting SSH Connections](troubleshooting-ssh.md)\.

8 # Troubleshooting Access Errors and AWS CodeCommit<a name="troubleshooting-ae"></a>

9

10 The following information might help you troubleshoot access errors you might see when connecting with AWS CodeCommit repositories\.

11

12 **Topics**

13 + [Access Error: Prompted for AWS User Name When Connecting to an AWS CodeCommit Repository](#troubleshooting-ae1)

14 + [Access Error: Prompted for User Name and Password When Connecting to an AWS CodeCommit Repository from Windows](#troubleshooting-ae1w)

15 + [Access Error: Public Key Denied When Connecting to an AWS CodeCommit Repository](#troubleshooting-ae2)

16

17 ## Access Error: Prompted for AWS User Name When Connecting to an AWS CodeCommit Repository<a name="troubleshooting-ae1"></a>

18

19 **Problem:** When you try to use Git to communicate with an AWS CodeCommit repository, a message appears prompting you for your AWS user name\.

20

21 **Possible fixes:** Configure your AWS profile or make sure the profile you are using is the one you configured for working with AWS CodeCommit\. For more information about setting up, see [Setting Up](setting-up.md)\. For more information about IAM, access keys, and secret keys, see [Managing Access Keys for IAM Users](http://docs.aws.amazon.com/IAM/latest/UserGuide/ManagingCredentials.html) and [How Do I Get Credentials?](http://docs.aws.amazon.com/IAM/latest/UserGuide/IAM_Introduction.html#IAM_SecurityCredentials)\.

22

23 ## Access Error: Prompted for User Name and Password When Connecting to an AWS CodeCommit Repository from Windows<a name="troubleshooting-ae1w"></a>

24

25 **Problem:** When you try to use Git to communicate with an AWS CodeCommit repository, you see a pop\-up dialog box asking for your user name and password\.

26

27 **Possible fixes:** This might be the built\-in credential management system for Windows\. Depending on your configuration, do one of the following:

28 + If you are using HTTPS with Git credentials, your Git credentials are not yet stored in the system\. Provide the Git credentials and continue\. You should not be prompted again\. For more information, see [For HTTPS Users Using Git Credentials](setting-up-gc.md)\.

29 + If you are using HTTPS with the credential helper for AWS CodeCommit, it is not compatible with the Windows credential management system\. Choose **Cancel**\.

30

31 This might also be an indication that you installed the Git Credential Manager as part of installing Git for Windows\. The Git Credential Manager is not compatible with AWS CodeCommit\. Consider uninstalling it\.

32

33 For more information, see [For HTTPS Connections on Windows with the AWS CLI Credential Helper](setting-up-https-windows.md) and [Git for Windows: I Installed Git for Windows, but I Am Denied Access to My Repository \(403\)](troubleshooting-ch.md#troubleshooting-windowshttps)\.

34

35 ## Access Error: Public Key Denied When Connecting to an AWS CodeCommit Repository<a name="troubleshooting-ae2"></a>

36

37 **Problem:** When you try to use an SSH endpoint to communicate with an AWS CodeCommit repository, an error message appears containing the phrase `Error: public key denied`\.

```
38
39 **Possible fixes:** The most common reason for this error is that you have not completed set up
       for SSH connections\. Configure a public and private SSH key pair, and then associate the
       public key with your IAM user\. For more information about configuring SSH, see [For SSH
       Connections on Linux, macOS, or Unix](setting-up-ssh-unixes.md) and [For SSH Connections on
       Windows](setting-up-ssh-windows.md)\.
40
41
42
43
44 # Troubleshooting Configuration Errors and AWS CodeCommit<a name="troubleshooting-cf"></a>
45
46 The following information might help you troubleshoot configuration errors you might see when
       connecting with AWS CodeCommit repositories\.
47
48 **Topics**
49 + [Configuration Error: Cannot Configure AWS CLI Credentials on macOS](#troubleshooting-cf1)
50
51 ## Configuration Error: Cannot Configure AWS CLI Credentials on macOS<a name="troubleshooting-
       cf1"></a>
52
53 **Problem:** When you run `aws configure` to configure the AWS CLI, you see a `ConfigParseError`
       message\.
54
55 **Possible fixes:** The most common cause for this error is that a credentials file already
       exists\. Browse to \~/\.aws and look for a file named `credentials`\. Rename or delete that
       file, and then run aws configure again\.
56
57
58
59
60 # Troubleshooting Console Errors and AWS CodeCommit<a name="troubleshooting-cs"></a>
61
62 The following information might help you troubleshoot console errors you might see when using
       AWS CodeCommit repositories\.
63
64 **Topics**
65 + [Access Error: Encryption Key Access Denied for an AWS CodeCommit Repository from the Console
       or the AWS CLI](#troubleshooting-ae3)
66 + [Console Error: Cannot Browse the Code in an AWS CodeCommit Repository from the Console](#
       troubleshooting-cs1)
67
68 ## Access Error: Encryption Key Access Denied for an AWS CodeCommit Repository from the Console
       or the AWS CLI<a name="troubleshooting-ae3"></a>
69
70 **Problem:** When you try to access AWS CodeCommit from the console or the AWS CLI, an error
       message appears containing the phrase `EncryptionKeyAccessDeniedException` or `User is not
       authorized for the KMS default master key for CodeCommit 'aws/codecommit' in your account`\.
71
72 **Possible fixes:** The most common cause for this error is that your AWS account is not
       subscribed to AWS Key Management Service, which is required for AWS CodeCommit\. Open the
       IAM console, choose **Encryption Keys**, and then choose **Get Started Now**\. If you see a
       message that you are not currently subscribed to the AWS Key Management Service service,
       follow the instructions on that page to subscribe\. For more information about AWS
```

CodeCommit and AWS Key Management Service, see [AWS KMS and Encryption](encryption.md)\.

74 ## Console Error: Cannot Browse the Code in an AWS CodeCommit Repository from the Console<a name
="troubleshooting-cs1"></a>

75

76 **Problem:** When you try to browse the contents of a repository from the console, an error
message appears denying access\.

77

78 **Possible fixes:** The most common cause for this error is that an IAM policy applied to your
AWS account denies one or more of the permissions required for browsing code from the AWS
CodeCommit console\. For more information about AWS CodeCommit access permissions and
browsing, see [Authentication and Access Control for AWS CodeCommit](auth-and-access-control
.md)\.

79

80

81

82

83 # Troubleshooting Triggers and AWS CodeCommit<a name="troubleshooting-ti"></a>

84

85 The following information might help you troubleshoot issues with triggers you might see in AWS
CodeCommit\.

86

87 **Topics**

88 + [Trigger Error: A Repository Trigger Does Not Run When Expected](#troubleshooting-ti1)

89

90 ## Trigger Error: A Repository Trigger Does Not Run When Expected<a name="troubleshooting-ti1
"></a>

91

92 **Problem:** One or more triggers configured for a repository does not appear to run or does not
run as expected\.

93

94 **Possible fixes:** If the target of the trigger is a AWS Lambda function, make sure you have
configured the function's resource policy for access by AWS CodeCommit\. For more
information, see [Example 2: Create a Policy for AWS Lambda Integration](auth-and-access-
control-iam-identity-based-access-control.md#access-permissions-lambda-int)\.

95

96 Alternatively, edit the trigger and make sure the events for which you want to trigger actions
have been selected and that the branches for the trigger include the branch where you want
to see responses to actions\. Try changing the settings for the trigger to **All repository
events** and **All branches** and then testing the trigger\. For more information, see [Edit
Triggers for a Repository](how-to-notify-edit.md)\.

97

98

99

100

101 # Authentication and Access Control for AWS CodeCommit<a name="auth-and-access-control"></a>

102

103 Access to AWS CodeCommit requires credentials\. Those credentials must have permissions to
access AWS resources, such as AWS CodeCommit repositories, and your IAM user, which you use
to manage your Git credentials or the SSH public key that you use for making Git connections
\. The following sections provide details on how you can use [AWS Identity and Access
Management \(IAM\)](http://docs.aws.amazon.com/IAM/latest/UserGuide/introduction.html) and
AWS CodeCommit to help secure access to your resources:

104 + [Authentication](#authentication)

105 + [Access Control](#access-control)

106

107 ## Authentication<a name="authentication"></a>

108

109 Because AWS CodeCommit repositories are Git\-based and support the basic functionality of Git, including Git credentials, we recommend that you use an IAM user when working with AWS CodeCommit\. You can access AWS CodeCommit with other identity types, but the other identity types are subject to limitations, as described below\.

110

111 Identity types:

112 + **IAM user** - An [IAM user](http://docs.aws.amazon.com/IAM/latest/UserGuide/id_users.html) is simply an identity within your AWS account that has specific custom permissions\. For example, an IAM user can have permissions to create and manage Git credentials for accessing AWS CodeCommit repositories\. **This is the recommended user type for working with AWS CodeCommit\.** You can use an IAM user name and password to sign in to secure AWS webpages like the [AWS Management Console](https://console.aws.amazon.com/), [AWS Discussion Forums](https://forums.aws.amazon.com/), or the [AWS Support Center](https://console.aws.amazon.com/support/home#/)\.

113

114 You can generate Git credentials or associate SSH public keys with your IAM user\. These are the easiest ways to set up Git to work with your AWS CodeCommit repositories\. With Git credentials, you generate a static user name and password in IAM\. You then use these credentials for HTTPS connections with Git and any third\-party tool that supports Git user name and password authentication\. With SSH connections, you create public and private key files on your local machine that Git and AWS CodeCommit use for SSH authentication\. You associate the public key with your IAM user, and you store the private key on your local machine\.

115

116 In addition, you can generate [access keys](http://docs.aws.amazon.com/IAM/latest/UserGuide/id_credentials_access-keys.html) for each user\. Use access keys when you access AWS services programmatically, either through [one of the AWS SDKs](https://aws.amazon.com/tools/) or by using the [AWS Command Line Interface \(AWS CLI\)](https://aws.amazon.com/cli/)\. The SDK and CLI tools use the access keys to cryptographically sign your requests\. If you 'dont use the AWS tools, you must sign the requests yourself\. AWS CodeCommit supports *Signature Version 4*, a protocol for authenticating inbound API requests\. For more information about authenticating requests, see [Signature Version 4 Signing Process](http://docs.aws.amazon.com/general/latest/gr/signature-version-4.html) in the *AWS General Reference*\.

117 + **AWS account root user** - When you sign up for AWS, you provide an email address and password that is associated with your AWS account\. These are your *root credentials*, and they provide complete access to all of your AWS resources\. Certain AWS CodeCommit features are not available for root account users\. In addition, the only way to use Git with your root account is to configure the AWS credential helper, which is included with the AWS CLI\. You cannot use Git credentials or SSH public\-private key pairs with your root account user \. For these reasons, we do not recommend using your root account user when interacting with AWS CodeCommit\.

118 **Important**

119 For security reasons, we recommend that you use the root credentials only to create an *administrator user*, which is an *IAM user* with full permissions to your AWS account\. Then, you can use this administrator user to create other IAM users and roles with limited permissions\. For more information, see [IAM Best Practices](http://docs.aws.amazon.com/IAM/latest/UserGuide/best-practices.html#create-iam-users) and [Creating an Admin User and Group](http://docs.aws.amazon.com/IAM/latest/UserGuide/getting-started_create-admin-group.html) in the *IAM User Guide*\.

120 + **IAM role** - Like an IAM user, an [IAM role](http://docs.aws.amazon.com/IAM/latest/UserGuide/id_roles.html) is an IAM identity that you can create in your account to grant specific permissions\. It is similar to an IAM user, but it is not associated with a specific person \. Unlike an IAM user identity, you cannot use Git credentials or SSH keys with this identity type\. However, an *IAM role *enables you to obtain temporary access keys that you can use to access AWS services and resources\. IAM roles with temporary credentials are useful in the following situations:

121 + **Federated user access** - Instead of creating an IAM user, you can use preexisting user identities from AWS Directory Service, your enterprise user directory, or a web identity provider\. These are known as *federated users*\. AWS assigns a role to a federated user when access is requested through an [identity provider](http://docs.aws.amazon.com/IAM/latest/UserGuide/id_roles_providers.html)\. For more information about federated users, see [Federated Users and Roles](http://docs.aws.amazon.com/IAM/latest/UserGuide/introduction_access-management.html#intro-access-roles) in the *IAM User Guide*\.

122 **Note**

123 You cannot use Git credentials or SSH public\-private key pairs with federated users\. In addition, user preferences are not available for federated users\.

124 + **Cross\-account access** - You can use an IAM role in your account to grant another AWS account permissions to access your 'accounts resources\. For an example, see [Tutorial: Delegate Access Across AWS Accounts Using IAM Roles](http://docs.aws.amazon.com/IAM/latest/UserGuide/tutorial_cross-account-with-roles.html) in the *IAM User Guide*\.

125 + **AWS service access** - You can use an IAM role in your account to grant an AWS service permissions to access your 'accounts resources\. For example, you can create a role that allows AWS Lambda to access an AWS CodeCommit repository on your behalf\. For more information, see [Creating a Role to Delegate Permissions to an AWS Service](http://docs.aws.amazon.com/IAM/latest/UserGuide/id_roles_create_for-service.html) in the *IAM User Guide*\.

126 + **Applications running on Amazon EC2** - Instead of storing access keys within an EC2 instance for use by applications running on the instance and for making AWS API requests, you can use an IAM role to manage temporary credentials for these applications\. To assign an AWS role to an EC2 instance and make it available to all of its applications, you can create an instance profile that is attached to the instance\. An *instance profile* contains the role and enables programs running on the EC2 instance to get temporary credentials\. For more information, see [Using Roles for Applications on Amazon EC2](http://docs.aws.amazon.com/IAM/latest/UserGuide/id_roles_use_switch-role-ec2.html) in the *IAM User Guide*\.

127

128 ## Access Control<a name="access-control"></a>

129

130 You can have valid credentials to authenticate your requests, but unless you have permissions you cannot create or access AWS CodeCommit resources\. For example, you must have permissions to view repositories, push code, create and manage Git credentials, and so on\.

131

132 The following sections describe how to manage permissions for AWS CodeCommit\. We recommend that you read the overview first\.

133 + [Overview of Managing Access Permissions to Your AWS CodeCommit Resources](auth-and-access-control-iam-access-control-identity-based.md)

134 + [Using Identity\-Based Policies \(IAM Policies\) for AWS CodeCommit](auth-and-access-control-iam-identity-based-access-control.md)

135 + [AWS CodeCommit Permissions Reference](auth-and-access-control-permissions-reference.md)

136

137

138

139

140 # Overview of Managing Access Permissions to Your AWS CodeCommit Resources<a name="auth-and-access-control-iam-access-control-identity-based"></a>

Every AWS resource is owned by an AWS account\. Permissions to create or access a resource are governed by permissions policies\. An account administrator can attach permissions policies to IAM identities \(that is, users, groups, and roles\)\. Some services, such as AWS Lambda, also support attaching permissions policies to resources\.

Note

An *account administrator* \(or administrator user\) is a user with administrator privileges\. For more information, see [IAM Best Practices](http://docs.aws.amazon.com/IAM/latest/UserGuide/best-practices.html) in the *IAM User Guide*\.

When granting permissions, you decide who gets the permissions, the resources they get permissions for, and the specific actions that you want to allow on those resources\.

Topics
+ [AWS CodeCommit Resources and Operations](#arn-formats)
+ [Understanding Resource Ownership](#understanding-resource-ownership)
+ [Managing Access to Resources](#managing-access-resources)
+ [Resource Scoping in AWS CodeCommit](#resource-scoping)
+ [Specifying Policy Elements: Resources, Actions, Effects, and Principals](#actions-effects-principals)
+ [Specifying Conditions in a Policy](#policy-conditions)

AWS CodeCommit Resources and Operations<a name="arn-formats"></a>

In AWS CodeCommit, the primary resource is a repository\. Each resource has a unique Amazon Resource Names \(ARN\) associated with it\. In a policy, you use an Amazon Resource Name \(ARN\) to identify the resource that the policy applies to\. For more information about ARNs, see [Amazon Resource Names \(ARN\) and AWS Service Namespaces](http://docs.aws.amazon.com/general/latest/gr/aws-arns-and-namespaces.html) in the *Amazon Web Services General Reference*\. AWS CodeCommit does not currently support other resource types, which are referred to as subresources\.

The following table describes how to specify AWS CodeCommit resources\.

Resource Type	ARN Format
Repository	arn:aws:codecommit:*region*:*account\-id*:*repository\-name*
All AWS CodeCommit repositories	arn:aws:codecommit:*
All AWS CodeCommit repositories owned by the specified account in the specified region	arn:aws:codecommit:*region*:*account\-id*:*

Note

Most AWS services treat a colon \(:\) or a forward slash \(/\) in ARNs as the same character\. However, AWS CodeCommit requires an exact match in resource patterns and rules\. When creating event patterns, be sure to use the correct ARN characters so that they match the ARN syntax in the resource\.

For example, you can indicate a specific repository \(*MyDemoRepo*\) in your statement using its ARN as follows:

"Resource": "arn:aws:codecommit:us-west-2:111111111111:MyDemoRepo"

2 To specify all repositories that belong to a specific account, use the wildcard character \(*\) as follows:

"Resource": "arn:aws:codecommit:us-west-2:111111111111:*"

1
2 To specify all resources, or if a specific API action does not support ARNs, use the wildcard character \(*\) in the `Resource` element as follows:

"Resource": "*"

1
2 You can also use the wildcard character\(*\) to specify all resources that match part of a repository name\. For example, the following ARN specifies any AWS CodeCommit repository that begins with the name `MyDemo` and that is registered to the AWS account `111111111111` in the `us-east-2` AWS Region:

arn:aws:codecommit:us-east-2:111111111111:MyDemo*

1
2 For a list of available operations that work with the AWS CodeCommit resources, see [AWS CodeCommit Permissions Reference](auth-and-access-control-permissions-reference.md)\.
3
4 ## Understanding Resource Ownership<a name="understanding-resource-ownership"></a>
5
6 The AWS account owns the resources that are created in the account, regardless of who created them\. Specifically, the resource owner is the AWS account of the [principal entity](http://docs.aws.amazon.com/IAM/latest/UserGuide/id_roles_terms-and-concepts.html) \(that is, the root account, an IAM user, or an IAM role\) that authenticates the resource creation request \. The following examples illustrate how this works:
7 + If you create an IAM user in your AWS account and grant permissions to create AWS CodeCommit resources to that user, the user can create AWS CodeCommit resources\. However, your AWS account, to which the user belongs, owns the AWS CodeCommit resources\.
8 + If you use the root account credentials of your AWS account to create a rule, your AWS account is the owner of the AWS CodeCommit resource\.
9 + If you create an IAM role in your AWS account with permissions to create AWS CodeCommit resources, anyone who can assume the role can create AWS CodeCommit resources\. Your AWS account, to which the role belongs, owns the AWS CodeCommit resources\.
10
11 ## Managing Access to Resources<a name="managing-access-resources"></a>
12
13 To manage access to AWS resources, you use permissions policies\. A *permissions policy* describes who has access to what\. The following section explains the options for creating permissions policies\.
14
15 **Note**
16 This section discusses using IAM in the context of AWS CodeCommit\. It doesn't provide detailed information about the IAM service\. For more information about IAM, see [What Is IAM?](http://docs.aws.amazon.com/IAM/latest/UserGuide/introduction.html) in the *IAM User Guide*\. For information about IAM policy syntax and descriptions, see [AWS IAM Policy Reference](http://docs.aws.amazon.com/IAM/latest/UserGuide/reference_policies.html) in the *IAM User Guide*\.
17
18 Permissions policies that are attached to an IAM identity are referred to as identity\-based policies \(IAM policies\)\. Permissions policies that are attached to a resource are referred to as resource\-based policies\. Currently, AWS CodeCommit supports only identity\-based policies \(IAM policies\)\.

19

20 **Topics**

21 + [Identity\-Based Policies \(IAM Policies\)](#identity-based-policies)

22 + [Resource\-Based Policies](#resource-based-policies-overview)

23

24 ### Identity\-Based Policies \(IAM Policies\)<a name="identity-based-policies"></a>

25

26 To manage access to AWS resources, you attach permissions policies to IAM identities\. In AWS CodeCommit, you use identity\-based policies to control access to repositories\. For example, you can do the following:

27 + **Attach a permissions policy to a user or a group in your account** - To grant a user permissions to view AWS CodeCommit resources in the AWS CodeCommit console, attach an identity\-based permissions policy to a user or group that the user belongs to\.

28 + **Attach a permissions policy to a role \(to grant cross\-account permissions\)** - Delegation, such as when you want to grant cross\-account access, involves setting up a trust between the account that owns the resource \(the trusting account\), and the account that contains the users who need to access the resource \(the trusted account\)\. A permissions policy grants the user of a role the needed permissions to carry out the intended tasks on the resource\. A trust policy specifies which trusted accounts are allowed to grant its users permissions to assume the role\. For more information, see [IAM Terms and Concepts](http://docs.aws.amazon.com/IAM/latest/UserGuide/id_roles_terms-and-concepts.html)\.

29

30 To grant cross\-account permissions, attach an identity\-based permissions policy to an IAM role\. For example, the administrator in Account A can create a role to grant cross\-account permissions to another AWS account \(for example, Account B\) or an AWS service as follows:

31

32 1. Account A administrator creates an IAM role and attaches a permissions policy to the role that grants permissions on resources in Account A\.

33

34 1. Account A administrator attaches a trust policy to the role identifying Account B as the principal who can assume the role\.

35

36 1. Account B administrator can then delegate permissions to assume the role to any users in Account B\. Doing this allows users in Account B to create or access resources in Account A\. If you want to grant an AWS service permission to assume the role, the principal in the trust policy can also be an AWS service principal\. For more information, see Delegation in [IAM Terms and Concepts](http://docs.aws.amazon.com/IAM/latest/UserGuide/id_roles_terms-and-concepts.html)\.

37

38 For more information about using IAM to delegate permissions, see [Access Management](http://docs.aws.amazon.com/IAM/latest/UserGuide/access.html) in *IAM User Guide*\.

39

40 The following example policy allows a user to create a branch in a repository named *MyDemoRepo*:

```
{ "Version": "2012-10-17", "Statement" : [ { "Effect" : "Allow", "Action" : [ "codecommit:CreateBranch" ],
"Resource" : "arn:aws:codecommit:us-east-2:111111111111:MyDemoRepo" } ] }
```

1

2 To restrict the calls and resources that users in your account have access to, create specific IAM policies, and then attach those policies to IAM users\. For more information about how to create IAM roles and to explore example IAM policy statements for AWS CodeCommit, see [Overview of Managing Access Permissions to Your AWS CodeCommit Resources](#auth-and-access-control-iam-access-control-identity-based)\.

3
Resource\-Based Policies<a name="resource-based-policies-overview"></a>

5
Some services, such as Amazon S3, also support resource\-based permissions policies\. For example, you can attach a resource\-based policy to an S3 bucket to manage access permissions to that bucket\. AWS CodeCommit doesn't support resource\-based policies\.

7
Resource Scoping in AWS CodeCommit<a name="resource-scoping"></a>

9
In AWS CodeCommit, you can scope identity\-based policies and permissions to resources, as described in [AWS CodeCommit Resources and Operations](#arn-formats)\. However, you cannot scope the `ListRepositories` permission to a resource\. Instead, you must scope it to all resources \(using the wildcard `*`\)\. Otherwise, the action fails\.

11
All other AWS CodeCommit permissions can be scoped to resources\.

13
Specifying Policy Elements: Resources, Actions, Effects, and Principals<a name="actions-effects-principals"></a>

15
You can create policies to allow or deny users access to resources, or allow or deny users to take specific actions on those resources\. AWS CodeCommit defines a set of public API operations that define how users work with the service, whether that is through the AWS CodeCommit console, the SDKs, the AWS CLI, or by directly calling those APIs\. To grant permissions for these API operations, AWS CodeCommit defines a set of actions that you can specify in a policy\.

17
Some API operations can require permissions for more than one action\. For more information about resources and API operations, see [AWS CodeCommit Resources and Operations](#arn-formats) and [AWS CodeCommit Permissions Reference](auth-and-access-control-permissions-reference.md)\.

19
The following are the basic elements of a policy:
+ **Resource** - To identify the resource that the policy applies to, you use an Amazon Resource Name \(ARN\)\. For more information, see [AWS CodeCommit Resources and Operations](#arn-formats)\.
+ **Action** - To identify resource operations that you want to allow or deny, you use action keywords\. For example, depending on the specified `Effect`, the `codecommit:GetBranch` permission either allows or denies the user to perform the `GetBranch` operation, which gets details about a branch in an AWS CodeCommit repository\.
+ **Effect** - You specify the effect, either allow or deny, that takes place when the user requests the specific action\. If you don't explicitly grant access to \(allow\) a resource, access is implicitly denied\. You can also explicitly deny access to a resource to make sure that a user cannot access it, even if a different policy grants access\.
+ **Principal** - In identity\-based policies \(IAM policies\), the only type of policies that AWS CodeCommit supports, the user that the policy is attached to is the implicit principal\.

25
To learn more about IAM policy syntax, see [AWS IAM Policy Reference](http://docs.aws.amazon.com/IAM/latest/UserGuide/reference_policies.html) in the *IAM User Guide*\.

27
For a table showing all of the AWS CodeCommit API actions and the resources that they apply to, see [AWS CodeCommit Permissions Reference](auth-and-access-control-permissions-reference.md)\.

29
Specifying Conditions in a Policy<a name="policy-conditions"></a>

³¹

³² When you grant permissions, you use the access policy language for IAM to specify the conditions under which a policy should take effect\. For example, you might want a policy to be applied only after a specific date\. For more information about specifying conditions in a policy language, see [Condition](http://docs.aws.amazon.com/IAM/latest/UserGuide/reference_policies_elements.html#Condition) and [Policy Grammar](http://docs.aws.amazon.com/IAM/latest/UserGuide/reference_policies_grammar.html) in the *IAM User Guide*\.

³³

³⁴ To express conditions, you use predefined condition keys\. There are no condition keys specific to AWS CodeCommit\. However, there are AWS\-wide condition keys that you can use as appropriate\. For a complete list of AWS\-wide keys, see [Available Keys for Conditions](http://docs.aws.amazon.com/IAM/latest/UserGuide/reference_policies_elements.html#AvailableKeys) in the *IAM User Guide*\.

³⁵

³⁶

³⁷

³⁸

³⁹ # Using Identity\-Based Policies \(IAM Policies\) for AWS CodeCommit<a name="auth-and-access-control-iam-identity-based-access-control"></a>

⁴⁰

⁴¹ The following examples of identity\-based policies demonstrate how an account administrator can attach permissions policies to IAM identities \(users, groups, and roles\) to grant permissions to perform operations on AWS CodeCommit resources\.

⁴²

⁴³ **Important**

⁴⁴ We recommend that you first review the introductory topics that explain the basic concepts and options available to manage access to your AWS CodeCommit resources\. For more information, see [Overview of Managing Access Permissions to Your AWS CodeCommit Resources](auth-and-access-control-iam-access-control-identity-based.md)\.

⁴⁵

⁴⁶ **Topics**

⁴⁷ + [Permissions Required to Use the AWS CodeCommit Console](#console-permissions)

⁴⁸ + [AWS Managed \(Predefined\) Policies for AWS CodeCommit](#managed-policies)

⁴⁹ + [Customer Managed Policy Examples](#customer-managed-policies)

⁵⁰

⁵¹ The following is an example of an identity\-based permissions policy:

{ "Version": "2012-10-17", "Statement" : [{ "Effect" : "Allow", "Action" : ["codecommit:BatchGetRepositories"], "Resource" : ["arn:aws:codecommit:us-east-2:111111111111:MyDestinationRepo", "arn:aws:codecommit:us-east-2:111111111111:MyDemo*"] }] }

¹

² This policy has one statement that allows a user to get information about the AWS CodeCommit repository named `MyDestinationRepo` and all AWS CodeCommit repositories that start with the name `MyDemo` in the **us\-east\-2** Region\.

³

⁴ ## Permissions Required to Use the AWS CodeCommit Console<a name="console-permissions"></a>

⁵

⁶ To see the required permissions for each AWS CodeCommit API operation, and for more information about AWS CodeCommit operations, see [AWS CodeCommit Permissions Reference](auth-and-access-control-permissions-reference.md)\.

⁷

⁸ To allow users to use the AWS CodeCommit console, the administrator must grant them permissions for AWS CodeCommit actions\. For example, you could attach the AWSCodeCommitPowerUser managed policy or its equivalent to a user or group, as shown in the following permissions

policy:

{ "Version": "2012-10-17", "Statement": [{ "Effect": "Allow", "Action": ["codecommit:BatchGet*", "codecommit:Get*", "codecommit:List*", "codecommit:Create*", "codecommit:DeleteBranch", "codecommit:Describe*", "codecommit:Put*", "codecommit:Post*", "codecommit:Merge*", "codecommit:Test*", "codecommit:Update*", "codecommit:GitPull", "codecommit:GitPush"], "Resource": "" }, { *"Sid": "CloudWatchEventsCodeCommitRulesAccess", "Effect": "Allow", "Action": ["events:DeleteRule", "events:DescribeRule", "events:DisableRule", "events:EnableRule", "events:PutRule", "events:PutTargets", "events:RemoveTargets", "events:ListTargetsByRule"], "Resource": "arn:aws:events:::rule/codecommit"* }, { "Sid": "SNSTopicAndSubscriptionAccess", "Effect": "Allow", "Action": ["sns:Subscribe", "sns:Unsubscribe"], "Resource": "arn:aws:sns:::codecommit*" }, { "Sid": "SNSTopicAndSubscriptionReadAccess", "Effect": "Allow", "Action": ["sns:ListTopics", "sns:ListSubscriptionsByTopic", "sns:GetTopicAttributes"], "Resource": "" }, { *"Sid": "LambdaReadOnlyListAccess", "Effect": "Allow", "Action": ["lambda:ListFunctions"], "Resource": ""* }, { "Sid": "IAMReadOnlyListAccess", "Effect": "Allow", "Action": ["iam:ListUsers"], "Resource": "" }, { *"Sid": "IAMReadOnlyConsoleAccess", "Effect": "Allow", "Action": ["iam:ListAccessKeys", "iam:ListSSHPublicKeys", "iam:ListServiceSpecificCredentials", "iam:ListAccessKeys", "iam:GetSSHPublicKey"], "Resource": "arn:aws:iam:::user/${aws:username}"* }, { "Sid": "IAMUserSSHKeys", "Effect": "Allow", "Action": ["iam:DeleteSSHPublicKey", "iam:GetSSHPublicKey", "iam:ListSSHPublicKeys", "iam:UpdateSSHPublicKey", "iam:UploadSSHPublicKey"], "Resource": "arn:aws:iam:::*user/${aws:username}"* }, { *"Sid": "IAMSelfManageServiceSpecificCredentials", "Effect": "Allow", "Action": ["iam:CreateServiceSpecificCredential", "iam:UpdateServiceSpecificCredential", "iam:DeleteServiceSpecificCredential", "iam:ResetServiceSpecificCredential"],* "Resource": "arn:aws:iam:::user/${aws:username}" }] }

1
2 In addition to permissions granted to users by identity\-based policies, AWS CodeCommit requires
     permissions for AWS Key Management Service \(AWS KMS\) actions\. An IAM user does not need
     explicit `Allow` permissions for these actions, but the user must not have any policies
     attached that set the following permissions to `Deny`:

1   "kms:Encrypt",
2   "kms:Decrypt",
3   "kms:ReEncrypt",
4   "kms:GenerateDataKey",
5   "kms:GenerateDataKeyWithoutPlaintext",
6   "kms:DescribeKey"

1
2 For more information about encryption and AWS CodeCommit, see [AWS KMS and Encryption](
     encryption.md)\.
3
4 ## AWS Managed \(Predefined\) Policies for AWS CodeCommit<a name="managed-policies"></a>
5
6 AWS addresses many common use cases by providing standalone IAM policies that are created and
     administered by AWS\. These AWS managed policies grant required permissions for common use
     cases\. The managed policies for AWS CodeCommit also provide permissions to perform
     operations in other services, such as IAM, Amazon SNS, and Amazon CloudWatch Events, as
     required for the responsibilities for the users who have been granted the policy in question
     \. For example, the AWSCodeCommitFullAccess policy is an administrative\-level user policy
     that allows users with this policy to create and manage CloudWatch Events rules for
     repositories \(rules whose names are prefixed with `codecommit`\) and Amazon SNS topics for
     notifications about repository\-related events \(topics whose names are prefixed with `
     codecommit`\), as well as administer repositories in AWS CodeCommit\.
7
8 The following AWS managed policies, which you can attach to users in your account, are specific
     to AWS CodeCommit:

9 + **AWSCodeCommitFullAccess** - Grants full access to AWS CodeCommit\. Apply this policy only to
   administrative\-level users to whom you want to grant full control over AWS CodeCommit
   repositories and related resources in your AWS account, including the ability to delete
   repositories\.

10

11 The AWSCodeCommitFullAccess policy contains the following policy statement:

{ ”Version”: ”2012-10-17”, ”Statement”: [{ ”Effect”: ”Allow”, ”Action”: [”codecommit:*”], ”Resource”: ”” }, { ”Sid”: ”CloudWatchEventsCodeCommitRulesAccess”, ”Effect”: ”Allow”, ”Action”: [”events:DeleteRule”, ”events:DescribeRule”, ”events:DisableRule”, ”events:EnableRule”, ”events:PutRule”, ”events:PutTargets”, ”events:RemoveTargets”, ”events:ListTargetsByRule”], ”Resource”: ”arn:aws:events:::rule/codecommit*” }, { ”Sid”: ”SNSTopicAndSubscriptionAccess”, ”Effect”: ”Allow”, ”Action”: [”sns:CreateTopic”, ”sns:Delete-Topic”, ”sns:Subscribe”, ”sns:Unsubscribe”, ”sns:SetTopicAttributes”], ”Resource”: ”arn:aws:sns:::codecommit*” }, { ”Sid”: ”SNSTopicAndSubscriptionReadAccess”, ”Effect”: ”Allow”, ”Action”: [”sns:ListTopics”, ”sns:ListSubscriptionsByTopic”, ”sns:GetTopicAttributes”], ”Resource”: ”” }, { ”Sid”: ”LambdaRead-OnlyListAccess”, ”Effect”: ”Allow”, ”Action”: [”lambda:ListFunctions”], ”Resource”: ”” }, { ”Sid”: ”IAMReadOnlyListAccess”, ”Effect”: ”Allow”, ”Action”: [”iam:ListUsers”], ”Resource”: ”” }, { ”Sid”: ”IAMReadOnlyConsoleAccess”, ”Effect”: ”Allow”, ”Action”: [”iam:ListAccessKeys”, ”iam:ListSSHPublicK-eys”, ”iam:ListServiceSpecificCredentials”, ”iam:ListAccessKeys”, ”iam:GetSSHPublicKey”], ”Resource”: ”arn:aws:iam:::user/${aws:username}” }, { ”Sid”: ”IAMUserSSHKeys”, ”Effect”: ”Allow”, ”Action”: [”iam:DeleteSSHPublicKey”, ”iam:GetSSHPublicKey”, ”iam:ListSSHPublicKeys”, ”iam:UpdateSSHPublicKey”, ”iam:UploadSSHPublicKey”], ”Resource”: ”arn:aws:iam:::user/${aws:username}” }, { ”Sid”: ”IAMSelfMan-ageServiceSpecificCredentials”, ”Effect”: ”Allow”, ”Action”: [”iam:CreateServiceSpecificCredential”, ”iam:Up-dateServiceSpecificCredential”, ”iam:DeleteServiceSpecificCredential”, ”iam:ResetServiceSpecificCredential”], ”Resource”: ”arn:aws:iam:::user/${aws:username}” }] }

1 + **AWSCodeCommitPowerUser** - Allows users access to all of the functionality of AWS CodeCommit
   and repository\-related resources, except it does not allow them to delete AWS CodeCommit
   repositories or create or delete repository\-related resources in other AWS services, such
   as Amazon CloudWatch Events\. We recommend that you apply this policy to most users\.

2

3 The AWSCodeCommitPowerUser policy contains the following policy statement:

{ ”Version”: ”2012-10-17”, ”Statement”: [{ ”Effect”: ”Allow”, ”Action”: [”codecommit:BatchGet*”, ”codecommit:Get*”, ”codecommit:List*”, ”codecommit:Create*”, ”codecommit:DeleteBranch”, ”codecom-mit:Describe*”, ”codecommit:Put*”, ”codecommit:Post*”, ”codecommit:Merge*”, ”codecommit:Test*”, ”code-commit:Update*”, ”codecommit:GitPull”, ”codecommit:GitPush”], ”Resource”: ”” }, { ”Sid”: ”Cloud-WatchEventsCodeCommitRulesAccess”, ”Effect”: ”Allow”, ”Action”: [”events:DeleteRule”, ”events:De-scribeRule”, ”events:DisableRule”, ”events:EnableRule”, ”events:PutRule”, ”events:PutTargets”, ”events:Remove-Targets”, ”events:ListTargetsByRule”], ”Resource”: ”arn:aws:events:::rule/codecommit” }, { ”Sid”: ”SNSTopi-cAndSubscriptionAccess”, ”Effect”: ”Allow”, ”Action”: [”sns:Subscribe”, ”sns:Unsubscribe”], ”Resource”: ”arn:aws:sns:::codecommit*” }, { ”Sid”: ”SNSTopicAndSubscriptionReadAccess”, ”Effect”: ”Allow”, ”Action”: [”sns:ListTopics”, ”sns:ListSubscriptionsByTopic”, ”sns:GetTopicAttributes”], ”Resource”: ”” }, { ”Sid”: ”LambdaReadOnlyListAccess”, ”Effect”: ”Allow”, ”Action”: [”lambda:ListFunctions”], ”Resource”: ”” }, { ”Sid”: ”IAMReadOnlyListAccess”, ”Effect”: ”Allow”, ”Action”: [”iam:ListUsers”], ”Resource”: ”” }, { ”Sid”: ”IAMReadOnlyConsoleAccess”, ”Effect”: ”Allow”, ”Action”: [”iam:ListAccessKeys”, ”iam:ListSSH-PublicKeys”, ”iam:ListServiceSpecificCredentials”, ”iam:ListAccessKeys”, ”iam:GetSSHPublicKey”], ”Re-source”: ”arn:aws:iam:::user/${aws:username}” }, { ”Sid”: ”IAMUserSSHKeys”, ”Effect”: ”Allow”, ”Action”: [”iam:DeleteSSHPublicKey”, ”iam:GetSSHPublicKey”, ”iam:ListSSHPublicKeys”, ”iam:UpdateSSHPublicKey”, ”iam:UploadSSHPublicKey”], ”Resource”: ”arn:aws:iam:::user/${aws:username}” }, { ”Sid”: ”IAMSelfMan-ageServiceSpecificCredentials”, ”Effect”: ”Allow”, ”Action”: [”iam:CreateServiceSpecificCredential”, ”iam:Up-dateServiceSpecificCredential”, ”iam:DeleteServiceSpecificCredential”, ”iam:ResetServiceSpecificCredential”], ”Resource”: ”arn:aws:iam:::user/${aws:username}” }] }

1 + **AWSCodeCommitReadOnly** - Grants read\-only access to AWS CodeCommit and repository\-related
   resources in other AWS services, as well as the ability to create and manage their own AWS

CodeCommit\-related resources \(such as Git credentials and SSH keys for their IAM user to use when accessing repositories\)\. Apply this policy to users to whom you want to grant the ability to read the contents of a repository, but not make any changes to its contents\.

The AWSCodeCommitReadOnly policy contains the following policy statement:

{ "Version": "2012-10-17", "Statement": [{ "Effect": "Allow", "Action": ["codecommit:BatchGet*", "codecommit:Get*", "codecommit:Describe*", "codecommit:List*", "codecommit:GitPull"], "Resource": "" }, { "Sid": "CloudWatchEventsCodeCommitRulesReadOnlyAccess", "Effect": "Allow", "Action": ["events:DescribeRule", "events:ListTargetsByRule"], "Resource": "arn:aws:events:::rule/codecommit" }, { "Sid": "SNSSubscriptionAccess", "Effect": "Allow", "Action": ["sns:ListTopics", "sns:ListSubscriptionsByTopic", "sns:GetTopicAttributes"], "Resource": "" }, { "Sid": "LambdaReadOnlyListAccess", "Effect": "Allow", "Action": ["lambda:ListFunctions"], "Resource": "" }, { "Sid": "IAMReadOnlyListAccess", "Effect": "Allow", "Action": ["iam:ListUsers"], "Resource": "" }, { "Sid": "IAMReadOnlyConsoleAccess", "Effect": "Allow", "Action": ["iam:ListAccessKeys", "iam:ListSSHPublicKeys", "iam:ListServiceSpecificCredentials", "iam:ListAccessKeys", "iam:GetSSHPublicKey"], "Resource": "arn:aws:iam:::user/${aws:username}" }] }

For more information, see [AWS Managed Policies](http://docs.aws.amazon.com/IAM/latest/UserGuide/access_policies_managed-vs-inline.html#aws-managed-policies) in the *IAM User Guide*\.

Customer Managed Policy Examples<a name="customer-managed-policies"></a>

You can create your own custom IAM policies to allow permissions for AWS CodeCommit actions and resources\. You can attach these custom policies to the IAM users or groups that require those permissions\. You can also create your own custom IAM policies for integration between AWS CodeCommit and other AWS services\.

Topics
+ [Customer Managed Identity Policy Examples](#customer-managed-policies-identity)
+ [Customer Managed Integration Policy Examples](#integration-policy-examples)

Customer Managed Identity Policy Examples<a name="customer-managed-policies-identity"></a>

The following example IAM policies grant permissions for various AWS CodeCommit actions\. Use them to limit AWS CodeCommit access for your IAM users and roles\. These policies control the ability to perform actions with the AWS CodeCommit console, API, AWS SDKs, or the AWS CLI\.

Note
All examples use the US West \(Oregon\) Region \(us\-west\-2\) and contain fictitious account IDs\.

Examples
+ [Example 1: Allow a User to Perform AWS CodeCommit Operations in a Single Region](#identity-based-policies-example-1)
+ [Example 2: Allow a User to Use Git for a Single Repository](#identity-based-policies-example-2)
+ [Example 3: Allow a User Connecting from a Specified IP Address Range Access to a Repository](#identity-based-policies-example-3)
+ [Example 4: Deny or Allow Actions on Branches](#identity-based-policies-example-4)

Example 1: Allow a User to Perform AWS CodeCommit Operations in a Single Region<a name="identity-based-policies-example-1"></a>

27 The following permissions policy uses a wildcard character \(`"codecommit:*"`\) to allow users to perform all AWS CodeCommit actions in the us\-east\-2 Region\.

{ "Version": "2012-10-17", "Statement" : [{ "Effect" : "Allow", "Action" : ["codecommit:"], "Resource" : "arn:aws:codecommit:us-east-2:" }] }

1

2 #### Example 2: Allow a User to Use Git for a Single Repository<a name="identity-based-policies-example-2"></a>

3

4 In AWS CodeCommit, the `GitPull` IAM policy permissions apply to any Git client command where data is retrieved from AWS CodeCommit, including git fetch, git clone, and so on\. Similarly, the `GitPush` IAM policy permissions apply to any Git client command where data is sent to AWS CodeCommit\. For example, if the `GitPush` IAM policy permission is set to `Allow`, a user can push the deletion of a branch using the Git protocol\. That push is unaffected by any permissions applied to the `DeleteBranch` operation for that IAM user\. The `DeleteBranch` permission applies to actions performed with the console, the AWS CLI, the SDKs, and the API, but not the Git protocol\.

5

6 The following example allows the specified user to pull from, and push to, the AWS CodeCommit repository named `MyDemoRepo`:

{ "Version": "2012-10-17", "Statement" : [{ "Effect" : "Allow", "Action" : ["codecommit:GitPull", "codecommit:GitPush"], "Resource" : "arn:aws:codecommit:us-east-2:111111111111:MyDemoRepo" }] }

1

2 #### Example 3: Allow a User Connecting from a Specified IP Address Range Access to a Repository<a name="identity-based-policies-example-3"></a>

3

4 You can create a policy that only allows users to connect to an AWS CodeCommit repository if their IP address is within a certain IP address range\. There are two equally valid approaches to this\. You can create a `Deny` policy that disallows AWS CodeCommit operations if the IP address for the user is not within a specific block, or you can create an `Allow` policy that allows AWS CodeCommit operations if the IP address for the user is within a specific block\.

5

6 You can create a `Deny` policy that denies access to all users who are not within a certain IP range\. For example, you could attach the AWSCodeCommitPowerUser managed policy and a customer\-managed policy to all users who require access to your repository\. The following example policy denies all AWS CodeCommit permissions to users whose IP addresses are not within the specified IP address block of 203\.0\.113\.0/16:

{ "Version": "2012-10-17", "Statement": [{ "Effect": "Deny", "Action": ["codecommit:"], "Resource": "", "Condition": { "NotIpAddress": { "aws:SourceIp": ["203.0.113.0/16"] } } }] }

1

2 The following example policy allows the specified user to access an AWS CodeCommit repository named MyDemoRepo with the equivalent permissions of the AWSCodeCommitPowerUser managed policy only if their IP address is within the specified address block of 203\.0\.113\.0/16:

{ "Version": "2012-10-17", "Statement": [{ "Effect": "Allow", "Action": ["codecommit:BatchGetRepositories", "codecommit:CreateBranch", "codecommit:CreateRepository", "codecommit:Get*", "codecommit:GitPull", "codecommit:GitPush", "codecommit:List*", "codecommit:Put*", "codecommit:Test*", "codecommit:Update*"], "Resource": "arn:aws:codecommit:us-east-2:111111111111:MyDemoRepo", "Condition": { "IpAddress": { "aws:SourceIp": ["203.0.113.0/16"] } } }] }

1

2 #### Example 4: Deny or Allow Actions on Branches<a name="identity-based-policies-example-4"></a
  >

3

4 You can create a policy that denies users permissions to actions you specify on one or more
  branches\. Alternatively, you can create a policy that allows actions on one or more
  branches that they might not otherwise have in other branches of a repository\. You can use
  these policies with the appropriate managed \(predefined\) policies\. For more information,
  see [Limit Pushes and Merges to Branches in AWS CodeCommit](how-to-conditional-branch.md)\.

5

6 For example, you can create a `Deny` policy that denies users the ability to make changes to a
  branch named master, including deleting that branch, in a repository named *MyDemoRepo*\.
  You can use this policy with the **AWSCodeCommitPowerUser** managed policy\. Users with
  these two policies applied would be able to create and delete branches, create pull requests
  , and all other actions as allowed by **AWSCodeCommitPowerUser**, but they would not be able
   to push changes to the branch named *master*, add or edit a file in the *master* branch in
  the AWS CodeCommit console, or merge a pull request into the *master* branch\. Because `Deny
  ` is applied to `GitPush`, you must include a `Null` statement in the policy, to allow
  initial `GitPush` calls to be analyzed for validity when users make pushes from their local
  repos\.

7

8 **Tip**

9 If you want to create a policy that applies to all branches named *master* in all repositories
  in your AWS account, for `Resource`, specify an asterisk \(`*` \) instead of a repository
  ARN\.

  { "Version": "2012-10-17", "Statement": [{ "Effect": "Deny", "Action": ["codecommit:GitPush", "code-
  commit:DeleteBranch", "codecommit:PutFile", "codecommit:MergePullRequestByFastForward"], "Resource":
  "arn:aws:codecommit:us-east-2:80398EXAMPLE:MyDemoRepo", "Condition": { "StringEqualsIfExists": {
  "codecommit:References": ["refs/heads/master"
  ] }, "Null": { "codecommit:References": false } } }] }

1

2 The following example policy allows a user to make changes to a branch named master in all
  repositories in an AWS account\. You might use this policy with the AWSCodeCommitReadOnly
  managed policy to allow automated pushes to the repository\. Because the Effect is `Allow`,
  this example policy would not work with managed policies such as AWSCodeCommitPowerUser\.

  { "Version": "2012-10-17", "Statement": [{ "Effect": "Allow", "Action": ["codecommit:GitPush"], "Resource":
  "*", "Condition": { "StringNotEqualsIfExists": { "codecommit:References": ["refs/heads/master"] } } }] }

1

2 ### Customer Managed Integration Policy Examples<a name="integration-policy-examples"></a>

3

4 This section provides example customer\-managed user policies that grant permissions for
  integrations between AWS CodeCommit and other AWS services\. For specific examples of
  policies that allow cross\-account access to an AWS CodeCommit repository, see [Configure
  Cross\-Account Access to an AWS CodeCommit Repository](cross-account.md)\.

5

6 **Note**

7 All examples use the US West \(Oregon\) Region \(us\-west\-2\) when a region is required, and
  contain fictitious account IDs\.

8

9 **Examples**

10 + [Example 1: Create a Policy That Enables Cross\-Account Access to an Amazon SNS Topic](#access
   -permissions-sns-int)

11 + [Example 2: Create a Policy for AWS Lambda Integration](#access-permissions-lambda-int)

238

12

13 #### Example 1: Create a Policy That Enables Cross\-Account Access to an Amazon SNS Topic<a name
="access-permissions-sns-int"></a>

14

15 You can configure an AWS CodeCommit repository so that code pushes or other events trigger
actions, such as sending a notification from Amazon Simple Notification Service \(Amazon SNS
\)\. If you create the Amazon SNS topic with the same account used to create the AWS
CodeCommit repository, you do not need to configure additional IAM policies or permissions\.
You can create the topic, and then create the trigger for the repository\. For more
information, see [Create a Trigger for an Amazon SNS Topic](how-to-notify-sns.md)\.

16

17 However, if you want to configure your trigger to use an Amazon SNS topic in another AWS account
, you must first configure that topic with a policy that allows AWS CodeCommit to publish to
that topic\. From that other account, open the Amazon SNS console, choose the topic from
the list, and for **Other topic actions**, choose **Edit topic policy**\. On the **Advanced
** tab, modify the policy for the topic to allow AWS CodeCommit to publish to that topic\.
For example, if the policy is the default policy, you would modify the policy as follows,
changing the items in *red italic text* to match the values for your repository, Amazon SNS
topic, and account:

{ "Version": "2008-10-17", "Id": "__default_policy_ID", "Statement": [{ "Sid": "__default_statement_ID",
"Effect": "Allow", "Principal": { "AWS": "*" }, "Action": ["SNS:Subscribe", "SNS:ListSubscriptionsByTopic",
"SNS:DeleteTopic", "SNS:GetTopicAttributes", "SNS:Publish", "SNS:RemovePermission", "SNS:AddPermission",
"SNS:Receive", "SNS:SetTopicAttributes"], "Resource": "arn:aws:sns:us-east-2:111111111111:NotMySNSTopic",
"Condition": { "StringEquals": { "AWS:SourceOwner": "111111111111" } } }, { "Sid": "CodeCommit-
Policy_ID", "Effect": "Allow", "Principal": { "Service": "codecommit.amazonaws.com" }, "Action": "SNS:Pub-
lish", "Resource": "arn:aws:sns:us-east-2:111111111111:NotMySNSTopic", "Condition": { "StringEquals": {
"AWS:SourceArn": "arn:aws:codecommit:us-east-2:80398EXAMPLE:MyDemoRepo", "AWS:SourceAccount":
"80398EXAMPLE" } } }] }

1

2 #### Example 2: Create a Policy for AWS Lambda Integration<a name="access-permissions-lambda-int
"></a>

3

4 You can configure an AWS CodeCommit repository so that code pushes or other events trigger
actions, such as invoking a function in AWS Lambda\. For more information, see [Create a
Trigger for a Lambda Function](how-to-notify-lambda.md)\.

5

6 If you want your trigger to run a Lambda function directly \(instead of using an Amazon SNS
topic to invoke the Lambda function\), and you do not configure the trigger in the Lambda
console, you must include a policy similar to the following in the function's resource
policy:

{ "Statement":{ "StatementId":"Id-1", "Action":"lambda:InvokeFunction", "Principal":"codecommit.ama-
zonaws.com", "SourceArn":"arn:aws:codecommit:us-east-2:80398EXAMPLE:MyDemoRepo", "SourceAc-
count":"80398EXAMPLE" } }

1

2 When manually configuring an AWS CodeCommit trigger that invokes a Lambda function, you must
also use the Lambda [AddPermission](http://docs.aws.amazon.com/lambda/latest/dg/
API_AddPermission.html) command to grant permission for AWS CodeCommit to invoke the
function\. For an example, see the [To allow AWS CodeCommit to run a Lambda function](how-to
-notify-lambda-cc.md#how-to-notify-lambda-create-function-perm) section of [Create a Trigger
for an Existing Lambda Function](how-to-notify-lambda-cc.md)\.

3

4 For more information about resource policies for Lambda functions, see [AddPermission](http://docs.aws.amazon.com/lambda/latest/dg/API_AddPermission.html) and [The Pull/Push Event Models](http://docs.aws.amazon.com/lambda/latest/dg/intro-invocation-modes.html) in the *AWS Lambda Developer Guide*\.

5

6

7

8

9 # AWS CodeCommit Permissions Reference<a name="auth-and-access-control-permissions-reference"></a>

10

11 The following tables list each AWS CodeCommit API operation, the corresponding actions for which you can grant permissions, and the format of the resource ARN to use for granting permissions\. The AWS CodeCommit APIs are grouped into tables based on the scope of the actions allowed by that API\. Refer to it when setting up [Access Control](auth-and-access-control.md#access-control) and writing permissions policies that you can attach to an IAM identity \(identity\-based policies\)\.

12

13 When you create a permissions policy, you specify the actions in the policy's `Action` field\. You specify the resource value in the policy's `Resource` field as an ARN, with or without a wildcard character \(*\)\.

14

15 To express conditions in your AWS CodeCommit policies, use AWS\-wide condition keys\. For a complete list of AWS\-wide keys, see [Available Keys](http://docs.aws.amazon.com/IAM/latest/UserGuide/reference_policies_elements.html#AvailableKeys) in the *IAM User Guide*\.

16

17 **Note**

18 To specify an action, use the `codecommit:` prefix followed by the API operation name \(for example, `codecommit:GetRepository` or `codecommit:CreateRepository`\.

19

20 **Using Wildcards **

21

22 To specify multiple actions or resources, use a wildcard character \(*\) in your ARN\. For example, `codecommit:*` specifies all AWS CodeCommit actions and `codecommit:Get*` specifies all AWS CodeCommit actions that begin with the word `Get`\. The following example grants access to all repositories with names that begin with `MyDemo`\.

arn:aws:codecommit:us-west-2:111111111111:MyDemo*

1

2 You can use wildcards only with the *repository\-name* resources listed in the following table\. You can't use wildcards with *region* or *account\-id* resources\. For more information about wildcards, see [IAM Identifiers](http://docs.aws.amazon.com/IAM/latest/UserGuide/reference_identifiers.html) in *IAM User Guide*\.

3

4 **Topics**
5 + [Required Permissions for Git Client Commands](#aa-git)
6 + [Permissions for Actions on Branches](#aa-branches)
7 + [Permissions for Actions on Pull Requests](#aa-pr)
8 + [Permissions for Actions on Individual Files](#aa-files)
9 + [Permissions for Actions on Comments](#aa-comments)
10 + [Permissions for Actions on Committed Code](#aa-code)
11 + [Permissions for Actions on Repositories](#aa-repositories)
12 + [Permissions for Actions on Triggers](#aa-triggers)
13 + [Permissions for Actions on AWS CodePipeline Integration](#aa-acp)

14
15 ## Required Permissions for Git Client Commands<a name="aa-git"></a>

16
17 In AWS CodeCommit, the `GitPull` IAM policy permissions apply to any Git client command where data is retrieved from AWS CodeCommit, including git fetch, git clone, and so on\. Similarly, the `GitPush` IAM policy permissions apply to any Git client command where data is sent to AWS CodeCommit\. For example, if the `GitPush` IAM policy permission is set to `Allow`, a user can push the deletion of a branch using the Git protocol\. That push is unaffected by any permissions applied to the `DeleteBranch` operation for that IAM user\. The `DeleteBranch` permission applies to actions performed with the console, the AWS CLI, the SDKs, and the API, but not the Git protocol\.

18
19 `GitPull` and `GitPush` are IAM policy permissions\. They are not API actions\.

20
21 If you see an expand arrow \(****\) in the upper\-right corner of the table, you can open the table in a new window\. To close the window, choose the close button \(**X**\) in the lower \-right corner\.

22
23
24 **AWS CodeCommit Required Permissions for Actions for Git Client Commands**

25
26 | AWS CodeCommit Permissions for Git | Required Permissions | Resources |
27 | --- | --- | --- |
28 | GitPull | `codecommit:GitPull` Required to pull information from an AWS CodeCommit repository to a local repo\. This is an IAM policy permission only, not an API action\. | arn:aws:codecommit:*region*:*account\-id*:*repository\-name* |
29 | GitPush | `codecommit:GitPush` Required to push information from a local repo to an AWS CodeCommit repository\. This is an IAM policy permission only, not an API action\. If you create a policy that includes a context key and a `Deny` statement that includes this permission, you must also include a `Null` context\. For more information, see [Limit Pushes and Merges to Branches in AWS CodeCommit](how-to-conditional-branch.md)\. | arn:aws:codecommit:*region*:*account\-id*:*repository\-name* |

30
31 ## Permissions for Actions on Branches<a name="aa-branches"></a>

32
33 The following permissions allow or deny actions on branches in AWS CodeCommit repositories\. These permissions pertain only to actions performed in the AWS CodeCommit console and with the AWS CodeCommit API, and to commands performed using the AWS CLI\. They do not pertain to similar actions that can be performed using the Git protocol\. For example, the **git show \-branch \-r** command displays a list of remote branches for a repository and its commits using the Git protocol\. It's not affected by any permissions for the AWS CodeCommit `ListBranches` operation\.

34
35 If you see an expand arrow \(****\) in the upper\-right corner of the table, you can open the table in a new window\. To close the window, choose the close button \(**X**\) in the lower \-right corner\.

36
37
38 **AWS CodeCommit API Operations and Required Permissions for Actions on Branches**

39
40 | AWS CodeCommit API Operations for Branches | Required Permissions \(API Actions\) | Resources |
41 | --- | --- | --- |
42 | [CreateBranch](http://docs.aws.amazon.com/codecommit/latest/APIReference/API_CreateBranch.

html) | `codecommit:CreateBranch` Required to create a branch in an AWS CodeCommit repository\. | arn:aws:codecommit:*region*:*account\-id*:*repository\-name* |

43 | [DeleteBranch](http://docs.aws.amazon.com/codecommit/latest/APIReference/API_DeleteBranch.html) | `codecommit:DeleteBranch` Required to delete a branch from an AWS CodeCommit repository\. | arn:aws:codecommit:*region*:*account\-id*:*repository\-name* |

44 | [GetBranch](http://docs.aws.amazon.com/codecommit/latest/APIReference/API_GetBranch.html) | `codecommit:GetBranch` Required to get details about a branch in an AWS CodeCommit repository\. | arn:aws:codecommit:*region*:*account\-id*:*repository\-name* |

45 | [ListBranches](http://docs.aws.amazon.com/codecommit/latest/APIReference/API_ListBranches.html) | `codecommit:ListBranches` Required to get a list of branches in an AWS CodeCommit repository\. | arn:aws:codecommit:*region*:*account\-id*:*repository\-name* |

46 | [UpdateDefaultBranch](http://docs.aws.amazon.com/codecommit/latest/APIReference/API_UpdateDefaultBranch.html) | codecommit:UpdateDefaultBranchRequired to change the default branch in an AWS CodeCommit repository\. | arn:aws:codecommit:*region*:*account\-id*:*repository\-name* |

47

48 ## Permissions for Actions on Pull Requests<a name="aa-pr"></a>

49

50 The following permissions allow or deny actions on pull requests in AWS CodeCommit repositories\. These permissions pertain to actions performed with the AWS CodeCommit console and the AWS CodeCommit API, and commands performed using the AWS CLI\. They do not pertain to similar actions that can be performed using the Git protocol\. For related permissions on comments, see [Permissions for Actions on Comments](#aa-comments)\.

51

52 If you see an expand arrow \(****\) in the upper\-right corner of the table, you can open the table in a new window\. To close the window, choose the close button \(**X**\) in the lower \-right corner\.

53

54

55 **AWS CodeCommit API Operations and Required Permissions for Actions on Pull Requests**

56

57 | AWS CodeCommit API Operations | Required Permissions \(API Actions\) | Resources |

58 | --- | --- | --- |

59 | BatchGetPullRequests | `codecommit:BatchGetPullRequests` Required to return information about one or more pull requests in an AWS CodeCommit repository\. This is an IAM policy permission only, not an API action that you can call\. | arn:aws:codecommit:*region*:*account\-id*:*repository\-name* |

60 | [CreatePullRequest](http://docs.aws.amazon.com/codecommit/latest/APIReference/API_CreatePullRequest.html) | `codecommit:CreatePullRequest` Required to create a pull request in an AWS CodeCommit repository\. | arn:aws:codecommit:*region*:*account\-id*:*repository\-name* |

61 | [DescribePullRequestEvents](http://docs.aws.amazon.com/codecommit/latest/APIReference/API_DescribePullRequestEvents.html) | Required to return information about one or more pull request events\. | arn:aws:codecommit:region:account\-id:repository\-name |

62 | [GetCommentsForPullRequest](http://docs.aws.amazon.com/codecommit/latest/APIReference/API_GetCommentsForPullRequest.html) | `codecommit:GetCommentsForPullRequest` Required to return comments made on a pull request\. | arn:aws:codecommit:*region*:*account\-id*:*repository\-name* |

63 | GetCommitsFromMergeBase | `codecommit:GetCommitsFromMergeBase` Required to return information about the difference between commits in the context of a potential merge\. This is an IAM policy permission only, not an API action that you can call\. | arn:aws:codecommit:*region*:*account\-id*:*repository\-name* |

64 | [GetMergeConflicts](http://docs.aws.amazon.com/codecommit/latest/APIReference/API_GetMergeConflicts.html) | `codecommit:GetMergeConflicts` Required to return information

information about merge conflicts between the source and destination branch in a pull request\. | arn:aws:codecommit:region:account\-id:repository\-name |

65 | [GetPullRequest](http://docs.aws.amazon.com/codecommit/latest/APIReference/API_GetPullRequest.html) | `codecommit:DescribePullRequest` Required to return information about a pull request\. | arn:aws:codecommit:*region*:*account\-id*:*repository\-name* |

66 | [ListPullRequests](http://docs.aws.amazon.com/codecommit/latest/APIReference/API_ListPullRequests.html) | `codecommit:ListPullRequests` Required to return information about the pull requests for a repository\. | arn:aws:codecommit:*region*:*account\-id*:*repository\-name* |

67 | [MergePullRequestByFastForward](http://docs.aws.amazon.com/codecommit/latest/APIReference/API_MergePullRequestByFastForward.html) | codecommit:MergePullRequestByFastForwardRequired to close a pull request and attempt to merge the source branch into the destination branch of a pull request using the fast\-forward merge option\. | arn:aws:codecommit:*region*:*account\-id*:*repository\-name* |

68 | [PostCommentForPullRequest](http://docs.aws.amazon.com/codecommit/latest/APIReference/API_PostCommentForPullRequest.html) | codecommit:PostCommentForPullRequest Required to post a comment on a pull request in an AWS CodeCommit repository\. | arn:aws:codecommit:*region*:*account\-id*:*repository\-name* |

69 | [UpdatePullRequestDescription](http://docs.aws.amazon.com/codecommit/latest/APIReference/API_UpdatePullRequestDescription.html) | codecommit:UpdatePullRequestDescription Required to change the description of a pull request in an AWS CodeCommit repository\. | arn:aws:codecommit:*region*:*account\-id*:*repository\-name* |

70 | [UpdatePullRequestStatus](http://docs.aws.amazon.com/codecommit/latest/APIReference/API_UpdatePullRequestStatus.html) | codecommit:UpdatePullRequestStatus Required to change the status of a pull request in an AWS CodeCommit repository\. | arn:aws:codecommit:*region*:*account\-id*:*repository\-name* |

71 | [UpdatePullRequestTitle](http://docs.aws.amazon.com/codecommit/latest/APIReference/API_UpdatePullRequestTitle.html) | codecommit:UpdatePullRequestTitle Required to change the title of a pull request in an AWS CodeCommit repository\. | arn:aws:codecommit:*region*:*account\-id*:*repository\-name* |

72

73 ## Permissions for Actions on Individual Files<a name="aa-files"></a>

74

75 The following permissions allow or deny actions on individual files in AWS CodeCommit repositories\. These permissions pertain only to actions performed in the AWS CodeCommit console, the AWS CodeCommit API, and to commands performed using the AWS CLI\. They do not pertain to similar actions that can be performed using the Git protocol\. For example, the `git push` command pushes new and changed files to an AWS CodeCommit repository by using the Git protocol\. It's not affected by any permissions for the AWS CodeCommit `PutFile` operation\.

76

77 If you see an expand arrow \(****\) in the upper\-right corner of the table, you can open the table in a new window\. To close the window, choose the close button \(**X**\) in the lower \-right corner\.

78

79

80 **AWS CodeCommit API Operations and Required Permissions for Actions on Individual Files**

81

82 | AWS CodeCommit API Operations for Individual Files | Required Permissions | Resources |

83 | --- | --- | --- |

84 | [GetBlob](http://docs.aws.amazon.com/codecommit/latest/APIReference/API_GetBlob.html) | `codecommit:GetBlob` Required to view the encoded content of an individual file in an AWS CodeCommit repository from the AWS CodeCommit console\. | arn:aws:codecommit:*region*:*account\-id*:*repository\-name* |

85 | [PutFile](http://docs.aws.amazon.com/codecommit/latest/APIReference/API_PutFile.html) | `codecommit:PutFile` Required to add a new or modified file to an AWS CodeCommit repository from the AWS CodeCommit console, AWS CodeCommit API, or the AWS CLI\. | arn:aws:codecommit:*region*:*account\-id*:*repository\-name* |

86

87 ## Permissions for Actions on Comments<a name="aa-comments"></a>

88

89 The following permissions allow or deny actions on comments in AWS CodeCommit repositories\. These permissions pertain to actions performed with the AWS CodeCommit console and the AWS CodeCommit API, and to commands performed using the AWS CLI\. For related permissions on comments in pull requests, see [Permissions for Actions on Pull Requests](#aa-pr)\.

90

91 If you see an expand arrow \(****\) in the upper\-right corner of the table, you can open the table in a new window\. To close the window, choose the close button \(**X**\) in the lower \-right corner\.

92

93

94 **AWS CodeCommit API Operations and Required Permissions for Comments in Repositories**

95

96 | AWS CodeCommit API Operations | Required Permissions \(API Actions\) | Resources |
97 | --- | --- | --- |
98 | [DeleteCommentContent](http://docs.aws.amazon.com/codecommit/latest/APIReference/API_DeleteCommentContent.html) | `codecommit:DeleteCommentContent` Required to delete the content of a comment made on a change, file, or commit in a repository\. Comments cannot be deleted, but the content of a comment can be removed if the user has this permission\. | arn:aws:codecommit:*region*:*account\-id*:*repository\-name* |
99 | [GetComment](http://docs.aws.amazon.com/codecommit/latest/APIReference/API_GetComment.html) | `codecommit:GetComment` Required to return information about a comment made on a change, file, or commit in an AWS CodeCommit repository\. | arn:aws:codecommit:*region*:*account\-id*:*repository\-name* |
100 | [GetCommentsForComparedCommit](http://docs.aws.amazon.com/codecommit/latest/APIReference/API_GetCommentsForComparedCommit.html) | `codecommit:GetCommentsForComparedCommit` Required to return information about comments made on the comparison between two commits in an AWS CodeCommit repository\. | arn:aws:codecommit:*region*:*account\-id*:*repository\-name* |
101 | [PostCommentForComparedCommit](http://docs.aws.amazon.com/codecommit/latest/APIReference/API_PostCommentForComparedCommit.html) | `codecommit:PostCommentForComparedCommit` Required to create a comment on the comparison between two commits in an AWS CodeCommit repository\. | arn:aws:codecommit:*region*:*account\-id*:*repository\-name* |
102 | [PostCommentReply](http://docs.aws.amazon.com/codecommit/latest/APIReference/API_PostCommentReply.html) | `codecommit:PostCommentReply` Required to create a reply to a comment on a comparison between commits or on a pull request\. | arn:aws:codecommit:*region*:*account\-id*:*repository\-name* |
103 | [UpdateComment](http://docs.aws.amazon.com/codecommit/latest/APIReference/API_UpdateComment.html) | `codecommit:UpdateComment` Required to edit a comment on a comparison between commits or on a pull request\. Comments can only be edited by the comment author\. | arn:aws:codecommit:*region*:*account\-id*:*repository\-name* |

104

105 ## Permissions for Actions on Committed Code<a name="aa-code"></a>

106

107 The following permissions allow or deny actions on code committed to AWS CodeCommit repositories\. These permissions pertain to actions performed with the AWS CodeCommit console and the AWS CodeCommit API, and commands performed using the AWS CLI\. They do not pertain to similar actions that can be performed using the Git protocol\. For related permissions on

comments on committed code, see [Permissions for Actions on Comments](#aa-comments)\.

Explicitly denying some of these permissions might result in unexpected consequences in the AWS CodeCommit console\. For example, setting `GetTree` to `Deny` prevents users from navigating the contents of a repository in the console, but does not block users from viewing the contents of a file in the repository \(if they are sent a link to the file in email, for example\)\. Setting `GetBlob` to `Deny` prevents users from viewing the contents of files, but does not block users from browsing the structure of a repository\. Setting `GetCommit` to `Deny` prevents users from retrieving details about commits\. Setting `GetObjectIdentifier` to `Deny` blocks most of the functionality of code browsing\. If you set all three of these actions to `Deny` in a policy, a user with that policy cannot browse code in the AWS CodeCommit console\.

If you see an expand arrow \(****\) in the upper\-right corner of the table, you can open the table in a new window\. To close the window, choose the close button \(**X**\) in the lower \-right corner\.

AWS CodeCommit API Operations and Required Permissions for Actions on Committed Code

AWS CodeCommit API Operations	Required Permissions \(API Actions\)	Resources
BatchGetCommits	`codecommit:BatchGetCommits` Required to return information about one or more commits in an AWS CodeCommit repository\. This is an IAM policy permission only, not an API action that you can call\.	arn:aws:codecommit:*region*:*account\-id*:*repository\-name*
[GetCommit](http://docs.aws.amazon.com/codecommit/latest/APIReference/GetCommit.html)	`codecommit:GetCommit` Required to return information about a commit\.	arn:aws:codecommit:*region*:*account\-id*:*repository\-name*
GetCommitHistory	`codecommit:GetCommitHistory` Required to return information about the history of commits in a repository\. This is an IAM policy permission only, not an API action that you can call\.	arn:aws:codecommit:*region*:*account\-id*:*repository\-name*
[GetDifferences](http://docs.aws.amazon.com/codecommit/latest/APIReference/API_GetDifferences.html)	`codecommit:GetDifferences` Required to return information about the differences between commit specifiers \(such as a branch, tag, HEAD, commit ID, or other fully qualified reference\)\.	arn:aws:codecommit:*region*:*account\-id*:*repository\-name*
GetObjectIdentifier	codecommit:GetObjectIdentifierRequired to resolve blobs, trees, and commits to their identifier\. This is an IAM policy permission only, not an API action that you can call\.	arn:aws:codecommit:*region*:*account\-id*:*repository\-name*
GetReferences	codecommit:GetReferencesRequired to return all references, such as branches and tags\. This is an IAM policy permission only, not an API action that you can call\.	arn:aws:codecommit:*region*:*account\-id*:*repository\-name*
GetTree	codecommit:GetTreeRequired to view the contents of a specified tree in an AWS CodeCommit repository from the AWS CodeCommit console\. This is an IAM policy permission only, not an API action that you can call\.	arn:aws:codecommit:*region*:*account\-id*:*repository\-name*

Permissions for Actions on Repositories<a name="aa-repositories"></a>

The following permissions allow or deny actions on AWS CodeCommit repositories\. These permissions pertain to actions performed with the AWS CodeCommit console and the AWS CodeCommit API, and to commands performed using the AWS CLI\. They do not pertain to similar actions that can be performed using the Git protocol\.

If you see an expand arrow \(****\) in the upper\-right corner of the table, you can open the table in a new window\. To close the window, choose the close button \(**X**\) in the lower \-right corner\.

AWS CodeCommit API Operations and Required Permissions for Actions on Repositories

AWS CodeCommit API Operations	Required Permissions \(API Actions\)	Resources
[BatchGetRepositories](http://docs.aws.amazon.com/codecommit/latest/APIReference/API_BatchGetRepositories.html)	`codecommit:BatchGetRepositories` Required to get information about multiple AWS CodeCommit repositories in an AWS account\. In `Resource`, you must specify the names of all of the AWS CodeCommit repositories for which a user is allowed \(or denied\) information\.	arn:aws:codecommit:*region*:*account\-id*:*repository\-name*
[CreateRepository](http://docs.aws.amazon.com/codecommit/latest/APIReference/CreateRepository.html)	`codecommit:CreateRepository` Required to create an AWS CodeCommit repository\.	arn:aws:codecommit:*region*:*account\-id*:*repository\-name*
[DeleteRepository](http://docs.aws.amazon.com/codecommit/latest/APIReference/API_DeleteRepository.html)	`codecommit:DeleteRepository` Required to delete an AWS CodeCommit repository\.	arn:aws:codecommit:*region*:*account\-id*:*repository\-name*
[GetRepository](http://docs.aws.amazon.com/codecommit/latest/APIReference/API_GetRepository.html)	`codecommit:GetRepository` Required to get information about a single AWS CodeCommit repository\.	arn:aws:codecommit:*region*:*account\-id*:*repository\-name*
[ListRepositories](http://docs.aws.amazon.com/codecommit/latest/APIReference/API_ListRepositories.html)	codecommit:ListRepositoriesRequired to get a list of the names and system IDs of multiple AWS CodeCommit repositories for an AWS account\. The only allowed value for `Resource` for this action is all repositories \(`*`\)\.	*
[UpdateRepositoryDescription](http://docs.aws.amazon.com/codecommit/latest/APIReference/API_UpdateRepositoryDescription.html)	codecommit:UpdateRepositoryDescriptionRequired to change the description of an AWS CodeCommit repository\.	arn:aws:codecommit:*region*:*account\-id*:*repository\-name*
[UpdateRepositoryName](http://docs.aws.amazon.com/codecommit/latest/APIReference/API_UpdateRepositoryName.html)	codecommit:UpdateRepositoryNameRequired to change the name of an AWS CodeCommit repository\. In `Resource`, you must specify both the AWS CodeCommit repositories that are allowed to be changed and the new repository names\.	arn:aws:codecommit:*region*:*account\-id*:*repository\-name*

Permissions for Actions on Triggers<a name="aa-triggers"></a>

The following permissions allow or deny actions on triggers for AWS CodeCommit repositories\.

If you see an expand arrow \(****\) in the upper\-right corner of the table, you can open the table in a new window\. To close the window, choose the close button \(**X**\) in the lower \-right corner\.

AWS CodeCommit API Operations and Required Permissions for Actions on Triggers

AWS CodeCommit API Operations	Required Permissions \(API Actions\)	Resources
[GetRepositoryTriggers](http://docs.aws.amazon.com/codecommit/latest/APIReference/API_GetRepositoryTriggers.html)	`codecommit:GetRepositoryTriggers` Required to return

information about triggers configured for a repository\. | arn:aws:codecommit:*region*:*account\-id*:*repository\-name* |

157 | [PutRepositoryTriggers](http://docs.aws.amazon.com/codecommit/latest/APIReference/API_PutRepositoryTriggers.html) | `codecommit:PutRepositoryTriggers` Required to create, edit, or delete triggers for a repository\. | arn:aws:codecommit:*region*:*account\-id*:*repository\-name* |

158 | [TestRepositoryTriggers](http://docs.aws.amazon.com/codecommit/latest/APIReference/API_TestRepositoryTriggers.html) | `codecommit:TestRepositoryTriggers` Required to test the functionality of a repository trigger by sending data to the topic or function configured for the trigger\. | arn:aws:codecommit:*region*:*account\-id*:*repository\-name* |

159

160 ## Permissions for Actions on AWS CodePipeline Integration<a name="aa-acp"></a>

161

162 In order for AWS CodePipeline to use an AWS CodeCommit repository in a source action for a pipeline, you must grant all of the permissions listed in the following table to the service role for AWS CodePipeline\. If these permissions are not set in the service role or are set to **Deny**, the pipeline does not run automatically when a change is made to the repository, and changes cannot be released manually\.

163

164 If you see an expand arrow \(****\) in the upper\-right corner of the table, you can open the table in a new window\. To close the window, choose the close button \(**X**\) in the lower \-right corner\.

165

166

167 **AWS CodeCommit API Operations and Required Permissions for Actions on AWS CodePipeline Integration**

168

169 | AWS CodeCommit API Operations | Required Permissions \(API Actions\) | Resources |

170 | --- | --- | --- |

171 | [GetBranch](http://docs.aws.amazon.com/codecommit/latest/APIReference/API_GetBranch.html) | `codecommit:GetBranch` Required to get details about a branch in an AWS CodeCommit repository\. | arn:aws:codecommit:*region*:*account\-id*:*repository\-name* |

172 | [GetCommit](http://docs.aws.amazon.com/codecommit/latest/APIReference/GetCommit.html) | `codecommit:GetCommit` Required to return information about a commit to the service role for AWS CodePipeline\. | arn:aws:codecommit:*region*:*account\-id*:*repository\-name* |

173 | UploadArchive | `codecommit:UploadArchive` Required to allow the service role for AWS CodePipeline to upload repository changes into a pipeline\. This is an IAM policy permission only, not an API action that you can call\. | arn:aws:codecommit:*region*:*account\-id*:*repository\-name* |

174 | GetUploadArchiveStatus | `codecommit:GetUploadArchiveStatus` Required to determine the status of an archive upload: whether it is in progress, complete, cancelled, or if an error occurred\. This is an IAM policy permission only, not an API action that you can call\. | arn:aws:codecommit:*region*:*account\-id*:*repository\-name* |

175 | CancelUploadArchive | codecommit:CancelUploadArchiveRequired to cancel the uploading of an archive to a pipeline\. This is an IAM policy permission only, not an API action that can be called\. | arn:aws:codecommit:*region*:*account\-id*:*repository\-name* |

176

177

178

179

180 # AWS CodeCommit Reference<a name="references"></a>

181

182 The following reference topics can help you better understand AWS CodeCommit, Git, AWS regions,

```
     product limitations, and more\.
183
184 **Topics**
185 + [Regions and Git Connection Endpoints for AWS CodeCommit](regions.md)
186 + [Limits in AWS CodeCommit](limits.md)
187 + [Temporary Access to AWS CodeCommit Repositories](temporary-access.md)
188 + [AWS Key Management Service and Encryption for AWS CodeCommit Repositories](encryption.md)
189 + [Logging AWS CodeCommit API Calls with AWS CloudTrail](integ-cloudtrail.md)
190 + [AWS CodeCommit Command Line Reference](cmd-ref.md)
191 + [Basic Git Commands](how-to-basic-git.md)
192
193
194
195
196 # Regions and Git Connection Endpoints for AWS CodeCommit<a name="regions"></a>
197
198 Each AWS CodeCommit repository is associated with an AWS region\. AWS CodeCommit offers regional
        endpoints to make your requests to the service\. In addition, AWS CodeCommit provides Git
        connection endpoints for both SSH and HTTPS protocols in every region where AWS CodeCommit
        is available\.
199
200 All the examples in this guide use the same endpoint URL for Git in US East \(Ohio\): `git-
        codecommit.us-east-2.amazonaws.com`\. However, when you use Git and configure your
        connections, make sure you choose the Git connection endpoint that matches the region that
        hosts your AWS CodeCommit repository\. For example, if you want to make a connection to a
        repository in US East \(N\. Virginia\), use the endpoint URL of `git-codecommit.us-east-1.
        amazonaws.com`\. This is also true for API calls\. When you make connections to an AWS
        CodeCommit repository with the AWS CLI or the SDKs, make sure you use the correct regional
        endpoint for the repository\.
201
202 **Topics**
203 + [Supported Regions for AWS CodeCommit](#regions-acc)
204 + [Git Connection Endpoints](#regions-git)
205 + [Server Fingerprints for AWS CodeCommit](#regions-fingerprints)
206
207 ## Supported Regions for AWS CodeCommit<a name="regions-acc"></a>
208
209 You can create and use AWS CodeCommit repositories in the following AWS regions:
210 + US East \(Ohio\)
211 + US East \(N\. Virginia\)
212 + US West \(N\. California\)
213 + US West \(Oregon\)
214 + EU \(Ireland\)
215 + EU \(London\)
216 + EU \(Paris\)
217 + EU \(Frankfurt\)
218 + Asia Pacific \(Tokyo\)
219 + Asia Pacific \(Singapore\)
220 + Asia Pacific \(Sydney\)
221 + Asia Pacific \(Seoul\)
222 + Asia Pacific \(Mumbai\)
223 + South America \(São Paulo\)
224 + Canada \(Central\)
225
```

226 For more information about regional endpoints for AWS CLI, service, and API calls to AWS
      CodeCommit, see [AWS Regions and Endpoints](http://docs.aws.amazon.com/general/latest/gr/
      rande.html#codecommit_region)\.

227

228 ## Git Connection Endpoints<a name="regions-git"></a>

229

230 Use the following URLs when you configure Git connections to AWS CodeCommit repositories:

231

232

233 **Git connection endpoints for AWS CodeCommit**

234

235 | Region Name | Region | Endpoint URL | Protocol |
236 | --- | --- | --- | --- |
237 | US East \(Ohio\) | us\-east\-2 | https://git\-codecommit\.us\-east\-2\.amazonaws\.com | HTTPS
      |
238 | US East \(Ohio\) | us\-east\-2 | ssh://git\-codecommit\.us\-east\-2\.amazonaws\.com | SSH |
239 | US East \(N\. Virginia\) | us\-east\-1 | https://git\-codecommit\.us\-east\-1\.amazonaws\.com
      | HTTPS |
240 | US East \(N\. Virginia\) | us\-east\-1 | ssh://git\-codecommit\.us\-east\-1\.amazonaws\.com |
      SSH |
241 | US West \(Oregon\) | us\-west\-2 | https://git\-codecommit\.us\-west\-2\.amazonaws\.com |
      HTTPS |
242 | US West \(Oregon\) | us\-west\-2 | ssh://git\-codecommit\.us\-west\-2\.amazonaws\.com | SSH |
243 | EU \(Ireland\) | eu\-west\-1 | https://git\-codecommit\.eu\-west\-1\.amazonaws\.com | HTTPS |
244 | EU \(Ireland\) | eu\-west\-1 | ssh://git\-codecommit\.eu\-west\-1\.amazonaws\.com | SSH |
245 | Asia Pacific \(Tokyo\) | ap\-northeast\-1 | https://git\-codecommit\.ap\-northeast\-1\.
      amazonaws\.com | HTTPS |
246 | Asia Pacific \(Tokyo\) | ap\-northeast\-1 | ssh://git\-codecommit\.ap\-northeast\-1\.amazonaws
      \.com | SSH |
247 | Asia Pacific \(Singapore\) | ap\-southeast\-1 | https://git\-codecommit\.ap\-southeast\-1\.
      amazonaws\.com | HTTPS |
248 | Asia Pacific \(Singapore\) | ap\-southeast\-1 | ssh://git\-codecommit\.ap\-southeast\-1\.
      amazonaws\.com | SSH |
249 | Asia Pacific \(Sydney\) | ap\-southeast\-2 | https://git\-codecommit\.ap\-southeast\-2\.
      amazonaws\.com | HTTPS |
250 | Asia Pacific \(Sydney\) | ap\-southeast\-2 | ssh://git\-codecommit\.ap\-southeast\-2\.
      amazonaws\.com | SSH |
251 | EU \(Frankfurt\) | eu\-central\-1 | https://git\-codecommit\.eu\-central\-1\.amazonaws\.com |
      HTTPS |
252 | EU \(Frankfurt\) | eu\-central\-1 | ssh://git\-codecommit\.eu\-central\-1\.amazonaws\.com |
      SSH |
253 | Asia Pacific \(Seoul\) | ap\-northeast\-2 | https://git\-codecommit\.ap\-northeast\-2\.
      amazonaws\.com | HTTPS |
254 | Asia Pacific \(Seoul\) | ap\-northeast\-2 | ssh://git\-codecommit\.ap\-northeast\-2\.amazonaws
      \.com | SSH |
255 | South America \(São Paulo\) | sa\-east\-1 | https://git\-codecommit\.sa\-east\-1\.amazonaws\.
      com | HTTPS |
256 | South America \(São Paulo\) | sa\-east\-1 | ssh://git\-codecommit\.sa\-east\-1\.amazonaws\.com
      | SSH |
257 | US West \(N\. California\) | us\-west\-1 | https://git\-codecommit\.us\-west\-1\.amazonaws\.
      com | HTTPS |
258 | US West \(N\. California\) | us\-west\-1 | ssh://git\-codecommit\.us\-west\-1\.amazonaws\.com
      | SSH |
259 | EU \(London\) | eu\-west\-2 | https://git\-codecommit\.eu\-west\-2\.amazonaws\.com | HTTPS |

260 | EU \(London\) | eu\-west\-2 | ssh://git\-codecommit\.eu\-west\-2\.amazonaws\.com | SSH |
261 | Asia Pacific \(Mumbai\) | ap\-south\-1 | https://git\-codecommit\.ap\-south\-1\.amazonaws\.com | HTTPS |
262 | Asia Pacific \(Mumbai\) | ap\-south\-1 | ssh://git\-codecommit\.ap\-south\-1\.amazonaws\.com | SSH |
263 | Canada \(Central\) | ca\-central\-1 | https://git\-codecommit\.ca\-central\-1\.amazonaws\.com | HTTPS |
264 | Canada \(Central\) | ca\-central\-1 | ssh://git\-codecommit\.ca\-central\-1\.amazonaws\.com | SSH |
265 | EU \(Paris\) | eu\-west\-3 | https://git\-codecommit\.eu\-west\-3\.amazonaws\.com | HTTPS |
266 | EU \(Paris\) | eu\-west\-3 | ssh://git\-codecommit\.eu\-west\-3\.amazonaws\.com | SSH |
267
268 ## Server Fingerprints for AWS CodeCommit<a name="regions-fingerprints"></a>
269
270 The following table lists the public fingerprints for Git connection endpoints in AWS CodeCommit \. These server fingerprints are displayed as part of the verification process for adding an endpoint to your known hosts file\.
271
272
273 **Public fingerprints for AWS CodeCommit**
274
275 | Server | Cryptographic hash type | Fingerprint |
276 | --- | --- | --- |
277 | git\-codecommit\.us\-east\-2\.amazonaws\.com | MD5 | a9:6d:03:ed:08:42:21:be:06:e1:e0:2a:d1:75:31:5e |
278 | git\-codecommit\.us\-east\-2\.amazonaws\.com | SHA256 | 3lBlW2g5xn/NA2Ck6dyeJIrQOWvn7n8UEs56fG6ZIzQ |
279 | git\-codecommit\.us\-east\-1\.amazonaws\.com | MD5 | a6:9c:7d:bc:35:f5:d4:5f:8b:ba:6f:c8:bc:d4:83:84 |
280 | git\-codecommit\.us\-east\-1\.amazonaws\.com | SHA256 | eLMY1j0DKA4uvDZcl/KgtIayZANwX6t8\+8isPtotBoY |
281 | git\-codecommit\.us\-west\-2\.amazonaws\.com | MD5 | a8:68:53:e3:99:ac:6e:d7:04:7e:f7:92:95:77:a9:77 |
282 | git\-codecommit\.us\-west\-2\.amazonaws\.com | SHA256 | 0pJx9SQpkbPUAHwy58UVIq0IHcyo1fwCpOOuVgcAWPo |
283 | git\-codecommit\.eu\-west\-1\.amazonaws\.com | MD5 | 93:42:36:ea:22:1f:f1:0f:20:02:4a:79:ff:ea:12:1d |
284 | git\-codecommit\.eu\-west\-1\.amazonaws\.com | SHA256 | tKjRkOL8dmJyTmSbeSdN1S8F/f0iql3RlvqgTOP1UyQ |
285 | git\-codecommit\.ap\-northeast\-1\.amazonaws\.com | MD5 | 8e:a3:f0:80:98:48:1c:5c:6f:59:db:a7:8f:6e:c6:cb |
286 | git\-codecommit\.ap\-northeast\-1\.amazonaws\.com | SHA256 | Xk/WeYD/K/bnBybzhiuu4dWpBJtXPf7E30jHU7se40w |
287 | git\-codecommit\.ap\-southeast\-1\.amazonaws\.com | MD5 | 65:e5:27:c3:09:68:0d:8e:b7:6d:94:25:80:3e:93:cf |
288 | git\-codecommit\.ap\-southeast\-1\.amazonaws\.com | SHA256 | ZIsVa7OVzxrTIf\+Rk4UbhPv6Es22mSB3uTBojfPXIno |
289 | git\-codecommit\.ap\-southeast\-2\.amazonaws\.com | MD5 | 7b:d2:c1:24:e6:91:a5:7b:fa:c1:0c:35:95:87:da:a0 |
290 | git\-codecommit\.ap\-southeast\-2\.amazonaws\.com | SHA256 | nYp\+gHas80HY3DqbP4yanCDFhqDVjseefVbHEXqH2Ec |
291 | git\-codecommit\.eu\-central\-1\.amazonaws\.com | MD5 | 74:5a:e8:02:fc:b2:9c:06:10:b4:78:84:65:94:22:2d |
292 | git\-codecommit\.eu\-central\-1\.amazonaws\.com | SHA256 |

```
       MwGrkiEki8QkkBtlAgXbYt0hoZYBnZF62VY5RzGJEUY |
293 |  git\-codecommit\.ap\-northeast\-2\.amazonaws\.com | MD5 | 9f:68:48:9b:5f:fc
       :96:69:39:45:58:87:95:b3:69:ed |
294 |  git\-codecommit\.ap\-northeast\-2\.amazonaws\.com | SHA256 |
       eegAPQrWY9YsYo9ZHIKOmxetfXBHzAZd8Eya53Qcwko |
295 |  git\-codecommit\.sa\-east\-1\.amazonaws\.com | MD5 | 74:99:9d:ff:2b:ef:63:c6:4b:b4:6a:7f:62:c5
       :4b:51 |
296 |  git\-codecommit\.sa\-east\-1\.amazonaws\.com | SHA256 | kW\+VKB0jpRaG/
       ZbXkgbtMQbKgEDK7JnISV3SVoyCmzU |
297 |  git\-codecommit\.us\-west\-1\.amazonaws\.com | MD5 | 3b:76:18:83:13:2c:f8:eb:e9:a3:d0
       :51:10:32:e7:d1 |
298 |  git\-codecommit\.us\-west\-1\.amazonaws\.com | SHA256 |
       gzauWTWXDK2u5KuMMi5vbKTmfyerdIwgSbzYBODLpzg |
299 |  git\-codecommit\.eu\-west\-2\.amazonaws\.com | MD5 | a5:65:a6:b1:84:02:b1:95:43:f9:0e:de:dd:ed
       :61:d3 |
300 |  git\-codecommit\.eu\-west\-2\.amazonaws\.com | SHA256 | rORwz5k/IHp/
       QyrRnfiM9j02D5UEqMbtFNTuDG2hNbs |
301 |  git\-codecommit\.ap\-south\-1\.amazonaws\.com | MD5 | da:41:1e:07:3b:9e:76:a0:c5:1e
       :64:88:03:69:86:21 |
302 |  git\-codecommit\.ap\-south\-1\.amazonaws\.com | SHA256 | hUKwnTj7\+
       Xpx4Kddb6p45j4RazIJ4IhAMD8k29itOfE |
303 |  git\-codecommit\.ca\-central\-1\.amazonaws\.com | MD5 | 9f:7c:a2:2f:8c:b5:74:fd:ab:b7:e1:fd:af
       :46:ed:23 |
304 |  git\-codecommit\.ca\-central\-1\.amazonaws\.com | SHA256 |
       Qz5puafQdANVprL1j6r0Qyh4lCNsF6ob61dGcPtFS7w |
305 |  git\-codecommit\.eu\-west\-3\.amazonaws\.com | MD5 | 1b:7f:97:dd:d7:76:8a:32:2c:bd:2c:7b
       :33:74:6a:76 |
306 |  git\-codecommit\.eu\-west\-3\.amazonaws\.com | SHA256 | uw7c2FL564jVoFgtc\+ikzILnKBsZz7t9\+
       CFdSJjKbLI |
307
308
309
310
311 # Limits in AWS CodeCommit<a name="limits"></a>
312
313 The following table describes limits in AWS CodeCommit\. For information about limits that can
       be changed, see [AWS Service Limits](http://docs.aws.amazon.com/general/latest/gr/
       aws_service_limits.html#limits_codecommit)\.
314
315
316 |  |  |
317 | --- |--- |
318 | Number of repositories |  Maximum of 1,000 per AWS account\. This limit can be changed\. For
       more information, see [AWS Service Limits](http://docs.aws.amazon.com/general/latest/gr/
       aws_service_limits.html)\.  |
319 | Regions |  AWS CodeCommit is available in the following regions: [\[See the AWS documentation
       website for more details\]](http://docs.aws.amazon.com/codecommit/latest/userguide/limits.
       html) For more information, see [Regions and Git Connection Endpoints](regions.md)\.  |
320 | Number of references in a single push | Maximum of 4,000, including create, delete, and update
       \. There is no limit on the overall number of references in the repository\. |
321 | Number of triggers in a repository |  Maximum of 10\.  |
322 | Repository names |  Any combination of letters, numbers, periods, underscores, and dashes
       between 1 and 100 characters in length\. Repository names cannot end in \.git and cannot
       contain any of the following characters: ****\! ? @ \# $ % ^ & \* \( \) \+ = \{ \} \[ \] \|
```

```
        \\ / > < \~ ` ' "   ; :****   |
```

323 | Branch names | Any combination of allowed characters between 1 and 256 characters in length\. Branch names cannot: [\[See the AWS documentation website for more details\]]\(http://docs. aws.amazon.com/codecommit/latest/userguide/limits.html) Branch names are references\. Many of the limitations on branch names are based on the Git reference standard\. For more information, see [Git Internals]\(https://git-scm.com/book/en/v2/Git-Internals-Git-References) and [git\-check\-ref\-format]\(https://git-scm.com/docs/git-check-ref-format)\. |

324 | Trigger names | Any combination of letters, numbers, periods, underscores, and dashes between 1 and 100 characters in length\. Trigger names cannot contain spaces or commas\. |

325 | User names in commits made in the console | Any combination of allowed characters between 1 and 1,024 characters in length\. |

326 | Email addresses in commits made in the console | Any combination of allowed characters between 1 and 256 characters in length\. Email addresses are not validated\. |

327 | Repository descriptions | Any combination of characters between 0 and 1,000 characters in length\. Repository descriptions are optional\. |

328 | Metadata for a commit | Maximum of 20 MB for the combined [metadata for a commit]\(https:// git-scm.com/book/en/v2/Git-Internals-Git-Objects) \(for example, the combination of author information, date, parent commit list, and commit messages\)\.   There is no limit on the number or the total size of all files in a single commit, as long as the metadata does not exceed 20 MB and a single blob does not exceed 2 GB\. |

329 | File size display limit in the AWS CodeCommit console | Maximum of 6 MB\. |

330 | File paths | Any combination of allowed characters between 1 and 4,096 characters in length\. File paths must be an unambiguous name that specifies the file and the exact location of the file\. File paths cannot exceed 20 directories in depth\. Additionally, file paths cannot :[\[See the AWS documentation website for more details\]]\(http://docs.aws.amazon.com/ codecommit/latest/userguide/limits.html) Filenames and paths must be fully qualified\. The name and path to a file on your local computer must follow the standards for that operating system\. When specifying the path to a file in an AWS CodeCommit repository, use the standards for Amazon Linux\. |

331 | Git blob size | Maximum of 2 GB\. There is no limit on the number or the total size of all files in a single commit, as long as the metadata does not exceed 6 MB and a single blob does not exceed 2 GB\. |

332 | Custom data for triggers | This is a string field limited to 1,000 characters\. It cannot be used to pass any dynamic parameters\. |

333 | Graph display of branches in the Commit Visualizer | 35 per page\. If there are more than 35 branches on a single page, the graph is not displayed\. |

334

335

336

337

338 # Temporary Access to AWS CodeCommit Repositories<a name="temporary-access"></a>

339

340 You can allow users temporary access to your AWS CodeCommit repositories\. For example, you might do this to allow IAM users to access AWS CodeCommit repositories in separate AWS accounts \(a technique known as *cross\-account access*\)\. For a walkthrough of configuring cross\-account access to a repository, see [Configure Cross\-Account Access to an AWS CodeCommit Repository]\(cross-account.md)\.

341

342 You can also configure access for users who want or must authenticate through methods such as:

343 + Security Assertion Markup Language \(SAML\)

344 + Multi\-factor authentication \(MFA\)

345 + Federation

346 + Login with Amazon

347 + Amazon Cognito

348 + Facebook

349 + Google

350 + OpenID Connect \(OIDC\)\-compatible identity provider

351

352 **Note**

353 The following information applies only to the use of the AWS CLI credential helper to connect to AWS CodeCommit repositories\. You cannot use SSH or Git credentials and HTTPS to connect to AWS CodeCommit repositories with temporary access credentials\.

354

355 To give users temporary access to your AWS CodeCommit repositories, complete the following steps \.

356

357 Do not complete these steps if all of the following requirements are true:

358 + You are signed in to an Amazon EC2 instance\.

359 + You are using Git and HTTPS with the AWS CLI credential helper to connect from the Amazon EC2 instance to AWS CodeCommit repositories\.

360 + The Amazon EC2 instance has an attached IAM instance profile that contains the access permissions described in [For HTTPS Connections on Linux, macOS, or Unix with the AWS CLI Credential Helper](setting-up-https-unixes.md) or [For HTTPS Connections on Windows with the AWS CLI Credential Helper](setting-up-https-windows.md)\.

361 + You have installed and configured the Git credential helper on the Amazon EC2 instance, as described in [For HTTPS Connections on Linux, macOS, or Unix with the AWS CLI Credential Helper](setting-up-https-unixes.md) or [For HTTPS Connections on Windows with the AWS CLI Credential Helper](setting-up-https-windows.md)\.

362

363 Amazon EC2 instances that meet the preceding requirements are already set up to communicate temporary access credentials to AWS CodeCommit on your behalf\.

364

365 ## Step 1: Complete the Prerequisites<a name="temporary-access-prerequisites"></a>

366

367 Complete the setup steps to provide a user with temporary access to your AWS CodeCommit repositories:

368 + For cross\-account access, see [Walkthrough: Delegating Access Across AWS Accounts Using IAM Roles](http://docs.aws.amazon.com/IAM/latest/UserGuide/roles-walkthrough-crossacct.html)\.

369 + For SAML and federation, see [Using Your Organization's Authentication System to Grant Access to AWS Resources](http://docs.aws.amazon.com/STS/latest/UsingSTS/STSUseCases.html#IdentityBrokerApplication) and [About AWS STS SAML 2\.0\-based Federation](http://docs.aws.amazon.com/STS/latest/UsingSTS/CreatingSAML.html)\.

370 + For MFA, see [Using Multi\-Factor Authentication \(MFA\) Devices with AWS](http://docs.aws.amazon.com/IAM/latest/UserGuide/Using_ManagingMFA.html) and [Creating Temporary Security Credentials to Enable Access for IAM Users](http://docs.aws.amazon.com/STS/latest/UsingSTS/CreatingSessionTokens.html)\.

371 + For Login with Amazon, Amazon Cognito, Facebook, Google, or any OIDC\-compatible identity provider, see [About AWS STS Web Identity Federation](http://docs.aws.amazon.com/STS/latest/UsingSTS/web-identity-federation.html)\.

372

373 Use the information in [Authentication and Access Control for AWS CodeCommit](auth-and-access-control.md) to specify the AWS CodeCommit permissions you want to temporarily grant the user \.

374

375 ## Step 2: Get Temporary Access Credentials<a name="temporary-access-get-credentials"></a>

376

377 Depending on the way you set up temporary access, your user can get temporary access credentials in one of the following ways:

378 + For cross\-account access, call the AWS CLI [assume\-role](http://docs.aws.amazon.com/cli/latest/reference/sts/assume-role.html) command or call the AWS STS [AssumeRole](http://docs.aws.amazon.com/STS/latest/APIReference/API_AssumeRole.html) API\.

379 + For SAML, call the AWS CLI [assume\-role\-with\-saml](http://docs.aws.amazon.com/cli/latest/reference/sts/assume-role-with-saml.html) command or the AWS STS [AssumeRoleWithSAML](http://docs.aws.amazon.com/STS/latest/APIReference/API_AssumeRoleWithSAML.html) API\.

380 + For federation, call the AWS CLI [assume\-role](http://docs.aws.amazon.com/cli/latest/reference/sts/assume-role.html) or [get\-federation\-token](http://docs.aws.amazon.com/cli/latest/reference/sts/get-federation-token.html) commands or the AWS STS [AssumeRole](http://docs.aws.amazon.com/STS/latest/APIReference/API_AssumeRole.html) or [GetFederationToken](http://docs.aws.amazon.com/STS/latest/APIReference/API_GetFederationToken.html) APIs\.

381 + For MFA, call the AWS CLI [get\-session\-token](http://docs.aws.amazon.com/cli/latest/reference/sts/get-session-token.html) command or the AWS STS [GetSessionToken](http://docs.aws.amazon.com/STS/latest/APIReference/API_GetSessionToken.html) API\.

382 + For Login with Amazon, Amazon Cognito, Facebook, Google, or any OIDC\-compatible identity provider, call the AWS CLI [assume\-role\-with\-web\-identity](http://docs.aws.amazon.com/cli/latest/reference/sts/assume-role-with-web-identity.html) command or the AWS STS [AssumeRoleWithWebIdentity](http://docs.aws.amazon.com/STS/latest/APIReference/API_AssumeRoleWithWebIdentity.html) API\.

383

384 Your user should receive a set of temporary access credentials, which include an AWS access key ID, a secret access key, and a session token\. Your user should make a note of these three values because they are used in the next step\.

385

386 ## Step 3: Configure the AWS CLI with Your Temporary Access Credentials<a name="temporary-access-configure-credentials"></a>

387

388 Your user must configure the development machine to use those temporary access credentials\.

389

390 1. Follow the instructions in [Setting Up](setting-up.md) to set up the AWS CLI\. Use the aws configure command to configure a profile\.

391 **Note**

392 Before you continue, make sure the git config file is configured to use the AWS profile you configured in the AWS CLI\.

393

394 1. You can associate the temporary access credentials with the user's AWS CLI named profile in one of the following ways\. Do not use the aws configure command\.

395   + In the `~/.aws/credentials` file \(for Linux\) or the `%UserProfile%.aws\credentials` file \(for Windows\), add to the user's AWS CLI named profile the `aws_access_key_id`, `aws_secret_access_key`, and `aws_session_token` setting values:

396

397   ```

398   [CodeCommitProfileName]

399   aws_access_key_id=TheAccessKeyID

400   aws_secret_access_key=TheSecretAccessKey

401   aws_session_token=TheSessionToken

402   ```

403

404   \-OR\-

405   + Set the **AWS_ACCESS_KEY_ID**, **AWS_SECRET_ACCESS_KEY**, and **AWS_SESSION_TOKEN** environment variables:

406

407   For Linux, macOS, or Unix:

408

```
409    ```
410    export AWS_ACCESS_KEY_ID=TheAccessKey
411    export AWS_SECRET_ACCESS_KEY=TheSecretAccessKey
412    export AWS_SESSION_TOKEN=TheSessionToken
413    ```
414
415    For Windows:
416
417    ```
418    set AWS_ACCESS_KEY_ID=TheAccessKey
419    set AWS_SECRET_ACCESS_KEY=TheSecretAccessKey
420    set AWS_SESSION_TOKEN=TheSessionToken
421    ```
422
423    For more information, see [Configuring the AWS Command Line Interface](http://docs.aws.amazon
       .com/cli/latest/userguide/cli-chap-getting-started.html) in the *AWS Command Line
       Interface User Guide*\.
424
425  1. Set up the Git credential helper with the AWS CLI named profile associated with the temporary
       access credentials\.
426    + [Linux, macOS, or Unix](setting-up-https-unixes.md)
427    + [Windows](setting-up-https-windows.md)
428
429    As you follow these steps, do not call the aws configure command\. You already specified
       temporary access credentials through the credentials file or the environment variables\.
       If you use environment variables instead of the credentials file, in the Git credential
       helper, specify `default` as the profile name\.
430
431  ## Step 4: Access the AWS CodeCommit Repositories<a name="temporary-access-use-credentials"></a>
432
433  Assuming your user has followed the instructions in [Connect to a Repository](how-to-connect.md)
       to connect to the AWS CodeCommit repositories, the user then uses Git to call git clone,
       git push, and git pull to clone, push to, and pull from, the AWS CodeCommit repositories to
       which he or she has temporary access\.
434
435  When the user uses the AWS CLI and specifies the AWS CLI named profile associated with the
       temporary access credentials, results scoped to that profile are returned\.
436
437  If the user receives the `403: Forbidden` error in response to calling a Git command or a
       command in the AWS CLI, it's likely the temporary access credentials have expired\. The user
       must go back to [step 2](#temporary-access-get-credentials) and get a new set of temporary
       access credentials\.
438
439
440
441
442  # AWS Key Management Service and Encryption for AWS CodeCommit Repositories<a name="encryption
       "></a>
443
444  Data in AWS CodeCommit repositories is encrypted in transit and at rest\. When data is pushed
       into an AWS CodeCommit repository \(for example, by calling git push\), AWS CodeCommit
       encrypts the received data as it is stored in the repository\. When data is pulled from an
       AWS CodeCommit repository \(for example, by calling git pull\), AWS CodeCommit decrypts the
       data and then sends it to the caller\. This assumes the IAM user associated with the push or
```

pull request has been authenticated by AWS\. Data sent or received is transmitted using the HTTPS or SSH encrypted network protocols\.

445

446 The first time you create an AWS CodeCommit repository in a new region in your AWS account, AWS CodeCommit creates an AWS\-managed key in that same region in AWS Key Management Service \(AWS KMS\) that is used only by AWS CodeCommit \(the `aws/codecommit` key\)\. This key is created and stored in your AWS account\. AWS CodeCommit uses this AWS\-managed key to encrypt and decrypt the data in this and all other AWS CodeCommit repositories within that region in your AWS account\.

447

448 **Important**

449 AWS CodeCommit performs the following AWS KMS actions against the default key `aws/codecommit `\. An IAM user does not need explicit permissions for these actions, but the user must not have any attached policies that deny these actions for the `aws/codecommit` key\. Specifically, your AWS account must not have any of the following permissions set to deny when creating your first repository:

450 `"kms:Encrypt"`
451 `"kms:Decrypt"`
452 `"kms:ReEncrypt"`
453 `"kms:GenerateDataKey"`
454 `"kms:GenerateDataKeyWithoutPlaintext"`
455 `"kms:DescribeKey"`

456

457 To see information about the AWS\-managed key generated by AWS CodeCommit, do the following:

458

459 1. Sign in to the AWS Management Console and open the IAM console at [https://console\.aws\. amazon\.com/iam/](https://console.aws.amazon.com/iam/)\.

460

461 1. In the service navigation pane, choose **Encryption Keys**\. \(If a welcome page appears, choose **Get Started Now**\.\)

462

463 1. In **Filter**, choose the region for your repository\. For example, if the repository was created in us\-east\-2, make sure the filter is set to US East \(Ohio\)\.

464

465 1. In the list of encryption keys, choose the AWS\-managed key with the alias **aws/codecommit **\. Basic information about the AWS\-managed key will be displayed\.

466

467 You cannot change or delete this AWS\-managed key\. You cannot use a customer\-managed key in AWS KMS to encrypt or decrypt data in AWS CodeCommit repositories\.

468

469 ## Encryption Context<a name="w3ab1c56c15c15"></a>

470

471 Each service integrated with AWS KMS specifies an encryption context for both the encryption and decryption operations\. The encryption context is additional authenticated information AWS KMS uses to check for data integrity\. When specified for the encryption operation, it must also be specified in the decryption operation or decryption will fail\. AWS CodeCommit uses the AWS CodeCommit repository ID for the encryption context\. You can find the repository ID by using the get\-repository command or by viewing repository details in the AWS CodeCommit console\. Search for the AWS CodeCommit repository ID in AWS CloudTrail logs to understand which encryption operations were taken on which key in AWS KMS to encrypt or decrypt data in the AWS CodeCommit repository\.

472

473 For more information about AWS KMS, see the [AWS Key Management Service Developer Guide](http://docs.aws.amazon.com/kms/latest/developerguide/)\.

Logging AWS CodeCommit API Calls with AWS CloudTrail<a name="integ-cloudtrail"></a>

AWS CodeCommit is integrated with CloudTrail, a service that captures all of the AWS CodeCommit API calls and delivers the log files to an Amazon S3 bucket that you specify\. CloudTrail captures API calls from the AWS CodeCommit console, your Git client, and from code calls to the AWS CodeCommit APIs\. Using the information collected by CloudTrail, you can determine the request that was made to AWS CodeCommit, the source IP address from which the request was made, who made the request, when it was made, and so on\.

To learn more about CloudTrail, including how to configure and enable it, see the [AWS CloudTrail User Guide](http://docs.aws.amazon.com/awscloudtrail/latest/userguide/)\.

AWS CodeCommit Information in CloudTrail<a name="service-name-info-in-cloudtrail"></a>

When CloudTrail logging is enabled in your AWS account, API calls made to AWS CodeCommit actions are tracked in CloudTrail log files, where they are written with other AWS service records\. CloudTrail determines when to create and write to a new file based on a time period and file size\.

All AWS CodeCommit actions are logged by CloudTrail, including some \(such as `GetObjectIdentifier`\) that are not currently documented in the [AWS CodeCommit API Reference](http://docs.aws.amazon.com/codecommit/latest/APIReference/) but are instead referenced as access permissions and documented in [AWS CodeCommit Permissions Reference](auth-and-access-control-permissions-reference.md)\. For example, calls to the `ListRepositories` \(in the AWS CLI, `aws codecommit list-repositories`\), `CreateRepository` \(`aws codecommit create-repository`\) and `PutRepositoryTriggers` \(`aws codecommit put-repository-triggers`\) actions generate entries in the CloudTrail log files, as well as Git client calls to `GitPull` and `GitPush`\. In addition, if you have an AWS CodeCommit repository configured as a source for a pipeline in AWS CodePipeline, you will see calls to AWS CodeCommit access permission actions such as `UploadArchive` from AWS CodePipeline\. Since AWS CodeCommit uses AWS Key Management Service to encrypt and decrypt repositories, you will also see calls from AWS CodeCommit to `Encrypt` and `Decrypt` actions from AWS KMS in CloudTrail logs\.

Every log entry contains information about who generated the request\. The user identity information in the log entry helps you determine the following:
+ Whether the request was made with root or IAM user credentials
+ Whether the request was made with temporary security credentials for a role or federated user, or made by an assumed role
+ Whether the request was made by another AWS service

For more information, see the [CloudTrail userIdentity Element](http://docs.aws.amazon.com/awscloudtrail/latest/userguide/cloudtrail-event-reference-user-identity.html)\.

You can store your log files in your Amazon S3 bucket for as long as you want, but you can also define Amazon S3 lifecycle rules to archive or delete log files automatically\. By default, your log files are encrypted with Amazon S3 server\-side encryption \(SSE\)\.

If you want to be notified upon log file delivery, you can configure CloudTrail to publish Amazon SNS notifications when new log files are delivered\. For more information, see [

Configuring Amazon SNS Notifications for CloudTrail](http://docs.aws.amazon.com/awscloudtrail/latest/userguide/getting_notifications_top_level.html)\.

500

501 You can also aggregate AWS CodeCommit log files from multiple AWS regions and multiple AWS accounts into a single Amazon S3 bucket\.

502

503 For more information, see [Receiving CloudTrail Log Files from Multiple Regions](http://docs.aws.amazon.com/awscloudtrail/latest/userguide/cloudtrail-receive-logs-from-multiple-accounts.html) and [Receiving CloudTrail Log Files from Multiple Accounts](http://docs.aws.amazon.com/awscloudtrail/latest/userguide/cloudtrail-receive-logs-from-multiple-accounts.html)\.

504

505 ## Understanding AWS CodeCommit Log File Entries<a name="understanding-service-name-entries"></a>

506

507 CloudTrail log files can contain one or more log entries\. Each entry lists multiple JSON\-formatted events\. A log event represents a single request from any source and includes information about the requested action, the date and time of the action, request parameters, and so on\. Log entries are not an ordered stack trace of the public API calls, so they do not appear in any specific order\.

508

509 **Note**

510 This example has been formatted for improved readability\. In a CloudTrail log file, all entries and events are concatenated into a single line\. In addition, this example has been limited to a single AWS CodeCommit entry\. In a real CloudTrail log file, you will see entries and events from multiple AWS services\.

511

512 **Contents**

513 + [Example: A log entry for listing AWS CodeCommit repositories](#integ-cloudtrail-listrepositories)

514 + [Example: A log entry for creating an AWS CodeCommit repository](#integ-cloudtrail-createrepository)

515 + [Examples: Log entries for pull requests to an AWS CodeCommit repository](#integ-cloudtrail-gitpull)

516 + [Example: A log entry for a successful push to an AWS CodeCommit repository](#integ-cloudtrail-gitpush)

517

518 ### Example: A log entry for listing AWS CodeCommit repositories<a name="integ-cloudtrail-listrepositories"></a>

519

520 The following example shows a CloudTrail log entry that demonstrates the `ListRepositories` action\.

521

522 **Note**

523 Although `ListRepositories` returns a list of repositories, non\-mutable responses are not recorded in CloudTrail logs, so `responseElements` is shown as `null` in the log file\.

```
{
"eventVersion":"1.05", "userIdentity": { "type":"IAMUser", "principalId":"AIDACKCEVSQ6C2EXAMPLE",
"arn":"arn:aws:iam::444455556666:user/Mary_Major", "accountId":"444455556666", "accessKeyId":"AKI-
AIOSFODNN7EXAMPLE", "userName":"Mary_Major" }, "eventTime":"2016-12-14T17:57:36Z",
"eventSource":"codecommit.amazonaws.com", "eventName":"ListRepositories", "awsRegion":"us-east-1",
"sourceIPAddress":"203.0.113.12", "userAgent":"aws-cli/1.10.53 Python/2.7.9 Windows/8 botocore/1.4.43",
"requestParameters":null, "responseElements":null, "requestID":"cb8c167e-EXAMPLE", "eventID":"e3c6f4ce-
EXAMPLE", "readOnly":true, "eventType":"AwsApiCall", "apiVersion":"2015-04-13", "recipientAccoun-
tId":"444455556666" }
```

1

2 ### Example: A log entry for creating an AWS CodeCommit repository<a name="integ-cloudtrail-
   createrepository"></a>

3

4 The following example shows a CloudTrail log entry that demonstrates the `CreateRepository`
   action in the US East \(Ohio\) Region region\.

{ ”eventVersion”: ”1.05”, ”userIdentity”: { ”type”: ”IAMUser”, ”principalId”: ”AIDACKCEVSQ6C2EXAM-
PLE”, ”arn”: ”arn:aws:iam::444455556666:user/Mary_Major”, ”accountId”: ”444455556666”, ”accessKeyId”:
”AKIAIOSFODNN7EXAMPLE”, ”userName”:”Mary_Major” }, ”eventTime”: ”2016-12-14T18:19:15Z”,
”eventSource”: ”codecommit.amazonaws.com”, ”eventName”: ”CreateRepository”, ”awsRegion”: ”us-east-
2”, ”sourceIPAddress”: ”203.0.113.12”, ”userAgent”: ”aws-cli/1.10.53 Python/2.7.9 Windows/8 botocore/1.4.43”,
”requestParameters”: { ”repositoryDescription”: ”Creating a demonstration repository.”, ”repositoryName”:
”MyDemoRepo” }, ”responseElements”: { ”repositoryMetadata”: { ”arn”: ”arn:aws:codecommit:us-east-
2:111122223333:MyDemoRepo”, ”creationDate”: ”Dec 14, 2016 6:19:14 PM”, ”repositoryId”: ”8afe792d-
EXAMPLE”, ”cloneUrlSsh”: ”ssh://git-codecommit.us-east-2.amazonaws.com/v1/repos/MyDemoRepo”, ”repositoryName”: ”MyDemoRepo”, ”accountId”: ”111122223333”, ”cloneUrlHttp”: ”https://git-codecommit.us-east-
2.amazonaws.com/v1/repos/MyDemoRepo”, ”repositoryDescription”: ”Creating a demonstration repository.”,
”lastModifiedDate”: ”Dec 14, 2016 6:19:14 PM” } }, ”requestID”: ”d148de46-EXAMPLE”, ”eventID”: ”740f179d-
EXAMPLE”, ”readOnly”: false, ”resources”: [{ ”ARN”: ”arn:aws:codecommit:us-east-2:111122223333:MyDe-
moRepo”, ”accountId”: ”111122223333”, ”type”: ”AWS::CodeCommit::Repository” }], ”eventType”: ”AwsApi-
Call”, ”apiVersion”: ”2015-04-13”, ”recipientAccountId”: ”111122223333” }

1

2 ### Examples: Log entries for pull requests to an AWS CodeCommit repository<a name="integ-
   cloudtrail-gitpull"></a>

3

4 The following example shows a CloudTrail log entry that demonstrates the `GitPull` action where
   the local repo is already up\-to\-date\.

{ ”eventVersion”: ”1.05”, ”userIdentity”: { ”type”: ”IAMUser”, ”principalId”: ”AIDACKCEVSQ6C2EXAM-
PLE”, ”arn”: ”arn:aws:iam::444455556666:user/Mary_Major”, ”accountId”: ”444455556666”, ”accessKeyId”:
”AKIAIOSFODNN7EXAMPLE”, ”userName”:”Mary_Major” }, ”eventTime”: ”2016-12-14T18:19:15Z”,
”eventSource”: ”codecommit.amazonaws.com”, ”eventName”: ”GitPull”, ”awsRegion”: ”us-east-2”, ”sourceIPAddress”: ”203.0.113.12”, ”userAgent”: ”git/2.11.0.windows.1”, ”requestParameters”: null, ”responseElements”:
null, ”additionalEventData”: { ”protocol”: ”HTTP”, ”dataTransferred”: false, ”repositoryName”: ”MyDemoR-
epo”, ”repositoryId”: ”8afe792d-EXAMPLE”, }, ”requestID”: ”d148de46-EXAMPLE”, ”eventID”: ”740f179d-
EXAMPLE”, ”readOnly”: true, ”resources”: [{ ”ARN”: ”arn:aws:codecommit:us-east-2:111122223333:MyDe-
moRepo”, ”accountId”: ”111122223333”, ”type”: ”AWS::CodeCommit::Repository” }], ”eventType”: ”AwsApi-
Call”, ”recipientAccountId”: ”111122223333” }

1

2 The following example shows a CloudTrail log entry that demonstrates the `GitPull` action where
   the local repo is not up\-to\-date and so data is transferred from the AWS CodeCommit
   repository to the local repo\.

{ ”eventVersion”: ”1.05”, ”userIdentity”: { ”type”: ”IAMUser”, ”principalId”: ”AIDACKCEVSQ6C2EXAM-
PLE”, ”arn”: ”arn:aws:iam::444455556666:user/Mary_Major”, ”accountId”: ”444455556666”, ”accessKeyId”:
”AKIAIOSFODNN7EXAMPLE”, ”userName”:”Mary_Major” }, ”eventTime”: ”2016-12-14T18:19:15Z”,
”eventSource”: ”codecommit.amazonaws.com”, ”eventName”: ”GitPull”, ”awsRegion”: ”us-east-2”, ”sourceIPAddress”: ”203.0.113.12”, ”userAgent”: ”git/2.10.1”, ”requestParameters”: null, ”responseElements”: null, ”additionalEventData”: { ”protocol”: ”HTTP”, ”capabilities”: [”multi_ack_detailed”, ”side-band-64k”, ”thin-pack”],
”dataTransferred”: true, ”repositoryName”: ”MyDemoRepo”, ”repositoryId”: ”8afe792d-EXAMPLE”, ”shallow”:
false }, ”requestID”: ”d148de46-EXAMPLE”, ”eventID”: ”740f179d-EXAMPLE”, ”readOnly”: true, ”resources”:
[{ ”ARN”: ”arn:aws:codecommit:us-east-2:111122223333:MyDemoRepo”, ”accountId”: ”111122223333”, ”type”:
”AWS::CodeCommit::Repository” }], ”eventType”: ”AwsApiCall”, ”recipientAccountId”: ”111122223333” }

1

2 ### Example: A log entry for a successful push to an AWS CodeCommit repository<a name="integ-cloudtrail-gitpush"></a>

3

4 The following example shows a CloudTrail log entry that demonstrates a successful `GitPush` action\. The `GitPush` action appears twice in a log entry for a successful push\.

{ "eventVersion": "1.05", "userIdentity": { "type": "IAMUser", "principalId": "AIDACKCEVSQ6C2EXAMPLE", "arn": "arn:aws:iam::444455556666:user/Mary_Major", "accountId": "444455556666", "accessKeyId": "AKIAIOSFODNN7EXAMPLE", "userName":"Mary_Major" }, "eventTime": "2016-12-14T18:19:15Z", "eventSource": "codecommit.amazonaws.com", "eventName": "GitPush", "awsRegion": "us-east-2", "sourceIPAddress": "203.0.113.12", "userAgent": "git/2.10.1", "requestParameters": null, "responseElements": null, "additionalEventData": { "protocol": "HTTP", "dataTransferred": false, "repositoryName": "MyDemoRepo", "repositoryId": "8afe792d-EXAMPLE", }, "requestID": "d148de46-EXAMPLE", "eventID": "740f179d-EXAMPLE", "readOnly": true, "resources": [{ "ARN": "arn:aws:codecommit:us-east-2:111122223333:MyDemoRepo", "accountId": "111122223333", "type": "AWS::CodeCommit::Repository" }], "eventType": "AwsApiCall", "recipientAccountId": "111122223333" }, { "eventVersion": "1.05", "userIdentity": { "type": "IAMUser", "principalId": "AIDACKCEVSQ6C2EXAMPLE", "arn": "arn:aws:iam::444455556666:user/Mary_Major", "accountId": "444455556666", "accessKeyId": "AKIAIOSFODNN7EXAMPLE", "userName":"Mary_Major" }, "eventTime": "2016-12-14T18:19:15Z", "eventSource": "codecommit.amazonaws.com", "eventName": "GitPush", "awsRegion": "us-east-2", "sourceIPAddress": "203.0.113.12", "userAgent": "git/2.10.1", "requestParameters": { "references": [{ "commit": "100644EXAMPLE", "ref": "refs/heads/master" }] }, "responseElements": null, "additionalEventData": { "protocol": "HTTP", "capabilities": ["report-status", "side-band-64k"], "dataTransferred": true, "repositoryName": "MyDemoRepo", "repositoryId": "8afe792d-EXAMPLE", }, "requestID": "d148de46-EXAMPLE", "eventID": "740f179d-EXAMPLE", "readOnly": false, "resources": [{ "ARN": "arn:aws:codecommit:us-east-2:111122223333:MyDemoRepo", "accountId": "111122223333", "type": "AWS::CodeCommit::Repository" }], "eventType": "AwsApiCall", "recipientAccountId": "111122223333" }

1

2

3

4

5 # AWS CodeCommit Command Line Reference<a name="cmd-ref"></a>

6

7 This reference will help you learn how to use AWS CLI\.

8

9 **To install and configure the AWS CLI**

10

11 1. On your local machine, download and install the AWS CLI\. This is a prerequisite for interacting with AWS CodeCommit from the command line\. For more information, see [Getting Set Up with the AWS Command Line Interface](http://docs.aws.amazon.com/cli/latest/userguide/cli-chap-getting-set-up.html)\.

12 **Note**

13 AWS CodeCommit works only with AWS CLI versions 1\.7\.38 and later\. To determine which version of the AWS CLI you have installed, run the `aws --version` command\.

14 To upgrade an older version of the AWS CLI to the latest version, see [Installing the AWS Command Line Interface](http://docs.aws.amazon.com/cli/latest/userguide/installing.html)\.

15

16 1. Run this command to verify the AWS CodeCommit commands for the AWS CLI are installed:

aws codecommit help

1

2 This command should return a list of AWS CodeCommit commands\.

3

4 1. Configure the AWS CLI with the configure command, as follows:

aws configure

1
2 When prompted, specify the AWS access key and AWS secret access key of the IAM user you will use
       with AWS CodeCommit\. Also, be sure to specify the region where the repository exists, such
       as `us-east-2`\. When prompted for the default output format, specify `json`\. For example:

AWS Access Key ID [None]: Type your target AWS access key ID here, and then press Enter AWS Secret Access
Key [None]: Type your target AWS secret access key here, and then press Enter Default region name [None]:
Type a supported region for AWS CodeCommit here, and then press Enter Default output format [None]: Type
json here, and then press Enter

1
2 To connect to a repository or a resource in another region, you must re\-configure the AWS CLI
       with the default region name for that region\. Supported default region names for AWS
       CodeCommit include:
3 + us\-east\-2
4 + us\-east\-1
5 + eu\-west\-1
6 + us\-west\-2
7 + ap\-northeast\-1
8 + ap\-southeast\-1
9 + ap\-southeast\-2
10 + eu\-central\-1
11 + ap\-northeast\-2
12 + sa\-east\-1
13 + us\-west\-1
14 + eu\-west\-2
15 + ap\-south\-1
16 + ca\-central\-1
17
18 For more information about AWS CodeCommit and regions, see [Regions and Git Connection Endpoints
       ](regions.md)\. For more information about IAM, access keys, and secret keys, see [How Do I
       Get Credentials?](http://docs.aws.amazon.com/IAM/latest/UserGuide/IAM_Introduction.html#
       IAM_SecurityCredentials) and [Managing Access Keys for IAM Users](http://docs.aws.amazon.com
       /IAM/latest/UserGuide/ManagingCredentials.html)\.
19
20 To view a list of all available AWS CodeCommit commands, run the following command:

aws codecommit help

1
2 To view information about a specific AWS CodeCommit command, run the following command, where *
       command\-name* is the name of the command \(for example, create\-repository\):

aws codecommit command-name help

1
2 To learn how to use the commands in AWS CLI, go to one or more of the following sections to view
       descriptions and example usage:
3 + [batch\-get\-repositories](how-to-view-repository-details.md#how-to-view-repository-details-
       with-names-cli)
4 + [create\-branch](how-to-create-branch.md#how-to-create-branch-cli)
5 + [create\-pull\-request](how-to-create-pull-request.md#how-to-create-pull-request-cli)
6 + [create\-repository](how-to-create-repository.md#how-to-create-repository-cli)
7 + [delete\-branch](how-to-delete-branch.md#how-to-delete-branch-cli)
8 + [delete\-comment\-content](how-to-commit-comment.md#how-to-commit-comment-cli-commit-delete)

```
 9 + [delete\-repository](how-to-delete-repository.md#how-to-delete-repository-cli)
10 + [describe\-pull\-request\-events](how-to-view-pull-request.md#describe-pull-request-events)
11 + [get\-blob](how-to-view-commit-details.md#how-to-view-commit-details-cli-blob)
12 + [get\-branch](how-to-view-branch-details.md#how-to-view-branch-details-cli-details)
13 + [get\-comment](how-to-commit-comment.md#how-to-commit-comment-cli-get-comment-info)
14 + [get\-comments\-for\-compared\-commit](how-to-commit-comment.md#how-to-commit-comment-cli-get-
      comments)
15 + [get\-comments\-for\-pull\-request](how-to-review-pull-request.md#get-comments-for-pull-
      request)
16 + [get\-commit](how-to-view-commit-details.md#how-to-view-commit-details-cli-commit)
17 + [get\-differences](how-to-view-commit-details.md#how-to-view-commit-details-cli-differences)
18 + [get\-merge\-conflicts](how-to-view-pull-request.md#get-merge-conflicts)
19 + [get\-pull\-request](how-to-view-pull-request.md#get-pull-request)
20 + [get\-repository](how-to-view-repository-details.md#how-to-view-repository-details-with-name-
      cli)
21 + [get\-repository\-triggers](how-to-notify-edit.md#how-to-notify-edit-cli)
22 + [list\-branches](how-to-view-branch-details.md#how-to-view-branch-details-cli)
23 + [list\-pull\-requests](how-to-view-pull-request.md#list-pull-requests)
24 + [list\-repositories](how-to-view-repository-details.md#how-to-view-repository-details-no-name-
      cli)
25 + [merge\-pull\-request\-by\-fast\-forward](how-to-close-pull-request.md#merge-pull-request-by-
      fast-forward)
26 + [post\-comment\-for\-compared\-commit](how-to-commit-comment.md#how-to-commit-comment-cli-
      comment)
27 + [post\-comment\-for\-pull\-request](how-to-review-pull-request.md#post-comment-for-pull-
      request)
28 + [post\-comment\-reply](how-to-commit-comment.md#how-to-commit-comment-cli-commit-reply)
29 + [put\-file](how-to-create-file.md#how-to-create-file-cli)
30 + [put\-repository\-triggers](how-to-notify-edit.md#how-to-notify-edit-cli)
31 + [test\-repository\-triggers](how-to-notify-test.md#how-to-notify-test-cli)
32 + [update\-comment](how-to-commit-comment.md#how-to-commit-comment-cli-commit-update)
33 + [update\-default\-branch](how-to-change-branch.md#how-to-change-branch-cli-default)
34 + [update\-pull\-request\-description](how-to-update-pull-request.md#update-pull-request-
      description)
35 + [update\-pull\-request\-status](how-to-close-pull-request.md#update-pull-request-status)
36 + [update\-pull\-request\-title](how-to-update-pull-request.md#update-pull-request-title)
37 + [update\-repository\-description](how-to-change-repository.md#how-to-change-repository-cli-
      description)
38 + [update\-repository\-name](how-to-change-repository.md#how-to-change-repository-cli-name)
39
40
41
42
43 # Basic Git Commands<a name="how-to-basic-git"></a>
44
45 You can use Git to work with a local repo and the AWS CodeCommit repository to which you've
      connected the local repo\.
46
47 The following are some basic examples of frequently used Git commands\.
48
49 For more options, see your Git documentation\.
50
51 **Topics**
52 + [Configuration Variables](#how-to-basic-git-configuration-variables)
```

262

57

58 ## Configuration Variables<a name="how-to-basic-git-configuration-variables"></a>

59

60

61 | | |

62 | --- |--- |

63 | Lists all configuration variables\. | `git config --list` |

64 | Lists only local configuration variables\. | `git config --local -l` |

65 | Lists only system configuration variables\. | `git config --system -l` |

66 | Lists only global configuration variables\. | `git config --global -l` |

67 | Sets a configuration variable in the specified configuration file\. | `git config [--local \| --global \| --system] variable-name variable-value` |

68 | Edits a configuration file directly\. Can also be used to discover the location of a specific configuration file\. To exit edit mode, typically you type `:q` \(to exit without saving changes\) or `:wq` \(to save changes and then exit\), and then press Enter\. | `git config [--local \| --global \| --system] --edit` |

69

70 ## Remote Repositories<a name="how-to-basic-git-remotes"></a>

71

72

73 | | |

74 | --- |--- |

75 | Initializes a local repo in preparation for connecting it to an AWS CodeCommit repository\. | `git init` |

76 | Can be used to set up a connection between a local repo and a remote repository \(such as an AWS CodeCommit repository\) using the specified nickname the local repo has for the AWS CodeCommit repository and the specified URL to the AWS CodeCommit repository\. | `git remote add remote-name remote-url` |

77 | Creates a local repo by making a copy of an AWS CodeCommit repository at the specified URL, in the specified subfolder of the current folder on the local machine\. This command also creates a remote tracking branch for each branch in the cloned AWS CodeCommit repository and creates and checks out an initial branch that is forked from the current default branch in the cloned AWS CodeCommit repository\. | `git clone remote-url local-subfolder-name` |

78 | Shows the nickname the local repo uses for the AWS CodeCommit repository\. | `git remote` |

79 | Shows the nickname and the URL the local repo uses for fetches and pushes to the AWS CodeCommit repository\. | `git remote -v` |

80 | Pushes finalized commits from the local repo to the AWS CodeCommit repository, using the specified nickname the local repo has for the AWS CodeCommit repository and the specified branch\. Also sets up upstream tracking information for the local repo during the push\. | `git push -u remote-name branch-name` |

81 | Pushes finalized commits from the local repo to the AWS CodeCommit repository after upstream tracking information is set\. | `git push` |

82 | Pulls finalized commits to the local repo from the AWS CodeCommit repository, using the specified nickname the local repo has for the AWS CodeCommit repository and the specified branch | `git pull remote-name branch-name` |

83 | Pulls finalized commits to the local repo from the AWS CodeCommit repository after upstream tracking information is set\. | `git pull` |

84 | Disconnects the local repo from the AWS CodeCommit repository, using the specified nickname the local repo has for the AWS CodeCommit repository\. | `git remote rm remote-name` |

```
85
86  ## Commits<a name="how-to-basic-git-commits"></a>
87
88
89  |   |   |
90  | --- |--- |
91  | Shows what has or hasn't been added to the pending commit in the local repo\.  | `git status
         ` |
92  | Shows what has or hasn't been added to the pending commit in the local repo in a concise
         format\. \(`M` = modified, `A` = added, `D` = deleted, and so on\)  | `git status -sb`  |
93  | Shows changes between the pending commit and the latest commit in the local repo\.  | `git
         diff HEAD`  |
94  | Adds specific files to the pending commit in the local repo\.  | `git add [file-name-1 file-
         name-2 file-name-N \| file-pattern]`  |
95  | Adds all new, modified, and deleted files to the pending commit in the local repo\.  | `git
         add `  |
96  | Begins finalizing the pending commit in the local repo, which displays an editor to provide a
         commit message\. After the message is entered, the pending commit is finalized\.  | `git
         commit`  |
97  | Finalizes the pending commit in the local repo, including specifying a commit message at the
         same time\.  | `git commit -m "Some meaningful commit comment"`  |
98  | Lists recent commits in the local repo\.  | `git log`  |
99  | Lists recent commits in the local repo in a graph format\.  | `git log --graph`  |
100 | Lists recent commits in the local repo in a predefined condensed format\.  | `git log --
         pretty=oneline`  |
101 | Lists recent commits in the local repo in a predefined condensed format, with a graph\.  | `
         git log --graph --pretty=oneline`  |
102 | Lists recent commits in the local repo in a custom format, with a graph\. \(For more options,
         see [Git Basics \- Viewing the Commit History](http://git-scm.com/book/en/Git-Basics-
         Viewing-the-Commit-History)\)  | `git log --graph --pretty=format:"%H (%h) : %cn : %ar : %s
         "`  |
103
104 ## Branches<a name="how-to-basic-git-branches"></a>
105
106
107 |   |   |
108 | --- |--- |
109 | Lists all branches in the local repo with an asterisk \(`*`\) displayed next to your current
         branch\.  | `git branch`  |
110 | Pulls information about all existing branches in the AWS CodeCommit repository to the local
         repo\.  | `git fetch`  |
111 | Lists all branches in the local repo and remote tracking branches in the local repo\.  | `
         git branch -a`  |
112 | Lists only remote tracking branches in the local repo\.  | `git branch -r`  |
113 | Creates a new branch in the local repo using the specified branch name\.  | `git branch new-
         branch-name`  |
114 | Switches to another branch in the local repo using the specified branch name\.  | `git
         checkout other-branch-name`  |
115 | Creates a new branch in the local repo using the specified branch name, and then switches to
         it\.  | `git checkout -b new-branch-name`  |
116 | Pushes a new branch from the local repo to the AWS CodeCommit repository using the specified
         nickname the local repo has for the AWS CodeCommit repository and the specified branch name
         \. Also sets up upstream tracking information for the branch in the local repo during the
         push\.  | `git push -u remote-name new-branch-name`  |
```

117 | Creates a new branch in the local repo using the specified branch name\. Then connects the new branch in the local repo to an existing branch in the AWS CodeCommit repository, using the specified nickname the local repo has for the AWS CodeCommit repository and the specified branch name\. | `git branch --track new-branch-name remote-name/remote-branch-name` |
118 | Merges changes from another branch in the local repo to the current branch in the local repo \. | `git merge from-other-branch-name` |
119 | Deletes a branch in the local repo unless it contains work that has not been merged\. | `git branch -d branch-name` |
120 | Deletes a branch in the AWS CodeCommit repository using the specified nickname the local repo has for the AWS CodeCommit repository and the specified branch name\. \(Note the use of the colon \(`:`\)\.\) | `git push remote-name :branch-name` |
121
122 ## Tags<a name="how-to-basic-git-tags"></a>
123
124
125 | | |
126 | --- |--- |
127 | Lists all tags in the local repo\. | `git tag` |
128 | Pulls all tags from the AWS CodeCommit repository to the local repo\. | `git fetch --tags` |
129 | Shows information about a specific tag in the local repo\. | `git show tag-name` |
130 | Creates a "lightweight" tag in the local repo\. | `git tag tag-name commit-id-to-point-tag-at` |
131 | Pushes a specific tag from the local repo to the AWS CodeCommit repository using the specified nickname the local repo has for the AWS CodeCommit repository and the specified tag name\. | `git push remote-name tag-name` |
132 | Pushes all tags from the local repo to the AWS CodeCommit repository using the specified nickname the local repo has for the AWS CodeCommit repository\. | `git push remote-name --tags` |
133 | Deletes a tag in the local repo\. | `git tag -d tag-name` |
134 | Deletes a tag in the AWS CodeCommit repository using the specified nickname the local repo has for the AWS CodeCommit repository and the specified tag name\. \(Note the use of the colon \(`:`\)\.\) | `git push remote-name :tag-name` |
135
136
137
138
139 # AWS CodeCommit User Guide Document History<a name="history"></a>
140
141 The following table describes the important changes to the documentation since the last release of the *AWS CodeCommit User Guide*\.
142 + **API version:** 2015\-04\-13
143 + **Latest documentation update:** May 16, 2018
144
145
146 | Change | Description | Date Changed |
147 | --- | --- | --- |
148 | New topic | The [Limit Pushes and Merges to Branches](how-to-conditional-branch.md) topic has been added\. The [AWS CodeCommit Permissions Reference](auth-and-access-control-permissions-reference.md) topic has been updated\. | May 16, 2018 |
149 | New section | The [Working with Files in AWS CodeCommit Repositories](files.md) section has been added\. The [AWS CodeCommit Permissions Reference](auth-and-access-control-permissions-reference.md) and [Getting Started with AWS CodeCommit Tutorial](getting-started-cc.md)

topics have been updated\. | February 21, 2018 |

150 | New topic | The [Configure Cross\-Account Access to an AWS CodeCommit Repository](cross-account.md) topic has been added\. | February 21, 2018 |

151 | New topic | The [Integrate AWS Cloud9 with AWS CodeCommit](setting-up-ide-c9.md) topic has been added\. The [Product and Service Integrations](integrations.md) topic has been updated with information about AWS Cloud9\. | December 1, 2017 |

152 | New section | The [Working with Pull Requests in AWS CodeCommit Repositories](pull-requests.md) section has been added\. The [Authentication and Access Control for AWS CodeCommit](auth-and-access-control.md) section has been updated with information about permissions for pull requests and commenting\. It also includes updated managed policy statements\. | November 20, 2017 |

153 | Updated topics | The [Product and Service Integrations](integrations.md) topic has been updated to include links for customers who want to update their existing pipelines to use Amazon CloudWatch Events to start pipelines in response to changes in an AWS CodeCommit repository\. | October 11, 2017 |

154 | New topics | The [Authentication and Access Control for AWS CodeCommit](auth-and-access-control.md) section has been added\. It replaces the Access Permissions Reference topic\. | September 11, 2017 |

155 | Updated topics | The [Manage Triggers for a Repository](how-to-notify.md) section has been updated to reflect changes in trigger configuration\. Topics and images have been updated throughout the guide to reflect changes in the navigation bar\. | August 29, 2017 |

156 | New topic | The [Working with User Preferences](user-preferences.md) topic has been added\. The [View Tag Details](how-to-view-tag-details.md) topic has been updated\. The [Product and Service Integrations](integrations.md) topics has been updated with information about integrating with Amazon CloudWatch Events\. | August 3, 2017 |

157 | New topics | The [Integrate Eclipse with AWS CodeCommit](setting-up-ide-ec.md) and [Integrate Visual Studio with AWS CodeCommit](setting-up-ide-vs.md) topics have been added\. | June 29, 2017 |

158 | Updated topic | AWS CodeCommit is now available in two additional regions: Asia Pacific \(Mumbai\), and Canada \(Central\)\. The [Regions and Git Connection Endpoints](regions.md) topic has been updated\. | June 29, 2017 |

159 | Updated topic | AWS CodeCommit is now available in four additional regions: Asia Pacific \(Seoul\), South America \(São Paulo\), US West \(N\. California\), and EU \(London\)\. The [Regions and Git Connection Endpoints](regions.md) topic has been updated\. | June 6, 2017 |

160 | Updated topic | AWS CodeCommit is now available in four additional regions: Asia Pacific \(Tokyo\), Asia Pacific \(Singapore\), Asia Pacific \(Sydney\), and EU \(Frankfurt\)\. The [Regions and Git Connection Endpoints](regions.md) topic has been updated to provide information about Git connection endpoints and supported regions for AWS CodeCommit\. | May 25, 2017 |

161 | New topic | The [Compare Branches](how-to-compare-branches.md) topic has been added\. The contents of the [Working with Branches](branches.md) section have been updated with information about using the AWS CodeCommit console to work with branches in a repository\. | May 18, 2017 |

162 | New topic | The [Compare Commits](how-to-compare-commits.md) topic has been added with information about comparing commits\. The structure of the user guide has been updated for working with [repositories](repositories.md), [commits,](commits.md), and [branches](branches.md)\. | March 28, 2017 |

163 | Updated topic | The [View Commit Details](how-to-view-commit-details.md) topic has been updated with information about viewing the difference between a commit and its parent in the console, and using the get\-differences command to view differences between commits using the AWS CLI\. | January 24, 2017 |

164 | New topic | The [Logging AWS CodeCommit API Calls with AWS CloudTrail](integ-cloudtrail.md) topic has been added with information about logging connections to AWS CodeCommit using AWS CloudFormation\. | January 11, 2017 |

165 | New topic | The [For HTTPS Users Using Git Credentials](setting-up-gc.md) topic has been added with information about setting up connections to AWS CodeCommit using Git credentials over HTTPS\. | December 22, 2016 |

166 | Updated topic | The [Product and Service Integrations](integrations.md) topic has been updated to include information about integration with AWS CodeBuild\. | December 5, 2016 |

167 | Updated topic | AWS CodeCommit is now available in another region, EU \(Ireland\)\. The [Regions and Git Connection Endpoints](regions.md) topic has been updated to provide information about Git connection endpoints and supported regions for AWS CodeCommit\. | November 16, 2016 |

168 | Updated topic | AWS CodeCommit is now available in another region, US West \(Oregon\)\. The [Regions and Git Connection Endpoints](regions.md) topic has been updated to provide information about Git connection endpoints and supported regions for AWS CodeCommit\. | November 14, 2016 |

169 | New topic | The [Create a Trigger for a Lambda Function](how-to-notify-lambda.md) topic has been updated to reflect the ability to create AWS CodeCommit triggers as part of creating the Lambda function\. This simplified process streamlines trigger creation and automatically configures the trigger with the permissions required for AWS CodeCommit to invoke the Lambda function\. The [Create a Trigger for an Existing Lambda Function](how-to-notify-lambda-cc.md) topic has been added to include information about creating triggers for existing Lambda functions in the AWS CodeCommit console\. | October 19, 2016 |

170 | New topic | AWS CodeCommit is now available in another region, US East \(Ohio\)\. The [Regions and Git Connection Endpoints](regions.md) topic has been added to provide information about Git connection endpoints and supported regions for AWS CodeCommit\. | October 17, 2016 |

171 | Topic update | The [Product and Service Integrations](integrations.md) topic has been updated to include information about integration with AWS Elastic Beanstalk\. | October 13, 2016 |

172 | Topic update | The [Product and Service Integrations](integrations.md) topic has been updated to include information about integration with AWS CloudFormation\. | October 6, 2016 |

173 | Topic update | The [For SSH Connections on Windows](setting-up-ssh-windows.md) topic has been revised to provide guidance for using a Bash emulator for SSH connections on Windows instead of the PuTTY suite of tools\. | September 29, 2016 |

174 | Topic update | The [View Commit Details](how-to-view-commit-details.md) and [AWS CodeCommit Tutorial](getting-started-cc.md) topics have been updated to include information about the Commit Visualizer in the AWS CodeCommit console\. The [Limits](limits.md) topic has been updated with the increase to the number of references allowed in a single push\. | September 14, 2016 |

175 | Topic update | The [View Commit Details](how-to-view-commit-details.md) and [AWS CodeCommit Tutorial](getting-started-cc.md) topics have been updated to include information about viewing the history of commits in the AWS CodeCommit console\. | July 28, 2016 |

176 | New topics | The [Migrate a Git Repository to AWS CodeCommit](how-to-migrate-repository-existing.md) and [Migrate Local or Unversioned Content to AWS CodeCommit](how-to-migrate-repository-local.md) topics have been added\. | June 29, 2016 |

177 | Topic update | Minor updates have been made to the [Troubleshooting](troubleshooting.md) and [For HTTPS Connections on Windows with the AWS CLI Credential Helper](setting-up-https-windows.md) topics\. | June 22, 2016 |

178 | Topic update | The [Product and Service Integrations](integrations.md) and Access Permissions Reference topics have been updated to include information about integration with AWS CodePipeline\. | April 18, 2016 |

179 | New topics | The [Manage Triggers for a Repository](how-to-notify.md) section has been added\. New topics include examples, including policy and code samples, of how to create, edit, and delete triggers\. | March 7, 2016 |

180 | New topic | The [Product and Service Integrations](integrations.md) topic has been added\. Minor updates have been made to [Troubleshooting](troubleshooting.md)\. | March 7, 2016 |

181 | Topic update | In addition to the MD5 server fingerprint, the SHA256 server fingerprint for AWS CodeCommit has been added to [For SSH Connections on Linux, macOS, or Unix](setting-up-

ssh-unixes.md) and [For SSH Connections on Windows](setting-up-ssh-windows.md)\. | December 9, 2015 |

182 | New topic | The [Browse Files in a RepositoryCreate or Add a FileEdit the Contents of a File](how-to-browse.md) topic has been added\. New issues have been added to [Troubleshooting](troubleshooting.md)\. Minor improvements and fixes have been made throughout the user guide \. | October 5, 2015 |

183 | New topic | The [For SSH Users Not Using the AWS CLI](setting-up-without-cli.md) topic has been added\. The topics in the [Setting Up](setting-up.md) section have been streamlined\. Guidance to help users determine which steps to follow for their operating systems and preferred protocols has been provided\. | August 5, 2015 |

184 | Topic update | Clarification and examples have been added to the SSH key ID steps in [SSH and Linux, macOS, or Unix: Set Up the Public and Private Keys for Git and AWS CodeCommit](setting-up-ssh-unixes.md#setting-up-ssh-unixes-keys-unixes) and [SSH and Windows: Set Up the Public and Private Keys for Git and AWS CodeCommit](setting-up-ssh-windows.md#setting-up-ssh-windows-keys-windows)\. | July 24, 2015 |

185 | Topic update | Steps in [SSH and Windows: Set Up the Public and Private Keys for Git and AWS CodeCommit](setting-up-ssh-windows.md#setting-up-ssh-windows-keys-windows) have been updated to address an issue with IAM and saving the public key file\. | July 22, 2015 |

186 | Topic update | [Troubleshooting](troubleshooting.md) has been updated with navigation aids\. More troubleshooting information for credential keychain issues has been added\. | July 20, 2015 |

187 | Topic update | More information about AWS Key Management Service permissions has been added to the [AWS KMS and Encryption](encryption.md) and the Access Permissions Reference topics\. | July 17, 2015 |

188 | Topic update | Another section has been added to [Troubleshooting](troubleshooting.md) with information about troubleshooting issues with AWS Key Management Service\. | July 10, 2015 |

189 | Initial release | This is the initial release of the *AWS CodeCommit User Guide*\. | July 9, 2015 |

190
191
192
193
194 # AWS Glossary<a name="glossary"></a>
195
196 For the latest AWS terminology, see the [AWS Glossary](http://docs.aws.amazon.com/general/latest /gr/glos-chap.html) in the *AWS General Reference*\.

www.ingramcontent.com/pod-product-compliance
Lightning Source LLC
LaVergne TN
LVHW082037050326
832904LV00005B/217